morality USA

Published with assistance from the Margaret S. Harding
Memorial Endowment honoring the first director of the
University of Minnesota Press.

morality USA

ellen g. friedman
corinne squire

University of Minnesota Press
Minneapolis
London

Published by the University of Minnesota Press
111 Third Avenue South, Suite 290
Minneapolis, MN 55401-2520
http://www.upress.umn.edu

Library of Congress Cataloging-in-Publication Data

Friedman, Ellen G., 1939– *1949*
    Morality USA / Ellen G. Friedman, Corinne Squire.
        p.   cm.
    ISBN 0-8166-2748-7 (hc : alk. paper). — ISBN 0-8166-2749-5
(pbk. : alk. paper)
    1. United States—Moral conditions.   2. United States—Social
conditions—1980–   3. Social values—United States.   I. Squire,
Corinne, 1958–   .   II. Title.
    HN90.M6F75   1998
    306'.0973—dc21   98-2999

Printed in the United States of America on acid-free paper

The University of Minnesota is an equal-opportunity educator and employer.

10 09 08 07 06 05 04 03 02 01 00 99 98   10 9 8 7 6 5 4 3 2 1

To Dino & Sam,
My favorite aunt &
uncle who taught me to love
books and a child & that
started everything.
Love,
Ellen

For Max, Rebecca, and Sonia
— EGF

For Ruby, Peggy, and Neil
— CS

Contents

Acknowledgments

Many people supported this book over the years. The following people and groups have our gratitude for their insightful observations of portions of the book and for their help in thinking through a number of knotty issues with us: Kum-Kum Bhavnani, Ann Phoenix, Michelle Fine, Mun Wong, Jane Ussher, Gisela Engel, Gerda Lauerbach, Renate Kroll, Helmut Winter, Richard Kamber, Miriam Fuchs, Paula Rothenberg, Sherrie Rosen, Drew Giorgi, Ann Graham, Renae Bredin, Barry Novick, Melinda Roberts, Simon Barrett, John Munford, Steve Nicholls, Wendelien van Oldenborg, Neil Turok, the Gender Group at the Institute for American and English Studies at Johann Wolfgang von Goethe University, Frankfurt, and the brown-bag-lunch forum at the College of New Jersey. Many thanks to Jennifer Moore at the University of Minnesota Press for good advice, meticulous editing, and careful shepherding of the manuscript through production.

The librarians at the College of New Jersey were indefatigable and ingenious in their search for obscure references and sources. Although many of them helped us with this project, we particularly wish to acknowledge Patricia Beaber and Elizabeth Maziarz. In the Women's and Gender Studies Office at the College of New Jersey, Patricia Karlowitsch, Ellen G. Friedman's secretary, and undergraduate and graduate assistants Amy Clauss, Pam Cummings, Jill Edwards-Cifelli, Christine Sasso, Jackie Lugg, Jennifer Marshall, and especially Deborah Gepner Salvaggio facilitated this book with their intelligent and efficient accomplishment of dozens of essential tasks. Many thanks too to Ruth Smith and her family, Evelyn Babb, Young Ping and her family, and Karen and Lorenza Banks, for the help with child care without which Corinne Squire could not have coauthored this book.

The F.I.R.S.L. committee at the College of New Jersey; Brunel University, London; and the University of Central England, Birmingham, provided us with grants of released time and assistance without which this book would not have been possible.

Rosalind Coward's and Larry McCaffery's critical readings of early drafts of several chapters both encouraged us and helped us make the book better. We particularly thank Brian McHale, who contributed extensive, valuable, and incisive commentary both at the book's inception and when we had almost completed it. All of these people contributed positively to the book, but its flaws are, of course, our own.

Introduction

The highest ethical life ... consists at all times in the breaking of rules which have grown too narrow for the actual case.
William James, *The Moral Philosopher and the Moral Life*

There are no moral phenomena at all, only a moral interpretation of phenomena.
Friedrich Nietzsche, *Beyond Good and Evil*

People like me are what stand between us and Auschwitz. I see evil around me every day.
Newt Gingrich, *The Wit and Wisdom of Newt Gingrich*

The Debate about Morality

In 1991, in the middle of an August night, a ship sank off Cape Town. The captain was one of the first to go ashore. He said he had left to direct the rescue operation better, and all 561 passengers were indeed saved. Over the next couple of days, the U.S. news media chewed over the incident. Should the captain have left? And what criterion should we use to make such a decision: the likely effectiveness of the rescue; an individual's right to save himself or herself; a humanitarian duty to care for others; professional responsibilities; or the traditional rule that the captain leaves last (*New York Times,* 11 August 1991)? Was the captain, as the New York tabloid the *Daily News* sniped, just a "chicken of the sea" (6 August 1991)?

In that same summer, a forty-two-year-old South Dakota woman was pregnant after artificial insemination with her son-in-law's sperm. At birth, the child was to be given to him and the woman's infertile daughter to bring up as their child. Pictures of the woman and her family were ubiquitous in the press. Arguments about the gains to be won from new reproductive technologies, the good sense of employing a known, sympathetic surrogate, and the ultimate motherly love involved in the act jostled with powerful

1

convictions that the situation was unnatural, even incestuous. Many of those who thought the procedure made sense nevertheless voiced suspicions that it was strange or wrong (Nash, 1991; *New York Times,* 5–6 August 1991).

In 1990, four members of an African American Illinois family set off to visit cousins in Arkansas. They never got there; their car dove off a bridge into a river, and all of them drowned. Police took a month to discover what had happened. For some commentators, the delay was the sad consequence of police mistakes, nothing more. Others claimed the mistake would not have happened if the family had been rich, white, or both, and saw the incident as simply an extreme example of the ubiquitous racialization of justice. Many thought the bodies might never have been found if the media had not taken up the case. The family and its supporters vowed to prosecute the Illinois chief of police. The promised Senate investigatory committee never materialized.

In the aftermath of the O. J. Simpson "not guilty" verdict at the first, criminal trial, the media conducted an angstfest on the racially divided response, contrasting cheering black women in battered women's shelters with angry white men railing at "black" justice. But racial polarity did not exhaust the reactions: there was something for everyone. Black jurors interviewed after the verdict insisted on their devotion to an unraced justice. Many whites and blacks thought that justice had been bought, and the National Organization for Women said the verdict sanctioned domestic violence. Some accused television of perverting the law. Simpson's future became surrounded with ethical debate: should he have custody of his children? appear on pay-TV? get sponsorship deals? The Simpson aftermath mixed up debates about racist justice, race as moral metaphor, and moralities of gender and class with apprehension about the media's power to shape and supersede morality.

Questions of morality stimulate extensive and agitated cultural debate in the United States. Since the late 1980s, the debate has taken on a millennial urgency; the moral state of the nation is discussed everywhere. In bookstores, thick jeremiads slamming the moral zeitgeist sell well. In politics, moral positions such as the Contract with America and "family values" drive policy. In churches and law courts, supermarket tabloids and upscale monthlies, in the growing number of journals on professional ethics, in schools and workplaces and in front of the television, intense moral arguments take place on a wide span of issues. Some of these issues—professional responsibility, the technologizing of reproduction, the questionable reality of the media, racialized justice—emerge from the stories just described. Other contested issues include information technologies and privacy, environmental controls, affirmative action and identity politics, the legal rights of homosexuals, sexual harassment and date rape, child abuse, crime and punishment, and assisted suicide for the terminally ill. Sporadically, too, the personal lives of public figures provoke agonized bouts of national self-criticism that fascinate and bemuse the rest of the world.

What is morality? We, like the philosopher Alasdair MacIntyre, take it to mean rules of right conduct, rules that go beyond the sphere of public convention claimed by etiquette or manners and that have their own rationale, separate from religion, the law, and aesthetics (MacIntyre, 1984: 39). We are interested not in prescribing a morality but in exploring how popular representations describe and constitute different, often conflicting sets of moral rules.[1]

For a country that often accuses itself of having no morality, the United States says a lot about it. Perhaps this logorrhea occurs because morality is, like sexuality, a highly culturally charged issue, subject to intense scrutiny and ubiquitous control. Moreover, definitions of morality change. They are contingent, making sense only in relation to immorality, and aspects of them seem impossible to pin down in words. As a result, moral debates in the United States often sound as if they are repeating themselves endlessly, going nowhere. There seem to be no common assumptions, no agreement on what makes a valid argument, no shared ground where arguments can be resolved. This unresolvable uncertainty is omnipresent in *The Day America Told the Truth* (1991), James Patterson and Peter Kim's survey of what people in the United States think is right and wrong. "As we entered the 1990s," Patterson and Kim say, "it became suddenly and urgently clear that a tumultuous change was occurring in America and the world around us.... Yesterday's verities had vanished. Unpredictability and chaos became the norm" (3). Some people view such uncertainty as offering an opportunity for intercultural exchange or as holding out the possibility of new moral frames. More frequently, though, moral uncertainty evokes anxiety, nostalgia, or cynicism. And when, as usually happens, moral uncertainty is interpreted as moral decline or disorder, it generates fear, hostility, and attempts to impose a firmer frame of moral judgment.

This book examines the complications and contradictions in contemporary U.S. representations of morality. It gives an account of what moral uncertainties consist of, and suggests that they may be more productive than they appear. The book is not a work of philosophy, although it examines the conceptual structuring of moral discourses. It is not history, although it pays attention to the histories inhering in moral discourses and coloring their effects. Rather, it is an account of how morality appears in different cultural domains. The book analyzes how journalists, educators, novelists, artists, and advertisers, in cultural settings from academia through New Age stores to television talk shows, present moral issues. It describes how these presentations play out in regard to topics with strong moral resonances, for instance, justice, family, the body, and politicial correctness; and in regard to particular cases that exemplify moral confusion, such as those of Tawana Brawley and Baby M. It is concerned with both the contemporary shape of moral discourses and their possible futures.

Probably the most noticeable response to the current climate of moral indecision is outrage—the apoplectic sputtering of a Pat Buchanan, for instance, who opposes the "moral bankruptcy" of U.S. reactions to AIDS with his own solution, "stop the sodomizing" (*New York Post*, 2 December 1987), and wants to turn the nation into a moral fortress, locking up the deviant. Some regret is more reasoned and provisional. In *The End of History and the Last Man* (1992), one book from the many shelves of recent texts mulling over moral decline, Francis Fukuyama argues that since the decline of the Soviet Union, liberal democracies have no more worthy goal than to raise the standard of living. They have lost the ability to think ethically (323ff.). Andrew Delbanco thinks we have lost not only a language of but also a necessary sense of evil (1995: 226–28). MacIntyre himself writes of the impossibility of understanding the contemporary world, which presents us with "not only an uninterpreted, but an uninterpretable world" (1984: 79). Gertrude Himmelfarb blames the abdication of Victorian values for moral vacuity (1994: 158–61), while Christopher Lasch (1991: 49–81) attributes the decline in civic responsibility and hope to the culture's obsession with progress. Another take on moral confusion is enthralled apocalypticism, such as that of Jean Baudrillard, who writes about our captivation by media (1989a). For others, morality is recoupable only as nostalgia, because universal ideas of good and evil seem to them impossible in the postmodern world (Lyotard, 1993: 210).

At the far end of the spectrum of dismay is a highly noticeable and much-discussed response: strategic dissociation, exemplified in Bret Easton Ellis's *American Psycho* (1991). In this novel, the narrator kills lightly, baroquely, and with impunity. Identity is indeterminate: homeless people are indistinguishable from one another, and one yuppie is forever looking another in the eye and calling him by the wrong name. The reader can neither determine the motivations for characters' actions nor predict their consequences. *American Psycho* evokes the large uncertainties about right and wrong that permeate contemporary U.S. culture. Despite its dispassion, the book cannot avoid reading like a moral commentary. The narrator's 1980s materialism is fingered on every page, a memento mori of twentieth-century America.

Moral uncertainty also generates stacks of would-be solutions. The highest-profile corrective is a conservative and Moral Majority smorgasbord of allegedly traditional measures. These include restrictions on contraception, abortion, pornography, and homosexual rights; mandatory school prayer; cutting welfare and balancing budgets; stripped-down government; a tougher judiciary; back-to-basics education; church attendance, and gun ownership. The menu attracts motley support. Its absolutism appeals to disillusioned liberals and get-tough Clintonian Democrats as well as to the Right. Individual items can generate weird alliances: C. Delores Tucker, chair of the national Political Congress of Black Women, uniting with the conservative William Bennett, editor of *The Book of Virtues* (1993), to oppose Warner Brothers' rap roster (Alexander, 1995); House Speaker Newt Gingrich and convicted drug dealer Mayor Marion Barry collaborating to restore inner-city Washington (Goldberg, 1995: 58). In wrangles over high and low culture, too, conservatives and radicals unite in moral absolutism, fulminating about television talk shows, slasher videos, or cyberspace as signs of cultural apocalypse. As the art theorist Charles Jencks puts it, "Many people, faced with fragmentation, panic and become moralists" (1992).

Perhaps the most popular corrective to moral uncertainty, despite the titular claim of the Moral Majority, is a crude, can-do pragmatism, a school of optimistic short-term troubleshooting that aims to cure the moral malaise of the United States not by comprehensive reform but by tackling doable problems one at a time with a finessing mix of improved management, better communication, and caring. Patterson and Kim's improvement plan belongs to this school:

> Problem: America has no leaders. Solution: ... The American political system must supply clear choices, then more of us have to choose intelligently. ... Problem: Greed is impoverishing America. Solution: Make productivity pay. ... Problem: The earth is sick. Solution: Make the environment an important unifying cause. (1991: 226–27)

Haunting the diagnoses of moral ills and schemes for improvement is nostalgia for a past era of moral certainty. The nostalgia fixes on a variety of dates: most often the 1950s, although increasingly the 1960s and the Victorian era, and sometimes the time of the New Deal or the writing of the Constitution. Occasionally the nostalgia is hidden, hardly known to those who speak it. *American Psycho,* for instance, in its bilious catalog of 1980s wrongs, often seems like the voice of a disillusioned hippie born out of time. Frequently the nostalgia is out in the open, as with Patterson and Kim, who repeatedly hark back to the "moral consensus" of the 1950s and early 1960s, "our parents' generation," when issues appeared not in "shades of grey," as now, but in "black and white.... Some would say that we've lost our moral backbone" (1991: 25, 32). However, nostalgia is rarely tested against the conflicted thoughts and behavior of the past. Regrets for the past sanctity of marriage ignore the historical reality of divorce as part of the American way of life since the seventeenth century (Riley, 1991: 9–33). Nostalgia for Victorian decency and order downplays the exploitation in that era of poor women and children by treating such phenomena as "anti-Victorian," as hangovers from the previous era or as precursors of the twentieth-century "cult of the self" (Collier, 1991: 64; Himmelfarb, 1995). Nor do nostalgia-mongers reflect on what their nostalgia means in circumstances that, as they themselves often acknowledge, present new and newly complex moral problems.

Moral Uncertainty

In this book, we do not want to repeat the unexamined yearnings for the past, the dismissals of the present, and the alternately sanctimonious and glib exhortations for the future of many contemporary moral commentaries. We are going to discuss the uncertainties in debates about morality not as marks of amorality or moral decline but simply *as* uncertainties—as multiplicities, ambiguities, and conflicts within the debates.

The irresolvability of contemporary moral argument is not so much a symptom of morality's absence or loss as an indication of pluralism, which needs careful analysis. This pluralism is not the tolerant exchange of viewpoints that agree to differ. It is, rather, a troubled coexistence of incompatible opinions, a babble of unmatched voices (MacIntyre, 1984: 10). For us to understand moral discourse, we need to sort out and detail these fragments. This book describes the different positions that manifest themselves around controversial moral issues and, in doing so, gives a picture of the uneasy moral pluralism in the United States.

Moral debate is complicated by the powerful histories and circumstances that shape different viewpoints. To hear your viewpoint interrogated by others or engulfed in general uncertainty is to hear your interests, your very self, put in question. When, for instance, the popular media give saturation coverage to a woman bearing a child for her infertile daughter, mothers, daughters, fathers, and sons-in-law across the country may start to question these family identities. Morality is intimately tied up with conflict, "conflict between ideals, conflict between obligations, conflict between essential, but incompatible, interests" (Hampshire, 1983: 1).

If your interests and identity are not socially powerful, your moral viewpoint will also lack power. But the challenge that viewpoint presents to dominant perspectives may still provoke disturbing uncertainty. A poor black family may not be able to prove racism in the Illinois police department, but it can challenge the department's moral authority where race is involved. Those who cite racism in the justice system to explain their support of O. J. Simpson or Mike Tyson may not persuade many others of their case, but they keep before everyone questions about the moral legitimacy of a country so racially polarized. The campaign for sexual harassment to be taken seriously and to be made a crime began in the 1970s in a culture that accepted men's sexual power over women in the workplace. At that time, as Catharine MacKinnon, the feminist legal theorist most associated with the campaign, says, "the facts that amount to sexual harassment did not amount to sexual harassment" (1989: 106). Although today the phenomenon is recognized by most women, many men still excuse it; yet they must live with its social and legal unacceptability.

Because class is a slippery category in the United States, it rarely generates clear moral challenges. The poor and the rich come together with everyone else as members of what Benjamin DeMott has called the "imperial middle" class. Because the ideology of this class is of classlessness, it focuses on meritocracy, the nuclear family, government nonintervention, individual freedom, and self-improvement (DeMott, 1990: 43). This ideology withstood even the economic polarization of the Reagan-Bush era. Clinton, too, the president of the imperial middle, promised to keep his hands off middle-class wage packets and restricted reform, especially of health care, on this account. "No new taxes," "the checkbook is closed," and the call for welfare to become workfare proved more effective arguments than outcries about fat-cat corruption and the plight of the deserving poor. Nevertheless, because these outcries happen again and again, they give class a hidden presence in moral argument. When the poor lose their right to food stamps but do not show up at food kitchens, we know that they are still being poor somewhere else and that tomorrow, that somewhere else may be our backyard.

Some moral uncertainties, then, can be understood as signs of resistance to the established order. The current climate of moral uncertainty can partly be explained as an outcome of the civil rights, women's, and gay liberation movements of the late 1950s, 1960s, and 1970s; of more recent campaigns for educational multiculturalism; and of environmentalism, whose ideological persuasiveness and political power have multiplied since the 1980s. These arguments for social change have not been won, but they have gained a place in everyone's mind. And they have disrupted the racism, sexism, homophobia, and economic and ecological complacency of the postwar period, factors integral to the period's ideas of what was right and wrong, to its moral certainty. Contemporary pundits such as Patterson and Kim, who fondly invoke 1950s-vintage moral certainty, usually overlook the discriminatory underpinnings of that certainty. In this book, we will try not just to describe current uncertainties in moral argument but also to sort out the conflicts of power that are bound up with these uncertainties.

Angst about moral confusion comes largely from those with the most to lose from social change movements. White men made up almost the whole of the nihilistic "brat pack" of early- and mid-1980s fiction writers for example, who documented cultural and ethical decay. *American Psycho*'s narrator, who personifies moral chaos, is the degenerate scion of an old family, turned unprincipled yuppie. The author, cynical yet condemning, implicitly speaks from a firmer position of moral power: the "imperial" male white middle class. Writers who are white women or people of color tend to have more precise agendas than the description of moral paralysis: the analysis of past injustices, the understanding of current ambiguities, the imagining of possible futures.

Social power, though, is not an infallible guide to moral position. Our moral frames draw on fantasies and possibilities as well as social realities. Even if you are working in a minimum-wage job and struggling to get by, you may nevertheless denounce workers who are arguing for a higher minimum-wage for pricing themselves out of a job if you believe, despite the evidence, that with hard work you are sure to make good (*New York Times*, 22 May 1992). Moreover, we all internalize the multiple and contradictory moral positions around us. When contemplating sexual harassment and other forms of sexual assault, women often use reasoning that is not in their interest but that nonetheless seems more persuasive to them than a feminist analysis. This moral identification with the oppressor may lead women, like men, to speculate on a female victim's contributory negligence, sexual history, or even dishonesty.

Political perspectives themselves often contain moral ambiguities of the kind they seem, by their absolutism, to rule out. The Reaganite discourse of traditional values, for instance, was accompanied by radical economic and social policies of deregulation and laissez-faire. Backing people before government, Reaganism supported popular culture before intellectual culture—although the popular variety brought into every decent home the sitcom world of lone parents and recombined families, the soaps' incest and adultery, police-show shoot-outs, and reality programming's blurring of reportage with fiction. By the 1990s, the rhetoric of values was no longer conservatives' alone. Clintonian Democrats surmounted the contradiction between "family values" and popular culture simply by defining "family" more broadly, so that moral rectitude could go hand in hand with almost any lifestyle, on television or off. The potential problems of such morality-by-redefinition became obvious in early 1998. As allegations of President Clinton's affair with Monica Lewinsky surfaced, it was reported that the president had scoured the Bible to prove extramarital oral sex was not infidelity. This sophist "eatin' ain't cheatin'" morality stimulated debate on, for instance, *Nightline*, hosted by Ted Koppel. Usually, though, political discourse's homogenization of values and practices does not get debated. Instead, it throws a veil over moral uncertainties without resolving them.

Moral uncertainty is not always a matter of social, personal, or political conflicts. The uncertainty that troubles us is also the result of a more radical undecidability that stems from questions about identity and community. One place where such radical moral uncertainty has become more and more prominent over the past twenty years is within social change movements. Despite accusations of dogmatism by opponents of political correctness, feminist, civil rights, and lesbian and gay rights movements became increasingly self-critical in the 1970s and 1980s, qualifying and nuancing their explanations of the world. Lesbians and gay men moved away from fixed notions of what it is to be lesbian or gay, with an emphasis on particular sexual or social practices, toward more fluid definitions of identity. Post-AIDS queer culture, for instance, has to include men of color who do not identify primarily as gay, lesbians who may sometimes have sex with men, and the legacy of those who have died. Although passions still gather around the representation of African Americans, the range of allowable representations has increased to take in films as different, for instance, as the gangster movie *Menace II Society* (1993), the *House Party* teen comedies (the last was *House Party 3* in 1994), "chick flicks" such as *Waiting to Exhale* (1996), and art house movies such as *To Sleep with Anger* (1990) and *Daughters of the Dust* (1991). The Million Man March of African Americans in Washington two weeks after the first O. J. Simpson trial concluded brought together men of diverse ages, classes, and beliefs, and presented a face of black masculinity different from Simpson's: patriarchal but collective, aimed at redeeming the past, and pledged to the future.[2] As definitions of identity and community become more complicated, moral clarity surrenders to undecidability.

Moral undecidability is also a result of a developing awareness of complexity in social relations. There is a growing recognition that the politics of race and gender, for instance, cannot be separated out, as was demonstrated in the conflicted public and media reactions to Anita Hill's and Clarence Thomas's testimonies. Although such complications make it more difficult to write prescriptions for social change, they also shift feminism, civil rights, and lesbian and gay rights in a more democratic direction. The recent history of U.S. social change movements thus suggests that in this country a turn toward social equity is a morally uncertain one. The increasing complexity of these movements is incompatible with universalizing, grand moral narratives.

Moral undecidability is a fundamental part of the Enlightenment thinking that guides contemporary U.S. moral discourse. For three hundred years, people in the West have assumed that humanity is a potential source of rational, universal, progressive values. But the construction of an encompassing moral framework is always undone by the impossibility of deciding, now that religious certainties have less force, what a rational morality might look like for irrational, passionate creatures such as ourselves (MacIntyre, 1984: 51ff.). There is no way, in post-Enlightenment moral thinking, to pass from what "is" to what "ought to be." We can make pronouncements about good and bad morals, of course, but these are anomalies, hangovers from the era of absolute belief, what MacIntyre calls "linguistic survivals from the practices of classical theism which have lost the context provided by those practices" (60). Moral undecidability is the price the West pays for the Enlightenment's liberal individualism, its unchaining of religious tradition into autonomous moral agency. The resulting moral bricolage of liberal individualism consistently opposes slavery and non-egalitarian social practices, for instance, but is unable to ground this opposition in a general principle. Liberal democracies cannot provide absolute definitions of truth or right because they must always cobble together the often conflicted interests of individuals and communities, minorities and majorities.[3]

Moral undecidability has been intensified by a series of breaks in moral certainty that have accompanied twentieth-century events. For the 1920s "lost generation," the First World War was one of these breaks. The Second World War also seemed to many to drain meaning from categories of good and bad. For some, such as Elie Wiesel (1982) and George Steiner

(1976), Nazism constituted a moral break. For Jean-François Lyotard (1989), the events gathered together under the name "Auschwitz" signaled the beginning of an overwhelming doubt about the possibility of meaning. The war had other effects on moral thinking. In the United States, as in Europe, postwar reforms, particularly the widening of access to education, expanded "morality" to include people's democratic entitlement, regardless of origin, to social opportunities. Further complications of moral argument peculiar to the United States can be traced to the Vietnam War, the assassinations of Martin Luther King, Jr. and John F. Kennedy, McCarthyism, and cases such as the 1921 Sacco-Vanzetti trial, an event that galvanized and then disillusioned a generation of hitherto politically quiescent intellectuals and artists. With Watergate, the U.S. electorate ended its romance with politicians. The spirit of *Camelot* (1967)—the wistful optimism in the musical and movie, and in their inspiration, the Kennedy administration— ceded to the outright nihilism of *The Texas Chainsaw Massacre* (1974), a film made, its director claimed, in a post-Watergate mood of disillusionment and anger (Carson, 1986). Watergate also produced a public acceptance of political corruption that allowed little surprise at the Irangate rerun and that continues to undermine people's hopes for the political future. Now, the best that politicians can expect is to be represented as self-interested but good-hearted, as in the anonymously authored book *Primary Colors* (1996), rather than self-interested and deeply corrupt, like the sadistic sleazeball president in the film *Absolute Power* (1996).

In the 1990s, the increasingly challenged moral authority of the United States was emblematized by a cluster of events: the civil unrest in Los Angeles and the impasses reached by the Clinton administration at home and in its efforts to make the world safe for democracy in Haiti, Somalia, and Bosnia. In 1995 and 1997, the Simpson trials, apotheoses to the world of the American dream as racial nightmare, became emblems of moral confusion. By the mid-1990s, economic stability and the power of the United States to dictate, if not control, the international order of things were widely said to have produced a "feel good" mood. But the precariousness of that complacency was apparent in the new national fear of domestic terrorism, moral rot from within. In movies such as *Independence Day* (1996) and *Men in Black* (1997), this threat appears as dangerous aliens, the delinquent offspring of friendly 1970s visitors like E. T., knowingly recreating their monstrous grandparents from 1950s B movies. More prosaically, after the Oklahoma City bombing in 1995, news media repeatedly displayed to us armed and angry white men living in trailer parks, on the cultural edges—hostile viruses seeking weak points in the benevolent body of the host society.

Although it is tempting to believe that during your lifetime, as Isaiah Berlin says of his, "more dreadful things occurred than at any other time in history," we are not arguing that events that have broken the moral frame are unique to this century (*Guardian,* 5 November 1991). There is a long history of moral contest in liberal democracy. Moreover, although even the most apparently monolithic of political and moral systems have cracks, such cracks are especially obvious in liberal democracies. The events of the twentieth century in the United States have generated a series of small breaks in the social order that have, in turn, induced breaks in moral thinking. As we live through the events, the established moral order finds it harder and harder to claim consensus.

Moral uncertainty is also heightened by our suspension between moral traditions. We are shaped, as Nietzsche puts it, "by *differing* moralities; our actions shine in differing colors, they are seldom unequivocal— and there are cases enough in which we perform *many-colored* actions" (1973: 148). Individuals draw on their own set of strongly felt traditions, and the uncertainty of moral thinking is partly a result of this unconscious multiplicity.[4] The tradition in which Alasdair MacIntyre sees most hope is Aristotelianism, which locates the good in a life lived by the rules for social good upon which a particular community decides. Despite the problems of defining "community," groups often voice this last principle. In cities such as Detroit, some African Americans claim a right to Ujaama schools exclusively for black males in order to multiply the numbers of male achievers, leaders, and responsible fathers. Schools in neighborhoods where religious fundamentalism is strong may not teach evolution.

Although religion inflects moral discourse, in Patterson and Kim's surveys only 27 percent of the respondents attended services regularly, and few deferred morally to organized religion (1991: 199–200).[5] But moral language is affected indirectly by theology. The Bernhard Goetz case, vigilante movies such as the *Death Wish* series (the first, *Death Wish,* appearing in 1974, and the last, *Death Wish 5,* in 1993), and women's revenge movies such as *Thelma and Louise* (1991) all demonstrated that perpetrators of violence can be excused of their crimes if they are on the right side of a biblically retributive "eye for an eye" take on justice. A Puritan notion of deservingness is also often discernible. Balanced budgets are touted as moral, not just good economic sense. In the William Kennedy Smith rape trial, the media verdict was that Patricia Bowman was poor and undeserving, compromised by her sexual history, unmarried motherhood, and drug use.

The 1980s also produced a flock of grand theories of feminine morality, variously concerned with maternity, social relationships, pacifism, ecology, language, and the body. The most convincing has been that of Carol Gilligan, whose book *In a Different Voice* described a female-associated ethical voice. Unlike the authoritative male voice that spells out universal moral principles, this voice is caring and responsible; it seems to carry a quasi-sacred promise of redemption, "the truth of an ethic of care" (1982: 173).

In addition, there exists a Nietzschean tradition that assumes that all metaphysical concepts—reason, truth, the good—are false. In the new era of the "extramoral," morality becomes irrelevant: "We sail straight over morality and past it" (Nietzsche, 1973: 54, 63, 148; see also MacIntyre, 1991). Outside art, crime, especially motiveless crime, seems best to represent this tradition. The media presentation of serial killers such as Charles Manson as celebrities and of the O. J. Simpson police chase as entertainment is evidence to many of the poverty of concepts of right and wrong. But the Nietzschean tradition is also an undertone in many ordinary people's moral thinking. It exists in uneasy symbiosis with more recognized moral frameworks, a disgruntled sidekick muttering in one's ear about the sanctimoniousness of religion, the hypocrisy of community, and the self-interest of individuals.

Across multiple moral frameworks and histories, moral uncertainty is unavoidable. Patterson and Kim are tersely sure of the negative implications. "We've become wishy-washy as a nation," they say (1991: 32). However, positions that assume absolute rights or wrongs and try to get everyone to adopt the same frame of judgment are out of place today. The incursion into moral debate of women, children, and the sexual, racial, and national "others" previously excluded complicates conventional ideas of reason and right constructed from a male European perspective (Kristeva, 1986: 300). We are now likely to see the world as "postmodern," beyond the certainties of Euro-American modernity—postindustrial, postpatriarchal, postcolonial, and multicultural. Dick Hebdige calls this condition simply the "Post" (1987: 48). It is a condition that supports numerous, apparently unrelated moralities. To many, it looks like a new and worrying embrace of moral relativism.

Moral Relativism and Emotivism

Although moral relativism has become closely associated in the last two decades with postmodernity, multiple moralities and moral undecidability are not exclusively contemporary phenomena. We can almost always discern a plurality of arguments in historical records of moral debates, and relativism often comes into play when these conflicting frameworks of morality are hard to resolve. Relativistic tactics can be used to resolve a Christian belief in God with agnostic skepticism, for instance. Pascal decided that it would be safer to believe in God, just in case he existed, than not to, since the cost of wrongheaded skepticism would be infinite and eternal. In making this wager, Pascal did not arbitrate between Christian and skeptical frames of thinking; instead, he relativistically accepted the validity of each frame (Hirst, 1990: 15–16). Questioning gender and sexual identities can generate relativism, too. In late-nineteenth-century Europe and North America, the struggles between irreconcilable moral viewpoints about gender and sexuality produced a sense of "sexual anarchy," with homosexuals, "free-lovers," and single, working, and "odd" women all exercising a public voice (Showalter, 1991). In the 1960s and 1970s, a similar sense of sexual and moral unruliness reasserted itself.

Compared with the seventeenth and nineteenth centuries, moral relativism today is more various and more secular. For MacIntyre, the moral undecidability inherent in liberal individualism has also acquired a specific twentieth-century form, that of emotivism. Emotivism grounds moral judgments in people's opinions and in how they feel. It is the belief that "all moral judgments are *nothing but* expressions of preference, expressions of attitude or feeling" (1984: 12). It becomes a matter of personal conviction, for instance, whether you think rules of conduct are spelled out in the Bible, are determinable by the scientific study of societies, emerge from human biology, or are simply up to you to decide. Contemporary emotivism casts even pleasurable feelings as the moral right of every U.S. citizen.

Emotivism dominates moral thinking even when other bases for judgment—for instance, Christianity or Marxism—are claimed: "To a large degree people now think, talk and act *as if* emotivism were true, no matter what their avowed theoretical standpoint may be" (MacIntyre, 1984: 22). Patterson and Kim's rapid tour through the moral states of the Union tells the same tale. "We have established ourselves as the authority on morality," they say. "Sin is defined by our own consciences" (1991: 201–3). In the movie *Contact* (1997), personal and religious doubts fuel a search for something "out there," in "empty" space. Astronomer Eleanor Arroway finds God, hope, and moral renewal for all of us, the movie suggests, in a scientifically unprovable transformative experience—an encounter with an alien. In a society where psychological concepts are widely used to explain social and political, as well as personal, events, accounts of morality that center on feelings fit comfortably with the established explanatory order. Adding to this user-friendliness is emotivism's ability to cohabit with diverse political philosophies: liberalism, social democracy and democratic socialism, capitalism, left and right libertarianism. It even manages to look rational.[6]

Feelings are finally, despite their commonalities, inaccessible to rational discussion between individuals and often opaque to the individuals who experience them. You may not be able to identify why something feels wrong to you, let alone understand the emotional-moral grid of someone else. Consequently, we expect the meaning even of a traditional narrative to vary wildly from person to person. The woman who bore a child for her daughter, and the daughter herself, for instance, were devout Catholics. For them, Catholicism's affirmation of sacred rather than human, secular control of reproduction did not apply to reproduction's enhancement. Emotivism therefore makes moral judgment fundamentally uncertain for individuals and for societies. If individuals cannot comprehend others' moral judgments, or even their own, they cannot collectively develop rules of conduct.

Although emotivism helps support the arguments against professionalism so prevalent in the United States, professionals are also very often called on to supplement emotivism with their own expert ethics (MacIntyre, 1984: 23). Doctors who decide on treatment for terminally ill patients can refer to a professionalized ethics regarding outcome, quality of life, and patient wishes, coded by the American Medical Association, that protects them from allegations of murder as well as from the intimate, non-negotiable emotions of patients' families. The profession that preeminently and finally makes moral rules, though, is the law. Although the courts have a fairly unproblematic mandate to regulate lawbreakers, large sections of society sometimes reject a legal decision. After their apparent settlement in the 1950s, 1960s, and 1970s, the return of school desegregation, abortion, and affirmative action cases to the Supreme Court—the ultimate arbiter of the arbitrating profession—is an example. The law may also have to borrow the authority of other professions by calling expert witnesses. Psychology, a discipline that has grown up alongside emotivist forms of explanation in this century, plays a big part in the legal system. Psychologists themselves see this alliance as ethically troubling, referring to colleagues who give legal testimony as "crystal ball" gazers, "hired guns," and "whores" (Pope and Vetter, 1992). Moreover, people are required to operate professional standards in arenas previously conceived of as private, for instance, in volunteer work, a sphere that used to connote only philanthropy or devoutness, and in parenting. The moral authority and responsibility of the professions is thus dispersing, passing to individuals.

Emotivism cohabits with different professionalisms in moral discourse, producing odd vacillations between personal feelings and complacent know-how. The legal system oversees the regulation of child abuse, for example, and an army of professionals—psychologists, social workers, police, teachers, and academic researchers—implements the regulation. But the definition of child abuse oscillates between professional criteria—checklists of behavioral risk indicators, for instance—and expressions of feelings. A child's assertions that an adult's touch "felt" wrong will be weighed alongside empirical assessments of genital or anal trauma, STDs, sleeplessness, and unusual sexual interest or aggression.

How do we manage this vacillation between emotivism and professionalism? The answer seems to be, by calling on a utilitarian cost-benefit morality that papers over the differences between them (MacIntyre, 1984: 62). Such utilitarian analyses allow us to assume that an individual's emotivist assessment of morality is "good" because it is the best the person can do at the time, and that professional judgments on moral issues are "good" because they aim for the greatest social benefit. From this perspective, when a patient decides whether or not to kill herself on the basis of what "feels" right, her feeling is a reckoning of the costs and gains of the two possible courses of action. When the captain left his sinking ship and said he could direct the rescue better from the shore, he was calculating that his professional use was greater there; he could save more lives than if he stayed on board. Patterson and Kim, who think the ship of U.S. moral certainty is sinking, are prophets of such a cost-benefit morality. They want us all to stand on the same unambitious but profitable moral ground, improving education, for instance, to help stop the Japanese from "beating us on the production line" (1991: 232).

A cost-benefit logic allows us to reconcile morality as a matter of individual feeling with morality as a set of rules, and to bear with the variability in our own and others' moral feelings and conduct. It fits easily with the pragmatic commitment—philosophically and politically strong in the United States—to practicality rather than to the fruitless striving to do what ought to be done. But such a utilitarian reliance on a vaguely defined social good as the criterion of what is right provides no conceptual frame in which to consider the moral confusions that trouble us. Patterson and Kim say that better education is a nationally shared goal, but they recognize that the question remains, whose values should it transmit (1991: 233)? Social good is often defined emotively, as the maximizing of individuals' good feelings, and frequently it seems the individuals who count here are the powerful ones. Utilitarian morality can look unpleasantly like opportunism (MacIntyre, 1984: 64). At its bucks-for-babies crudest, paying unmarried pregnant women if they agree to adoption, it slips into authoritarian social engineering (*New York Times,* 12 November 1995).

In the public response to allegations of President Clinton's adultery with Monica Lewinsky, however, a cost-benefit analysis offered not resolution but a welcome truce between conflicting feelings of morality. Polls in the early days of the scandal showed only 20 percent of respondents thought the allegations were untrue, but 56 percent approved of "the way Bill Clinton is handling his job as President" (*Economist,* 31 January 1998: 53). A president shouldn't cheat, lie, or encourage perjury, people said, but he was doing good things for the country, such as helping the economy, education, and women. Feminists were conspicuous among such utilitarian advocates. On the one hand, Betty Friedan could "believe" Clinton was framed; on the other, she speculated about his "very complex" marriage. In the end, she based her moral convictions on measurable gains, ignoring her more personal ethical feelings: "Whether it's a fantasy, a set-up, or true, I simply don't care . . . Clinton has started the national childcare policy, and appointed some very strong women. He has also stood firm on abortion" (1998).

Inconsistencies, lacunae, and variability in the telling have always fractured grand moral narratives. An emotivist morality intensifies this uncertainty. Attempts to correct the shortcomings of emotivist understandings through professionalism and calculations of moral costs and benefits do not extricate us. Definitions of professional ethics and of social good are also incommensurable, returning us to the moral frame of "feeling." And when nonnegotiable internal states are the ground on which all moral narratives stand, we have, indeed, spun off into relativism.

Relativism's Limits

Many critics of the postmodern condition argue that its relativism leaves us trapped in our individual perspectives, with no possibility of understanding others' views. Such relativism, critics say, makes moral consensus, which requires an exchange of views, very difficult. They see relativism as the prelude to a postmorality that either will endlessly repeat the moral status quo or, worse, will give rise to an antidemocratic morality resting on individual or state power. These fears about the politics of relativism are one-sided, though. First, relativism never attains absolute freedom from judgment, the pure disinterestedness that some fear it to be (Hampshire, 1983: 36–37). Even to declare that moral positions are unrelated, you must try to relate them to one another. Moreover, positions that sound relativist often turn out to possess, in their everyday living-out, a high degree of historical and social integration (Bellah et al., 1985: 281–83). Second, in a world of diverse, conflicting moral traditions, moral relativism of a necessarily limited kind can, by subverting grand moral narratives, help maintain a democratic approach to moral issues. Thwarting efforts to impose a single perspective, relativism discourages us from pursuing destructive and brutal conflicts between different, rigid perspectives (Hirst, 1990: 21). An acceptance of multiple moral discourses and a commitment to moral persuasion and negotiation are more appropriate today than narratives that impose a single violently homogenizing ethics. Indeed, more self-conscious uncertainty about moral judgments—more moral relativism—is valuable in the "Post" world.

The questions asked by relativists, though, do not make a morality. We want something more out of debates about morality than a realization that everyone has a different position.[7] Merely documenting such an atomized plurality does not get us very far. If moral relativism is limited, we want to know what its limitations are, as well as their effects. There turn out to be a number of ways to conceptualize a limited moral relativism. One way of being relativist without endorsing atomization is to *redescribe* the moral order, accepting its diversity but relying on language to reshape it into a single, benignly homogeneous ethic. Richard Rorty (1990) suggests we pursue such redescriptions. In his view, new words can make a new reality. But his version of pragmatism skims over politics and history by assuming that people can adopt a convenient amnesia about events that formed their moral positions. Cornel West says that Rorty is thereby "deceptively shrugging off the weight of the dead" (1986: 138). Rorty's position assumes that a gentleman's agreement can be reached, smoothing over moral conflict.

Perhaps what is amiss with current uncertainties in morality is not that they exist but that we view them too complacently and gloss over conflicts between different forms of thinking. How can it be that senators measure the suitability of a candidate for public office, such as Clarence Thomas, simultaneously by such different criteria as professional expertise, political convictions, race, and personal worth, without any attempt to evaluate these criteria against one another? George Bush's response to the mess of issues raised in the Thomas hearings—sexual harassment, racism, sexism, professional competence, a politicized justice system—was to sideline them all in the hunt for who leaked Anita Hill's statement about Thomas. The answer, according to MacIntyre, is to pay more attention to disentangling moral traditions, formulating the differences between them, and understanding that for certain problems, one tradition may be better than another (1984: 276–77).[8]

A tradition can be shown to be inconsistent or inadequate both in its own terms and in those of another, better-argued, and more comprehensive tradition. Just because you speak one moral language does not mean that you cannot come to understand and speak another, and even to see that its arguments encompass and improve upon those made in your first language. Indeed, because we live in and draw on a number of moral traditions, we are all morally multilingual to some degree. Moreover, narratives, the tales we tell, transmit moralities across time:

> It is through hearing stories about wicked stepmothers, lost children, good but misguided kings, younger sons who receive no inheritance but must make their own way in the world . . . that children learn or mislearn both what a child and what a parent is, what the cast of characters may be in the drama into which they have been born, and what the ways of the world are. (MacIntyre, 1984: 216)

Given a renewal of community, MacIntyre says, it should be possible for us to develop stories of morality that are comprehensible across traditions as well as time, narratives that can establish local moral consensuses at least temporarily. MacIntyre's concern to define moral traditions exactly makes him cautious about the possibilities of consensus, for even when moral traditions are well understood, negotiations often founder or go off course. For him, though, a renewal of Aristotelian community ethics remains a possible solution.

Such visions of community as the source of moral traditions and the agent of their development and change are powerful. But "community" today seems hard to define and more complicated than MacIntyre allows for. Communities that are defined variously by geography, ethnicity, or interest, for instance, do not all function in the same way regarding morality. How are the communities of race, gender, age, or nation to which we are socially assigned related to "elective communities," those of religion, politics, or sexuality (Weeks, 1989: 130)? Some groups that call themselves communities are much bigger, more coherent, or more powerful than others. Are they therefore morally better communities? What about individuals—do they have any power within a community? Because communities are homogeneous, they tend to stifle moral dissent and to create barriers between themselves and others (Bauman, 1995: 275).[9]

We would suggest that moral negotiations depend not on finding or building communities but on recognizing or developing shared rhetorics, patterns of speech and writing that have a common persuasiveness. Such convergences make it possible for us to describe past moral traditions in our speech and writing and to refer to moral arguments that are not our own. They are also necessary if there is to be moral negotiation. They let us argue through competing, incompatible rhetorics to reach jointly held ones, and, thus, they allow us to modify and restrict relativism. The process is not, as in Rorty, a polite conversational exchange between equals; it is messy, incomplete, and rude. But it allows transitory, local agreement on morality to be attained. The mother who bore a child for her daughter, for instance, was justified throughout the media by a rhetoric of maternalism that glossed over the intrusive technology and the hint of incest in the story. *People* magazine, in a piece titled "A Mother's Priceless Gift," covered the medical facts briefly, sidelined the biological father to a marginal appearance in one photo, and concentrated on the bond between mother and daughter (Plummer, 1991). In this case, warring rhetorics of individualism, science, religion, feminism, and the family were maneuvered into a temporary media truce by a rhetoric of maternal care that sanctioned the event while leaving residues of moral contest and unease.

Political factors partly determine the validity of a moral rhetoric.[10] But rhetorics can still provide us with consistent moral criteria. We can usually tell the difference between someone with a good persuasive argument and someone who is simply using his or her power to impose an argument. Particularly blatant marriages of influence and virtue mark the corporate world. Multinationals such as Exxon have the power even to adjudicate their own wrongdoings; a company such as Ben and Jerry's is a bit player in comparison. However, within the realm of rhetoric, Exxon's ads in the aftermath of the *Exxon Valdez* oil spill that portrayed the company as ecologically responsible fell flat because of their mismatch with the company's actions. By contrast, Ben and Jerry's, with its "1 percent for peace" fund, seems to live up to its more modest rhetoric of social responsibility.

If we are to negotiate moralities, we must relate to people different from ourselves. Since communities do not offer a model for such negotiable differences, how else might we understand them? Emmanuel Levinas suggests that ethics must depend on respect for an "Other" who may be your neighbor or may have nothing in common with you. "I understand responsibility," he writes, "as responsibility for what is not my deed, or for what does not even matter to me" (1985: 294, 295). This Otherness, although it may be a shifting category, also has a quality of absoluteness that seems antithetical to negotiation (Cornell, 1993). If we say there is a "black," "gay," or "women's" morality, for instance, we are drawing borders around these categories that, as with "community," may limit exchange and make them impermeable to other moral discourses. The social theorist Chantal Mouffe's (1992a) notion of equivalence between citizens as the basis for changes in the political and moral order offers a broader field of respect for the other, relatively independent of identity categories and community.

Descriptions of moral negotiation often appear in writings about societies fractured by cultural difference. These writings suggest that when societies see themselves in moral dissolution, moral reformulation, based on a sense of equivalence, may be going on, unremarked, at the same time. Homi Bhabha analyzes how cultural differences are breaking up the monolith of "nation," making it flexible (1994). To describe such flexibility is to see something else in the moral disorder denounced in books such as *The Day America Told the Truth* (Patterson and Kim, 1991), something that supports moral reconstruction. In the United States, flexibility around nation has clear implications for moral discourse. A Bush campaign ad demonized the black criminal Willie Horton; then-Vice President Dan Quayle blamed the 1992 L.A. riots on irresponsible black fathers; even the Million Man March put forward similar ideas when it showed black men atoning for past irresponsibility. But the staid, white, national family implied in Grant Wood's *American Gothic* and often resurrected in politics, for instance, in the Norman Rockwell-collecting Ross Perot, has largely been supplanted by its black *Cosby Show* version; by a black Miss Liberty, Oprah Winfrey, holding aloft a microphone rather than a torch; and above all by the heroic figure of the black American athlete—Michael Jordan, Shaquille O'Neal, or Dennis Rodman, for instance. This changed image of the United States marks a moral shift. When blacks rather than whites are national symbols, the subtext is not moral assurance but moral reconstruction—improving democracy, righting wrongs.

At the same time, though, media playings out of moral debates through the figures of African American men often point up the disunity of a nation that pursues such debates by racialized allegory. Tyson, the Mike we don't want to be like, was not just the apotheosis of national degradation and helplessness as he bit into his opponent's ear, but also a replay of a tired old racial stereotype—"magnificent and horrible," as *Sports Illustrated* put it (Hoffer, 1997: 37). By his second trial, O. J. Simpson had turned not only into the media's own benchmark of media-fostered inauthenticity, but also into a figure so racialized as to be a cipher. The insistence of race in even the most apparently nonracialized of these representations is itself a kind of moral negotiation, breaking "nation" apart.

An analysis of moral negotiation must take seriously the pleasures people get from identifying with moral positions and from moral debate, even when those pleasures cannot be justified in terms of their social benefits and are difficult to understand. People enjoy identifying with moral positions, recognizing and feeling a part of them. Parts of an argument may be enjoyable even if we do not endorse the overall position, as with the exciting Nintendo-like visuals of the Persian Gulf War on TV, for instance. We may enjoy aspects of a moral argument that are incidental to the argument itself—images of sexual acts appearing briefly in an antipornography slide show, for example. The forms in which moral argument are expressed may be pleasurable too: the narrative progression in written and spoken stories; the visual patterns of film and television; the display of text and image on a page; the familiar voices or familiar faces in advertising, on political broadcasts, or on the nightly news. These seemingly marginal aspects of a moral discourse are often impossible to describe, let alone quantify, in a utilitarian calculation of costs and benefits. They can, nevertheless, lead us to support or reject a moral discourse: they contribute to its persuasiveness.[11] Emotivism goes further, claiming pleasurable feelings as the right of every U.S. citizen. Although emotivist pleasure is not an adequate moral argument, it is important to recognize the pleasure we get from morality and to acknowledge that we want to keep this pleasure.

The convolutions and imperfections involved in moral negotiation mean that it could go on forever, never reaching a consensus, always exploring new areas of uncertainty. Pursuing moral negotiation in a practical way, therefore, demands pragmatism: we must aim for a particular effect and stop when that effect is achieved. In the United States, where pragmatism has made a strong impression on intellectual life, politics, and everyday decision making, this orientation is both suitable and inevitable. Pragmatism may be "the best America has to offer itself and the world" (West, 1989: 8). But to say that moral negotiation entails pragmatism is not to say that it is a matter of easy compromise or utilitarian concentration on narrowly defined ends. Such tactics would not be compatible with other important aspects of moral negotiation: its entanglement with history and social relations, its infusion with apparently useless pleasures, and the necessity to understand competing moral frameworks. What is involved is a pragmatism that mixes elements of utopianism and uncertainty, suspicion about grand plans as well as concrete programs for change—"a rich and revisable tradition that serves as the occasion for cultural criticism and political engagement" (West, 1989: 239).[12]

Negotiating Morality

We have suggested that negotiations between moral traditions are possible, despite the traditions' variable characters and powers. Such negotiations pit more powerful perspectives against less powerful but nevertheless troublesome ones. They are skirmishes, not games played out between equals. They operate in and through rhetoric, and the agreements they reach are local and impermanent.

Sometimes moral negotiations appear as confrontations. The preacher and activist Al Sharpton, for instance, made demands on the justice system that often seemed nonnegotiable, but simply by spelling them out against the racist failings of the existing system and within the existing media, he negotiated with the prevailing moral order. The extreme nature of his position was perhaps a necessary counterpoint to the ineffectual reformism of elected African Americans and white liberals. It could be argued that O. J. Simpson's lawyer Johnnie Cochran operated a similar strategy when he repeatedly and exorbitantly drove racism into the initial spousal abuse frame of the case, thus forcing a national discussion on race (Monroe, 1996: 31).

Negotiation by confrontation happens in everyday situations too. Homeless people asking for money sometimes deliver a confrontational narrative of their own destitution and the good salaries, full stomachs, and happy home lives of passersby. Those accosted often interpret this narrative as a threat, but the homeless are rarely in a position to force a donation: the tales they tell are openers to negotiation, not extortion. Moral confrontations also appear in the popular media and in art. The recession movie *Roger and Me* (1989) adopted an unusual in-your-face strategy for a mainstream movie, berating General Motors and its CEO for closing its Flint, Michigan, plant and, in the process, closing down Flint itself. The film was funny enough to make its bitterness watchable, even understandable, to politically indifferent or opposed audiences. The photographer Barbara Kruger has put such negotiation by confrontation into the frame of the poster. In an image critiquing consumerism, for example, she uses a familiar and classical-looking picture of an outstretched, grasping hand, placing above it the Cartesian-genre slogan "I shop therefore I am."

At times, moral confrontation proceeds by affirmation. The movie *Boyz N the Hood* (1991) set a precedent that has since been followed by many television sitcoms, such as *Parent 'Hood* and *The Gregory Hines Show*, by presenting a vision of good African American fatherhood that directly opposed the culturally prevalent discourse of the absent or inadequate African American father. Years before, *The Cosby Show* had tackled stereotypes of the black family similarly, showing images of caring fathers, responsible mothers, and achieving, respectful children. Born-again Christians also conduct a kind of negotiation by affirmation. Their loud proclamations of the living presence of Jesus resist the national consensus

Figure 1. New Jack City. © *1991 Warner Bros. Inc.*

that God is an abstract, even metaphorical entity, closer perhaps to a deep sense of self than to a force in the world (Bloom, 1990: 257–59).

Most moral negotiations are muddier, depending neither on clear opposition nor affirmation. Homeless people, for instance, set up complex juxtapositions when they politely ask for money or "shake the cup" outside restaurants or alongside lines for movies or clubs, physically counterpointing consumption with hunger, enjoyment with suffering, disposable income with zero assets. Some people also develop ironic narratives. While many panhandlers on the New York City subway tell straightforward stories of personal tragedy, one man used to follow speculations about home-going commuters' dinner and entertainment plans—a big Chinese meal, maybe a movie—with an account of his own meager food intake. Another New York panhandler, an African American man, regularly requested donations to the "United Negro Pepperoni Pizza Fund," a line that paid off well except for the unavoidable gifts of pizza slices the man did not want.

This example raises a problem in pursuing moral negotiation by juxtaposition: you may get stuck in the irony. Negotiation by juxtaposition works best in art, literature, movies, and television, which can legitimately settle for an analysis or even a sketch of a moral problem without aiming for a solution. A major theme in coming-of-age books by writers of color—

Figure 2. Barbara Kruger, I Shop Therefore I Am, *1987. Courtesy Mary Boone Gallery, New York.*

such as Sandra Cisneros's *The House on Mango Street* (1991), Lorene Cary's *Black Ice* (1991), and Brent Staples's *Parallel Time: Growing Up in Black and White* (1994)—is the negotiation of the moral dissonance between their culture of origin and the dominant U.S. culture they live in. A fear of betraying their origin vies with a drive to be liberated from its constraints; a desire to be part of the writing culture competes with a reluctance to become what the elite culture demands. All reach a determined but uneasy resolution in the product of this ambivalence—the published writing. Moral negotiation by juxtaposition is prevalent in sitcoms. In one episode of *The Simpsons,* Homer, the breadwinner father, is helped in his efforts to prove himself in a top job by his guardian angel, a male secretary who encourages him to believe he can succeed. This morality tale of the virtue of being true to yourself transports itself into another register when it appears—briefly, ironically—that the secretary who helps Homer out of

Figure 3. I Am Out Therefore I Am, *1989. Courtesy Adam Rolston. Crack-and-peel sticker, offset lithography, 3⅞" x 3⅞".*

selfless love is gay. Some popular representations are adept at containing contrasting moral positions by using a familiar and pleasurable form. *New Jack City* (1991), a good-looking action movie with a sophisticated rap soundtrack, juxtaposed a picture of the euphoric money and power highs of the drug trade, in which a man can say, "My education's slow / But I got long dough"; a story of rogue cops, one black, one white; a critique of the dangers of crack-engendered greed, the destruction of poor African American urban neighborhoods, and the oppression and neglect acting on those neighborhoods; and a call for community responsibility. Something of this contradictory argument came out in Ice-T's "New Jack Hustler," a track played over the opening sequence of a street cop chasing a small-time dealer: "Lock me up / That's genocidal catastrophe / There'll be another one after me."

Representational juxtapositions can be effective when used politically. The AIDS Coalition to Unleash Power (ACT UP) redeployed Kruger's "I shop therefore I am" image (1987) on posters and T-shirts with a different slogan, "I am out therefore I am." With this plagiarized image, ACT UP reclaimed the pleasure of shopping from Kruger's critique and displaced it onto being "out." The image read, too, as a moral affirmation of open gay identity in a time of AIDS and homophobia. The hand in the image now looked as if it were reaching not for consumer goods but for recognition and for rights.

Moral negotiations of the kinds discussed here are minor blips in the calm tenor of conventional morality. Do these blips really matter? Doesn't their transient irony reinforce the authority of the conventional moralities that come before and after them? Aren't their hints of moral resistance about and for people who are not very powerful—few in numbers, socially marginalized, or both? In any case, aren't most of them the products of worthless, formulaic popular media? We could read all the examples in this way. The media often referred to Sharpton, for example, as their own creature, as dependent on them as they were interested in him. Can change really come about through such figures? Kruger's slogan, a popular postcard image, could be read as a funny but uncritical confession of self as shopper. A feminist might dismiss *Boyz N the Hood* as a new take on the old story of the greater value of men as parents. *Cosby* looks a lot like a middle-class white sitcom played, fashionably and lucratively, in blackface. The differences get swallowed up in consumption, "vanishing amid the percolators, stainless steel, mahogany and fabric" of the Cosby abode (Miller, 1988: 69). Homelessness is a large and intractable social problem, and to consider the styles by which homeless people raise money may seem irrelevant or patronizing. We could interpret Cisneros's, Cary's, and Staples's narratives as expressions of the anguish of those well out of danger; Homer's gay angel as one of those fairly common moments on network television that look startling but mean nothing and have no effects; *New Jack City*'s juxtapositional morality as dangerous vacillation; and ACT UP's "I am out therefore I am" as simplistic identity politics.

These criticisms can be countered. We have to accept the significance of popular media within contemporary culture, whether we think them valuable or disparage them. If mainstream cultural institutions often exploit and take over ironically resistant elements of popular culture, we can at least remember that, as a friend of Simone de Beauvoir's said of those who liked her writing but opposed her politically, "They swallow you; but it means they have to swallow your attacks as well; it all helps their ideological breakdown" (1968: 593). Does the minority status of many of the negotiations described here, diminish their significance? The term "minority" in the US must now be understood in terms of the country's realignment by Asian and Latin American, as well as African and European, diasporas. "Minority" cultural production is perhaps the most powerful part of what *Ebony* calls the "browning" of America (Whitaker, 1992). These are discourses that the United States in the time of the "Post" must not only tolerate but solicit and study closely: it needs them. For this reason, "minority" definitions and negotiations of moral positions have an important place in this book's arguments, though "minority" is a term insufficient to describe them.

What, though, of the contention that the kinds of moral negotiation we have been discussing are incidental, not because of cultural marginality but because one side lacks the power to impel serious negotiation, so that it will never really get anywhere? Outside the popular media, art, and literature, the demand that moral negotiations reach a pragmatic solution becomes intense. Arguments by confrontation, affirmation, and juxtaposition all have to stop at some pragmatic end. This necessity is especially obvious when the negotiation takes place in the time-limited fields of medicine and law.

A 1992 attempt to change the legal definition of death provides illustrations of both the failure and the success of such necessary pragmatism. In Coral Springs, Florida, parents of an anencephalic child, born with a brain stem but no cortex, tried to get her declared brain-dead so that her organs, before they deteriorated, could be donated to children who needed transplants. The legal definition of brain death requires that the brain stem cease functioning. But the medical consensus is that the brain stem is not what makes us human: it's "what goes on upstairs in the brain" that counts, because human brain stems "do not differ substantially from the brain stem of a fish" (*New York Times*, 31 March 1992). Anencephalic children thus seem to be an exceptional medical case that the law has overlooked. The parents of the child went to court to confront the inadequate legal definition. Some medical ethicists raised the problem of the slippery slope: after anencephalics, it might be said that other malformed babies, even mentally retarded babies, could be organ donors. Other ethicists suggested that the natural life span of anencephalic children ought to be respected. Caught in this imbroglio, the infant died after ten days. By then, none of her organs could be used for transplants.

The family wanted to follow up the case. But the medical establishment's conclusion was that the difficulties of pursuing the conflict legally would be insupportable. The establishment invoked utilitarian criteria of economic cost and the small number of children involved, and of potential social harm. As the medical ethicist Robert Levine said, transplant surgeons want to avoid the possibility of using anencephalics "not for ethical reasons but because it creates ill will in the community" (*New York Times,* 29 March 1992). More importantly, though, the conflict's likely ideological intractability, though not quantifiable, seemed to make it practically insoluble (*New York Times,* 31 March 1992; see also *New York Times,* 29 March and 5 April 1992). A considered, pragmatic limitation of moral negotiation can, then, be a justifiable end to such negotiation; it is not the same as a refusal to consider the issues or a self-interested calculation of costs and benefits.

Even a moral negotiation with very limited pragmatic aims can sometimes be effective. Popular discourse on the Lewinsky allegations provides a good example. Often this discourse was straightforwardly emotivist, picturing Clinton as a "charming rogue" or, forgivingly, a sex addict, and explaining Lewinsky as a habitual liar, a sad case, or a brave survivor speaking truth. Popular discourse tried to disentangle and define the moral traditions at play in this scandal, and the interests that drove them. Was the case about sex or the law, people asked, and which was the appropriate moral turf on which to fight it out? The Clinton-Lewinsky events became a movable moral feast, the center of a nexus of explanations that included all of the following, and more: a chivalrous far-right crusade against the satanic sexual harasser in the White House; a conspiracy by anti-Clintonian business and financial interests, or by the independent counsel, Kenneth Starr; opportunism in a Democratic Party prepared to ditch Clinton in pursuit of another term; a delusionally omnipotent and complacent White House; the common sense or lack of principle of Clinton-friendly feminists like Friedan.

If Lewinsky's allegations should be proved, *Time* columnist Andrew Ferguson suggested, the public's "elastic morality" could stretch no further; people would "turn from the very idea of public responsibility" (1998). Even at the start of the scandal, "the public," believing but dismissing the allegations, started stretching morality in new directions as it pragmatically evaluated what was at stake, and for whom, in the affair. The popular analyses suggested a plural "public," variable investments in the state, and diverse levels of collective responsibility and citizenship. Moral negotiation here had as its pragmatic, limited achievement a map of moral traditions and interests. Perhaps, in these complex and ambiguous circumstances, such mapping of the moral terrain was the only kind of negotiation possible.

In this book, we aim, once we have described the positions around particular moral issues, to indicate where and how negotiations between them might and do happen. Moreover, we want to suggest that, if there were more commitment to negotiating between positions, we would bring about more convergences between moralities. It might not be necessary, for instance, for a feminist to view Hedda Nussbaum as a product of patriarchy, a total victim. (Nussbaum is the New York woman who was battered by her partner, Joel Steinberg, who in 1987 killed their adopted child, Lisa.) A more complex evaluation of Nussbaum's behavior could be achieved without deserting or undermining the feminist agenda. And it is possible to establish, within white and African-American discourse, both that the U.S. justice system is institutionally racist and that it occasionally moves beyond racism, as in the second Rodney King trial.

Moral Discourses and Conduct

We have been discussing the uncertainty that currently besets moral discourses and how we can address this uncertainty. We have concentrated on trying to understand spoken, written, and visual representations of morality. These representations demand analysis, not just because of the confused structure of moral thinking but because of the strong relationships between such representations and conduct.

Popular and academic concern about moral uncertainty is closely connected with concern about people's behavior. Public anxiety about a crime victim, for instance, feeds sociological attempts to understand criminality. Politicians trumpeting the need to place the family at the moral center expect that ideal family to deliver lower deviance and higher educational attainment. So how do discourses of morality relate to the moral practicalities that ground our concerns and trouble so many? Moral discourses and moral conduct have mutual *effects*, in the double sense of this word: that is, each has properties of the other as well as consequences for the other.

Moral discourses reflect, to some extent, the current universe of moral action. Developments in reproductive technology that allow a woman to bear her son-in-law's child for her daughter introduce new uncertainties into notions of family. The ability to build vast cross-referenced computer databases intensifies debate about the right to privacy. However, moral discourses can persist beyond the historical circumstances that created them. The captain who left his sinking ship may have made an appropriately modern judgment, but other captains have not followed suit, and a professional board of investigation found him and his senior officers guilty of negligence. Moral discourses, moreover, are often espoused by constituencies that act against them. In the 1980s, voters elected two presidents with strong antiabortion positions, Reagan and Bush, yet most of these voters wanted to retain reproductive choice. Statistically, it is likely that many of them had had or would later have abortions themselves.

Discourses of morality can themselves powerfully affect conduct. They do not produce moral and immoral acts, but they define and order these acts. Extensive public discussion of child abuse cases, such as the death of Lisa Steinberg, make school officials, social workers, and therapists more alert to the symptoms of child abuse and more apt to intervene. The film *JFK* (1991) stimulated yet another media and public evaluation of allegations that John F. Kennedy's assassination resulted from a conspiracy by the CIA, Mafia, or powerful government officials. Some of the practical results of moral discourses are less obvious. What were the effects of Moral Majority paeans to the nuclear-heterosexual family, positions supported by most people in the United States but not implemented by them, as divorce and reported adultery rates indicate (Patterson and Kim, 1991: 94)? Maybe the Moral Majority's nostalgic script—its focus on Christianity, responsibility, hard work, and the family—was one that many liked to hear, though few followed it. The script's effect was, perhaps, that it reassured and comforted us, providing us with satisfying, lulling reminders of a bygone era.

This book is not a nostalgic call to return to moral certainties. Such calls do not address the complicated conditions of contemporary life. We cannot ignore the associations of moral certainty with sexism, racism, homophobia, and totalitarianism, with historical arrogance and cultural complacency. The breaks in the comforting grand moral narratives induced by a series of twentieth-century events, beginning with World War I and Auschwitz, have made the maintenance of universalized ideas of good and evil impossible and irrelevant, and have precipitated an emotivism that mixes personal, professional, and cost-benefit judgments. The contemporary sign of this change is a widespread, benumbing confusion in debates about morality, as in the muddled controversies about sea rescue, mother surrogacy, racial justice, and media power with which we began.

We are arguing both that this confusion is valuable and that more negotiation of morality is desirable and possible. This approach does not require a new universal moral order. Tentative, temporary, local, and negotiated settlements and a committed, historically and socially acute pragmatism fit better with the diverse communities and conflicting agendas in U.S. culture than general solutions and ideological dogmas do. To be a nation that engages productively with moral issues, there is no need to have a single, simple set of morals. Morality can live side by side with complexity.

1 | Strangers to Ourselves: Movies, Books, Art

"My sister in the end jumped naked from the window of the top floor of a seven-story building. This was after a long string of events. She couldn't get her license back. The state had made her take a drunken-driving evaluatory test and, because of this, she fell in with some dangerous characters—a kind of guru who made her think that what she did made no difference at all. Such were the fates of the heroes in ancient Greece: some perished under seven-gated Thebes, which was one battle; others died in Troy, fighting for Helen. These were the sons of gods and mortal women."
Tama Janowitz, *Slaves of New York*

It is part of morality not to be at home in one's home.
Theodor Adorno, *Minima Moralia*

Moral Tales

Titles appear over an out-of-focus river scene shot in tones of gray. The camera pans to a young boy on a bridge looking at a doll. Color and clarity replace grainy grays on the screen. With a look of determination, the boy throws the doll into the river, and it floats downstream. As the camera follows it, howls break the silence. The camera cuts to a dead girl, eyes open, who lies on the river bank. Beside her, a high school boy rocks back and forth. The camera zooms in on one of the corpse's hands, turned up in a grasping gesture. The scene ends with the young boy bicycling across the bridge and out of the frame.

This cryptic beginning to the 1987 movie *River's Edge* introduces its main themes. Even the lack of focus in the opening shot signals the fuzziness that in the film typifies contemporary ideas of good and evil. The boy "drowns" his sister's doll and then bikes nonchalantly away. The adolescent has strangled his girlfriend, and although he howls, he does not regret his act. He may feel self-disgust or angst, but not guilt.

In *River's Edge*, adolescents confront the murder of one friend by another. This plot allows the film to explore the loss of criteria for making

Figure 4. River's Edge. *High school students surrounding body of their dead friend.*

moral decisions. The movie was inspired by a real-life incident in which an adolescent strangled his girlfriend in November 1981 in Milpitas, California. After depositing her on a hill overlooking Milpitas, he invited his friends to view the corpse. As was detailed in *California* magazine, these teenagers did not report the murder, and except for bringing additional people to view the corpse, they went on with their lives, leaving the corpse to rot for twelve days (Kaye, 1982). Responding to the film's retelling of this story, a reviewer called it a "cultural event" that "suddenly forces you to see your culture, your history . . . in a different light" (Rosenbaum, 1987: 80). The movie seemed so striking an emblem of the culture's moral predicament that another reviewer judged it the "most disturbing movie" he had seen in his entire reviewing career (Denby, 1987: 90).

    River's Edge presents various dissonant discourses of morality in the responses of the teenagers to the murder of their friend. Their responses are vague or adopted from convenient models in movies and television. Patriotism, gang loyalty, self-defense, and love are all invoked as the characters attempt to fold the murder into their lives. One youth says, "We've got to test our loyalty against all odds. . . . I feel like Chuck Norris." Another youth thinks someone should tell the police, because, "It might be me next." Although these teenagers' contending moral discourses are kept in play even after one of them "narks" and the police get involved, none is convincingly developed. In *River's Edge,* the point is moral illiteracy, so that despite the variety of moral discourses put forward, each is cast as deficient or flawed.

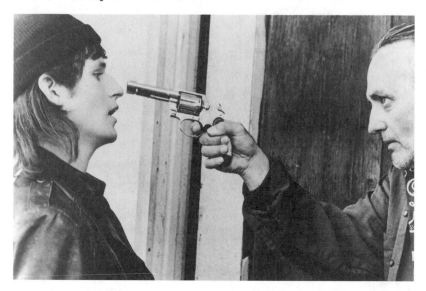

Figure 5. River's Edge. Left, *Layne (Crispin Glover) and* right, *Feck (Dennis Hopper).*

     The film's power to disturb comes from its presentation of a moral universe that seems strange but not completely alien. The film isolates positions of moral uncertainty that the viewer recognizes, but, separated from daily life and accumulated in cinematic sequences, they have the power to shock. This strategy of shocking, really a strategy of estrangement, is familiar to literary theorists. For instance, in 1917, Victor Shklovsky wrote that poetic language is partially a matter of foregrounding, of wrenching a semantic element out of its usual context and bringing it forward in an unexpected way. Such foregrounding makes this element strange and thereby, Shklovsky argued, poetic (1989: 741). Shklovsky's theory is useful in giving an account of artistic representations that, like those discussed in this chapter, isolate elements of the culture's moral life and, by making them strange, turn them into objects of deliberation. In these texts, the role of estrangement often goes beyond that of aesthetic device and describes an existential condition. When it comes to morality, something that is thought to be *of* us, such strangeness reflects on us and reflects us, in Nietzsche's phrase, as strangers to ourselves (1989: 15). The quality of strangeness, of foreignness, though, is always incomplete.[1] Because we recognize it and respond, it has an element of familiarity. This quality of strangeness haunted by the familiar inheres in many representations of moral uncertainty.

     The moral perversity of the *River's Edge* universe, which is also our own, is one source of a sense of estrangement. The feeling of strangeness also strikes when you step into uncharted moral terrain. In the last scene of Ariel Dorfman's play *Death and the Maiden* (1992a), a woman, her husband, and the man who raped and tortured her sit side by side dressed in evening clothes in a concert hall, listening to an orchestra play Schubert. The play explores how Chile's hope of sustaining a new and fragile democracy rests on the peaceful coexistence of those who were torturers in the Pinochet dictatorship and those who were tortured by them. *Death and the Maiden* is a vehicle for contemplating the disturbing moral ambiguities that such a situation provokes. In the play's afterword, Dorfman asks:

> How do we keep the past alive without becoming its prisoner? How do we forget it without risking its repetition in the future? And what are the consequences of suppressing that past and the truth it is whispering or howling to us . . . ? And perhaps the greatest dilemma of them all: how to confront these issues without destroying the national consensus which creates democratic stability? (59)

The play is a raw exposition of the situation's moral ambiguities. Does the cost of democracy include not punishing the man who raped and tortured you? Refusing accommodation and reconciliation would mean imitating the bloody practices of the preceding regime, turning yourself into a torturer. However, the accommodation between victim and oppressor, their uneasy reconciliation, could erode the very morality that democracy is meant to support. In a letter to the *New York Times,* Dorfman writes that the play "demands of the community that it examine its own complicity in the events happening on stage; it lodges the tragedy of the protagonists in the fractures and failings of society" (1992b). The play depicts a moral dilemma that extends beyond Chile, confronting, for instance, Germany, South Africa, the Balkans, and the republics of the former Soviet Union. Indeed, the dilemma appears wherever people who have had irreconcilable differences must live together—whether in the exploded neighborhoods of Crown Heights in Brooklyn and South Central Los Angeles or in families where violence or sexual abuse has occurred.

When past moral scripts can no longer be applied to the present, that present may separate from the body of tradition and appear as a Habermasian postmodern moment. That is, the moment we are living feels transitional and creates a sense of disequilibrium for the future as well (Smith, 1992: 23). This disequilibrium translates into moral uncertainty and results in a sense of strangeness. As well as being a textual effect, this strangeness often afflicts characters in stories of moral uncertainty. In Don DeLillo's novel *White Noise* (1985), traditional notions of morality are dissipated in the postmodern "noise" of media networks, computerized information, the deluge of ads, the blitz of products in supermarkets and malls, and redefined households in which "mother," "father," and "child" may refer to disparate people who are not linked by blood and who, because of divorces and re-marriages, may live in separate houses. Jack Gladney, the protagonist, is a "postmodern" man, adrift in a realm without convincing authorities or cer-tainties. Although he yearns for a fixed perspective, none seems tenable. Meditating on a "picture of Kennedy and the Pope in heaven" in a Catholic hospital, he asks Sister Hermann Marie, "Is it still the old heaven, like that, in the sky?" She replies, "Do you think we are stupid?" (317). The most she can offer him is the rationale that the church sustains the pretense of such beliefs: "Our pretense is a dedication. . . . As belief shrinks from the world, people find it more necessary than ever that *someone* believe" (319). Even when he plans to kill his wife's lover, Gladney cannot sustain an idea of the lover as evil and as deserving death. Confronted with the actual man bleed-ing from the gunshot wounds Gladney inflicted, he is unable to maintain the narrative of wronged husband seeking revenge. In the end, he switches moral scripts and saves the man's life (310–15).

Almost everything you see and read—novels, films, TV, photography—is preoccupied, if not obsessed, with demonstrating or interrogating the moral ambiguities of contemporary culture. Although these representations of moral ambiguity infect us all with a sense of strangeness, they offer a wide range of judgments—from a conviction that contemporary culture offers no moral limits, as in Bret Easton Ellis's novel *American Psycho* (1991), to a preacherly insistence on bolstering traditional institutions to stem the tide of moral decay, as in John Singleton's film *Boyz N the Hood* (1991), which argues that proper fathering is critical for saving inner-city black youth from death and jail. More often, though, a movie or novel explores and details moral uncertainty and then abandons it without recommending action. Woody Allen moves toward such a stalemate in *Crimes and Misdemeanors* (1991) by setting contemporary scenes of today's muddled morality next to clips from old movies. Juxtapositions with 1940s films are meant to demonstrate a discrepancy in moral attitude between the earlier era and the present. The moral positions in the old films are neither equivocal nor equivocated, as they are in the contemporary scene. Allen, unlike the social reformer Singleton, is fascinated by the turn to uncertainty and makes it his object to put it before the public.

However directors, novelists, and playwrights judge the culture's moral ambiguity, art and morality are linked. Art has always helped set an agenda for morality. It distills moral positions, isolates them in representa-tions, and puts them out again into the public domain. Art's analyses of moral discourses focus on locating symptomatic moments and emblematic acts. But art is under no pressure to negotiate moral complexities or produce solutions. It is more preoccupied with sifting moral ambiguities and mapping the historical breaks that provoke such ambiguities. Art also traces the deep nostalgia that results from moral uncertainty and the anxiety the culture exhibits as it moves toward a more complex moral condition.

The artistic representations that tumble out of movie studios, word processors, and darkrooms portray contemporary morality as in search of itself or frozen in ambiguity or sometimes even in panic. Moral uneasiness seems particularly entrenched in images of the U.S. family and justice system. When the family is used as a metaphor to convey such uneasiness, it is portrayed as decentered or ambivalent. Television has nearly abandoned the happy, nuclear family as a vehicle of moral indoctrination. From the sitcom *Married with Children* to the weekly docudramas, the aberrations and permutations of the media family—ranging from insult to incest—crystallize the culture's troubled relationship to morality. Even in art, the family has come under scrutiny: the Sally Mann photography exhibit *Immediate Family* (1992) and the New York Museum of Modern Art exhibit *Pleasures and Terrors of Domestic Comfort* (Galassi, 1991) are two examples. In family photographs, Mann evokes the disturbing undercurrents that are now part of the discourse of family relationships. She repeatedly sexualizes her prepubescent children, thus gathering contemporary anxieties about physical and sexual abuse in traditional families into the frame of her compositions. She tracks the ambiguities in viewers' fears and assumptions concerning family life. Where a viewer first sees radical exploitation and perversion of emotional and economic dependencies within the traditional family, as in the photo *The Terrible Picture, 1989*—a nude shot of Mann's younger daughter at age four with her eyes closed and her body covered with suspicious marks—the child has, in reality, been playing in the dirt. Although it turns out that this photo does not depict child abuse, the suggestion has been made.[2] The child may in fact be abused in other ways, emotionally perhaps, or she may be thought to represent other abused children who themselves are not easily identified. By such subversion of viewers' expectations, Mann explores the multiple uncertainties that haunt contemporary family relationships.

Tina Barney uses a more subtle photographic lexicon to depict the isolation experienced in family life. *Sunday New York Times* (1982), in *Pleasures and Terrors of Domestic Comfort,* features members of Barney's family assembled in a dining room (Galassi, 1991: 39). The photographic composition, as well as the title, leads the viewer to expect a traditional family

Figure 6. Tina Barney, Sunday New York Times, *1982. Courtesy Janet Borden Gallery, New York.*

Sunday morning scene. But Barney captures a moment in which mother, father, grandmother, husband, wife, and who goes with whom cannot be discerned, as with the dispersed family portrayed in DeLillo's novel. The family's interest is focused mainly on various sections of the *New York Times* rather than on one another. Eleven people, no more than two talking to one another—most in postures of isolation or contemplation—constitute a portrait that questions the nuclearity of the contemporary family and emphasizes, as do Mann's photographs, the moral unease and alienation that now accompany membership in the family group.

Macabre portraits of moral ambivalence through the family metaphor have garnered large audiences. Jane Smiley's bestseller *A Thousand Acres* (1991) looks under the carpets of a Midwest millionaire farming dynasty to find incest and strangling patriarchal control that ultimately destroys the dynasty, the farm, and the meanings they held of shared hard work, family solidarity, and a vision of a progressively prosperous future. *A Thousand Acres* probes gangrenous attachments of love and duty between siblings, neighbors, husbands and wives, and fathers and daughters. Smiley's, however, does not match the macabre family of the 1991 film *The Grifters,* based on Jim Thompson's novel. Here, maternal and filial love are integral elements in a drama of incest and murder. Although vestiges of traditional familial affection remain, the mother does not hesitate to impoverish her son or to risk his life so that she may escape from the mob, from which she is caught stealing. When he refuses to give her his money, she attempts sexual seduction. In the final, stunning scene, she accidentally murders him. Nevertheless, she composes herself, gathers his money, now bloodstained, and goes on with her life. The shifting and ambivalent relationship between real and convenient love in the transactions of mother and son gives the film its powerful cultural resonance.

Like the family, the justice system often serves as an emblem of moral confusion. In films and novels, justice is depicted as pathologically bureaucratic, immune to the issue of right and wrong. It is baffled by the exhaustive distinctions of legal codes, such as those between degrees and kinds of murder, assault, and robbery; by prosecutors' low expectations for conviction and the political proclivities of a particular judge or district attorney; and by professionals—such as psychologists, social workers, doctors, forensic experts, and spokespersons representing advocacy groups—each of whom has only a partial perspective. The bafflement of justice cuts across class lines, from the yuppies in novels such as *The Bonfire of the Vanities* by Tom Wolfe (1987) and *American Psycho* by Bret Easton Ellis (1991) to the poor black youths in the films *Juice* (1992) and *New Jack City* (1991). In *New Jack City,* a black youth who has risen to become an all-powerful cocaine king battles police who are intent on saving their neighborhood from him, but the fact that the cops finally capture him is irrelevant. The justice system is so incapacitated by its tangle of laws and procedures that moral action is impossible. The cocaine king is confident that he will be out of jail in a few months. He knows that because guilt and innocence have been reduced to two elements among dozens in the judicial drama, he will be able to manipulate decisions to fall in his favor. In fiction, as in many legal cases, "guilt" and "innocence" are terms with an inappropriately archaic ring or are inadequate to contemporary events.

Morality and Nostalgia

The past is a ubiquitous presence in artistic representations of morality. In Woody Allen's *Crimes and Misdemeanors* (1989), a scene in which the film's protagonist and his mistress argue over his wish to end their relationship is juxtaposed with a clip with a similar subject from Alfred Hitchcock's 1941 film *Mr. and Mrs. Smith.* Compared with the confusions of contemporary morality, the clip evokes an era when moral postures were fairly certain, when everyone seemed to know and agree upon what good and bad meant, when their fixity was assumed. In Hitchcock's screwball comedy, the misunderstanding concerns the legitimacy of a marriage certificate and is resolved when the couple is reunited. In Allen's black comedy, the quarrel is resolved with a murder. The past, or at least the nostalgic view of it represented by the Hitchcock clip, is offered as a measure of the muddled present.

Many cultural representations express nostalgia for the moral certainties of recent pasts (Friedman, 1993: 240–44). The success of Broadway shows reviving old musicals and films; of TV reruns from the 1950s, 1960s, and 1970s; of pop music, which recycles these decades; of films and television shows that tap into nostalgia, such as *The Wonder Years, Driving Miss Daisy* (1989), and *A League of Their Own* (1992); and of the resurrected careers of figures such as John Travolta, Tony Bennett, and Rosemary Clooney demonstrates the pull of these moral lost paradises. The 1950s seem to have a special place in the lexicon of nostalgia as an emblem of moral simplicity and stability so powerful that nostalgia can be transmitted by a hint of 1950s musical or visual style.[3] *The Grifters* plays off these connotations by using an indeterminate retro look at odds with its moral perversity. More straightforwardly, the resurgence of 1950s styling in advertising in the midst of the booming economy of the 1980s emphasized the seductiveness of morally sanitized 1950s images. It was more appealing to sell expensive perfume, clothes, or cars with a black-and-white image of old-style sophistication than with a full-color image of a contemporary yuppie consumer.

The description of the past as a time of moral stability is only one role among many that the past is playing in the effort to define contemporary moral ambiguity. When President Bush blamed the May 1992 Los Angeles riots, following the Rodney King verdict, on failed Great Society programs of the 1960s, he was like many who reach into the past to seek causes of contemporary moral ineptitude and confusion.[4] The past often acts as a matrix for understanding the present. It may be pictured as the scene of irreparable harm or the scene of irrecoverable paradise. It can serve as the repository of moral rectitude, the site of explanation, or the context of blame. The nostalgic view, the longing for a paradisial past, is often taken in the most pessimistic representations of the current moral condition, which present it as bleak and doomed. Movies, novels, and artworks reflect contemporary culture as confused and hopeless of future remedy. They show discomfort at having to negotiate moral contingency and change, and call on the past as refuge and antidote. Such representations are so common that U.S. culture sometimes seems suffused with moral homesickness, with longing for an imagined time before the fall from moral certainty.

Forrest Gump (1994) goes even further, transforming events associated with the turn to moral uncertainty into nostalgic flash cards. The movie features a character with an IQ of seventy-five and the Hollywoodized values of the 1950s. Here dumb and dumber means moral and more moral. As Gump sprints (he's a runner) through recent U.S. history, including the Vietnam War and Watergate, he turns it into, as Howard Hampton terms it, a "Hallmark sympathy card" (1994: 2). Viewed through Gump's point of view, the past is reinvented in a "back-to-the-future attempt to perform the cosmetic, reconstructive surgery of 'reillusionment'" (3). The familiar images of Vietnam, Kennedy, and Nixon offer the film's audience the nostalgic pleasures of gazing at a past cleansed of complex historical meaning by Gump's intellectual limitations, which the film offers as his moral strengths.[5]

Many contemporary works find in the past not the rush of transient events nor the actualities of history but a sense of timelessness, a metaphysical or atemporal perspective from which values hold firm. Nostalgia for the past ignores history or idealizes it in the search for unshakable certainty. Jean-François Lyotard writes that nostalgia is part of the postmodern condition, expressing yearning for the grand explanatory stories that used to make sense of the world but no longer do. He describes these stories as "great narratives by means of which we attempt to order the multitude of events." An example is the story that history is progressive, that, for instance, oppressed people will be emancipated and that the world strives, with ultimate success, toward a universal good, implying agreement on what is moral. In the postmodern condition, argues Lyotard, such narratives no longer compel belief, because our sense of the universal has eroded, if not disappeared (1989: 315).

Nostalgia for the lost great narratives seems a stable element of texts that concern themselves with what they view as the postmodern condition. Deeply felt yearning for the timeless narrative of family drives Gladney's nostalgia in *White Noise*. In Jay McInerney's *Bright Lights, Big City* (1984), nostalgia for any timeless story consumes the main character. In one scene, he longingly meditates on the Hasidim populating his subway car. He contemplates a Hasid who is sitting beside him:

> He is reading from his Talmud, running his finger across the page. . . .
> This man has a God and a History, a Community. He has a perfect
> economy of belief in which pain and loss are explained in terms of a

> transcendental balance sheet, in which everything works out in the end
> and death is not really death. Wearing black wool all summer must
> seem like a small price to pay. (57)

In comparison, the protagonist, a yuppie with writerly pretensions who is
on a treadmill of drugs, one-night stands, and a meaningless job, feels "like
an integer in a random series of numbers." Rastafarians also inspire his envy,
and he thinks, "Sometimes you feel like the only man in the city without
group affiliation" (57). The past overtakes him in the form of freshly baked
bread, reminding him of his mother's. The bread becomes his vehicle of redemption. Awakening from a cocaine high to the smell of fresh bread, his
abused nose bleeding, he trades his Ray-Bans for a bag of hard rolls in a gesture to retrieve the transcendent narrative of family: "You get down on your
knees and tear open the bag. The smell of warm dough envelops you. The
first bite sticks in your throat and you almost gag. You will have to go slowly.
You will have to learn everything all over again" (182). Here, going backward is the preferred direction, because going forward can be imagined only
as a continuation of the vicious present.

Nostalgia is the remedy of choice for moral homesickness even in
more traditional texts. In John Updike's *Rabbit at Rest* (1990), nostalgia for
an enduring moral story drives Rabbit, seriously ill with heart disease, to
play basketball competitively with a young man. Rabbit makes a desperate
effort, which ultimately costs him his life, to return to his youth, when the
macho morality he subscribed to provided terms he recognized and could
negotiate. His current life, on the other hand, includes social workers,
twelve-step programs to break various dependencies, clinics, and dread diseases like AIDS, born of what are for him unspeakable acts. Terrifying to
him, these terms are associated with weird and unmanning shrink talk and
a bewildering ethics of sensitivity and forgiveness. Unlike the terms of his
youth, they have rules he cannot respect and a mysterious vocabulary he
cannot speak.

In another pattern of nostalgia, a past space of moral clarity is used
by writers and filmmakers as the repository of redemptive fantasies. In *New
Jack City,* justice can be applied to the corruptions and knots that paralyze
the legal system only if it comes from another time, as an aberration from
a past when there was moral confidence. The film fulfills its nostalgic yearning for certain justice by bringing the past to usurp the present. It personifies morally certain justice as an old man with an old-time morality, who is
willing to risk his life to get rid of evil. He, rather than the justice system,
gives the cocaine king his due by shooting him. We cannot, this film argues,

expect justice within contemporary legal institutions. Justice is a relic, an occasional chance gift from the past. But the hope held out in *New Jack City* is less than unreliable; it is unreal. Nostalgia spins fairy tales about the past. As seen through the homogenizing view of *Forrest Gump*, the catastrophies of Vietnam, Kennedy's assassination, and Watergate are rendered simply as familiar moments from the past, exploiting audience nostalgia as blatantly as do greeting card images.

For some, the present is so denuded that even nostalgia has become damaged; thus, the past as a repository of values is a useless well from which to draw. Tama Janowitz, in *Slaves of New York* (1986), adopts this view. She is less confident that the past can be read meaningfully in a diminished present than are the other New York City "brat pack" writers, Bret Easton Ellis and Jay McInerney. Her most profound theme, in fact, is missed or impoverished interpretation. The meaning of events is blank to her characters, and although they do not seem to mind, the territory they negotiate seems morally blank as well.

Janowitz has gleaned techniques from the comic strip—from the alliteration of her characters' names (e.g., Marley Mantello) to the inappropriateness of their desires and actions. Her flat, exaggerated, and uninterpreted presentation of a bizzarely bankrupt universe in which religion, politics, and even greed bubble out of characters' mouths but are not connected to a convincing libido is an alternate strategy for portraying a morally vacuous universe. Vestiges of life before the fall from moral certainty are indicated in the empty vocabularies used by her characters, yet they do not add up to mourning a prelapsarian, unrecoverable past. They suggest only that rescue is *not* at hand, for what these vocabularies once contained has become vague or forgotten—cultural refuse.

In an episode of *Slaves of New York* titled "Ode to a Heroine of the Future," Janowitz proposes that these older vocabularies are inappropriate to current events. Lessons drawn from them aid in the individual's and the culture's self-delusion. Marley Mantello, the artist-narrator, tells the story of his sister's death. He attributes to her heroic stature the fact that his "sister in the end jumped naked from the window of the top floor of a seven-story building." She had the fate of "the heroes in ancient Greece: . . . my sister was a throwback to these earlier times." He also rhapsodizes on "the first race of man," who "was made of gold" (245). These paeans seem to have something to do with his sister and her death, but he never explains what. He believes that the mere proximity of the two—the gods and his sister—in his thoughts is sufficient to connect them. He backs away from a direct confrontation of the sordidness of his sister's condition by this means. On the night she dies, he meets her and her boyfriend in a club called the Gulag Archipelago. After noting her black eye, her ill health, and symptoms of cocaine use, he plays Frank Sinatra on the jukebox, a way of denying the sordid present by associating it with sentimental icons of the past. Later that night, Mantello's sister climbs on the window ledge of her boyfriend's apartment while high on cocaine, totters, and then slips off.

Mantello searches for a way to make sense of her death. He describes his few remaining thoughts as "something quite defunct and forgotten in the closet: an old cheese sandwich, perhaps, or a half-empty bottle of root beer" (259). Cheese sandwiches and root beer evoke a more innocent time; they are 1950s food, now stale and unusable, for in the present he has no context in which to put his sister's death. Then he fastens on the fantasy of the Greek gods. As the episode's title announces, he imagines that in the future his sister's death will have a heroic meaning. Janowitz's attitude toward nostalgic images that convey a complete moral order, such as the Greek heroes, is not like that of Woody Allen or McInerney. Not only do they speak a different moral vocabulary, but even the alphabet in which they are written is strange. Comparison or application to contemporary events can be only comically inappropriate. The name of the nightclub, the Gulag, for instance, implies the gap between the historical allusion and contemporary times. Janowitz does not intend the name of the club to represent the severe condition of the present. The gulag represents true tragedy, evokes radical evil and heroic resistance. There is nothing in the events of "Ode to a Heroine of the Future" remotely to deserve such an allusion, and it is the very distance between the historical event and its diminished meaning in the present that Janowitz is measuring. If such measurements imply nostalgia, it is a nostalgia that has forgotten the object of its yearning.

The Past as Explanation

Although nostalgia is one approach to the past in artistic representations of morality, in another the past becomes the site of explanation. Such representations find the origins of moral sickness there. A historical event almost compulsively linked to a turn in morality is the Holocaust. Under the name of Auschwitz, philosophers and artists have described a transformed moral horizon. In philosophical texts, Auschwitz functions as an explanatory myth for the modern condition. Elie Wiesel declares that after Auschwitz, infinity can no longer be measured by goodness. The infinite must henceforth be gauged by imagining the limit of evil (1982: 3–11). Theodor Adorno believes that Auschwitz introduced a profound cleavage in Western thought. Adorno speaks of the legacy of Auschwitz in Western culture, proposing that "after Auschwitz," ideas of God and of death changed: "After Auschwitz there is no word tinged from on high, not even a theological one, that has any right unless it underwent a transformation"; "In the camps death has a novel horror; since Auschwitz, fearing death means fearing worse than death" (1973: 367, 371). Cornel West identifies the Holocaust with "the end of the European Age (1492–1945)." He argues that it "shattered European self-confidence and prompted intense self-criticism, even self contempt" (1989: 235). For Jürgen Habermas, "Since then [the Holocaust,] a *conscious* life is no longer possible without mistrust for continuities that assert themselves without question and also want to draw their validity out of their questionlessness" (1990: 208). In an appraisal of the Auschwitz effect, Lyotard attributes to it a "sorrow in the *Zeitgeist*." This sorrow emerges from a post-Holocaust loss of belief in material progress and sociohistorical change:

> Following Theodor Adorno, I use the name Auschwitz to point out the irrelevance of empirical matter . . . in terms of the modern claim to help mankind to emancipate itself. What kind of thought is able to sublate (*Aufheben*) Auschwitz in a general . . . process towards universal emancipation? So there is a sort of sorrow in the *Zeitgeist*." (1986: 9)

"Auschwitz" (Hitler, Nazis, concentration camps, the Holocaust) is repeatedly raised in current representations—TV documentaries, movies, books, and fine art. Although not all of these works make contemporary moral uncertainty their central theme, it is nearly always presented as one of the Auschwitz effects. For many writers, directors, and artists, Auschwitz has become an iconographic event—an explanation of or gloss on our moral condition. In DeLillo's *White Noise*, Gladney is fixated on Hitler because of the connection between the events that the word "Hitler" signifies and the uncertainties and ambiguities of the postmodern moral life that inform Gladney's melancholy.

Auschwitz is presented as having definitive explanatory power over the present; it clarifies certain incapacities. It is construed as both cause and symbol of a loss of confidence in moral certainties and universals. The European-produced film *Zentropa*, released in 1992 and shown in art theaters throughout the United States, presents Auschwitz as an abiding weight on our present and future, an event that taints and corrupts all healing or ameliorating efforts—repentance, forgiveness, forgetting. *Zentropa*'s Danish director, Lars Von Trier, used AIDS patients to play concentration camp victims—a fact announced in film publicity—clearly burdening the present with Auschwitz associations.

Auschwitz is a persistent encumbrance on the present in many narratives. The relentless focus of *The Grey Zone* (1996), a play by Tim Blake Nelson that takes place in "Number One Crematorium, Auschwitz II—Birkenau" in autumn 1944, is the plague on moral certitude that the death camps let loose. Nelson's letter to the cast confesses the personal effect of the Holocaust: "In spite of its taking place before I was born, [it] is as personal, and in a sense as deeply confessional, as any piece I'll write. . . . This play proposes that there's criminality in being alive."[6] In the already morally contracted universe of "Number One Crematorium, Auschwitz II—Birkenau," the play concerns the Sonderkommando, a special unit of male prisoners, mainly Jews, who had to assist in the gassing and burning of their own people or face death themselves.[7] The play describes the moral ambivalence of their forced collaboration, an ambivalence that is carried into the present. It opens on a scene in which one of them has attempted suicide after assisting in the extermination of his family. The play is relentless in its moral pessimism. Life-saving, moral acts are sabotaged, and opportunities to act ethically are either missed or bungled. With each instance of morality betrayed, a sense of helplessness grows, communicating the sorrow that Lyotard describes as suffusing the zeitgeist. *The Grey Zone*'s last monologue belongs to the ghost of a cremated girl:

> The first part of me rises in dense smoke that mingles with the smoke of others. Then there are the bones, which settle in ash, and these are swept up to be carried to the river. And last, bits of our dust, that simply float there in air beside the workings of the men. These bits of dust are grey. We settle on their shoes and on their faces and in their lungs, and they become so used to us that soon they don't cough and they don't brush us away. (78–79)

The river and men, the play suggests, carry these bones and ashes beyond Auschwitz into a melancholy future.

Although Auschwitz is among the best-theorized and most widely cited breaks in moral certainty, it is most meaningful to intellectuals and artists who place themselves in the European tradition. Other historical moments have also been identified as eroding positions of moral certainty. Native American writers, such as Leslie Marmon Silko in *Ceremony* (1977) and *Almanac of the Dead* (1991), repeatedly return to the European conquest. For many African American writers, the significant historical referent is slavery. The tracing of current moral ambiguities, uncertainties, and transgressions to slavery contributes to the plots of many contemporary African American narratives—for instance, Toni Morrison's *Beloved* (1987), Carolivia Herron's *Thereafter Johnnie* (1991), Gloria Naylor's *Mama Day*

(1989), and, to a lesser extent, John Edgar Wideman's *Philadelphia Fire* (1990) and Jamaica Kincaid's *Lucy* (1991). Even when slavery is not a major plot element, it may have an explanatory function nevertheless. Wideman devotes a single paragraph in *Philadelphia Fire* to slave times, citing an incident in which slaves danced in a burying ground (1990: 98). That reference operates as a gloss on black life now, which, according to the novel, is self-destructively forgetful of the past.

In contrast to historical breaks in moral certainty attributed to events such as the Holocaust, the liberation movements of the 1960s, and the assassinations of John F. Kennedy and Martin Luther King, Jr., slavery encompasses a less discrete time period. It is also further in the past than other commonly cited breaks in moral continuity. Perhaps for these reasons, slavery is often depicted as a history that must be overcome rather than one that defines the present. It has the power of explanation but not determination. This possibility of going beyond the past becomes evident at the conclusions of Carolivia Herron's *Thereafter Johnnie* and Toni Morrison's *Beloved*. In Herron's narrative, elements from ancient Greek incest myths of origins are woven together with the Judeo-Christian myth of redemption. Herron tracks tragic contemporary conditions of black life to a myth of incest and rape: the slave Laetitia is first raped by her father, who is also her white owner, and then by his white son, her half-brother. To retain their power over her, they kill or sell the male issue of their unions. These original transgressions have directed the course of black life, and they have generated a permeating sorrow:

> "And from these origins has there come this great curse upon our house: 'The females shall be raped and the males shall be murdered.' And the males that are not murdered shall be sold, and to certain ones of the males that are neither murdered nor sold, to certain of those few males come late into the house marrying, and to certain of the males born to the house but who neveretheless survive murder and slavery— to these shall be given the power of revenge upon the females of their own house who consented with the white males for their destruction, these males shall be given the female children of their own house, and these shall be raped. And raped again." (1991: 239–40)

Redemption is imagined in the text as a certain "light" that holds out the promise of a future in which slavery will function as Greek or biblical myths do now—with historical antecedents transformed into cultural explanatory myth.

With *Beloved*, Toni Morrison, like Herron, presents slavery as an explanatory legacy for African Americans. However, it is a legacy that does not necessarily decide the future. Morrison is less interested in attributing the origins of the contemporary condition to slavery than in exploring the crushing moral dilemmas that slavery fosters and in imagining the terms by which a future may be projected. Unlike many writers and intellectuals on Auschwitz, contemporary black writers often emphasize future scripts more than the sorrowful imprint of the past on the present. Based on a historical incident, *Beloved* tells the story of an escaped slave who murders her baby, Beloved, and threatens to murder all of her children rather than turn them over to the white man who owns her. An emblem of courage, guilt, and self-destructiveness, Sethe, who commits the infanticide, figures the complicated legacy of slavery. Like Sethe, the novel suggests, African Americans need to come to terms with the legacy of slavery for a future not limited by that legacy. Obsession with the past, with ghosts and memory—as Sethe is obsessed until the last pages of the narrative—breeds a mutilating insularity, if not psychosis. Morrison resurrects the past to appraise its effects in the present and its meaning for the future, how it can be accepted into identity without completely overwhelming it so that an individual can imagine and plan for "tomorrow." Sethe's lover, Paul D, tells her, "Me and you, we got more yesterday than anybody. We need some kind of tomorrow" (1987: 273). As in Dorfman's *Death and the Maiden,* the past is not forgotten. It has authority in the present but cannot completely account for it, thus leaving room, creating an opportunity for a future over which the individual has some power (see Michaels, 1996: 4–8). For Morrison, the future, though severely qualified by moral ambivalence, can truly be entered.

As Auschwitz and slavery figure in philosophical and artistic explanations of the current state of morality, the 1960s dominate such explanations in more popular representations and, of course, in politics. In his 1960s bashing, Newt Gingrich, following the Republicans before him, found it politically expedient to locate the beginnings of current moral dilemmas in that era: "The belief that there are no general rules of behavior . . . began to supplant the centuries-old struggle to establish universal standards of right and wrong" (1995: 30). *Forrest Gump,* despite the intense nostalgia through which it views the 1960s, also targets that decade. On the body of Gump's one true love, Jenny, the film records the decade's moral consequences. A civil rights and antiwar protester, she becomes a drug addict and sex worker in the 1970s and leaves the 1980s in a coffin, the victim of AIDS, the movie intimates. Yet no matter how sinister or benign the characterization, the 1960s are seen as a break in postures of moral confidence and certainty, a social rupture that can explain the present. Cornel West writes that in the

United States, the "sixties constitute the watershed period" that "shattered male WASP cultural pretension and predominance" (1989: 238).

Both benign and sinister interpretations of the 1960s are given play in *River's Edge,* which uses this era as a context for analyzing contemporary moral ambiguity. In an early scene, John, the adolescent who murdered his girlfriend, wants dope and so drives to the house of Feck, a crazy 1960s biker with a peg leg whose companion is a sex-shop doll. Armed with a gun, Feck answers the door with the words, "I shot a girl once." Thereafter, viewers are invited to compare Feck's and John's motivations. Feck claims he killed out of love, John because "she was talking shit." Feck's act defines him. Forever after, he lives in the shadow of this murder. For John, however, the murder is a matter of indifference.

Civil rights, civil disobedience, feminism—all are invoked in the film as legacies of the 1960s. The decade of which Feck is one representative is both claimed as a morally purer era and blamed for the confused moral condition of the film's youthful characters. The film deliberately makes a causal link between the political movements of the 1960s and the moral ambiguities of the present, marking a break from times of moral clarity. The promises of the 1960s have deteriorated into current moral uncertainties. The climactic scene in which Feck kills John reiterates the film's argument regarding the relationship between the 1960s and the present. Feck murders John because John cannot adequately explain his act, an egregious, unforgivable sin in Feck's weird 1960s morality of civil disobedience for just cause. In a high school history class on the 1960s, a teacher proclaims, "We turned public sentiment around. . . . There was meaning in the madness." This assertion elicits two student responses, both missing the teacher's point that 1960s protesters affected the social and political system positively: While one student has learned to ask, "Isn't violence bad?" another has learned from the 1960s that "wasting people is great."

The film also suggests that the 1960s have been misinterpreted. The 1960s explosion of authoritarian patterns left a legacy not of freedom and justice but of alienation, license, and arbitrariness. Tim, the boy who "drowns" his sister's doll, has a mother, a product of the 1960s with a full-time job and a live-in boyfriend who, as substitute father, is willing to take on only the role of disciplinarian. Tim's older brother, Matt, and their mother argue over her marijuana cache. The *California* magazine account of the story on which the film is based relates that one of the killer's friends was indeed turned out by his mother because he stole her marijuana (Kaye, 1982). When Tim stays out all night, the exasperated mother screams, "I give up this mother bullshit! I'm nobody's mother!" words connected to, perhaps even made possible by, the women's movement, which came later but often gets blurred into the 1960s.

Despite the blame it casts on the 1960s, *River's Edge* also looks back to the earlier time with some nostalgia for the certainties that drove the decade's political activism. Even the loose morality of the 1960s functions as an instructive contrast to the current paralyzed morality. The film's ambivalence drives the scene in which Feck shoots John. Feck explains his act by saying John didn't love the girl he shot. He didn't feel a thing. Feck doesn't like killing people, but sometimes it is necessary. Some reviewers think this scene argues that even a 1960s homicidal maniac has a surer morality than contemporary middle-class adolescents. However, in casting the twisted Feck as the film's moral arbiter, the film interrogates its own nostalgia, as well as the contemporary moral climate.

The truism that "everyone" remembers what he or she was doing when President Kennedy was shot still gets repeated. In a 1996 novel that takes place in Canada, the protagonist ruminates on November 22, 1963: "'Where were you when JFK was shot?' It was a landmark in all of their lives. . . . She will remember thinking as she stepped back into the street afterwards that everything looked the same but was not" (Schoemperlen, 1996: 223). The Kennedy assassination, an event contributing to the moral break of the 1960s, is itself repeatedly cited as particularly corrosive on the nation's moral life. This specific break occupies DeLillo's *Libra* (1988), a novel that provides the Kennedy assassin Lee Harvey Oswald with a biography and details a conspiracy leading to the shooting. The warning the book delivers, like dozens of other fictional and nonfictional accounts, is that an outlaw, underground network—albeit loosely organized and perhaps the work of chance—is the real power moving history. The assassination was also the subject of Oliver Stone's movie *JFK* (1991), which mined and gathered into a single narrative widely divergent conspiracy theories about Kennedy's assassination that Stone reiterated in his 1995 sequel, *Nixon*. *JFK* proposes a grand plan by the "military-industrial complex"— including the CIA, generals, members of Congress, and Vice President Johnson—as well as the Mafia, to assassinate Kennedy because of his "soft on Communism" policies. The print and broadcast media were obsessed with the film, the theory it expounds, and its implications for political morality. Those who had and even those who had not seen the film could be heard talking about it on subways, in corporate elevators, at lunch counters, and in classrooms. The *New York Times* alone carried more than forty articles on the film and the assassination in the five months after *JFK* was released. After the film, physicians and surgical residents who participated in the

Kennedy autopsy battled one another in books and medical journals over how many bullets struck the president and where they entered and exited. The *JFK* craze even affected history professors, who assessed its accuracy in the *American Historical Review* (1992). Congress was not immune to the film's influence; it was prompted by reactions to the film to lock horns with the FBI and the CIA over reclassifying assassination material to make it available to investigators.

Kennedy assassination mania may be a symptom of the need that people in the United States feel for explanations of generalized moral uneasiness. The assassination took on the function, comparable to that of Auschwitz, of explaining the people's dissatisfaction with the morality of national political life. The grand conspiracy theory that Stone puts forward in his film is factually dubious. Its explanatory power does not lie primarily with its historical accuracy. Its deepest imprint is in the emotions, where it has a compelling validity. Although people may not believe in Stone's film as history, they believe in his depiction of subterranean, illegal negotiations that result in history. It validates our gut feeling that politicians' actions often have undisclosed subtexts. It provides a context for understanding such phenomena as the Iran-Contra episode, in which high government officials circumvented Congress to pursue a privatized foreign policy—as was asserted by the special prosecutor on Iran-Contra, Lawrence E. Walsh, in January 1994. It also serves the psychological purpose of putting people's moral confusion over how to judge issues and candidates in a setting that allows them to persist in this confusion, that justifies and excuses it, since the significant action, *JFK* teaches, is played out by a conspiracy of forces beyond people's knowledge and control.

Moral Privatization in Art

Specific historical breaks such as Watergate and the Kennedy assassination legitimate individual moral confusion. Moreover, the accretion of dramatic historical instances of moral failure contributes to a sense that contemporary institutions are not capable of defending morality. When history appears thus to have exhausted itself, people retreat to emotional frames of moral judgment and to spheres traditionally characterized in the United States as private, spheres where emotivism is least contested. *JFK* feeds into this privatization with its conspiracy narrative. The public sphere of politics becomes an irrelevant object of moral judgment as well as an inadequate purveyor of society's morality.

The privatization of morality, however, has sources other than a retreat from political moral failure. It reflects Americans' love affair with the authority of the individual vision, no matter how eccentric or hurtful. The habit of feting lawlessness, doubting institutions, distrusting the establishment, and esteeming personal vision in arenas such as religion, which are heavily institutionalized, has contributed to current privatized practices regarding morality. The reverence for individual choice, a quality connected to the founding ideals of the United States, extends to a national tradition of glorifying criminals. Witness the popularity of *Butch Cassidy and the Sundance Kid* (1969), the *Godfather* movies (1972–1990), and the folk-hero status of John Dillinger and Al Capone.[8] Organized crime and fascinating murderers are staples of the American cinema. From *Little Caesar* (1930) to *Silence of the Lambs* (1991), *Natural Born Killers* (1994), and *Dead Man Walking* (1995), the criminal has something of the romantic hero about him—the antiestablishment figure uncontainable in the circumscribed negotiations of the straight life. Even though such films more often than not punish these demonic heros, their seduction of the camera and the audience is clear.

Veneration of the extreme personal vision and the concomitant acceptance of lawlessness has often been traced to the ideal of religious tolerance that is part of the mythology of the colonial period in the United States. The allowing of "other" explanations of the universe led not only to religious pluralism but also, in order to protect this pluralism, to an individualization and privatization of religion (Bellah, et al., 1985: 225). In offering characters whose religious obsessions range from demonology to extreme asceticism, Joyce Carol Oates's gothic novel *Bellefleur* (1980) explores the negative implications of such privatization. Like inhabitants of the United States, her characters feel entitled to shop in the department store of religions and take home whatever suits them, mixing and matching at will to carve out their own religion and their own morality. A privatized ethics, based in individual feeling, defines the Bellefleur family, whose members will do anything, even murder, to advance their individual obsessions. In accord with U.S. culture, the Bellefleurs believe that whatever one feels is right.[9] The individual, rather than the legal system or a church institution, is the final arbiter of right and wrong. Typical of the many imperial characters in *Bellefleur* is Leah, an Amazonian woman whose size is a correlative to her megalomaniacal obsession to restore the family estate to its original 3 million acres. Jean Pierre Bellefleur, having just acquired a pardon arranged by Leah despite his conviction for mass murder, looks on the spectacle of the Bellefleurs and thinks, "What maddened mind, deranged by unspeakable lust, had imagined all this into being. . . ?" (359). Like most of us, the Bellefleurs make moral judgments based on their emotions, but they do not suffer from cultural amnesia; they are aware of various moral traditions. They simply will not privilege these external authorities over their own private emotions when it comes to morality. If this kind of emotivist moral reasoning is scrutinized in films such as *River's Edge,* in *Bellefleur* Oates traces this reasoning to the founding individualist myths of the United States and, with images of vampires, haunted castles, and nonreflecting mirrors, paints U.S. history and morality as a gothic novel.

Emotivism's licensing of individual moral agency presents a more general problem. By locating general moral judgment in individual feelings, we set hurdles to understanding others' judgments. Thus, this eminently democratic formulation of morality does not provide for the development of democratic consensus of moral issues, because it makes a full and rational exchange of moral views difficult. In *Bellefleur,* for instance, the hopelessness of moral consensuses among family members leads one exasperated character to blow up the Bellefleur house and its inhabitants.

At the individual level, others' moralities, and possibly also our own, remain opaque to us. Our private moral sovereignty is bought at the cost of remaining moral strangers to one another and perhaps even to ourselves. This strangeness is exacerbated in novels, films, and art, both because texts concerned with moral uncertainty exaggerate that uncertainty by isolating it and because art has no particular imperative to negotiate individual or eccentric moralities to arrive at consensus.

A liberal humanist version of moral privatization that assumes individual values are progressive, even redemptive, continues to be powerful within artistic representations of morality. It underpins the nostalgia in *Bright Lights, Big City* and is a less defined presence in the hopeful moments of *Death and the Maiden, River's Edge,* and *Thereafter Johnnie.* Liberal humanism is also often yoked to an ecumenical spiritualism that gives the voice of individual moral feeling greater legitimacy. In *New Jack City,* the old man who finally applies justice, although acting out of an idiosyncratic sense of what is right, is a patriarchal figure speaking Old Testament verses.[10]

Morrison's *Beloved* testifies to the persuasiveness of a privatized liberal humanist moral discourse in the most extreme circumstances. Although neither justifying nor condemning Sethe's murder of her infant, the narrative offers a context similar to that in David Rousset's 1946 description of prisoners in *L'univers concentrationnaire,* a "concentrationary universe," where acts that would be condemned as immoral outside the concentration camp are within moral limits in the inverted universe of the camps. This inverted morality is expressed in *Beloved* in Sethe's individual act. But the momentary reversal does not rule out a future in which individuals—Sethe

and Paul D—reassert liberal humanist moral values. Even in this redemptive version, though, moral privatization leads to its usual impasse: how are
we to be sure of the worth of values if they are generated and judged individually? Uneasiness shadows *Beloved*'s concluding sentiments. We can
hope, but not be sure, that individual moral agents transcend a legacy of
slavery and murder.

Moral privatization of an ostensibly redemptive nature received a
euphoric endorsement in the movie *Thelma and Louise* (1991). Like *Butch
Cassidy and the Sundance Kid, Thelma and Louise* is a road movie about two
lawbreakers who at the end must capitulate to the legal establishment or
die. These lawbreakers are women, and the rationale for their increasing
lawlessness is personal revenge against a series of misogynist men, including a Neanderthal husband and a rapist. The movie was panned as preach-
ing "man-hating" feminism by some reviewers and touted as liberating by
others. Yet Thelma's and Louise's criminal acts are either so carefully justified or carried out in such a winning spirit of adventure that audience sympathy is theirs. The women are quite emphatically on the side of justice,
while the men, representing male institutions such as the police and the FBI,
are only on the side of the law, which is portrayed as having less moral value.
Justice and law confront each other regularly in representations of morality,
whether in this movie, where, with sirens screaming, the police and FBI and
the women face off at the edge of the Grand Canyon, or in TV series such as
Law and Order and *Homicide*. In such representations, the law is usually
given the lesser value, as an arbitrary and manipulable code, while justice,
although in the possession of the mere individual, seems to derive from a
higher authority. In these dramas, the individual stands in for that unde-
fined authority.

A darker side of a privatized, emotivist morality is taken up in Pete
Dexter's elegantly sinister novel *Paris Trout* (1988). In this book, as in Oates's
Bellefleur, individualized morality is criminal and psychotic rather than redemptive or romantic. Set in the segregated South of the 1950s, *Paris Trout*
measures personal morality against justice and law. Each of the main characters speaks for one of these three competing moralities. The title character, Paris Trout, is a white businessman in Cotton Point, Georgia. He is
racist, misogynist, violent, and increasingly mad. He sells a car on credit to
Henry Ray, a young black man. Henry Ray has an accident that reveals the
shiny car to be a rusted junk heap. He returns it to Trout, telling him he will
not pay for it. Trout, armed with rifles and accompanied by his hired gun,
pursues Henry Ray to his home, intent on revenge. When he does not find
him at home, he shoots Ray's sister, Rosie, and Ray's mother. Rosie dies as

a result of her wounds, but the mother survives, though she carries Trout's bullet in her chest. The murder is so coldly executed and the victim so clearly innocent that even Cotton Point's racist establishment is moved to arrest Trout. Trout, however, feels he has done nothing wrong: "There was a contract he'd made with himself a long time ago that overrode the law, and being the only interested party, he lived by it. He was principled in the truest way. His right and wrong were completely private" (47). Trout, who has a law degree, understands that he cannot flagrantly violate the law, but his privatized morality tells him that the law is not there to protect blacks. When the prosecutor reminds him that there is one rule in the penal code for both black and white and that when a person breaks it, the code requires an "eye for an eye," Trout responds, "Those ain't the same kind of eyes . . . and they ain't the same kind of rules" (48).

In contrast to Trout's privatized morality are those of his wife and his lawyer. Hannah's and Seagraves's moralities are structured by a distinction between the laws of the gods and the laws of humanity, a distinction Sophocles makes in *Antigone* that still informs accounts of morality. Just as Antigone defies the law of the kingdom to give her brother a religious burial, Hannah's morality is carved out of the sacred and contrasts with Seagraves's, which is carved out of the profane. When Seagraves tries to convince Hannah to keep up appearances during the trial, they have the following exchange:

> He said, "What if I proved that your husband was defending his life by dischargin' those shots?"
>
> Her expression turned unfriendly. "You can't prove what didn't happen," she said.
>
> "It's for a court of law to determine."
>
> She shook her head. "There is no story you can tell in your court that will change what happened in that house. . . ."
>
> "That is a misperception," he said, "that an act is, of itself, a crime or a perversion. It becomes such only after it is judged. . . ."
>
> "The misperception," she said, "is that the law, and lawyers, decide what already happened." (136)

Paris Trout explodes the dialectic of higher justice versus earthly law that traditionally animates texts centered on moral choice, by introducing the third term of privatized morality. This third term subverts the other two, so that no sense of common systems of morality can be maintained. In *Paris Trout,* neither God's law nor humanity's is relevant, because neither moves events nor resolves dilemmas. Rather, Trout's individual morality wins out: at the end of the book, he kills almost all of the principals, including Sea-

Figure 7. A scene from Larry Clark's Kids.

graves and himself. Although Hannah survives, her morality, privileged by Dexter, does not prevail. She returns to the life of a teacher, having made no difference in the tragic drama her husband initiated. In Sophocles' play, Antigone is sacrificed so that her community can learn what is due the gods. In Dexter's novel, no purpose is served through the sacrifice of Rosie or the others whom Trout kills. By expanding this ancient conflict, Dexter dramatizes the deadly extreme to which the canonization of a privatized morality may lead.

An equally powerful but more indirect representation of the inadequacies of emotivist moral privatization can be found in the Larry Clark film *Kids* (1995), which, like *River's Edge,* focuses on a group of adolescents, this time from New York City and of mixed economic, ethnic, and racial backgrounds.[11] *Kids* has even fewer adult characters than *River's Edge* has. The adults who do appear are used exclusively as (usually unwilling) sources of money or food. The plot turns on two characters: Telly, a seventeen-year-old whose aim is to seduce very young virgins, and Jennie, a fifteen-year-old who searches for Telly after she finds out that he has infected her with HIV. The handheld camera work and the repeated close-ups of the kids give the film both a documentary and a claustrophobic feel. The revelation that Jennie was infected some time ago by Telly, the only boy she has slept with, gravely revalues the morality attached to the opening scenes, in which he seduces a barely pubescent girl now at risk for HIV, as well as to his boast to his friend Casper, "Who am I? Who am I? The motha fuckin' virgin surgeon." Although less explictly than in *Paris Trout, Kids* judges the inadequacy of moral privatization by its public effects. By the end of the movie, Jennie has not told Telly about being infected with AIDS, but this condition invests with tragic irony his last speech about his need to have sex: "Sometimes when you're young, the only place to go is inside. That's just it. Fucking is what I love. Take that away from me, and I really got nothin'." The film's last words, the most morally explicit it offers, belong to Casper, who raped Jennie the night before while she was unconscious on drugs: "Jesus Christ. What happened?"[12] A moral daze is the most these emotivist narcissists can come up with.

Some artists argue that their images are not required to have a public meaning. In suggesting that their works have an untranslatable private iconography or that translation is not the point, they sanction emotivist moral privatization. Andres Serrano and Robert Mapplethorpe, for instance, attempt to sequester the morality attached to their images in a privatized moral frame. Unlike Dexter, who summons the privatized frame to excoriate it, or Clark, who wants to share his ambivalent fascination with it, Serrano and Mapplethorpe treat it uncritically and, indeed, privilege it above other moral frames. Serrano's works include the notorious *Piss Christ* (1987), a photograph of a plastic crucifix submerged in the artist's urine. The photo has obvious cultural meaning—the contamination of an image of the sacred by plastic and urine. Yet the cultural associations of this image jar with Serrano's private moral iconography. On the one hand, he asserts that his work is fundamentally religious: the photo "reflects my Catholic upbringing, and my ambivalence to that upbringing, being drawn to Christ yet resisting organized religion." On the other hand, his account is eccentric and emotivist: he describes the urine as one of "life's vital fluids," like blood and milk. He used it, he claims, because it produced a "vivid and vibrant color" (*New York Times*, 16 August 1989). His interpretations describe a personal religious iconography. Similarly, Mapplethorpe claims the photos in his *X Portfolio*, which include *Lou*, a photo of a finger in an erect penis, and *Helmut and Brooks*, a photo of one man's fist up another man's anus, for a private moral quest. In a 1988 *Art News* article, he says, "I wasn't trying to educate anyone. I was interested in examining my own reactions." In following his private moral odyssey, Mapplethorpe reached a border that became the site of self-estrangement: "There were certain pictures I took, certain areas I went into, that I decided were not places I wanted to be" (qtd. in Weiley, 1988: 108; see also R. Hughes, 1992: 21). Yet despite the pains Serrano and Mapplethorpe take to protect their images with a privatized morality, it is an oxymoron in a public photograph. The dramatic subjects of the photos can be read only as calculated to seize the viewer's attention by their quantum leap beyond expectation. Like *Paris Trout* and *Kids,* Serrano's and Mapplethorpe's photographs testify that there is a public consequence to privatized morality, whether that consequence is to interrogate the relation of privatized and traditional justice and law, as in Dexter's novel, to suggest the public repercussions of personal codes, as in *Kids,* or to dramatize how the placing of a personal image in public space affects the moral resonance of that image.

For some, moral privatization engenders simply cynicism, a Nietzschean disbelief in the moral sincerity of others. Ellis's *American Psycho* is one of a flood of works that adopt such a cynical posture. Robert Altman's film about Hollywood, *The Player* (1992), delivers the cynical message that as long as you can make lots of money, nothing you do—not even your committing murder—will be held against you, and nothing you desire denied you, not even white-picket-fenced happiness with the girlfriend of the man you have killed. Even the Western has abandoned its solid perch of moral certitude for the quicksand of cynical moral privatization. In Clint Eastwood's *Unforgiven* (1992), the sheriff and the outlaw have not simply switched positions, they have invented new ones. This shifting moral syntax makes their ethics unreadable. The sheriff is sometimes a cruel villain who dispatches justice with his fists, his boots, and a bullwhip. Yet his cruel image is confused by his warm smile, his accomplished storytelling, and his charming incompetence as a carpenter. The killer, whom we see murdering for money with cold-blooded efficiency, is an abstemious widower struggling to scratch together a living for his two children.

Unforgiven reiterates a certain cynical position in which only the vocabulary of morality persists, and this vocabulary is mouthed only robotically or in parody. A more complex example of moral discourse frozen in cynicism occurs in the 1991 film by Joel and Ethan Coen, *Barton Fink.* The film, set in the 1930s, centers on a Hollywood scriptwriter newly arrived from New York. In the hotel where the scriptwriter stays, a neighbor who introduces himself as an insurance salesman turns out to be a serial killer who later decapitates a woman while Fink sleeps with her. The murderer, with whom Fink stays on friendly terms, hands him a box containing her head, which Fink carries around with him. In the last scene, Finks meets a beautiful woman on the beach, an embodiment of the woman in a picture on his hotel room wall on which the camera focuses repeatedly throughout the film. As the woman gazes at the sea, a gull swoops down and captures its prey while Fink sits behind her, observing, the box beside him. This picture insists that the predatory, the beautiful, and the maniacal populate the same life narrative without an outside point of view to distinguish between them. The insight that there is no power calibrating the moving spectacle of life is delivered through a surreal, distorted plot and hyperbolic and parodic images. Even Fink's hotel room wallpaper, oozing white slime, is grotesque beyond sense. These techniques of exaggeration are employed to interrogate our sense of causality, to suggest its suspension or perversion. Fink's writer's block disappears after the murder, and, in a fever of creativity, he writes what he considers his best work while the box containing the head presides on his typewriter table as a sort of bodiless muse. The studio president, who once kissed Fink's feet, later calls him a stupid kike. The anti-Semitism emphasizes the 1930s setting and evokes the moral break associated with it. In the world of *Barton Fink,* the meanings of the words "neighbor," "author," "beauty," "love," "fidelity," "art," "friendship," and "loyalty" have been emptied. If all discourse is empty, how does one speak? If morality is special to each person, it cannot be communicated, so how can one talk meaningfully about it? The cynical answer that the Coens provide is that one speaks in clichés.

The Search for Moral Borders

The belief that ideas of morality have become so tied to personal emotions that they cannot truly be communicated results in texts expressing moral panic, anxiously conveying a sense that good and evil no longer have definition. In explaining his motivation for the exorbitant, unhinged events in *American Psycho,* Ellis sounds this note of panic: "If violence in films, literature and in some heavy-metal and rap music is so extreme . . . it may reflect the need to be terrified in a time when the sharpness of horror-film tricks seems blunted by repetition on the nightly news" (1990: 1). The cultural limits of the acceptable, as tested on the news each night, seem to Ellis to be perpetually receding beyond the horizon. *American Psycho* is a mad reach for that horizon, for a limit that seems to have cultural agreement. Within mainstream publishing, the novel takes a long flight into the taboo.[13] Much of the violence in *American Psycho is* against women, as many have observed, but Patrick Bateman, the novel's protagonist, also tortures and murders the homeless, the blind, children, dogs, and his male friends.[14] One chapter title is "Tries to Cook and Eat a Girl." A murderous three-page sequence—a warm-up for the more extreme events that follow—begins as follows:

> Effortlessly I'm leaping in front of her, blocking her escape, knocking her unconscious with four blows to the head from the nail gun. I drag

her back into the living room, laying her across the floor over a white Voilacutro cotton sheet, and then I stretch her arms out, placing her hands flat on thick wooden boards, palms up, and nail three fingers on each hand, at random, to the wood by their tips. (1991: 245)

Ellis learned his use of description from Ernest Hemingway. It is flat, cold, and precise. Hemingway, though, relied on the reader to fill in the emotional subtext. He would provide, he said, the "tip of the iceberg," while the reader filled in what was below the surface. In *American Psycho,* there is only surface. Bateman describes the murders he performs in as much obsessive, reportorial detail as he describes the clothes and possessions that belong to him and his friends, and with equal interest and dispassion.

According to Ellis, the emphasis on surfaces and simulations in postmodern culture discourages the effort to locate anything else; it promotes concentration on appearances. On the opening page, Bateman's friend explains the exemption from blame for his whole group, attributing his impunity to his social class: "I'm creative, I'm young, unscrupulous, highly motivated, highly skilled. In essence what I'm saying is that society can *not* afford to lose me. I'm an *asset*." Bateman is an "asset" in part because he works for a Wall Street investment firm. But he is mostly an "asset" in appearance. He does not spend much time working. He occupies his day lunching, exercising, shopping, and getting high—that is, when he is not murdering or torturing. Surface in this novel is everything. Bateman and his fellow investment bankers buy recognition of their professional status through their clothes, haircuts, and "hard" bodies. If they look right, they are accepted into the fold. Bateman looks the part of an investment banker; therefore, that is what he is. Even when he confesses to crimes in detail, he is not believed.

In this novel, moral feeling has migrated from the internal recesses of the individual to the surface. Jake in *The Sun Also Rises* thinks that morality is "things that made you disgusted afterwards. No, that must be immorality" (Hemingway, 1926: 149). The sentence articulates the lostness of the lost generation. Although Jake has lost God, he retains the ability to feel good and bad viscerally, as disgust. Moreover, his disgust is the tip of the iceberg in his visceral but fully developed morality. A strict, if privatized, code of good and evil clings to a whole range of experiences in Jake's universe— from fishing and bullfighting to love and friendship. Echoing Jake, Bateman confesses that "there wasn't a clear identifiable emotion within me, except for greed and possibly total disgust" (Ellis, 1991: 282). But there is no depth to his disgust. In contrast to Jake, who is disgusted because his sexual jealousy makes him want to beat someone up, Bateman, who kills with indifference, is disgusted by an improperly prepared sauce for his dinner or a non-designer tie. *American Psycho* suggests that the breaks in moral thinking between the First World War and now have wrought an increasingly privatized emotivist morality. Jake's individually decided ethics have objects of some worth and are communicable to his circle of acolytes. In the late twentieth century, Ellis laments, these objects have been reduced to surface qualities: "Surface, surface, surface was all that anyone found meaning in" (375). In *American Psycho*, a yuppie uniform constructs identity. It communicates to others the totality of a person's life, including one's morality—regardless of what one actually believes and does. In this novel, morality thus attached to surfaces is virtual, not real, and the moral value of acts is so private that it has no public register. Morality is a country without a border, Ellis mourns.

American Psycho became an icon around which commentators tested definitions of morality. Protests were staged by several groups, including representatives of NOW. Simon & Schuster decided to pull the book, despite having given Ellis a $300,000 advance (Adler, 1990a). Even the ACLU waffled; one ACLU spokesperson, referring to the violence in Ellis's text, asked, "If this is acceptable what's the next step?" (Kennedy, 1991: 426). Reviewers characterized the book as a "bestseller from hell" (Harrison, 1991: 148) and as a "Black Bible" (Corliss, 1991: 56). Norman Mailer, who in *An American Dream* (1965) depicted this dream as murdering your wife and raping your mistress, puzzled over Bateman's motivations: If "God and the devil do not war with each other over the human outcome," then evil is banal and human beings absurd (1991: 221). But Ellis is not primarily concerned with metaphysical battles over the human soul or with a final, defining authority over good and evil.

American Psycho exemplifies the search for moral borders, a search propelled by the fear of limitlessness. To execute this search, Ellis embarks on a flight into the weird and the taboo. It is part of his cautionary strategy to keep his readers locked in a psychopathic culture without escape routes. To the gratuitous question "Why?" that someone poses, Bateman replies in the novel's last lines:

> Well, though I know I should have done *that* instead of not doing it, I'm twenty-seven for christ sakes and this is, uh, how life presents itself in a bar or in a club in New York, maybe *anywhere,* at the end of the century and how people, you know, *me,* behave. . . . Above one of the doors covered by red velvet drapes in Harry's is a sign and on the sign

in letters that match the drapes' color are the words THIS IS NOT AN EXIT. (1991: 399)

There is no exit in Bateman's claustrophobic world.

With this allusion to Sartre's *No Exit* (1947) and with the allusion to Dante's *Inferno* in the novel's first line, "Abandon all hope ye who enter here" (1991), Ellis invites comparisons among these three visions of hell. In the seven hundred years since Dante, hell has remained a powerful concept, powerful enough to be useful to Sartre, an atheist. He was able to construct a play around the metaphor of hell because there was general cultural consensus on the meanings of sin, guilt, responsibility, and punishment. He could count on his audience's understanding the constellation of moral elements that went into the concept of hell, whether or not they or he subscribed to a specific religion. Dante and Sartre share basic assumptions about the meaning of good and evil. In both of their versions of hell, sinners are punished on the basis of their actions.

Ellis's world contains no such equation. It is a post-Holocaust, post–civil rights, postfeminist, technological lawyers' world where it is taken for granted that the justice system is corrupted by, for example, classism and racism, the factors that allow Bateman's murders to go unpunished. In Ellis's text, as well as in so many contemporary representations, all of these factors are affected, one way or another, by the power that personal convictions of right and wrong have. The staples of Dante's and Sartre's worlds—sin, guilt, punishment, responsibility—survive in the vocabulary of television ministries, but they have been destabilized and diffused in the larger culture. In *American Psycho*, the result is that the complexities invading legal judgments also inflect moral judgments to produce a sense of general moral relativism. Bateman makes the end point of this relativism frighteningly clear in his statement, "I am blameless. Each model of human behavior must be assumed to have some validity" (1991: 377).

To draw a clear picture of hell, one that is uncompromised by such complexities, Ellis seems compelled to travel an extreme distance, the border of hell having receded almost beyond imagining in the forty-plus years since *No Exit*—indeed, as Bateman argues, beyond the usual boundaries of the human: "I had all the characteristics of the human being—flesh, blood, skin, hair—but my depersonalization was so intense, had gone so deep, that the normal ability to feel compassion had been eradicated, the victim of a slow, purposeful erasure" (282).

American Psycho collapses into cynicism: "Justice is dead. Fear, recrimination, innocence, sympathy, guilt, waste, failure, grief, were things, emotions, that no one really felt anymore. Reflection is useless, the world is senseless. Evil is its only permanence. God is not alive. Love cannot be trusted. . . . This was civilization as I saw it, colossal and jagged" (375). The search for moral borders has failed as expected, and, rather than reframe the search, Ellis maintains the text at a uniformly cynical pitch.

Competing Discourses

The search for moral borders, cynicism, nostalgia, and emotivist moral privatization are lenses of analysis in artistic representations. The representations themselves attempt to unravel the present and expose threads that have been ignored, underestimated or hidden. Their domain is description or examination of what is. Art has no call to be pragmatic, because its office is not to provide solutions. What it does is render the past, insist on the present, or express desires for the future. The characterizations of moral uncertainty offered in this chapter—the nature and effect of its birth in the past, its location and dimension in the present, its fate in the future—are contested and in competition, and add up to a cacophony of explanations. DeLillo's *White Noise*, for instance, insists on the present. The protagonist, Gladney, is not allowed to linger in the old certainties and dead narratives of the past. In DeLillo's account, he must reconcile himself to the Habermasian postmodern moment, portrayed as a bleak, chaotic present. *American Psycho* and *Barton Fink* imagine an even bleaker present than DeLillo's, one without hope of reconciliation. Their pessimism is so absolute that you can either deny their vision or join in their moral cynicism. Where the past is imagined as having monarchal power over the present, the present is to some degree paralyzed. The moral certainty represented by old movies in *Crimes and Misdemeanors* cannot now be approached. It is a failure that in Allen's film refuses negotiation. Allen's vision is limited by his nostalgic insistence on a lapsed moral certainty. He clings to a moral narrative that no longer has general legitimacy. In *JFK*, Stone uses the past to provide an account of political immorality so powerful and omniverous that, for Stone converts, only political paralysis or revolution seems an adequate response. *The Grey Zone*, in contrast, presents the past as a sorrowful specter haunting the present. Herron's *Thereafter Johnnie* and Morrison's *Beloved* picture the paralysis that the past can exert over the present, yet they allow a bargain to be made with the past that permits a move into the future. Herron puts forward a religious moral discourse to make this bargain. Morrison makes a similar bargain with a liberal humanist morality. In some representations, the present is a private, emotivist moment, inarticulate and thus unshareable. Dexter interprets such privatization as moral bankruptcy, Serrano and

Mapplethorpe seize it as an opportunity for solipsistic quests, and Clark follows it to death's door.

Some representations, such as *River's Edge,* take on competing emotivist discourses to demonstrate a crippling moral limbo. Other representations may not only accept such competition but also squeeze some hopeful possibilities out of it. Spike Lee's *Jungle Fever* (1991), dedicated to Yusef Hawkins, a sixteen-year-old black youth who was shot in 1989 during a racial incident in Bensonhurst, Brooklyn (*New York Times,* 8 August 1989), takes on clashing moralities in order to point beyond them. The plot turns on an affair between a married black architect from Harlem and his working-class Italian secretary from Bensonhurst. This situation gives Lee the opportunity to juxtapose stereotypes of race and class in various degrees of malignancy. Whites are racist but sexually curious about blacks, educated blacks disdain working-class Italian Americans but are also sexually curious about them, black women curse the self-hatred that drives their best men into the arms of white women, and an elderly black preacher uses the Old Testament as armor against the moral chaos that is outside the "good book." These perspectives, though stereotypical, are emotionally powerful. Yet the contending perspectives lose definition as several of the characters reach beyond bigotry and received ideas. Unlike Spike Lee's earlier movie *Do the Right Thing* (1989), the competing discourses of race and class are eventually negotiated by some characters into a discourse of the future that counters racism and classism with simple, sure gestures: the Italian American secretary moves out of Bensonhurst, away from an obligation to conform to racist ethics; the architect returns to his wife, knowing that he is not just following his preacher father's Old Testament script for the moral life. No longer do his actions seem to him morally neutral, or "complex," as he puts it earlier in the film. In the optimism of this ending lies the conviction that flexibility inhabits even the most obstinate conflicts about race. Indeed, in this film it is the move toward uncertainty that makes for optimism.

Jungle Fever, then, provides a kind of qualified back talk to analyses that doom the future, if moral uncertainty persists, or that, like *Forrest Gump,* deal with this uncertainty by proposing to kill off its representatives, such as Jenny. Even Auschwitz, as a permanent scar on the moral life of the West, gets some back talk, most prominently in Steven Spielberg's *Schindler's List* (1993). This elegiac film does not, like Jean-François Lyotard and Elie Wiesel, or *Zentropa* and *The Grey Zone,* view the present as a footnote to Auschwitz. Perhaps, as some reviewers complained, it does focus too lovingly on Oskar Schindler, a Nazi party member and swindler who nevertheless saved eleven hundred Jews from death. Yet as the film bursts into color at the end, leaving the black and white with which the horrific past is depicted, and parades Schindler's Jews and their children and grand-children in Israel, it talks back in a vocabulary of hope and an ethical be-yond. This vocabulary is, of course, sentimental and, we must remember, not universal. The film's back talk to Holocaust-inspired sorrow in the zeit-geist has limited communicability. For instance, seventy Oakland, Cali-fornia, students, mostly black and poor, brought by their teachers to see *Schindler's List* on Martin Luther King Jr. Day, laughed at some of the vio-lence on the screen. For them it was another horror film, albeit weirder than most.[15] Such responses remind us that each representation of morality, al-though having perhaps some elasticity, is restricted to those who under-stand it.

Because the city can accommodate almost any account of morality, it is often the setting for representational attempts at moral negotiation.[16] Most often the city is a metaphor for the Habermasian idea of the post-modern with which this chapter began: it is a place that feels transitional and fosters disequilibrium, a sense that anything can happen, and where one is always, as a stranger in relation to most others, a little anxious, morally disturbed. This sense of the city prevails in a long list of films and novels—*New Jack City, Juice, Escape from New York* (1981), *The Grifters, American Psycho, The Bonfire of the Vanities, Kids, Pulp Fiction* (1994), and *Clockers* (1995). The city's association with transition, disequilibrium, and estrangement, as well as its pluralism, can make productive the uncertainty that these qualities provoke. One example is John Sayles's film of city life, *City of Hope* (1991). The city in the film is a place where corruption, protest, drunkenness, religiosity, love, betrayal, and madness dissolve and reappear, swinging into and out of focus in turn. Here, hope depends on mutability, on the opportunities created by uncertainty and instability. The film ends with a sense that whatever moral solution is negotiated is tentative and con-tingent. In the concluding scenes, we get a dialogue between a white pro-fessor of urban relations and the black youth who beat him up, a march by angry blacks against political hacks who have been conspiring to throw them out of the neighborhood, and a reconciliation between a corrupt fa-ther and his dying son. In proposing the city as a metaphor for productive uncertainty, the film does not ignore the difficulties in such a proposal. *City of Hope* closes, after all, on a cracked character called Asteroid, who com-pulsively cries, "Help." The cry of this stock madman-in-the-city suggests that rescue as well as abandonment is among the possibilities the city offers.

Jungle Fever and *City of Hope* use the instabilities in city landscapes to talk back to fatalistic accounts of "postmodern" moral uncertainty. Sayles's film suggests the possibilities in the anxiety and estrangement of city life. The film imagines that if we understand that we are strangers to ourselves, to paraphrase Julia Kristeva (quoting Nietzsche), we can use that understanding to live with others who are strangers to us (1991: 170). In McInerney's 1996 novel *The Last of the Savages,* the moral impasse of nostalgia that marks *Bright Lights, Big City* is left behind for this Kristevan encounter with otherness. Grimly determined to sever ties with his corrupt, racist, southern, aristocratic father, Will Savage, the only remaining Savage son, moves west to California, land of America's manifest destiny. Here he tentatively spells out that destiny as making the stranger a part of the family, making him familiar: a rich, white, heterosexual entrepreneur with a low sperm count, Savage marries a southern black woman and asks his white, homosexual, Catholic northern friend to provide the sperm so he can have a baby.

The child of this miscegenation carries the name of his Savage father, but on him the meaning of that name has become productively uncertain, detached from bigotry, corruption, and unearned privilege. The narrator, who is also the sperm donor, asks, "Will he combine our strengths, this mulatto boy, or be divided against himself? . . . I wondered whether a child of two races might redeem the original sin of our heritage. Or whether, at least, he might be happier with who he is than we were" (270). In *The Last of the Savages,* as well as in *City of Hope* and *Jungle Fever,* moral certainty is associated with racism, sexism, and a crippling nostalgia. Moral uncertainty and ambiguity can accommodate negotiation between various moral discourses that looks beyond such certainties. McInerney questions the ease of taking such "twelve steps into a brave new life": "If we log on to the Internet, eat the right foods and exercise religiously, surely we will forget our differences and begin to love one another. But then the riots break out again in the City of Angels" (271). Such representations, even when they are heavy-handed or skeptical, help us imagine what the benefits might be of surrendering authoritarian moral frames for a plurality of competing and uncertain moves toward contingent, revisable, negotiated solutions.

2 | Justice Post-Tawana

My name is Tawana Brawley and I'm not a liar and I'm not crazy. I simply just want justice and then I want to be left alone.
Tawana Brawley, 29 September 1988

What is the problem here, anyway? Why do so many people, male and female alike, feel threatened by the concept of women shooting rapists?
Sonny Jones, *Women and Guns*

[Justice] . . . is simultaneously both oppressive and near, but in the nearness, we call it injustice.
Ingeborg Bachmann, *Malina*

Compromising Justice

Early one afternoon in November 1987, a woman in Dutchess County, upstate New York, saw a girl in a green garbage bag in front of the empty house next door. When the police arrived, they found a black teenager whose body was smeared with excrement and whose chest and stomach were marked with the words "cunt," "KKK," and "nigger." Although the girl did not speak to police, in the hospital she scrawled "white cop" when a black officer asked who had attacked her. Later her mother and aunt said she told them that six white men had abducted her and, over the course of four days, had raped and sodomized her. The girl's name was Tawana Brawley, and she was fifteen.

Two African American lawyers, Alton Maddox and C. Vernon Mason, and activist-preacher Al Sharpton stepped in to represent the Brawleys. These men pressured the governor, Mario Cuomo, to appoint a special prosecutor. When Cuomo chose Robert Abrams, they rejected him as racist and incompetent and counseled the family not to cooperate with the grand jury that Abrams assembled. African Americans gave Brawley extensive support: Bill Cosby and *Essence* magazine offered a $25,000 reward for information leading to the arrest of the rapists; boxing promotor Don King pledged $100,000 toward her education; Mike Tyson visited her and gave her his diamond-studded Rolex watch and $50,000. Publicly, Brawley continued to say nothing. Maddox, Mason, and Sharpton became her voice, adding information that they said came from her—most importantly, the identities of three of the assailants, one a local assistant prosecutor.

The media initially painted a picture of the fifteen-year-old Brawley as a cheerful, conscientious young woman, a good student, a cheerleader, and a member of the track team. But family members, friends, and townspeople soon provided competing accounts: she stayed out all night, had lots of boyfriends, took drugs, and lied to and fought with her family, especially her stepfather. A neighbor reported seeing her get into the garbage bag. Perry McKinnon, an ex-chauffeur for Sharpton, Maddox, and Mason, told reporters that the team had fabricated evidence and that Sharpton privately called Brawley's story "bull———" (Kunen, 1988). The case stalled in the courts but continued to generate heated disagreements and scorching rhetoric in newspapers and on radio and television. An episode of the *Donahue* show was broadcast from the Bethany Baptist Church, Brooklyn, where in September 1988, ten months after the story broke, Tawana and her mother, Glenda, took sanctuary from a grand jury subpoena and arrest warrant for Mrs. Brawley. In the same month, the grand jury decided that Tawana's story was not true and dropped the case. The media circus that had gathered around the case disbanded. But a smaller sideshow erupted in 1989 when Darryl Rodriguez, who presented himself as Brawley's boyfriend, said he heard from her own mouth that the story was a hoax (*New York Newsday,* 27 April 1989). The following year, six *New York Times* journalists resurrected the case with the book *Outrage,* their attempt at a definitive account (McFadden et al., 1990). Then, in 1997, when Steven Pagones, the assistant prosecutor accused of raping Brawley, sued her defense team, many of the debates and legal confrontations were surreally replayed.

Public images of the Tawana Brawley case were jumbled and contradictory. Was Brawley a young black girl whose victimization was reminiscent of the horrors of slavery, or a manipulative adolescent willing to stand the world on its head to avoid the anger of her violent stepfather, or a disturbed, abused teenager who needed psychiatric help? The activism and egos of Brawley's lawyers contributed to the muddle. Was a fifteen-year-old in need of legal advice being sacrificed on the altar of fame and spurious politics? For some, the Brawley case reinforced their belief that women and blacks fabricate injustices. The *New York Post* bought into this position toward the end of the grand jury deliberations when it editorialized, "The teenager's lurid tale of kidnapping and sexual abuse never really rang true" (28 September 1988). Another common complaint was that all accounts of racist injustice would now be suspect. "After Tawana Brawley, who will believe the next black woman who says she was raped by white men?" columnist Pete Hamill wrote (*New York Post*, 28 September 1988). For segments of the black press, however, the Brawley story's truth was not in question: the case simply demonstrated the bankruptcy of the white justice system.

Interpretations of the affair as an instance of race and gender oppression vied with convictions that political manipulation or simple bad faith were at work, making the story incoherent and its main issues elusive. The history of black-white relations in the United States, sociological characterizations of African Americans as welfare mothers and teen gangsters, whites' denials of discrimination, and personal, professional, and political interests all contributed to the incoherence. Initial sympathy for a young black girl who said she had been raped by six whites gradually had to accommodate the many contradictory accounts of the incident. Brawley's lawyers opposed the grand jury subpoena seeking Glenda Brawley's testimony with an argument about "400 years of oppression," a position that the judge, Angelo Ingrassia, conceded had merit. At the same time, Sharpton was alleged to boast, "If we can win this Tawana thing, we'll be the biggest niggers in New York" (McFadden et al., 1990: 309).[1] At the messy conclusion of the case, no one felt that justice had really been done. An *Essence* story by Audrey Edwards, published a year after Brawley was discovered in the garbage bag, begins: "A few months ago I stopped having any opinion at all in the matter of Tawana Brawley ... for by then the case ... had become so muddled, confused and mired in racism and our own pathology that it became almost impossible to know what to think, much less to know what the truth was" (1988: 79).

The questions that the case raised persisted in debates of subsequent high-profile cases in the late 1980s and the 1990s, creating a post-Tawana confusion in matters of justice and relegitimizing suspicion of blacks and women. A climate of doubt hung over black women's words, such as those of Anita Hill at the Clarence Thomas Supreme Court confirmation hearings. Suspicion surrounded the testimony of Desiree Washington, a black woman who accused Mike Tyson of rape, and of the black female St. John's University student who alleged rape by four white members of the college lacrosse team and whose sexual history was the object of extensive legal and tabloid speculation. This deepening mistrust also affected white women, such as Patricia Bowman when she said William Kennedy Smith had raped her, and a seventeen-year-old from Glen Ridge, New Jersey, generally regarded as "mentally defective," who alleged rape by four schoolmates. In the highly raced first O. J. Simpson trial, such doubts encouraged the impugning of the murdered woman, a "party girl" rumored to use drugs and to have promiscuous sex.

Post-Tawana, even the murders of young black people by whites were shadowed by lingering distrust of the black victim. In August 1989, Yusef Hawkins was shot by an Italian American youth in Bensonhurst when he went to buy a used car. The tabloids speculated on whether he might really have had theft in mind, and treated sympathetically the claim of other Bensonhurst youths that they thought Hawkins was going to see a white girl in the neighborhood. The Brawley case also underlined the ambivalent relationship between nonwhites and the police. Communities of color may mistrust the police, yet the police are sometimes their only hope. This ambivalence peaked after the first Simpson verdict, when black jurors' criteria for reasonable doubt about police evidence appeared, to many white observers, to be much lower than their own.

By emphasizing the plurality of tenable moral positions that adhere to a single event, the Brawley case called attention to the competing perspectives held about any justice issue. This new normalization of moral disorder was apparent, for instance, in the case of Gavin Cato, a seven-year-old Carribean American boy from Crown Heights, Brooklyn, who was killed accidentally by a Hasidic driver. At the scene, angry blacks confronted Hasidim, the private Hasidic ambulance did not take the boy, and the driver who killed him was not arrested. Media accounts were able to describe the events, which sparked a series of confrontations, demonstrations, and attacks in the neighborhood, simultaneously as a tragic accident and as an instance of one community's indifference, even malice, toward others.

The personal emotions that muddled the Brawley case also foreshadowed the emotional complications now regularly explored around high-profile cases involving race, rape, and sexual abuse. In the California child sexual abuse trial of Peggy McMartin Buckey, owner of the McMartin Preschool, and her son Raymond, public outrage, the beliefs of interviewers and therapists, and children's own fears and fantasies vied with the evidence. As with Brawley's youthful, innocent, yet demonic media persona, childhood operated as the crystallization both of morality and of its absence. In 1990, six years after the investigation started, the court dismissed the remaining fifty-two charges of molestation (*New York Times*, 19 August 1991).

Because Brawley would not testify, the press conference became an alternate courtroom. Journalists questioned their own role: Mike Taibbi and Anna Sims-Phillips, respectively a reporter and a producer for CBS Television, called their book on the relationship between the press and justice *Unholy Alliances* (1989). Trial by media escalated in post-Brawley cases to such a point that although at the end of 1992, Mary Jo and Joey Buttafuoco, the Long Island, New York, couple in the Amy Fisher "fatal attraction" case, were cleared of any criminal action by the courts, they were "prosecuted" across several episodes of the *Donahue* show and found guilty.[2] Such litigation journalism reached its apogee during O. J. Simpson's criminal trial, when court TV helped structure the legal proceedings and constituted the viewing audience as the "thirteenth juror."

Uncertainties about justice did not emerge for the first time with the Brawley affair. A month before Brawley made her accusation, the Howard Beach trial ended. Police had arrested eleven youths for beating three African American men who had stopped to get a pizza in Howard Beach, in Queens, New York City. One, Michael Griffiths, was killed by a car as he fled. Of the three white youths charged, only one was sentenced, on manslaughter and assault charges. Around this case, too, racial politics had a higher profile than legal argument, victimhood was confused by implications of blame—Just what were these young men doing in a white area?— and the justice system seemed to be flailing around. Earlier, in 1984, Bernhard Goetz's vigilante shooting of four subway muggers in New York City mobilized debate about a "justice" that pitted black against white, also priming reactions to the Brawley case. In the same year, in the so-called Preppie Murder, a prep school dropout killed a rich young woman of his acquaintance in New York City's Central Park. As with Brawley, the media saw the fault everywhere: in the indulged youths, in their irresponsible parents, and in the greed that drove them all. In the Brawley case, many of these uncertainties about justice came together, and afterward they were more insistent and harder to overlook.

With Tawana Brawley on his arm, Al Sharpton appeared outside the courtroom where young African American men were being tried for allegedly raping and beating a white woman jogging in New York's Central Park, to "observe the differences in the court system black and white victims can expect" (*New York Times*, 30 July 1990). Five years after the Brawley case, Sharpton recognized the post-Tawana effect in matters of justice when he acknowledged that her story might not have been true, but he declared himself unrepentant because the issues that the case raised were so important. The black woman who, in March 1990, said she was raped by the four white St. John's students reported that she heard them say, "No one believed Tawana Brawley. So nobody will believe this one" (*New York Times*, 26 July 1991). Describing the media orgy of the Amy Fisher case, columnist

Marvin Kitman cited the Brawley precedent (*New York Newsday*, 1 January 1993).[3] It could be said that we are in a post-Tawana phase in debates about justice. "Post-Tawana," then, is a shorthand for the growing uncertainties about justice that the Brawley case emblematized.

Uncertain Justice

Post-Tawana uncertainties in justice seem ubiquitous. The word "justice" is itself uncertain: does it mean equity? the good? reform? punishment? revenge? From one perspective, the police are agents of justice meriting unquestioned support. From another, they betray the communities they are supposed to serve. Neighborhoods sometimes appreciate vigilante protection but deplore the rough justice that results. The law is our primary moral arbiter, yet legal precedent often seems insufficient for current circumstances. For instance, after prolonged feminist campaigning, lawyers now use a "battered woman" defense that says "provocation" can mean years of abuse rather than, as formerly, a few prior moments of physical assault. It also turns the reluctance of many victims to testify into evidence of their beaten-down state (*New York Times*, 6 June 1996). The Supreme Court, the ultimate guarantor of the country's justice, includes a member accused of sexual harassment, a charge that a large proportion of the population believes. The justice system is supposed to honor the line between public and private. But where does this line fall when military recruitment excludes gays, when police officers crack down on domestic violence, and when judges rule on who owns the baby in surrogacy cases such as that of Baby M?

Like justice practices, justice philosophies are obsessed with uncertainty. Whose justice? Which rationality? These are the questions posed by the title of a book by Alasdair MacIntyre (1989) that theorizes indeterminacy in justice. For MacIntyre, justice is intractable because each community has a different investment in justice and each tries to claim it. The cultural critic Stanley Fish agrees that there is no single immutable justice that transcends the historical and the situational. Even with an apparently fundamental matter such as justice, he says, we cannot choose our beliefs, for they are indissolubly bound to the culture (1990: 322–24).

These writers contest the mainstream argument, associated with John Rawls, that consensus on justice is still possible. Rawls writes, "Those who hold different conceptions of justice can . . . still agree that institutions are just when no arbitrary distinctions are made between persons in the assigning of basic rights and duties" (1972: 5). Such proclamations tend to forget that although blacks, women, and children have, by law, the same "rights and duties" as white men, their social disempowerment and the justice system's built-in indifference to it make them less apt to find equal treatment.[4]

We define morality through our concepts of justice and through our justice systems. Together, they make concrete our ideas of morality, of good and bad conduct. However, as the problems with Rawls's formulation suggest, the relationships between the justice system and our ideas of justice, and between justice in the present, past, and future, are not straightforward. It is in these intricacies that post-Tawana uncertainties about justice lie. The ethical ideal—the product of rational thinking or religious belief—is often at odds with the legal system, as well as with individual notions of morality (Cornell, 1992: 92). Again, Sophocles' Antigone symbolizes this conflict. When Antigone insists on burying her dishonored brother, she raises the ethical ideal, the laws of God, above the laws of the king, which forbid the burial. For Antigone, the ethical ideal of justice is absolute and nonnegotiable. In Sharpton's theatrical presentation, Brawley was a modern Antigone, an emblem of resistance to endemic racism in the name of an ideal justice. Onstage at a press conference, Brawley said, "My family and I thought we couldn't get any justice so we decided not to cooperate" (*New York Post*, 29 September 1988). But with Brawley, the ideal of justice became tangled with questions of truth, and then with the question, *whose* truth? At a Howard University conference titled "The Voice of Truth in a Time of Trouble," she shared the stage with the convicted drug offender and then ex-mayor of Washington, D.C., Marion Barry; and a black nationalist whom many condemn for anti-Semitism, Louis Farrakhan (*New York Times Book Review*, 29 July 1988).

It is impossible to describe fully the ideal, rational morality for which we are striving, or to measure accurately our progress toward it (MacIntyre, 1989: 3–4). Nevertheless, people operate on the assumption that an ethical ideal, with all its demands and unreachability, has a presence in the justice system. An ideal, after all, is something that we can never reach but for which we always aim. Although we may suspect the justice system of not living up to the ethical ideal, traces of this ideal always cling to it. As legal philosopher Drucilla Cornell writes, "The ethical is a necessity as well as an impossibility" (1992: 84). Throughout the 1998 case, Brawley's supporters claimed that theirs was an attempt to bring the justice system closer to the ethical ideal. When the grand jury subpoenaed Brawley's mother, William Jones, pastor of Bethany Baptist Church, complained that "Mafia dons' mothers are not subpoenaed." When Maddox contended that the district attorney and the police were following "Brawley law," the practice of discounting black women's accusations of rape against white men, he was demanding that the law operate in accordance with the ethical ideal (*Donahue,* 1988: 6, 14).

Ethical ideals vary, as do criteria for judging our distance from them. Such democratic plurality makes for uncertainty. The Brawley case abraded the already troubled relationship between the ethical ideal and the actualities of justice. Presenting the Brawleys' and their advisers' legal demands as bewilderingly irrational, liberal sectors of the media cast doubt on the ethics of the Brawley campaign. Sharpton, Maddox, and Mason "wanted oratory, not facts; they wanted heat, not illumination; they wanted conflict, not justice," Hamill asserted (*New York Post,* 28 September 1988).

A way to judge the relationship between the justice system and ethics is to assume that ethical ideals are embodied in particular groups' formulations of morality and to assess how close the justice system comes to these "community" formulations. In the Brawley case, competing community ethics—those of African Americans versus those of the legal establishment—qualified, more insistently than before, the notion of a universal ethical tradition. For Glenda Brawley, justice that came from whites was tainted: "First of all, the [medical] examiners, were they white? . . . I mean, there have [*sic*] been evidence that I will say have been covered up. . . . Who said there wasn't semen? Were you there?" (*Donahue,* 1988: 1). The white media did not ignore this community ethics so much as deliberately reject it. For the *New York Post* editorial writers, what the Brawley campaign called community solidarity was "racial huckstering," a mendacity directly opposed to ideals of justice. Of Sharpton, Mason, and Maddox, they claimed, "From now on, whenever they open their mouths in public, it will be safe to assume they're lying" (28 September 1988). Robert McFadden, coauthor of *Outrage,* characterized the battle as "the truth versus a kind of appeal . . . for black loyalty" (*Donahue,* 1990: 15). To the Brawley campaigners, liberal media people such as McFadden who called for the facts were governed not by rationality but by their own community interests. Each side, in its unshakable belief, operated as what MacIntyre calls a "community of prerational faith," reminiscent of earlier communities governed by faith in a religious principle (1989: 5).

What influence should a group's democratic decisions or its consensus on an issue have on moral principles that were set up to be timeless and universal? Should African Americans make charges and present evidence through the media, rather than the law, if they think that the law does not provide the impartial forum it is supposed to? When Sharpton, Mason, and Maddox told the media that Steven Pagones, a local assistant prosecutor, was one of Tawana's assailants, they cited judicial inaction to justify this publicity. Pagones first resorted to a symbolic $800 million libel suit, and years later sued for a smaller amount, to combat the personal harm he suffered from these accusations (McFadden et al., 1990: 369).

Post-Tawana uncertainties also emerged from the confused relationship between justice past, present, and future. When we call for justice, we are asking for a more equitable future. "Justice," whether it means a reformed justice system or an ethical ideal, is always beyond the horizon, something yet to come. But a precise vision of this future escapes us (Cornell, 1992: 135). We tend to see justice as something we bring with us from the past, in the procedures and precedents we set up then. This traditionalism is important, because it helps us remember past inequities and how we corrected them: slavery before the Thirteenth Amendment; child labor before the Fair Labor Standards Act (1938); school segregation before *Brown v. Board of Education* (1954); illegal abortion before *Roe v. Wade* (1973). References to the past thus work as a roll call of socially induced breaks in justice, beginning with the earliest U.S. struggles for democracy and including feminists', blacks', and advocates' challenges to white men's hold over civil rights.

The past of justice is not simple. The longer, better-defined histories of justice and injustice are the most powerful. Kimberlé Crenshaw says, for instance, that African Americans remember the long and powerful past of lynching but can find only a short and ambiguous past for sexual harassment (qtd. in *New York Times,* 17 July 1992). As a result, Clarence Thomas, in describing his confirmation hearings as a "high-tech lynching," was, whatever the truth of the allegations, more persuasive for many African Americans than Anita Hill, whose arguments rested on the second, less compelling history. In the first trial of the Los Angeles police officers accused of beating Rodney King, the officers were found not guilty. A white juror, empathizing with police officers' dangerous and apparently hopeless work in a poor neighborhood, said justice had a longer timescale than the three-minute video of King's beating. Other jurors, watching as defense attorneys screened the video frame by frame, saw justice as that one instant when the black man's arm could have been raised in attack and the police might "reasonably" be restraining him.[5]

Historical breaks in thinking about justice are also not absolute. In 1992, the Supreme Court qualified *Brown v. Board of Education* by ruling that schools segregated by virtue of residential patterns do not violate the Constitution. At such times, justice looks as if it is recapitulating the past. When we recall past injustices and reiterate past solutions, we are interpreting the past in the context of the present. A sense of the past meanings of justice can also, however, act as a way of holding on to justice in the present. In mourning her dead brother, Antigone mourns the justice of the past and thus keeps it alive in the present. Animating the Los Angeles riots of 1992 was a violent grief for betrayed promises of equitable justice. The initial acquittal of the four police officers who were videotaped beating Rodney King epitomized this betrayal.

To recall the past of justice is also to say something about its future. When we look to the past for help or as a warning, we are projecting backward the future we would like, "remembering the future" (Cornell, 1992: 147). Mourning past justice or making reparations for past injustice, then, can be a way of imagining a possible future as well as fighting for justice in the present. After the 1992 civil unrest in L.A., economic recovery was minimal, but pockets of hope developed where people parlayed remembered principles of freedom and equity into renewed commitment to volunteer projects, parenting classes for young women and men, and programs to get youths out of gangs (Broyles, 1992: 38; *Los Angeles Times,* 1 August 1992; *New York Times,* 1 November 1992). But remembering the past cannot address fully the present and future of justice. Conditions change, and strategies for pursuing justice must be modified. In the 1980s, for instance, social change movements shifted their emphasis toward the private domain. The women's movement transferred its campaigning focus from equal pay to domestic violence. Abuses suffered by children in the once sacrosanct domestic realm became objects of exhaustive investigation and prosecution in a procession of cases: the McMartin Preschool trial, the 1992 trial of workers at the New Jersey Wee Care day care center accused of a similarly bizarre list of sexual abuses; the death of Lisa Steinberg, the adopted daughter of a professional couple who fatally abused her; Oprah Winfrey's and Roseanne Barr's well-publicized revelations of abuse; and Woody Allen and Mia Farrow's custody battle.

The Brawley case intensified uncertainties about the relationship between justice and history. The case called up, in concentrated form, remembrances of past wrongs, old plans for reform, and imaginings of a future free of violence against blacks, women, and children. It was a progressive as well as a regressive break. On the one hand, black women's accusations of injustice were treated more skeptically afterward. On the other hand, it showed that justice issues that recall the past, by raising, for example, the history of women slaves raped by their owners, are not identical with that past; they have their own contemporary meanings too. Moreover, demands for justice now, like those that Brawley's supporters made, may have much more to do with the future than with current circumstances. Her supporters' focus was on future equity for blacks as much as it was on the young woman before them. After Tawana, it became even more difficult to think about justice only in the present.

The sense of urgency driving justice debates also gives rise to uncertainty. Injustices demand solutions and demand them immediately. The urgency driving justice debates impels those debates to engage explicitly with the uncertain relationships between ideal and actual justice, and between justice past, present, and future. This urgency of justice tames ethical ideals into legal compromise. Trying to move the jury to an expeditious decision confined to the law, the judge in the Glen Ridge case cautioned, "This is a criminal trial. . . . It is not a morality play" (*New York Times*, 7 March 1993). Their urgency also means that justice debates are too sensitive to the present to get swallowed up in backward- or forward-looking perspectives. The chant in Crown Heights after the car accident that killed Gavin Cato was, "What do we want? Justice! When do we want it? Now!" When Leona Benton imported the "abortion pill," RU 486, she immediately began a court battle for her right to use it. The pill has to be taken in the first eight weeks of pregnancy. In this case, the judge managed to rule against Benton before the eight weeks expired. But though the urgency of justice debates seems to reduce their uncertainty, really it just puts uncertainty on hold. Suspicions about the ethical failures of the justice system, fears of stasis or regression in the historical progress of justice, and utopian hopes for the future remain subtexts to the solutions we cobble together in a state of urgency.

Where justice issues are raised in novels or movies, a more relaxed agenda can be adopted. The bonds seller in Tom Wolfe's novel *The Bonfire of the Vanities* (1987) is being arraigned on a new charge when the book ends. The endlessness of his case is not a mirror of the legal system—for, despite appeals and retrials, cases do get settled—but a literary comment on the justice system's enormous distance from the ethical ideal. The underworld milieu in *The Grifters* (1991) raises philosophical questions about whether U.S. society endorses the survivalism and enterprise shown in the film, and the murder in *Barton Fink* (1991) asks whether the criminal breaking of taboos may be artistically liberating. A newspaper report of a crime might ask similar questions, but it would insist principally that the justice system solve the crime. Issues of justice that go beyond the justice system also appear more pressing when dealt with in the world outside art and popular media. A series of 1980s yuppie-bashing novels, such as *Bright Lights, Big City* (McInerney, 1984), were effective in describing the injustices of conspicuous consumption, but in politics such outrage needs to be accompanied by a corrective policy suggestion—the higher taxes for the rich, for example, that formed part of Bill Clinton's 1992 election platform. In cultural works, then, uncertainties about justice are less likely to be allied with a temporary, imperfect, pragmatic answer to them. However, some films, books, and artworks do display the characteristic urgency of justice debates. In the early 1990s, movies such as *City of Hope* (1991) and *Boyz N the Hood* (1991), in which justice is in question, presented a highly specific portrayal of conflicts in the city, especially concerning race, as well as possible resolutions to them. The lead actor in the latter film, the rapper Ice Cube, called the movie "a window into the black community"—for the first time, the suburban mainstream could see something of contemporary black urban life (*New York Times,* 14 July 1991).

Vacillating between realities and moral ideals, and directed not just toward present, future, or past but in all three directions, justice seems permanently confused. Since the Brawley case, we are even more prepared for justice issues to resolve themselves only temporarily and contingently, accompanied by an acute and persisting sense of doubt. After Tawana Brawley, justice, despite its urgency, seems likely to be always uncertain and complex, imbued with indeterminacy.

What Justice?

In 1992, a police officer shot and killed a nineteen-year-old Dominican, Jose Garcia, in the lobby of a Washington Heights, New York City, apartment building. The police officer said he was taking Garcia into the building for questioning when he thought he saw Garcia reach into his back pocket for a gun. Garcia had a record as a small-time drug peddler. His family and friends, however, said he was no longer dealing, talked of his fondness for his mother and siblings, and described him as a "grown-up kid." The police officer was not charged. Though he had a record of improper arrests, fellow officers called him "the cop we all want to be" (*New York Times,* 18 July 1992). Five days of angry, sometimes violent marches to New York City's Thirty-fourth Police Precinct and occasional looting followed Garcia's death. Mayor David Dinkins visited Garcia's family, and the police, seeing this as a no-confidence gesture, held an unruly demonstration in front of City Hall.

In September 1989, Congress passed a bill to limit the time served for contempt in Washington, D.C., custody cases. Introduced by Senator Orrin Hatch, the bill was designed to free Elizabeth Morgan, imprisoned for two years for refusing to reveal the whereabouts of her daughter or to allow court-ordered visits by her ex-husband. Public sympathy for Morgan, an Ivy League-educated cosmetic surgeon who alleged that her ex-husband had sexually abused their daughter, Hilary, contradicted repeated court judgments that the abuse was not proved and that her ex-husband should continue to see the child. Psychiatrists and therapists hired by both sides offered contesting and inconclusive testimony. By the time the bill was passed, seventeen lawyers and twelve expert witnesses had spoken. In November 1990, a New Zealand Family Court granted sole custody to Morgan, who had secretly taken Hilary there. The case continued in the 1990s, when Congress introduced a bill that would allow Elizabeth and Hilary Morgan to return to the United States without the child having to see her father. The father has opposed the bill (*New York Times,* 21 September 1996).

The most common way to make sense of the contradictory positions in such cases is to consult our feelings. The resulting emotivist, privatized language of justice assumes that emotions are universally felt. Everyone could understand that Morgan's desperate moves to protect her child were also comprehensible in the name of motherhood: she was sacrificing "her money, her career, and her freedom to protect her child" (Groner, 1991: 17). Such emotivist, privatized language may at first glance seem to manage uncertainty about justice, resolving it with the certainty of subjective experience. At the same time, however, this language of justice is relativist, for the emotions determining a decision on justice are individually owned and do not necessarily coincide with anyone else's. Emotivism engenders uncertainty by granting individuals a right to their own understanding of a problem and by not presuming to judge one understanding against another. Some social workers, lawyers, psychiatrists, and judges found Morgan manipulative and cruel in her pursuit of custody—not a good mother. Garcia's friends and relatives said he was a quiet neighborhood boy struggling to survive in a new country in the midst of a loving family. But the police saw him as a dangerous youth, the type who makes a neighborhood unsafe. Such contradictory feelings can result only in a relativist notion of justice that defines it as what each individual feels it is. Justice becomes something that cannot be negotiated or communicated even between individuals, let alone groups.

Some relativism may be inevitable, even valuable, but emotivism means that the categories of justice multiply until there is one for every individual, every subjective experience. How can we assess the Garcia family's tenderness toward their son against the police's absolute confidence in their colleague? How can we assess Clarence Thomas's feeling of being the object of media and legal racism against Anita Hill's feelings of humiliation and oppression; or a child's assertion that a father's touch was bad and abusive against the father's equally strong assertion that his touch was caring and loving; or a man's recall of consensual sex against a woman's memory of rape?

After Tawana, emotivist discourses of justice have a new legitimacy and a new fatalism. The domain of individual feelings that played such a large part in the Brawley case is now a constant factor in debates about justice and injustice. At the same time, people accept that this domain provides not answers so much as a realm of guaranteed uncertainty. By the time the media brought us the stories of Garcia's death and the fight between Hilary Morgan's parents, the jumble of personal perspectives on the events and their intractability to negotiation seemed normal.

An emotivist, privatized language of justice and an accompanying uncertainty are part of the fabric of the U.S. justice system. The "intent" of the founding fathers and the "plain meaning" of written and spoken words are the two myths, Stanley Fish says, with which U.S. legal interpretations justify themselves (1990: 322–24). These myths assume that we can understand the intent and the meaning of the founding fathers. Cracks in the myths appear every time constitutional interpreters, all claiming access to the true meaning and intent, clash. Both pro-choice and antiabortion advocates defend their views on constitutional grounds, for example, though according to Robert Bork, former Supreme Court nominee, "the inescapable fact is that the constitution contains not one word that can be tortured into the slightest relevance to abortion, one way or the other" (*New York Times*, 8 July 1992).

The privatization of constitutional guarantees of individual rights also encourages emotivism. Rights are cast negatively or passively—as the right not to do something or not to have something done to you. In the Constitution, " 'negative freedom'— staying out, letting be" far outweighs "positive, legal affirmations" (MacKinnon, 1989: 164). This framing emphasizes freedom from state interference in the realm we think of as "private." Thus, it gives a special moral legitimacy to the deep feelings associated with that realm. The judge's ruling suggested that Hilary Morgan's father had a right to an uninterrupted relationship with his daughter that overshadowed expert suspicions about abuse. In a British BBC2 documentary broadcast on 17 April 1996, *Ellen's in Exile*, the man himself explicitly claimed a constitutional status for his feeling that being a parent was the most important relationship in his life. If his daughter came back to the United States and he could not see her, he said, he would no longer be a person under the Constitution.

Popular debates about justice are also strongly emotivist. Often our evaluations of crime perpetrators and victims depend on whom we like bet-

ter. Did you prefer sweet, serene Nancy Kerrigan, the ice-skating assault victim, or Tonya Harding, her tough-talking, sassy competitor convicted of
planning the assault? Did O. J. Simpson seem to regret his spousal abuse?
Did he look like a good father? On television, Anita Hill appeared to some
as trustworthy and sincere, to others as a manipulative and pathological liar.
TV viewers' judgments about her personality largely determined what conclusions they reached about her charge.

Fictional representations of justice take on the same personal perspective. By the turn of the "greed is good" decade, movies such as *Wall
Street* (1988), *Crimes and Misdemeanors* (1989), *New Jack City* (1991), *City
of Hope* (1991), and *Thelma and Louise* (1991) were suggesting, with a procession of corrupt financial moguls, murderous ophthalmologists, cocaine
kings, mob-controlled mayors, and vigilante housewives, that the justice
system could be evaded if you were a compelling enough character. Today
at the movies, justice is the preserve of a few maverick individuals struggling on the frontier of anarchy to maintain their integrity. "They set aside
their laws as and when they wish. . . . All they have over us is tyranny and I
will not live under that yoke," says a colonial settler on the actual frontier
in the movie based on James Fenimore Cooper's 1826 frontier novel *The
Last of the Mohicans* (1992); the settler is talking not only about English justice in 1757 but also about the United States today. *Unforgiven* (1992) took
the privatization of justice further. In this movie, even cowboys—the archetypal lone guardians of justice—are too compromised by their past and
present relationship to brutality to serve as moral figures. One rejects violence but fails to deliver justice; the other sees that justice can come only
from the barrel of a gun, along with his own self-degradation. Conversely,
movie redemption can be a simple personal choice. In *Pulp Fiction* (1994),
a hit man, struck by a religious premonition, stops a robbery in progress in
the diner where he is eating, because, he says, he wants to put evil behind
him and become a good shepherd to the weak.

On television, fictional representations of police and lawyers have
moved away from their earlier focus on crime, punishment, and objective
investigation. Since the 1980s, the dominant television view of justice has
been a personal one. Jack Webb's "Just the facts, ma'am" has yielded to the
psychological dilemma of *L.A. Law's* Jonathan Rollins, who, though African
American himself, in one episode used racial stereotypes against a Japanese
CEO whom his Anglo client was suing for discrimination. The plot turned
on Rollins's ambivalence, his willingness to use racism to win the case despite his generally antiracist stance. Novels about crime and the law have
also made justice a matter of personal interpretation. In Scott Turow's *Pre-*

sumed Innocent (1987), the narrator is accused of the murder his wife commits. Questions close to the end of the narrative crystallize the book's personalized doubts about justice and the justice system: "But what is harder? Knowing the truth or finding it, telling it or being believed?" (418).

The emphasis on private emotions in discourse about justice is mirrored in privatized individual and community mechanisms for achieving justice. Owning a gun provides many individuals with a reassuring line of self-defense, and gun clubs, shooting lessons, and magazines such as *American Survival Guide* and *Women and Guns* increasingly shore up this strategy. Some people assume the responsibility of distributing justice themselves, stepping in, like Morgan, where the law seems to them to be failing. This vigilantism was emblematized in Ellie Nesler's 1993 killing of Daniel Driver, charged with molesting her son at a church camp, during a California court hearing at which Driver was likely to be let go. Calling on a private feeling that is assumed to be universal, she asked in justification, "What's a mother to do?" (*New York Times*, 3 April 1993). Such private retributions can be extremely idiosyncratic and partial: someone may be killed for being in another's yard or for a gesture or a word interpreted as threat or disrespect. In 1992, a homeowner in Baton Rouge, Louisiana, shot a sixteen-year-old Japanese exchange student who was looking for a nearby Halloween party. When the student did not respond to the command "Freeze!" which he did not know, the homeowner shot him.

Emotivist approaches to justice seem to provide solutions where, as with Brawley, the courts can only dither and reach a conclusion that satisfies no one. Moreover, the solutions are not as decisive as they appear. They are always haunted by cases' other meanings. Commentators on the Morgan case lamented the court's inattention to Hilary's right to a secure and happy childhood. Even when a group or an individual successfully responds to a problem—picketing and closing down a drugs operation, for instance—the relativist nature of such private justice leaves a hint of doubt in the answers. What about the people on the next block, where the drug dealers now set up shop?

Another way to manage the uncertainties about justice is to adopt a fixed set of professional practices. The police, the law, psychiatric and social services, and the media all have such practices, which provide criteria for judging and acting on justice issues. But the practices are often inadequate or compromised. Indeed, it is on their failures that many controversies about justice rest: those in the case of Jose Garcia, killed during police investigations; the Morgan case, stalemated by the law's helplessness and the endless interviews by psychiatrists; the police beating of Rodney King; and the Brawley case.

Each professional discourse of justice positions itself outside history, as if its methods are the only ones that can lead to the truth. Both sides in the Morgan case hired pediatricians, child psychiatrists, social workers, and therapists. Each side's experts measured and remeasured Hilary's vaginal opening and observed her play with anatomically correct dolls in attempts to show or disprove abuse. Their findings were either inconclusive or contradictory. Professionalized accounts of justice thus end up being laws unto themselves—only this time, it is the perspective of the profession, rather than the individual, that is the court of last resort.

One answer to the problems encountered by emotivist and professional discourses of justice is to set aside all hope of a common code of justice and to calculate instead the social costs and benefits of different actions. Such calculations are often financial. Columnist Pete Hamill explained his fury about the Brawley case partly in terms of the money it had cost—$750 million to $1 billion—and the good social uses to which that money could have been put: "to buy textbooks in Newburgh or Bed-Stuy, to rehab some apartments in The Bronx or bring health care into the welfare hotels" (*New York Post,* 28 September 1988). At other times a broader calculus of cost and benefit comes into play, for instance, allowing the police to weigh the economic and social rewards of pursuing small-time thieves against the large monetary and time costs of such work. The tabloids implicitly excused the murder of Yusef Hawkins, killed by young white men in Bensonhurst, by following reports of his death with reports of his parents' marital difficulties. This strategy tacitly subtracted the social cost of black familial instability from the social cost of the murder of a working-class black youth, and by this means diminished the injustice of the event.

Fictional representations are particularly able to rely on a costs-and-benefits morality without being obliged to provide a more consistent frame for justice judgments. Through the 1980s and 1990s, a string of "yuppies in crisis" movies—*Volunteers* (1985), *True Colors* (1991), *Defending Your Life* (1991), *Regarding Henry* (1991), and *The Doctor* (1991)—anxiously balanced yuppies' disproportionate, seemingly unjust hold on salaries and goods against their good works and citizenly concern. In an early example, *Lost in America* (1985), a yuppie couple journey through an America of poverty, insecurity, simple pleasures, and fulfilling relationships. When they return to their well-paying jobs at the end of the movie, they are justified in having what seemed at the beginning to be too much but what now (their having experienced poverty and having learned good values the hard way) seems to be what they truly deserve.

The trouble with cost-benefit evaluations of a justice issue is that we may make different calculations. Victims of small theft may value the social rewards of catching the thief far higher than do the police. Many tabloid readers would not accept that Hawkins's parents' marital problems mitigate the horror of the young man's murder. A veneer of consensus characterizes utilitarian discourses of justice, but the question remains, whose consensus? Post-Tawana, it may be easier to characterize justice as a matter of costs and benefits rather than ethics, but the rendering has become more difficult in the wake of the realization of how many and different the possible computations are.

Older discourses of justice still exist, providing more complete narratives of justice. When the grand jury accused Tawana and Glenda Brawley of subverting justice by withholding evidence, they took sanctuary in the Bethany Baptist Church, thus framing the case as a story of ungodly persecution. Though undercut by emotivism, concepts of guilt and innocence retain a theological force within the culture. Even a criminal act can be acceptable if the criminal is able to convey a quasi-theological sense of the crime as retribution. During the L.A. riots, as TV cameras rolled, white truck driver Reginald Denny was pulled from his cab and nearly beaten to death by what came to be known as the "L.A. 4+," seven young black men. With the races reversed, this footage seemed to parallel the Rodney King video. Joe Hicks, of the Southern Christian Leadership Conference, described many black people's response as, "They kicked that white boy's ass and good for them, because *we* get our ass kicked *all* the time." Naomi Bradley of the L.A. 4+ defense committee quoted Sistah Souljah: "Two wrongs don't make a right. But it sure does make things even" (qtd. in Cooper, 1993: 28). Personal retribution has become the stuff of cultural mythology in movies such as the *Death Wish* series (e.g., 1974, 1993), starring Charles Bronson, and, with a lower body count, *Thelma and Louise* (1991). We may not accept revengeful anger as a justification, but we understand its religious tone even when it can claim no theological underpinning.

Religious grand narratives are interwoven with the dominant privatized discourse. After the 1988 case, Tawana Brawley, converted to Islam, stood alongside Minister Louis Farrakhan on lecture platforms, clad in a long white gown, denouncing her detractors. In this scenario, declarations of faith became assertions of personal virtue, counters to the media picture of a naughty teenager given to byzantine and dishonest self-protection, alongside her complicitous mother. Post-Tawana, religious arguments about justice seem even more difficult to sustain without tying them to personal accounts, given all the undecidability that this connection brings.

Other grand narratives of justice, based on encompassing political or social theories, also persist. But attempts to explain injustice in social terms also lean heavily on psychological arguments and images. The media emblematized the social problems facing the city in the Central Park jogger's individual tragedy. She was cast as Miss Liberty, the symbol of a mythical city, efficient, safe, and white, while her attackers were symbols of the economic and social chaos threatening to engulf it.[6] Some feminists blame male violence for *Thelma and Louise* phenomena such as women carrying guns and wives killing abusive husbands or—in the Lorena Bobbitt case—cutting off their penises. But, like the movie, these explanations use feminism to justify highly individual feelings of anger, revenge, and pleasure. Private factors seem to be present in social and political accounts of justice with a new inevitability. This shift happened gradually throughout the 1980s and 1990s. However, personal factors of truthfulness and trustworthiness were so prevalent in the Brawley affair that it seems apt to characterize as "post-Tawana" the contemporary drive to reduce social and political explanations to private emotions.

Whose Justice?

Patricia Bowman spent the evening of Good Friday, 29 March 1991, at Au Bar, a popular drinking spot in Palm Beach, Florida. At about 3 A.M., she and a girlfriend, Michele Cassone, went with William Kennedy Smith, his cousin Patrick Kennedy, and Patrick's father, Senator Edward Kennedy, to the Kennedys' beach-front summer home. At 5:30 A.M., Bowman called her friend Anne Mercer to say she had been sexually assaulted. Mercer and her boyfriend drove to the Kennedy house to collect her. At 2 P.M. on Saturday, Bowman told police that Smith had raped her (Stephen, 1991: 17). Against previous policy and amid controversy, *NBC Nightly News* and the *New York Times* named Bowman. The case went to trial at the beginning of December 1991, with television cameras in the court. To protect what remained of Bowman's anonymity, television disguised her face with a fuzzy blue dot. As an alleged Kennedy victim, she raised the ghost of Mary Jo Kopechne. Nevertheless, she had to fight the Kennedy charisma and to answer to the court and the media for her single parenthood, her checkered work history, her drinking and traffic tickets, and her "little wild streak" (*New York Times,* 22 April 1991; *New York Times,* 26 April 1991; Taylor, 1992: 38).

The Bowman-Smith saga makes it clear that power relations, the patterns of control that social groups have over each other, are central to justice. Power relations, like those of class and gender in *Bowman v. Smith,* permeate the justice system and our concepts of justice. Justice has a clearer relationship to power than do other realms of moral uncertainty. For injustice is always suffered by someone, and it is in the name of that someone that the claim of injustice is made. "Whose justice?" is, thus, a question that is asked much more readily and more frequently than "Whose morality?"

Paralyzing moral angst comes predominantly from educated white men—from Bret Easton Ellis's brutal existential anguish in *American Psycho* (1991), or from Richard Sennett, bemoaning urban anarchy (1992). We may understand such angst as a lament not for the moral order whose breakdown the writers describe, but for the social power that the moral order once bestowed on them. Sennett contemplates the diversity and inequality fracturing "his" New York City. He describes an encounter with an Indian shopkeeper, a father, as Sennett is, and imagines discussing fatherhood with him. But in the end, he simply pays and goes, leaving an incompleteness in the encounter that he thinks is inevitable in contemporary city life (1992: 147–48). In contrast to these relatively privileged meditations on the insurmountability of difference, challenges to justice announced by women, people of color, lesbians and gay men, the poor and the working class, the homeless, the HIV-positive, and victims of violent crime can be heard as the sound of the disenfranchised arguing back. Less powerful social groups live and speak moral uncertainty as something specific—injustice. When Rev. Joseph Lowery, one of the founding ministers of the civil rights movement, says, "There is no sanctuary for the soul from the sorrow of the society in which we live," he does not stop there but names the sorrow: failure to extend jobless benefits, and boatloads of Haitian refugees turned back, many to sink (*New York Times,* 15 June 1992).

Women's actual and ideological confinement to a private realm outside justice makes them a good focus for examining the power relations of justice. Bowman's case involved an accumulation of feminine failings that compromised her innocence. She was both insufficiently private and inappropriately public: unmarried, with a child, she met Smith in a singles bar and agreed to drive to his home at 3 A.M. In the St. John's rape case, the fact that the complainant had been drinking, as well as her reported cooperation with some of the men's demands, worked against her claims. At one point, she turned to the defense attorneys and said, "I'm not the one on trial" (*Amsterdam [N.Y.] News,* 17 August 1991).[7] Women's accusations of sexual harassment or abuse are frequently treated as attention-seeking or, as with

Anita Hill, paranoia (Bhabha, 1992: 247). Even speaking removes believ-ability from women. The comatose Central Park jogger and, at first, the traumatized Brawley were silent figures of suffering. The press treats pub-licly vocal women—such as Bowman and Desiree Washington, raped by Mike Tyson—much more critically. Using plain words to describe private acts of ambiguous moral status, Hill lost her right to privacy. Although Clarence Thomas's continual appeals to this right were accorded some re-spect, the senatorial committee subjected Hill (though she was only a wit-ness, not a candidate) to personal scrutiny far beyond the subject of her tes-timony (Ross, 1992: 57).

The media subtly color-grade women's believability. When the press thought Brawley was telling the truth, it named her but still made her an honorary white. Her race was hardly mentioned; she was simply a pretty, shy cheerleader. Later, as her story began to fall apart and her silence was interpreted as sly, she became a bad girl and got metaphorically blacker.[8] Black men's and white women's voices can, though, get black women heard. Audrey Edwards points out how Brawley's ordeal was subordinated to black men's political agendas: "Why is it that three Black male advisors now figure more prominently and have received more attention than the victim her-self?" (1988: 136). Competition can even develop between whites and black men to claim the voices of black women. The mainstream white media in-fantilized and patronized Brawley, reducing her to the instrument of the black men speaking on her behalf.

When black women speak out against black men, they themselves may become proxies of the white establishment. Media support for Desiree Washington and Anita Hill, which whitened them into American princess and career woman respectively, was intimately linked with the demonizing of Mike Tyson and Clarence Thomas. Covering the Tyson trial, Joan Mor-gan summarized white journalists' response toward Washington as, "She doesn't seem black at all," and that toward Tyson as a classic animalization: "You can take the primate out of the jungle, but you can't expect to civilize him." (1992: 39).[9] Sections of the black media read cases such as those of Tyson, Thomas, Simpson, and the Central Park attackers as genocidal plots against the African American man. In these analyses, black men, especially powerful ones, are targets of the white establishment, black women accus-ing them are co-opted Aunt Jemimas, and white women such as Nicole Brown Simpson, accused of escalating an ordinary domestic tiff into a 911 call, are hysterical, fantasizing fools. But gender still sometimes outweighs race, an imbalance that was especially clear in the Thomas hearings. When

*Figure 8. Tawana Brawley. Courtesy Dave Rentas/*New York Post.

Thomas associated Hill's allegations and the senators' questioning with lynching, he helped legitimize sexual harassment for white as well as black men, leaving shared masculinity, rather than race, as the central term in the controversy. "If the lynched body is black," Homi Bhabha summarizes, its "real color is its gender. You can hear Thomas say to his interrogators, 'I may be accused of sexual harassment, but ain't I a man?'" (1992: 247).[10]

Representations of women in justice debates both recognize and deny the place of class. This vacillation leaves women sometimes defined by their class position, sometimes cut loose from it or declassed entirely, like Brawley—black but not urban, floating outside class. Class factors into calculations of white female victimhood. Hedda Nussbaum's culpability in the fatal abuse of her adopted daughter, Lisa, by Lisa's adopted father, Joel Steinberg, seemed almost impossible for the media to contemplate, because of Nussbaum's secure record of education and professional employment. Bowman's class was also a liability. She had a patchy work history and, though part of a well-off family, she was poor in contrast with her alleged attacker. Men's class enters into such equations too. How could Steinberg, who seemed an archetypal professional, a lawyer, be an abuser? For middle-class viewers of the Bowman trial, Smith's background of privilege also told against him.

Race and class are difficult to articulate together, however. Hill and Washington were more middle-class than black to most of their white supporters. This suppression of race also affects black men. Thomas was represented as a meritocratic success story, the deraced "hero of the American dream," as well as the black "hanged man of the American nightmare" (Bhabha, 1992: 242). It was indeed his deraced class position that let white men see him as simply another man victimized by a malicious woman. The middle-class status of the alleged Central Park attackers caused only minor hiccups in mainstream media representations of them as part of the black male threat identified, by cultural fiat, with an "underclass." For much of the black media, too, the issue of class did not arise in these cases: the women were presented simply as sisters, like Brawley, or as token whites, educated black women selling out black men, like Hill and Washington. Even feminists who supported the Central Park jogger's right as a woman to be safe in public spaces neglected the class nature of that freedom, the fact that going wherever you want, whenever you want, is a political priority primarily for middle-class women (Didion, 1992: 254).

Women's sexuality can cloud their victimhood or criminalize them before the act. Popular representations tie lesbian sexuality and female bisexuality to feminism, promiscuity, prostitution, sadomasochism, and murder in a miasma of criminality and predatory sexuality. While the media undermined Hill's testimony with innuendos that she could not sustain a relationship with a man and that her feminism made her a man hater, senators insinuated she had homosexual "proclivities" (qtd. in Ross, 1992: 59). In the film *Basic Instinct* (1992), the monogamous lesbian kills out of passion, comprehensibly, while the character who has sex with women *and* men is manipulative, dangerous, and eventually gets killed herself, her just desert, a complication of the long cinematic history of lesbians who kill. Coming after *Basic Instinct,* the media crush on the Florida highway murders, committed by a woman said to be both a lesbian and a prostitute, consolidated the contemporary mythology of murderous, sexually ambiguous women.

Attempts to explain justice issues in terms of power assume that every group with a particular interest has its own take on justice. But post-Tawana, group or "community" justice is difficult to get a fix on. People's identities are multiple and shifting, not stable enough to support clear discourses of community. Black women's educational and career success, black men's social and economic marginalization and high percentage of violent death, and black men's violence against black women increasingly divide by gender the justice aims of people united by race. In addition, the ideas of justice that you endorse and express cannot be transcribed directly from your social background. The range of African American responses to the Thomas hearings bears this out. Sociologist Orlando Patterson argued that Hill's insensitivity to Thomas's "down-home style of courtship" demonstrated her distance from black culture (qtd. in Bhabha, 1992: 237). Cornel West castigated black leaders for their "failure of nerve" in not speaking out against Thomas's lack of qualifications (1992: 391). Newark Mayor Sharpe James called the nomination "a disgrace and an affront" to African Americans (*Amsterdam [N.Y.] News,* 24 August 1991). Poet Maya Angelou gave him lukewarm support, convinced that it would be either Thomas or no blacks on the Supreme Court (*New York Times,* 25 August 1991). Afro-American studies professor Paula Giddings argued the destructiveness of unthinking black solidarity in the face of a "black-on-black sexual crime" (1992: 442).

If we raise race or gender loyalty over all other ethical considerations, we will do some violence to justice (Cornell, 1992: 8). Because communities are themselves unstable and heterogeneous, there is not much danger of this happening. If, though, we accept the need for an ethical ideal, even a temporary notion of a common good, then justice itself will inevitably do some violence in the name of the good. Pursuing the goodwill at times means repressing the demands for justice of the other. Even if women determined rules of evidence along with men, there would still be cases in which insufficient evidence would mean that a rapist went free. Given the meager evidence, it is hard to imagine a judicial system in which Bowman would have won her case, even if the jury had resisted the defense's attempts to discredit her.[11] Similarly, the grand jury was doing the right thing when it dismissed Brawley's allegations—even though this dismissal suppressed legitimate African American claims of unequal justice.[12]

The corollary of this necessary violence in the pursuit of justice is that even an act that seems violent and unjust to most people has *some* connection with an ethical ideal. In February 1991, a Korean worker at the C-Town supermarket in Elmhurst, Queens, hit an eleven-year-old black boy whom he thought was shoplifting, took him into a back room, and kept him there for half an hour until his mother was contacted and came to get him. The worker was clearly not an ethical exemplar, yet even his act aspired to an ethical ideal. Indeed, it was the Elmhurst incident, along with other similar events, that moved the Korean Grocers' Association to fund black radio appreciations of the late Thurgood Marshall and to have Al Sharpton as a guest at its annual awards dinner; and the Korean Produce Association cosponsored a minority scholarship project with Harlem's *Amsterdam News*. Even if you have very little power, your unavoidable encounters with the ambiguities of justice mean that you too are able to engage in negotiating the path toward the good. HIV-positive women, for instance, are predominantly African American or Latina and poor. They are not a powerful constituency. Yet they and their advocates forced the medical establishment to make the definition of AIDS, modeled on gay men, more equitable by including women's symptoms.

Equivalent Justices

During the hearings to confirm Clarence Thomas to the Supreme Court, senators called a black law professor from Oklahoma, Anita Hill, to give evidence. She alleged that while she was Thomas's assistant at the Education Department and the Equal Employment Opportunity Commission, he repeatedly asked her for dates. When she refused, he talked to her about porn movies and his own sexual exploits, calling himself Long Dong Silver. Senators' interrogation of Hill included questions about her character: Was she getting revenge because Thomas hadn't wanted a serious relationship? Hadn't she stolen the "Long Dong Silver" accusation from another sexual harassment case? Did she have a boyfriend? Couldn't she take a joke? The senators confirmed Thomas, but those up for reelection were almost unseated. Their working-over of Hill stimulated the "Year of the Woman," a campaign to give "women's issues" such as harassment, abortion, health care, education, and crime higher political priority and to get more women elected. In the longer term, by forcing sexual harassment into the open, Hill's testimony meant that relations between women and men around the watercooler would never be the same.

Uncertainties about justice seem to leave it, like other moral uncertainties, suspended between confused realities and impossible ideals. At times such uncertainties seem like dead ends, but they can lead, through negotiation, to change. Debates about justice demand solutions. To engi-

Figure 9. Anita Hill. Photo by Stanley Tretick. People Weekly. Copyright 1991 Stanley Tretick.

neer these solutions, we have to engage with dominant discourses of justice that rely on private emotions, professional criteria, or utilitarian calculations, even if we do not want to reproduce them. One strategy involves confronting the existing discourses of justice and offering a distinct alternative. Some interpreted the Thomas hearings along these lines, as a challenge to the political establishment. In front of millions of TV viewers, the senators, the country's ruling elite, seemed simply out of it—pompous, arrogant, or, like Ted Kennedy, absurdly unqualified as they questioned Thomas. In the Brawley case, Sharpton negotiated dramatically by confrontation, condemning the inequities of the police and the courts and calling for dismissals and prosecutions to clean them up. Rappers such as Public Enemy, Sister Souljah, Ice T, NWA, and Coolio generate word pictures of the abandonment of justice in inner-city communities and suggest didactic solutions. In "Not Wit' a Dealer," MC Lyte warns her friend Cecilia against drug dealers, men with "junk jewelry and no soul." The song ends with Cecilia's and her man's murder. As the Uzi roars, Lyte tersely points out the lesson: "See why it pays to be choosy?" In movies such as *Do the Right Thing* (1989),

New Jack City (1991), *Boyz N the Hood* (1991), *Straight out of Brooklyn* (1991), and *Juice* (1992), the morality tales about crime and punishment in inner-city communities are similarly polarized between education and family, on the one hand, and drugs, gangs, and death, on the other. Such confrontations can reinforce existing justice discourse by their vehement rejection of it; they generate little engagement with the ideals and potential futures of such discourse. However, they have an immediate and strong critical effect that does not entirely disperse.

Some efforts at negotiating in regard to justice are more complicated, employing a strategy of estranging juxtaposition. Anita Hill operated outside the culture's collusive silence about sexual harassment (Bhabha, 1992: 243). By naming sexual harassment, she turned herself into an "odd woman," but she also helped redefine relationships between men and women in the workplace. Juxtapositions are clearest in the popular media, the theater of cultural stability and normalcy, where we expect to see the good being praised or rewarded and wrongdoers being punished or pursued. To see the opposite—the police beating Rodney King, or John Gotti going free, for instance—is an estranging juxtaposition of a kind that goes back to the Watergate tapes. At present, it is as much through such media challenges as through the justice system itself that ideas of justice are called into question.

One possible way to speak across different concepts of justice is, as Emmanuel Levinas suggests, to adopt as a first principle a respect for the ethical difference of the Other (1985: 95–101). Such respect does not imply that we should celebrate otherness romantically, forgetting its realities. If we respect Anita Hill's ethical voice, we must recognize it as a particular black woman's voice, not the voice of black women everywhere or a timeless voice. It follows that we will have to multiply and change continually the names we give to those other than ourselves.

Respect for the other is one way we can manage the difficulties of collective life without withdrawing into individualism. We can modify this suggestion by arguing, like Iris Marion Young (1990), that the community, with its insistence on the sameness of all members, should not be our model of justice. Instead we should foreground the city, a key term in justice debates. The city, with its inexhaustible possibilities of encountering differences of all kinds and its ability to accommodate the ostracized, should show us how to think about justice. Differences are pleasurable, Young points out. They, not the sameness of community, are the stuff of most people's lives. Even the academics like Christopher Lasch (1991) who propose a return to small community structure as the answer to moral turpitude and uncertain justice, writes Young, "love to show visiting friends around the Boston or San Francisco or New York in which they live, climbing up towers to see the glitter of lights and sampling the fare at the best ethnic restaurants" (1990: 237).

The contemporary city that Young describes could, with minor modifications, be anywhere; it could be Nairobi as well as New York, a new suburban hub or an old, established urban center. It is a city of capital and poverty, of cultural atomism and exchange. It is not merely an emblem of modernity or a sign of racial division, as it was in media coverage of the Central Park jogger case. Rather, it signals a new "relationship of people to one another, to their own history and to one another's history" (1986: 20). It is defined not by tolerance of difference, as for Richard Rorty (1990), nor by responsibility to difference, as for Levinas (1985), but by its recognition of difference.

Chantal Mouffe suggests that such recognition of difference is both a utopian hope and a pragmatic plan, based on what is possible and exists. She maintains that we may reconcile our different identities, the various "communities of values, language, culture" to which we belong, within a "citizen" identity. This identity can uphold a general ethical standard. Citizenship can thus maintain a relationship of equivalence, a sense of "we-ness" in the face of antidemocratic forces that does not compromise difference (1992a: 30, 32). With this notion of an equivalent citizen identity, we can negotiate justice in ways that respect difference but do not fail in the face of it, reaching temporary ethical agreements. Equivalent justice aims at timely, consensual solutions that neither deny the variable past, present, and future nor negate the ethical beyond.

A sense of equivalence already frames some thinking about race and justice. To indicate the complexities of the riots in L.A., one African American gang member claimed that some Korean American groceries where the shopkeepers "treat you with respect" were not torched. Nevertheless, some Korean American businesses that were reported to be involved with African American organizations were burned, and sneaker stores seem to have been looted regardless of ownership (New York Times, 21 June 1992). Yet when an Asian shopkeeper, much liked by his black customers, was burned out by a Mexican American youth from outside the area, black youths from the shopkeeper's neighborhood reported the arsonist to the police. "You got homeys turning in a Mexican to the cops—who they hate—for burning a Jap store," the gangster said. "So it's not as simple as they say" (Broyles, 1992: 38).[13] Some African American commentators develop a similar strategy when they suggest ways of thinking about justice across race. Cornel West, writing in the black periodical Emerge in response to the failure to negotiate a common justice in Crown Heights in the aftermath of Gavin Cato's death and the killing of Yankel Rosenbaum during the ensuing violent anti-Jewish demonstrations, enumerates the historical oppression of blacks and Jews, their common involvement in progressive movements, and their points of conflict. He insists that each group must recognize this complex history respectfully and reflectively. Group identity, he writes, must be thought about ethically if there are to be fruitful discussions of justice: "Self-critical exchanges must take place within and across black and Jewish communities not simply about their own group interest but also, and more important, about what being black or Jewish means in *ethical* terms" (1993: 44).

In negotiating an equivalent justice, one group may represent justice for all, acting not as a metaphor for an ideal justice but as an indicator of a particular, persuasive moral stance. In the United States, the quincentennial of Columbus's landing was marked, more than anything else, by embarrassment. The Native American view that Columbus did not discover anything but only initiated genocide succeeded in making the anniversary so ethically dubious for the entire nation that celebrations fell flat. Women also anchor our negotiations of an equivalent justice. When Drucilla Cornell describes Antigone's conflict between the ideal and the practice of justice, she implies that women are all Antigones. As observers of the justice system, outside it yet implicated in it, women are apt to understand this conflict. Like Antigone, they often observe and preserve the history and future of justice through mourning. Whether in demonstrations for their disappeared sons and husbands in El Salvador, at funerals of slain ANC activists in South Africa, or at the funerals for Jose Garcia, Yusef Hawkins, and Yankel Rosenbaum, women mourn injustice for everyone.

Because in the United States your race as well as your gender assigns you a place inside or outside the justice system, Antigone is most likely to appear here as a black woman: someone who, even in the entertaining guise of Oprah Winfrey or Whoopi Goldberg, raises awkward issues; someone who calls stark attention to the justice system's failings, like Tawana Brawley, the St. John's victim, or Anita Hill. However bleached-out by class, Hill was heard as a black woman and, speaking in that voice, established a new equivalence among women in relation to sexual harassment. More women now recognize their susceptibility to sexual harassment, and every citizen—male and female—has been baptized in the sexual harassment discourse. With Hill, too, women gained a new model for forcing issues before the public eye: they could "Anita Hill" them (Quindlen, 1993). In 1992, many women candidates took up Hill's challenge to business-as-usual politics in regard to abortion, health, child care, education, and crime, as well as gender issues. Carol Mosely Braun, who had proclaimed her outrage at the Thomas hearings on TV, received six hundred calls asking her to run against Illinois senator Alan Dixon, who had voted for Thomas—and she beat him (*Philadelphia Inquirer*, 14 January 1992). For many black women, Hill's voice, and Washington's, also pointed up the equivalence of justice between black men and women, and that black women, while recognizing black men's oppression, must call them on their sexism and negotiate a new ethical relationship. As Joan Morgan, writing of Mike Tyson, put it, "He, like all black men who hurt and abuse us, must be held responsible for his actions. Saying so doesn't mean that we love black men any less; it simply means that we are not willing to let race loyalty buy us early tombstones" (1992: 39).

3 | Family

Baby M

On 27 March 1986, Mary Beth Whitehead, a New Jersey housewife and high school dropout, gave birth to a nine-pound two-ounce girl, whom she named Sara. Whitehead had contracted to give up the newborn for $10,000. Instead, she fled with the baby to Florida. Richard, Whitehead's husband, a sanitation worker, was the father of her two older children, but this baby's father was William Stern, a New Jersey biochemist. Stern and his wife, Elizabeth, a pediatrician, had hired Whitehead to be artificially inseminated by Stern. The surrogacy solved certain personal problems for the Sterns: Elizabeth, who had multiple sclerosis, did not have to risk her health further with a pregnancy. And William was able to continue his family line, which, except for him, the Nazis had ended. The Sterns tracked Whitehead to Florida and, with the aid of local police, took the baby and renamed her Melissa. Asserting her natural right to her baby, Whitehead fought back in the New Jersey courts, where the contest became known as the "Baby M" case.

Uncertainties poured out of the case. Commentators wondered whether the surrogacy was a womb rental or a baby sale. *Time* asked, "Whose child is this?" (Lacayo, 1987b). Katha Pollitt wrote that the Baby M case bore an "uncanny resemblance to the all-sales-final style of a used-car lot" (1987: 681). Anne Taylor Fleming voiced some of the more emotional uncertainties in a *New York Times Magazine* article: "Always, for women, there are questions: Could I have a baby and give it away? Could I pay someone to have a baby for me? . . . What about her husband who watches her grow large with another man's child? What about the babies themselves who will know they've been 'bought' and therefore 'sold'?" (1987: 32). *Time* sought biblical precedent, citing Hagar, who had Abraham's child when his wife Sarah was past childbearing age. Hagar was a slave, just as Whitehead, poorer and less powerful than the Sterns, could be construed as a modern-day slave. Yet Baby M lacked the divine sanction of the biblical case. The rights and wrongs of the case seemed undecidable (Lacayo, 1987b: 57). *People* magazine declared, "There are no bad people in this case" (Shaughnessy, 1987: 50).

The Baby M case brought to public consciousness the deeply felt doubts that attend reproductive technology, doubts that magnify as the repro-tech bar continues to be raised. In the decade after Baby M hit the news, in vitro fertilization went far beyond the romance of a sperm and an egg in a petri dish to include the precision of moving particular chromosomes from one egg to another (Kolata, 1997b). Whimsical moral speculations about Nobel-laureate sperm banks that could produce Einsteinian babies lost their sci-fi resonance when Scottish geneticist Ian Wilmut cloned a sheep named Dolly in his laboratory (*New York Times,* 24 February 1997).

Who Is the Mother, Father, Grandmother, Child?

The Baby M case threw into public debate and further uncertainty the issue of what constitutes a mother. Who is the mother, if not the biological mother? For Whitehead, the simple fact that she had had the baby legitimated her custody. Feminist defenses of Mary Beth Whitehead reduced the rights of the biological father to those of a receiver of a discretionary gift. Psychologists had other criteria for judging motherhood. Those who examined Whitehead for the court said she had an "emotional overinvestment" in her children and criticized her assumption that physically bearing the child gave her a mother's rights (Harrison, 1987: 309). As Barrie Thorne writes, "The same child may now have three different mothers: one who donates the egg, another who nurtures the fetus in her womb and gives birth, and a mother who gives primary care after birth" (1992: 11). Even such enumerations cannot cover all the questions asked about mothers in the unfolding drama of repro-tech, such as whether postmenopausal women have the right to become mothers or, as in cases in which older mothers carried babies for their adult children, whether a woman can be the mother of her own grandchildren.[1]

In addition, the Baby M case pushed to new ground the uncertainty already attached to fatherhood. Outside surrogacy, the identity of the father is a question of faith or of a DNA test. Here, even though the sperm donor was definitively known, his contribution, said Whitehead, did not make him a father. Judge Harvey Sorkow, who ruled on the case in New Jersey Superior Court, took a biological view of fatherhood: "A father cannot buy what is already his" (Lacayo, 1987a; 525 A. 2d N.J. Super. Ct. [1987]).[2]

Baby M's proliferation of possible mothers and fathers illustrated the seemingly new fluidity of moral and emotional claims that men, women, and children may have on one another. Not only does it make more ambiguous the question of who we are to one another, but it also complicates concomitant rights and responsibilities. By becoming a point at which discourses of family, morality, feminism, child custody, and new reproductive technologies collided, Baby M revealed the plasticity of definitions of family and the precarious status of morality within those definitions. Baby M, notes ethicist Arthur Caplan, "takes away a reference point" (qtd. in Hartouni, 1991: 49).[3]

If renting a stranger for surrogacy exacerbates moral uncertainty and explodes icons of parenthood, what does using your mother for the same purpose do? Cases of grandmother surrogates such as those in South Dakota and New York throw notions of family into chaos, violating the normal sense of generational progression, and evoke the specter of incest, the sin against which, according to Freud and Lévi-Strauss, the family is constructed. Debates surrounding these cases concerned who's who in the family: is the grandmother also the mother, and what is her new relationship to her child and to her or his partner? In fact, the Mayo Clinic in Minnesota turned down Arlette Schweitzer, the South Dakota woman who eventually became the surrogate for her daughter, because Minnesota law stipulates that the birth mother is the mother (*New York Times*, 11 August 1991).

Surrogate motherhood is not the only reproductive technology to hurl muddled family ethics into hyperdrive. Does a man have rights over his ex-wife's ova? Does *ex utero* fertilization enhance these rights or lessen them? And is the embryo property owned by the parents or an autonomous person with its own rights? In the Tennessee Supreme Court in 1992, a man won a suit preventing his ex-wife from implanting eggs he had fertilized.

The seven embryos, the perplexed judge wrote, are neither "'persons' nor 'property,' but occupy an interim category" (*New York Times,* 2 June 1992). Even when, as often happens, such cases are rescripted in the morally simpler universe of television fiction, the issues still seem terminally tangled. In an episode of the television drama *Picket Fences* (broadcast 5 February 1993), based on a real Long Island case, the parameters of family, as well as of life and death, were indecipherable or simply up to you: A doctor moves into town with his wife, who is on life-support equipment. Although she is legally dead, he wants to keep her organs alive for six more months to bring her pregnancy to term.[4] The wife's mother sues to have the tubes pulled, because her daughter's living will calls for it. The judge decides that because the wife had an organ donor card, her organs, as well as the body that supports them, should be used to continue the life of the fetus. Who has more right over the woman's body, the husband or the mother? Should the woman's wishes supersede the father's right to a child?

Disturbances in supposedly natural ties of affection between parents and children found extreme expression in the first custody case brought by a child, that of Gregory Kingsley, a Florida twelve-year-old who divorced his parents in 1992 to live with his foster parents. Because the case followed the paradigm of a divorce procedure, it suggested, more emphatically than ever before, that children should have choices concerning their family. Just as adults choose their marriage partners, this child wanted to choose his parents (*New York Times,* 8 July and 26 September 1992).[5] The child's claiming of the right to divorce his parents makes ambiguous profoundly entrenched patterns of family hierarchy. In addition, criteria for parenthood are again in question. Here, the foster parents claimed to be Kingsley's "psychological parents," while the mother's claim was the more traditional one of flesh and blood.

The Private, the Public, and the Family

One effect of new reproductive technologies is that the law and professionals have a more visible role in defining good families. The court's intrusion on what felt like private moral terrain in the matter of Baby M, transplanting into the legal realm what had seemed firmly biological, meant that it was brokering definitions of parenthood. In the debate about mothers and fathers that ensued, parenthood seemed suddenly elusive, turning on love, labor, and personal deservedness, as much as on ovum and sperm.

The court's encroachment on a realm that we generally regard as private, bounded at most by religious, moral protocols, involves it in decisions with little basis in legal precedent. As a result of Judge Sorkow's decision that Whitehead was not the mother of Baby M, the court OK'd the rewriting of Baby M's birth certificate to reflect Stern's paternity, a move that flouted the biological mother's conventional right to decide who else is listed on the birth certificate (525 A.2d 1175–76).[6] In the wake of the Baby M case, public interventions in definitions of parenthood proliferated. Twenty-seven state legislatures proposed regulating contract parenthood in what opponents of surrogacy called "bucks for baby" bills (Pollitt, 1987: 682).

The state's participation in family not only crosses the public/private divide in ways that feel transgressive but may also give the blessing of law to bias. In explaining why the private is political and should be state regulated, Catharine MacKinnon writes that for women, unlike men, the private is not a place of personal freedom but the domain of subordination without recourse to police or law (1989: 168). When the courts intervene in the private sphere, they often take their patriarchal assumptions with them. For feminists, Judge Sorkow's decision that Elizabeth Stern was Baby M's mother reduced women to their marital status: whoever is married to the sperm donor is the mother (Ehrenreich, 1989: 71). In this ruling Whitehead became a mere tool of production. Whitehead herself said, "It was like I was a breeder and they were just interested in what I could produce" (1986: 47). Although in an appeal a New Jersey Supreme Court judge ordered that Whitehead's parental status be restored, she still did not get custody, just visitation privileges (537 A. 2d N.J. 1227 [1988]).

Like reproductive technology, child abuse has helped move family discourse onto the couch and into the courts, from where it returns, professionalized, to talk shows and public discussion. The proliferation of therapies, laws, and talk about child abuse lessens the family as a moral body, blurring the boundaries of family responsibility for morality. Definitions of abuse are themselves murky: legal and psychological experts disagree about what constitutes child abuse and who should decide whether a child has been abused. The president of the National Coalition for Child Protection Reform, Elizabeth Vorenberg, makes the point that child protection agencies do not always distinguish between an abused child and a child living in poverty. She tells the story of James Norman of Illinois, whose children were put in foster care in 1993 while he was temporarily unemployed. With the electricity off and the food spoiling in the fridge, a social worker assumed the worst and took the kids. The professionals and the law dragged their feet, and Norman died of a heart attack before the court could rule to restore the children to their father (Vorenberg, 1993: A16).

In cases such as those of Baby M and James Norman, what feels like a violation of a clearly private, biological terrain is perhaps no more than a new sign of the fact that the family has always been a hybrid of the public and the private (Deleuze, 1979: x). Jacques Donzelot argues that the state traditionally defines family functions. In the nineteenth century, it made the family responsible for moral problems in order to deal with indigence, unemployment, and crime that it had difficulty managing (1979: 53–58). Although how you raise children seems your parental prerogative, you do it within a strict, state-mandated set of rules. The nuclear family has always been "permeable" to public institutions (Minson, 1985: 183). The state determines when and for how long your children go to school and what they learn. In August 1994, the United States Congress voted to cut funds to school districts that teach children that homosexuality is an alternative lifestyle (*New York Times,* 2 August 1994). If your method of discipline is corporal punishment, the state may define it as child abuse. It expects you to clean, dress, and feed your children according to its implicit standard. And it frowns on leaving children in the street, in the care of other children, or alone. Unlike the Christmas vacation in the 1990 Hollywood movie *Home Alone,* during which a clever kid, accidentally left home, frustrates the efforts of would-be burglars, a 1993 Acapulco vacation ended in arrest at the Mexican border for David and Sharon Schoo, of suburban Chicago, because they had left their two daughters, aged five and nine, home alone (*New York Times,* 12 July 1993). The family and the roles within it, although experienced privately, are "policed" by the culture to forward its aims of an educated citizenry that is healthy, sexually regulated, and whose members are responsible for one another. The family fulfills public objectives having to do with social control that range from disease to dissidence, and when families violate social norms, the state can walk into the family sphere to deal with those violations (Minson, 1985: 183).

Such policing depends on professionals and courts, the standards and guidelines of which are often slippery and ambiguous, leaving judgments to fall to individual feeling. ABC's *Nightline* repro-tech show on 7 April 1989 put it this way: "With new technologies peering into the womb, women have been forced to peer into their hearts" (qtd. in Hartouni, 1991: 39)—as have psychologists, gynecologists, lawyers, and judges. Inadequate as a moral blueprint, decisions such as the one regarding Baby M are good barometers of emotivist confusion. In the absence of convincing criteria for good parents and surrogacy, the experts filled the vacuum with emotivism—the felt rightness or wrongness of a particular course of action—dressed as psychological, legal, and feminist opinion. Because it was fraught with such emotivism, the Baby M case never seemed definitively morally decided.

Class and gender also complicate lawyers' and psychologists' emotivism in their policing of families. Although court officials and the experts they hired spoke in terms of the "best interests of the child," their judgments regarding the Baby M case seemed to turn more on emotionally determined class differentials. When Whitehead said she wanted to "give the gift of life," a court-appointed psychologist interpreted this phrase as evidence of "a deep seated narcissistic need" and concluded she had a mixed personality disorder. The Sterns, who had greater familiarity with psychological discourse, did not alienate the experts by using such quasi-religious terminology. Michelle Harrison points out that Whitehead's play with the baby was also subject to classed judgments: "Mary Beth Whitehead was said to have 'failed pattycake' by saying 'Hooray!' to the baby instead of 'pattycake'" (Harrison, 1987: 307). Whitehead herself describes one expert who condemned the stuffed panda she bought for the baby and said that ordinary "pots and pans or spoons" would be more developmentally appropriate (Whitehead, with Schwarz-Noble, 1989: 143). Judge Sorkow and the experts equated the best interests of the child with the heftier salary and academic degrees that the Sterns brought to child rearing. His Superior Court opinion dwells on Whitehead's poverty, the fact that she received public assistance, the two mortgages on her house that went into default, and her filing for bankruptcy in 1983 (525 A. 2d 1128, N.J. Super. Ch. [1987]: 1140–41). On the Sterns' side, the opinion pointed out the opportunities for music lessons and athletics for Baby M at the Sterns (1148). The judge discounted Whitehead's biological connection and her experience in already raising two children, and dismissed the nonbinding nature of the surrogacy contract she had signed. The Superior Court opinion on Baby M reads like the court's and experts' middle-class biases put forward as if they were the law.

Foundation Myths of Family

Family is the institution around which foundation myths of civilization have been built. Those myths, present in the Baby M decisions, haunt all contemporary discourse on the family. Both psychoanalytic theory and the Greek myths out of which this theory was formulated propose that civilization depends on a particular relationship between mother, father, and child. In psychoanalytic theory, the development of the self rests on separation from the mother and subsequent identification with the father, who stands for civilization—a process that Freud called oedipalization and Lacan associates with entry into culture, the order of law and language. To become part of the paternal, social world, the child turns away from the mother and represses desire for her. While the father's sphere is that of agency and desire, the mother is other, alien and horrific.

If in analytic theory the mother must be repressed, in Aeschylus's *Oresteia*, civilization depends upon her murder (Irigaray, 1991: 40–42). Matricide precedes the establishment of patriarchal law and makes possible reasoned civil order. After Orestes kills his mother because she murdered his father, Agamemnon, he is pursued by the female Furies. Their authority is overturned by Athena, a phallic woman born from her father's head. She saves Orestes by replacing the Furies with a court system ruled by an all-male jury, who personify reason. At Orestes' murder trial, Apollo invokes the Olympian father, Zeus, pronouncing that nothing can "match the power of the Father." Apollo argues that the father is the only true parent:

> The woman you call the mother of the child
> is not the parent, just a nurse to the seed,
> the new-sown seed that grows and swells inside her.
> The man is the source of life—the one who mounts.
> She, like a stranger for a stranger, keeps
> the shoot alive unless god hurts the roots. (ll. 665–70)

In the play, law and civil society depend on imperious patriarchs and disposable women. As is exemplified in the Baby M Superior Court judgment, such sentiments, privileging the rights of the father, are reproduced in much current discourse on the family. Although feminists resist narratives that support conventional notions of parenting and the family, these narratives persist and are everywhere reproduced, even by women. As Julia Kristeva argues, women find it difficult to refuse the name of the Father: Electra, Orestes' sister, who encourages him to kill his mother, represents "militants in the cause of the father" who emerge whenever "social consensus corners any woman who wants to escape her condition" (1986: 152).

Reduced to a "surrogate uterus," Whitehead was refused subjectivity by much of the press and, as the Superior Court judgment read, was subordinate to the father. Mary Jacobus writes that Whitehead was "bound to lose" this battle, "given the privileging of the Father in any system of representation that inscribes paternal, Oedipal, or divine desire as primary" (1990: 25).

Nostalgia

Nostalgia is the primary means by which the oedipal and oresteian specters circulate, filling felt absences in contemporary configurations of family. The increasing instability in the family constellation and its consequent moral ambiguity closely parallels the enormous attention paid to the ideal of the "traditional family" in U.S. culture. The gestures that nostalgically recall family and the name of the father are countered by transgressive moves on the traditional family constellation. For instance, in awarding custody to the Sterns, parents by contract, Judge Sorkow cited the fact that Elizabeth Stern "will not work full time because she is aware of the infant's needs that will require her presence" (1148).

Family is treated as a basic and universal social unit, the place where morality is modeled and produced. The expectation that it is the primary center for the inculcation of values and the ethical life is heard throughout the culture. Interpersonal family relationships, relying on nostalgic emotions rather than on religious doctrine or rational argument, are used as the template for morality. Across national discourses, whether in sociology texts or in political speeches, one repeatedly hears "the family" yearningly invoked as the fulcrum of the U.S. moral economy. In 1913, Bronislaw Malinowski's *The Family among the Australian Aborigines* set the terms of family discourse. The family, he argued, fills a universal human need and has three defining features: clear boundaries that distinguish insiders from outsiders, a location where family members can be together, and a connection solidified by the feelings of love and warmth that family members have for one another (see Collier, Rosaldo, and Yanagisako, 1992: 33). In addition to these criteria, most Americans take "family" to mean nuclear, heterosexual, with children, and for life. This configuration is equated with fundamental morality.

But in a demographic sense, this family is unreal. In 1987, only 7% of households fit the pattern of breadwinning father, full-time mother, and at least one child under the age of eighteen (Thorne, 1992: 9).[7] Although we think of a family as protecting children, 20% of U.S. children live in poverty, the majority of these living in female-headed households. Even the bare bones of the nuclear family—a married couple living with their own children— represents only about 17% of U.S. families (*New York Times,* 20 October 1992). Children with divorced parents who themselves get divorced as adults may live with six or seven "families" during their lifetimes. Moreover, the Murphy Brown phenomenon that former Vice President Dan Quayle complained about is growing: although single motherhood is still much more common among poor women and members of minority groups, the percentage of single professional women who became mothers tripled from 1983 to 1993 ("Week in Review," *New York Times,* 18 July 1993). Even Newt Gingrich has a lesbian half-sister, whom he says he loves and whom he points to as an exemplar of the American family's diversity (Udovitch, 1995: 158).

Economic necessity and social movements have sufficiently interrogated the rhetoric of stay-home nurturing mothers and breadwinning authoritative fathers, so that, although this rhetoric is still used to manipulate emotions for political purposes, we recognize that the "happy family" paradigm promoted in the popular textbook *The Happy Family*, by John Levy and Ruth Munroe, first printed in 1938 and reprinted nineteen times by 1964, has gone. The U.S. Census Bureau definition of a family—a household of two or more individuals related by blood or law—excludes many informally constituted families, such as those in *Paris Is Burning* (1991), but jettisons the patriarchal moral assumptions of *The Happy Family* and may soon include gay married couples in some states. Even Robert Frost's definition of home as "The place where, when you have to go there, / they have to take you in" ("The Death of the Hired Man") seems superannuated, assuming loyalties and commitments that are far from universal. Because the family seems like such an uncertain institution in the present, people seek out a surer model in the past. In idealizing this past, they intensify the uncertainty of the present. They distance themselves from contemporary problems to luxuriate in the stasis of looking back.

Unlike justice, about which there is little agreement, family, despite its infinite variations of form, is less contested in its ethical essence of nurturance, responsibility, altruism, and interdependence. Across ideologies, it is described as having an essential morality that places it above or beyond justice (Okin, 1989: 27–29). The nostalgia of this view, in which the family is internally just, goes unacknowledged. Susan Moller Okin summarizes this thinking: "The family is not characterized by the circumstances of justice, which operate only when interests differ and goods being distributed are scarce. An intimate group, held together by love and identity of interests, the family is characterized by nobler virtues" (25–26). Such a view recapitulates Rousseau's and Hume's argument that justice is not pertinent to the family because, unlike the state, it is governed by affection for its members (Okin, 1989: 26–27). Even feminist accounts reiterate these notions. The authors of *Families in Flux* offer a "modern" definition, which nevertheless maintains the family's emotional and moral power: "a unit of intimate, transacting and interdependent persons sharing resources, responsibility, and commitment over time" (Swerdlow et al., 1989: xii). The virtues of love and self-sacrifice that, in this idealized view, drive family relationships put the family's morality on a plane higher than the practical negotiations between self-interest and state interest that mark justice. This characterization makes the politics of family either irrelevant, endless, or endlessly disappointing. It is also the strategy by which patriarchal culture has segmented the family off from the general culture, creating a special zone, even within a democracy, in which democratic processes are partially suspended for the higher authority, the law of the Father. Traditionally, when the state polices the family, it has to have special cause and justification to question a particular familial government—although a family headed by a woman loses much of that immunity.

The entire national enterprise—the economy, crime rates, education, social policy is tied to a similar nostalgic, idealized notion of family. The Reagan administration even imaged defense as a matter of the government paternally protecting children from outside harm when it used a child's drawing of a stick figure family perched on a globe over which arched the Star Wars defense shield. "Star Wars," said Reagan, would protect the United States "just as a roof protects a family from rain" (*New York Times,* 18 August 1983). The shield metaphor from medieval romance literature is, of course, masculine, and in these family metaphors, the speaker implies a patriarch on whose protection and authority the safety of other family members is supposed to depend. Indeed, it is around the absence of this figure that the welfare debate revolves. When Paul Robeson Jr. and Mel Williamson attributed the crimes of the youths indicted for the Central Park jogger assault to the failures of *family* to deal with the "surroundings of drugs and violence [and] with what is seen on TV and in the movies," what they meant by the failures of family was the absence or weakness of fathers. Like many observers of the African American family, Robeson and Williamson extol the extended family paradigm that they say characterizes it. They suggest that African Americans can overcome the difficulties that families face in "trying to instill humane values" by the community's (doctors, lawyers, teachers, ministers, writers, journalists, athletes) taking on this "struggle for our children" (1989). They project the oedipal moment onto a "father" written into every figure of cultural authority.

All images of family, whether in politics, professional discourse, self-help literature, religion, or other grand narratives, hark back to an ideal past. This ideal becomes what is missing in families today. Yet the fantasy of, say, the 1950s family ignores problems that did not enter public consciousness until later and masks the public controversies that beset the real thing. Divorce rates dropped in the 1950s and marriages and childbearing went up, but the stable, happy nuclear family as perfect moral classroom never really existed. As Stephanie Coontz writes, "The reality of these families was far more painful and complex than the expurgated memories of the nostalgic would suggest" (1992: 29). Although homosexuality, children's rights, and incest and other domestic violence had not yet emerged into academic research on the family, abortion, divorce, sexuality, women's work, child discipline, the generation gap, and father or mother absence were hot topics (see, for example, Barber [1953]). The fragility of 1950s nostalgia is also evident from a quick glance at popular culture of the time, which was obsessed with, as one commentator put it, "the family and its discontent" (Dieckmann, 1987). Adultery is the central theme in movies such as *Peyton Place, East of Eden, Cat on a Hot Tin Roof,* and *The Seven Year Itch.* Popular women's magazines spelled out an agenda of family concern similar to today's. A June 1959 issue of *True Confessions* tackles adultery and incest ("Not Mine to Love"), children and divorce ("Why Cry—Nobody Cares"), irresponsible teenage motherhood ("She Was a Menace"), unloving parents ("Starved for a Father's Affection"), and children's abandonment and poverty ("Forced to Beg in the Streets"). Even the notion of divorce as a modern moral disease—spread, according to the political Right, by women's liberation—is debatable. Divorce, according to sociologist Glenda Riley, is an American tradition dating back to the Puritans. Even in the Victorian era, one in every fourteen marriages ended up broken. Part of the U.S. way of life, writes Riley, is to split up and, like the pioneers, go west to solve problems (1991: 124).

Although the Malinowski "Honey, I'm home" family—and the apple-pie, picket-fence, all-American emblem of it—is nowhere, it is, at the same time, everywhere. In Jennie Livingston's film *Paris Is Burning* (1991), the Harlem vogueing community is shown as constituted of "families" of biologically and legally unrelated gay men of color. One "mother," Pepper Labeija, describes the value of these self-generated families, which provide younger members with emotional and material nurturing and support, sometimes even homes. "Mothers" are idealized in traditional ways. For instance, Willi Ninja, mother to another "family," says, "The mother is the strongest one." Yet, also in the traditional pattern, the mother is a figure of which you can make fun. In one scene of sardonic humor, the "children" of Angie Xtravaganza brag about buying her tits for Christmas, pretend to nurse at them, and crow, "My mommy is a drag queen."

The idea that the ideal family is intrinsically benign obviously conflicts with family realities. To deal with the resulting confusion, the culture exhibits an obsessive nostalgia for reclaiming a nurturing, altruistic family in which all positions are stable and proper. This unexamined nostalgia is itself a stabilizing, though paralyzing, state. The family is a notion to which we obsessively return. In the words of Jacques Donzelot, "It has become an essential ritual of our societies to scrutinize the countenance of the family at regular intervals in order to decipher our destiny, glimpsing in the death of the family an impending return to barbarism, the letting go of our reasons for living; or indeed, in order to reassure ourselves at the sight of its inexhaustible capacity for survival" (1979: 4).

The Neofamily

Contemporary families deviate from the traditional model in many directions. Across all of these deviations, however, the traditional family's emotional economy remains. The neofamily, like the traditional, patriarchal one, is attached to a definite place, has a circumscribed membership, and delivers love and nurturing while demanding respect and responsibility. The neofamily generates moral ambiguity through its deviant structures, but at the same time, because of its nostalgia for the traditional family's emotional security, it is immobilized, held in place despite its variety. It responds to moral uncertainty by supporting beliefs in or fantasies of the traditional, patriarchal family. In the context of neofamilies, these beliefs and fantasies become more uncertain than usual and, because of their very fragility and failure to resolve uncertainties, are likely to demand perpetual restatement or reinvestment.

Often neofamilies develop nostalgic parallels with the old model to manage this fragility and failure. A felt resemblance to the traditional family may simply be declared. In *Paris Is Burning*, nonfamily groups are represented as families largely by naming their members "mothers," "fathers," and "children." Yet despite these groups' familylike emotional and structural organization, they are far from "family." You join by invitation; members support each other in the unfamilial goal of winning trophies at masquerade balls—"a family is a gay street gang," one performer says—and there is no prohibition against incest.[8] Though more conventionally deviant, Don DeLillo's *White Noise* household, like the households in *Paris Is Burning*, consists of family members who play the roles of mother, father, and children yet are not all related by blood, law, or nurturance. These roles are not theirs indefinitely but are rotated and exchanged, depending on circumstances and the chain of marriages and divorces. In both *Paris Is Burning* and *White Noise*, the nominal, declared family is sustained by a nostalgic fantasy of family that is in constant danger of dissipating.

Representations of neofamilies often have the look of a traditional family, because they reinstate old roles around new figures and contexts. Much contemporary gay fiction, such as the stories of David Leavitt, explores personal relationships in terms similar to fiction about heterosexuals; only the pronouns change. Mandy Merck has called this normalizing strategy a suburbanization of the gay novel, "maintaining its object choice while domesticating its stories and settings" (1990: 44). This strategy is evident in David Leavitt's novel, *Equal Affections* (1989), in which the homosexuality of the narrator is treated unexceptionally, as a fairly neutral character descriptor that occasionally flavors the conversation. In thinking about her fetus, acquired through artificial insemination, the narrator's sister, a lesbian, voices quite typical concerns: "If my baby's a boy . . . and he's gay, like his father and his uncle and his mother, then I want you . . . to take care of him, to see he turns out all right" (50). Stephen McCauley's *The Object of My Affection* (1987) can be thought of as a contemporary *Jane Eyre* (1847), with a gay man in the role of Charlotte Brontë's Jane, a woman in the role of St. John Rivers, and a gay man with an adopted son in the role of Rochester. The narrative is drenched with the yearning for normal family relationships, love, and a sense of permanence that characterizes *Jane Eyre*. A visual example of this suburbanization is a photo by Sage Sohier, *Gordon and Jim, with Gordon's Mother Margot, San Diego, California* (1987), included in the exhibition *Pleasures and Terrors of Domestic Comfort* (Galassi, 1991: 93). We see a middle-aged male couple on a flowered sofa, holding hands, one man with an arm around his elderly mother, the other with a dog at his feet. It is a loving family portrait in which intimacy drowns out the contended morality of same-sex "marriage." Such images dress up moral uncertainty to look like the normal emotional torments of the family romance. But the vehemence with which normalcy is asserted—through the deliberate "no comment" of a realist photograph and truth-telling photography itself, or through Leavitt's and McCauley's concentration on interiority, the ethics of emotions, as if the forms through which these emotions are lived are irrelevant—is evidence of the residual felt moral deviance of such neofamilies.

Even when the portrait is of an antifamily, a family removed from normal family ethics of connection by emotional autism, the image measures itself against the perfect family. Tina Barney's *Sunday New York Times* (1982; in Galassi, 1991: 39), which presents a moment of family fragmentation at Sunday breakfast, is a photograph that mocks ideals of family harmony. Nevertheless, by suggesting the gap between the photo and the ideal, Barney is engaged in a nostalgic recollection of the sustaining emotional ties that families are supposed to provide. The sitcom *Married with Children* comes closer to an uncompromised picture of an antifamily, an image of how abjectly horrible families can be. Here brutal self-interest replaces parental responsibility, and incest seems to be held in check only by stupidity and mutual hatred. Still, most of the laughs come from assumptions about how families *ought* to be. The credits drip pea-green gore while the song "Love and Marriage" plays, and we see shots of a slob of a father scratching his belly and a couch-potato mother clutching a cigarette and the remote control. Family members are presented as unnurturing, unhappy, oversexual, sexually inadequate, callous, dumb, poor, lazy, and unhygienic. But atonement for these aberrations is implicit in the family members' perpetual references to what a family should do and feel and in their intermittent attempts to measure up; in one episode, for instance, the mother cooks something to celebrate the daughter's much-delayed high school graduation.

Sometimes a figure maternalized by its nurturing grounds the emotional economy of a group, thus turning it into a neofamily. In *Murphy Brown*, for instance, a variety of figures nurture at different times, but this task usually rests on the character of the producer. The same is true in *NYPD Blue*, in which the captain, an African American man, often occupies a maternal position, making decisions that, though they may harm the precinct politically, uphold a feminized ethics of care and social responsibility. Even the Clintonian neofamily, a warm, fuzzy unit seemingly defined only by caring relationships, reinstates a maternal center. Clinton's expanded "family" was subtextually a response to a thirty-year government paranoia, dating from New York Senator Daniel Patrick Moynihan, about "deviant" single mothers, especially poor black mothers. Fatherless Clinton was thus speaking on behalf of mothers when he defined all nurturing relationships as families. In the Clintonian children's television ratings topper *Barney and Friends*, a purple dinosaur repeatedly invokes the notion of family to cover all caring relationships, such as those between him and his child friends. This familial ecumenism is conveyed in the show's signature song, "Family Is People": "They come in all different sizes and different kinds / But mine's just right for me." Yet the verses of the song also translate this ecumenism as the conventional family with nurturing women: a single mother or a "loving dear old Grandma." Such maternalizations reiterate fantasies of mothers without acknowledging the moral conflicts in contemporary motherhood.

Popular culture is endlessly inventive in attempting to absorb breaks in family structure. The Hallmark greeting card company recognizes that the numbers of recombinant households add up to a substantial market. The sentiments of the cards it produces for this market assimilate and normalize the proliferating kinds of family relationships by reconstituting the recombinant family as emotionally the same as the traditional one. As reporter Marilyn Shapiro discovered,

> Today a child who truly cares for a father's new wife may choose a card which reads, "To my Other Mother," "To Someone Who is Like a Mother to me," . . . or more oedipally, "To My Father's Wife." The divorced wife may send a card to her ex-husband's new wife that reads, "To Someone Who's Been Good To My Children." And if she's grateful to this woman for taking her husband off her hands, she may choose to send, "To Someone Who's Been Good To *Me*." (1991)

Hallmark is able to embrace these changes because it addresses people who are standing in the same place as the ideal family members, as if they fit the traditional model, people as interchangeable as the Stepford wife, husband, and child.

The postfeminist neofamily tries to absorb the ambiguities around family by trumping them with a doctrine of choice. Although it purports to offer an array of options, these options always reduce to one: a new traditionalism that salves the inequities of the traditional family by promising individual fulfullment in every role. Even "Dinkys" (dual income, no kids yet) can purchase the emotions of the traditional family. Advertising for upscale household goods evokes textually and pictorially a family's emotional security. In catalog photos, tables are set, beds made, flowers arranged, and coffee perks comfortingly on the stove. Out of sight, always just about to step back in, are the men and women whose paid and domestic labor made this scene possible and the children whose emotional security this material order represents. The *New York Times* also plays on the new traditionalism. Under the heading "I Read It My Way," the *Times* uses a photo of a smiling woman and her preppy son to justify women reading the paper as they live their lives however they want—choosing, as the advertisement says, the "sheer enjoyment" of the "Home" section and the "Parent and Child" and "Consumer Saturday" columns over the world news, for instance, just as the woman in the ad implicitly has opted for the pleasures of child care (financially supported, we have to assume, by a middle-class man) over work outside the home. These ads deliver the traditional family emotionally flawless and vacuum-sealed—free of dirty dishes and debates about women's sixty-three cents, child and wife abuse, and custody.

Interrogating Oedipus

The foundation myths persist, but they have become vulnerable. The father's authority is often interrogated at the same time that it is reproduced. Repeated judgments and insistent discourse that privilege fatherhood and equate patriarchy with culture are voiced against unsettling shifts in the traditional constellation of mother, father, and child.

Such mutations in the family body and their moral consequences are more exactingly calculated in serious fiction than by television or Hallmark. Sexual abuse is the target of some powerful fiction in which the traditional, patriarchal family comes apart. In Jane Smiley's *A Thousand Acres* (1991), the adult protagonist remembers that her father raped her as a child. As a result, the patriarchal thousand-acre estate dissipates, the central family falls to pieces, and the female narrator takes a job as a waitress and moves into a small apartment, a location that represents and critiques the tentativeness and atomism of postpatriarchal living arrangements. Dorothy Allison's autobiographical novel *Bastard out of Carolina* (1992), which details child abuse in a poor Greenville County, South Carolina, family, rejects the traditional response of simple condemnation. The book refuses to blame a mother who remains with the husband who raped her daughter, his step-daughter. Yet in the portrait of this decision and the childlike man for whom the mother makes it, Allison demonstrates how poverty and raw emotional need can distort the mythic family configuration. Joyce Carol Oates's *We Were the Mulvaneys* (1996) records the disintegration of an ideal wealthy American family after the cheerleader daughter is raped on prom night by the son of one of the town's leading families. The mother exiles her daughter to a distant relative to keep her out of view of the outraged father, who nevertheless leaves. But as years go by, the mother and daughter, as well as the other children, recover normal lives—though they are estranged and bear scars. The novel ends in cautious optimism with a Fourth of July family reunion, sans father, suggesting that family and America, as evoked by the holiday, can survive without patriarchy and that the morality that once held families together is flawed.

The novels of Oates, Allison, and Smiley, despite the complex morality they depict, provide hope, because they point to an ethical beyond, whether, as with Oates, at a family reunion, as with Allison, in authorship, or, as with Smiley, in a waitress job, a garden apartment, and an eight-year-old Toyota. Allison's fiction, made out of the moral cracks in family life, shows us a controlled and purposeful moral ambiguity, an ambiguity that has a literary point. Oates's Mulvaneys trade in their sense of family to develop individual lives. Allison's autobiographical story has made her a writer. Smiley's heroine, loosed from the embrace of her family and its thousand acres, is also redeemed, in this case by awakening to the truth that her father raped her and that therefore neither he nor his kingdom deserves preservation. More broadly, she is forced from the economic and sexual slavery of patriarchy.

Smiley's portrait of patriarchal corruption is extreme: the accumulation of a thousand acres for the ostensible purpose of keeping the family through the generations is really the rationale for creating a kingdom in which the patriarch has absolute power and is allowed anything, even his daughters. For Smiley, the suppression of incest is not the cost of civilization, as Freud asserts; rather, incest is the mechanism of domination. It is also the name for the patriarchal thrall from which women need to awaken. Smiley's use of the economic metaphor of a thousand acres for this thrall also suggests an engagement with the classic economic justification for women's subordination. Both Freud and Lévi-Strauss describe the family as ensuring the androcentric movement of property through its control of women's sexuality and its hierarchization of male power.[9] In all three novels, the ambiguities of abuse are lost either in the newfound certainty of the author's voice or in anti-oedipal protest. In real cases, the ambiguity around abuse is more difficult to absorb. We feel that abused and abuser should be clear moral categories and that we should be able to assign motives for abuse—poverty, mental illness, addiction. If the family is unable to act as the moral body, it should be ill. Such clarity provides hope, because if we can determine who and why, then we can imagine a cure in the beyond. Often, though, no such determinations seem possible and no solution presents itself.

When it broke in November 1987, the story of Lisa Steinberg's fatal abuse by her adoptive parents, Joel Steinberg and Hedda Nussbaum, dominated the media with a hysterical insistence. By all the usual measures, the Steinberg-Nussbaum family should have been upstanding citizens: they lived on a prestigious Greenwich Village street in a house that Mark Twain had once occupied. Steinberg was a wealthy lawyer and Nussbaum a children's book editor. Social agencies and school authorities repeatedly ignored obvious evidence of Lisa's abuse. Their assumptions were blasted by subsequent revelations: Lisa's bruises and unkemptness, Hedda's bashed-in prize-fighter's face and gangrenous legs, and the screams that often rang out from the apartment. This evidence, that even a middle-class, professional Jewish family's rectitude was uncertain, was a serious blow to the family's ability to represent morality. After Hedda and Lisa, the yuppie family unit seemed incipiently pathological.

Nussbaum herself was a mutation in the discourse of family and abuse. As mother, her role was to act as moral anchor of the family. Should she have rescued her child at all costs? The tabloids depicted Joel's abuse of Lisa and Hedda as Hedda's fault. Although Hedda was not put on trial, Emily Praeger called her a "Village zombie child abuser" (qtd. in Munk, 1988: 12). Everyone asked, "Why didn't she leave? Why didn't she protect her child?" They did not ask, "How could he do this? How do we stop it?" Steinberg, Erica Munk noted, "despite being under the whole country's eyes, has evaded our gaze" (1989: 16). Do we expect men to abuse, and therefore tend to blame them less than perhaps less culpable women? Are women to blame for their own domestic victimization, or does it make them blameless, stripping them of moral agency? Opinions were split about this case. On the one hand, Munk argues that Nussbaum, a classic victim of battered

Figure 10. Hedda Nussbaum. © New York Newsday.

woman syndrome, was infantilized and deprived of agency in a bizarre parody of women's general subordination in the family (1988: 16). Susan Brownmiller, on the other hand, arguing that Nussbaum was culpable, writes of the excuse that Nussbaum was in a state of cocaine psychosis the night Lisa died, saying that "the use of drugs . . . is not a legal, or a moral, excuse for failure to act responsibly." Nor, Brownmiller wrote, should women perpetuate the idea that they are "doomed to be victims of the abnormal psychology of love at all cost" (1989a).[10]

Love or Abuse?

What appears to some to be abuse may to others pass as moral action or be claimed as art. Curfews and parents' responsibility for enforcing them are newly acceptable, part of public order, the need for them attributed to the notion that America has lost its sense of right and wrong ("In the Name," 1996: 23–24). Professionals, parents, and the law find it difficult to weigh abuse against love and sometimes cannot distinguish between the two. In the case of fifteen-year-old Linda Marrero, whose parents in 1991 chained her to the radiator in their New York City living room to stop her from going out and getting high on crack, neighbors called the action "tough love," while the police charged the parents with "unlawful imprisonment." Marrero herself refused to press charges, stating that her parents acted in her interests (*New York Times*, 20 September 1991). According to syndicated columnist George Will, who made the act into a standard of good parenting, if people are "going to have children, they have an obligation to care about them as fiercely as Linda Marrero's parents care about her." She was "lucky" that "she has a father at home, and a mother who said to him, 'go buy me a chain and two locks'" (1991). Ejlat Feuer of West Orange, New Jersey, was arrested in 1995 on child endangerment charges when the manager of a photo processing lab turned his prints over to the police. He had taken nude photos of his six-year-old daughter for an art class. Similar cases were reported in Akron, Ohio, Boston, and San Francisco. In the Feuer case, the investigating detective was reported to have asked Mrs. Feuer whether she believed in God when she explained to him that the "nude body is really interesting. It's part of life" (*New York Times*, 30 January 1995). The detective grabbed at the only apparently straightforward moral vocabulary still available to him, showing up his moral confusion regarding proper relations between parents and children.

The photographer Sally Mann explores this line between love and abuse. Her exhibit *Immediate Family* (1992) repeatedly plays on the viewer's distress and confusion regarding the ambiguities attached to contemporary family life. For instance, in *Damaged Child,* a close-up of Mann's older daughter with one eye swollen, the child is not hurt in the way the photograph leads you to believe, but has been bitten by an insect. Nevertheless, as with *The Terrible Picture, 1989,* the photo evokes child abuse in all of its forms—emotional as well as physical. Even the relationship between the photographer mother and her photographic object, her child, may be construed as a mixture of love and abuse. Multiplying the ironies and complexities in this mother-photographer and daughter-subject relationship is the photo's title. In Mann's photographs, discourses interfere with one another, ultimately disclosing their limits: where are the borders of childhood innocence, parental benevolence, and artistic license?[11]

In the realm of the failed maternal, Nussbaum is a figure of the perplexity and fear we encounter at such moral borders. With her cauliflower ear, glazed stare, and passivity in the face of her violent history, she erupted into our comfortable consensus about mothers and family like a monster into a suburban living room. She was a figure of what Kristeva calls the abject, a force conjuring up both revulsion and desire. This woman was at the center of a discourse that never talked about her horrific combination of love and aggression but only about one or the other. At a time when the policing of families is focused on monitoring and controlling abuse, this abject mother marks the limit of the culture's ability to police the oedipal family, the extremity of ethical thought, and moral action.[12] Destabilizing phenomena, such as those represented by Nussbaum, Mann, Feuer, and, for that matter, Baby M and the morally contentious advances in reproductive technology that her case represents, transport the culture to its own border, put it face-to-face with its limitations, and give you a sense that some certainty should be there but is not, a certainty some understand as the ever-elusive "real" (Kristeva, 1982: 9). In such confrontations, the meanings of "mother," "father," and "child" blur beyond comprehension into a place where "meaning collapses," the repository of the unavailable real (2).

As with Nussbaum and Mary Beth Whitehead, the figure of the abject mother often symptomizes this confrontation with limits. Because she is a manifestation of the failures of the oedipal family, the abject mother repeatedly precipitates out of cultural moral anxiety, including feminist familial accounts—as with the mothers in *A Thousand Acres, Bastard out of Carolina,* and *We Were the Mulvaneys,* for example, who do little to oppose the abusers of their daughters. The significance of this figure is aptly expressed in the title of Kathy Acker's 1993 novel *My Mother: Demonology,* a text obsessed with the fault lines in the oedipal configuration. In the more popular medium of the Hollywood horror film, this mother appears as the *Alien* and reappears in *Aliens, Alien 3,* and *Alien 4: Resurrection.* Released in 1979, 1986, 1992, and 1997 respectively, these films of the maternal alien, a kind of abject mother, were released in the years when a "family values" agenda dominated national politics, an agenda that itself revealed familial anxieties provoked by feminism and the new reproductive technologies. The acts of real mothers—from Joan Crawford, as depicted in her daughter Christina's book *Mommie Dearest,* published in 1978, to Susan Smith, who, Medea-like, drowned her two small sons in South Carolina in 1994—get more attention in the media than do the acts of abusive fathers and husbands. People from all over the country sent money to pay for Smith's prosecution. Yet O. J. Simpson, who admitted abusing his wife and was alleged to have murdered her, became the star of a long-running TV courtroom drama that took reality programming and soap opera further than ever. The prosecution sought the death penalty for Smith. As in *The Oresteia,* mothers are singled out for special blame. Smith tried to shift her own abjection to black men when she claimed that a black man had abducted her children, but in engagements between the two, the black man may also transfer his abjectness to the woman—as defense arguments in the Simpson trials and the Clarence Thomas hearings suggested.

The Self-Help Family

Hedda Nussbaum and Joel Steinberg were moral isolates, acting according to a system of family ethics so privatized as to be a folie à deux. But the language that both Nussbaum and Steinberg used to explain themselves comes out of the self-help movement. They can be viewed, at least in part, as nightmare products of this movement, the vocabulary of which marked much of the detail of their lives together. With Lisa unconscious on the bathroom floor, Steinberg left for a business meeting, instructing Nussbaum to "relax, go with her. Stay in harmony with her" (qtd. in Kantrowitz, 1988: 58). Nussbaum claimed that when she first met him, Steinberg helped to build her self-esteem: "We had a kind of ESP." Nussbaum described their relationship as if it were a twelve-step program somehow gone awry. Explaining why Steinberg repeatedly moved a blowtorch (which he used for freebasing cocaine) around her body, burning her, she said, "Joel told me he did this to improve my coordination" (qtd. in Weiss, 1989: 89). Twelve-step language also affected those commenting on the case. Joyce Johnson, for instance, who wrote a book about the case, said of Nussbaum, "She became an addict—of a certain kind of poisoned love . . . and for thirteen years, she did not elect to be cured" (1990: 250).

The privatized moral universe of self-help, like that of Nussbaum and Steinberg, is built on an emotivist foundation. For MacIntyre, this emotivism is related to the growth of individualism, itself a precondition of a self-help sensibility: The "modern self . . . in acquiring sovereignty in its own realm lost its traditional boundaries provided by a social identity and a view of human life as ordered to a given end" (1984: 34). With the loss of such teleology and context for each human life, writes MacIntyre, "moral judgments lose any clear status and the sentences which express them . . . lose any undebatable meaning" (60). Consequently, the idea of the family unit changed emphasis from a coherent whole to a collection of individuals each with her or his own feelings. Thus, in addition to the mixed public and private regulation of the family, emotional individualism negotiates the relationship between the individual and the family. It is this relationship that the self-help movement pillages for its own ends.

According to personal growth literature, our diseased condition has as a principal source the dysfunctional family, and most families are dysfunctional. The United States is pathologically dependent on an institution that makes it sick, says self-help guru John Bradshaw: "Addiction has become our national lifestyle" (1987: 6). In the light of a national discourse preoccupied with family values, self-help seems like a counterdiscourse, an alternative to the failing oedipal structure. It speaks against family in the name of the self. Since the family no longer nurtures me, I must nurture myself. Since the family has made me sick, it cannot heal me. I must heal myself. Yet the self-help ethic is constructed on contradictions. As it denounces the family, it both builds its cure out of oedipalism and uses a nostalgic model of the perfect family in which the child is sacred and is the single focus of its parents. Bradshaw locates all family members in the self. He says you must find your own "inner child" before you can free yourself from pathological parental dependencies. Freedom from dependency, he claims, means acting as your own parents. You become mother and father to yourself. In twelve-step programs, too, family reduces to the self. If you are an adult child of an alcoholic, you must substitute yourself (Bradshaw, 1987: 217–24). Kathleen W., author of *Healing a Broken Heart* (1988), commands, "Become your own loving parent" (viii).

Self-parenting throws each person onto his or her own moral resources. You are your own community, your own measure of morality, the creator of a solipsistic ethical system that makes moral consensus irrelevant. Barbara Ehrenreich describes this perpetual moral kindergarten: "America has become, oxymoronically, a nation of 'adult children.' . . . Because we are 'adults,' we can see where [parents] went wrong; because we are 'children,' we are not responsible moral agents ourselves, at least not until the 'inner child' is cured" (1991a: 16). To offset the self-absorption that such a system encourages, Bradshaw cooks together a vague religiosity toward which the "recovered" should strive. Beginning from a base of ego psychology, Bradshaw stirs in some Zen, plus a good helping of nonspecific Christianity, and sprinkles the lot with spiritual-sounding homilies, such as "reverence for life" and "yearning for Bliss" (1987: 238). For Bradshaw, nirvana consists of an innocuous and homogenized multitraditioned spirituality that each person is to interpret and adapt individually, free of the shame that parenting rules impose on them—as, one might argue, Joel Steinberg and Hedda Nussbaum did. Even in twelve-step programs, where acknowledging a "Higher Power" is the first step to recovery, this power is defined individually and as an adjunct to the self's recovery: "Some spiritual truth came out of the pain" of being a compulsive caretaker, says Jacqueline Castine: "I must give to myself first" (1989: 8). The underlying assumption of recovery literature, then, despite its religious vocabulary, is that getting in touch with your feelings, an intrinsically good step, lets you oedipalize and thus morally cure yourself.

We can attribute the enormous popularity of the personal growth movement not only to increased reliance on emotivist morality but also to the self-help language that renders indeterminate moral relations in seemingly unambiguous terms, such as "addict" and "cure." As the Nussbaum case exemplified, self-help literature translates previously assumed questions of morality into questions of psychological well-being. It depicts most existential conditions as unhealthy: from drug addiction to single parenthood, from overeating to being old, we must pursue recovery. But this translation is flawed: illness never quite equals immorality; treatment, growth, and cure are not the same as moral struggle and improvement. The discourse of illness presents a morality free of agency or blame. Nussbaum cannot be at the same time a helpless addict, an irresponsible mother, and a figure of inexplicable evil.

The New Man

Literature and images coming out of the men's movement represent another ambiguous, emotivist effort to address gender conflicts and restabilize a moral family, this time by formulating a male reaction to thirty years of feminism. The movement uses the myth of male solidarity to cure the family. It has as its most general program lessons in the art of masculinity, an art that feminism is said to have obscured. As a British journalist put it, "There are lessons on everything in America. This is where you Learn To Be A Man" (Lawson, 1991).[13] Men share their feelings about the painful masculinities that their parents left them and try to reconstruct themselves as "Wild Men," strong but not violent, sensitive but not wimps.

Yet the men's movement reclaims the old pattern of the oedipal family as the solution to the softened boundaries of gender roles that have endangered male power. Robert Bly interprets the lessons of his emblematic myth, "Iron John," as "the importance of moving from the mother's realm to the father's realm" (1990: ix). Bly himself is an incarnation of this story. During the 1960s and 1970s, he claims, he was in the thrall of the Great Mother, about whom he led seminars all over the country. After a midlife crisis that included a divorce and remarriage, he changed his allegiance to Iron John, the Wild Man (Johnston, 1992: 8). Because the Wild Man is a postfeminist invention, it incorporates some awareness of changes in the family, but in its effort at re-oedipalization, it seems to retreat from the moral questions these changes raise.

Fatherhood literature tells a similar story. Books telling you how to raise your child used to be about being a good mother. New titles center on fatherhood: *How to Father, Expectant Father, Pregnant Fathers, The Birth of a Father, Father Power* (see Gibbs, 1993: 58). This situation has led Barbara Ehrenreich to quip, "Every man who changed a diaper has felt impelled . . .

to write a book about it" (1990: 140). It is no surprise that books on post-feminist men have been followed by those on postfeminist boys, "Iron John Jr.'s," including *The Trouble with Boys: A Wise and Sympathetic Guide to the Risky Business of Raising Sons* and *Raising a Son: Parents and the Making of a Healthy Son*, both published in 1994, which advocate "male mothering" and emphasize "intimacy" (Rubinstein, 1994). *Boyz N the Hood* (1991) literally and culturally reclaimed the fatherhood of boys from African American women for African American men, inscribing these fathers as newly in the mainstream while setting limits on women's power, responding to Moynihan and his more recent proponents while perversely endorsing them.

Bly's book and the fatherhood literature go beyond simple patriarchal reinscription by cannibalizing motherhood—claiming to share the skills, concerns, and feelings we conventionally associate with women. These writings present men with the emotions, even bodies, of women. A prosthesis of the "new man" is the empathy belly, the size and weight of a third-trimester fetus that lets a man feel pregnant. Bly's descriptions of Iron John add up to a male mother: all man, he watches over his charges with feminine devotion. Such blurring of masculinity is at the same time an example of and a response to the moral problems of family after feminism. The 1994 comedy *Junior* romanticizes the new man while at the same time satirizing pro-choice and reproductive technology discourse. In the movie, a pregnant Arnold Schwarzenegger responds to the suggestion that he terminate the pregnancy with the retort, "My body, my choice." When the woman with whose egg Schwarzenegger is impregnated says, "It's my baby," Danny Devito retorts, "Just because it's your egg, it doesn't make you the mother." Thus, newly feminized representations seem to be responding to feminism's moral demands when they portray nurturing, domestic (and pregnant) men.[14] Some women, though, charge that these representations take power from women in the only realm where they have conventionally held it—maternity. The focus of the representations on how men feel pays no attention to the conflicts between women and men that make contemporary family ethics unstable. Iron Johns, not their own parents so much as their own women, have a psychological completeness that makes women, let alone feminism, irrelevant. Often they appear more spontaneous and more sensitive and suffer more stoically than women. Where they nurture, they look like better mothers. In the TV sitcoms *Full House* and *My Two Dads* and the movie *Three Men and a Baby* (1987), girlfriend, mother, and grandmother figures have a necessary place, providing cursory girl talk and role modeling for the female children, implicitly guaranteeing those children's safety from sexual abuse by their fathers, or testifying to the central adult figures' hetero-sexuality. But it is the fathers who provide a better-than-Mom combination of economic security, basic care, and a relationship to the baby that is "play-ful, carefree, sensual," and unencumbered by career women's devotion to advancement (Kaplan, 1992: 196). Men are even claiming to experience vic-timhood better than women. Bly's Iron Johns claim the authority of the "ubervictim." After all, the argument goes, men represent nearly all of the soldiers killed in war, the large part of murder victims, two-thirds of our al-coholics, and most of the homeless, the suicides, the criminals, and the pris-oners (Johnson, 1992: 13).

The euphoric discourse about the new father often races beyond bet-ter motherhood to asserting that fathers have something extra to give. Bly claims that fathers should provide a psychological male womb, a specifi-cally male nurturing that is wild and wounding and has a hairy, phallic en-ergy associated with animals, hunting, and Dionysian excess. More re-strainedly, a *Time* cover story on the new fatherhood, "Bringing Up Father," stresses that fathers contribute something mothers cannot (Gibbs, 1993). The article quotes Communitarian David Blankenhorn, who, reprising Apollo in *The Eumenides*, dismisses the mother's role as merely biological and places responsibility for a child's character on the father: a "father produces not just children but socially viable children" (61).

New man's cannibalization of femininity, his assumption of a better womanhood, and his return to a phallic assertion over the maternal exhibit his awareness of the uncertainties that feminism introduces into family morality. Such self-reflectiveness distinguishes him from the mythological patriarchs and renders ambivalent his striving for masculinity. In the new patriarchy, men assert their superiority through feelings rather than through bigger paychecks or violence. However, they remain opposed to women in a double sense: they define themselves as not-women and, in their various stratagems against the feminist agenda, reveal a covert hostility toward women.

Crisis in the Family?

The emotivism of family discourses leaves untouched the uncertainties that circle family morality. These uncertainties have not led, as politicians claim, to the disappearance of the family. Donzelot writes that the "celebrated cri-sis of the family," rather than undermining the social order, allows for its development (1979: 8). The cracks and gaps perceived in family morality, its disequilibrium, are the mechanisms by which the culture and family values continually renegotiate their relationship.[15] The changes in family patterns—usually tied to divorce rates, the advancement of women, and children's rights—have been interpreted as a "crisis in the family" because the family is in conflict with the reproductive imperative of the patriarchy, the purpose of which is to keep property flowing along the patrilineage. However, for Donzelot, the family since the nineteenth century has been transformed through the efforts of women working mainly for their children's benefit in health, education, and self-development. It is a fluid institution with a reciprocal relationship to the social-political order.

Relationships within the family have changed from the hierarchical to the individual. Each person has rights within the family and has a separate relationship with the state, rather than having access to the state only through the father or the mother. In this explosion of children's, women's, and family rights legislation and legal precedents, the notion of a private sphere fades and the authoritarian figure in that sphere—the patriarch—loses power. A sphere emerges in which "private" matters are no longer sacred but open to the scrutiny of the courts and society. Such appropriation of the private recapitulates Enlightenment ideals and republican ethics, "which held that the transformation of private interests into contractual obligations and political compacts represented a higher morality than the expression of such family values as love or personal nurturance" (Coontz, 1992: 96–97). For John Adams, the "positive Passion for the public good" was "Superior to all private Passions" (qtd. in Coontz, 1992: 97). If we adopt this perspective, the change to more public oversight of family relations not only may protect those previously unprotected by the ideology of the private, but also may offer an alternative to the romantic notion that family morality is superior to public morality.

Even within the newly legislated field of the family, however, individuals' rights in relationships with other family members and with the state remain grounded in feeling. This emotivism leaves decisions idiosyncratic, not generalizable. Nevertheless, some change can happen within the democratic possibilities offered by the renewed emphasis on public/private fluidity, especially in its extension of rights. The notion of acting in the child's best interest allows us to expand ideas of what family is, including nontraditional families less oppressive to women and children than the conventional model. According to Jeffrey Minson, "The socio-legal formula 'in the best interests of the child' does not especially privilege the conjugal family." He argues for "increasing choice in living arrangements along the lines of social norms which were meant to be realised within a nuclear family but do not depend upon that arrangement" (1985: 216–17). Conversely, the rights of, for instance, gay men and lesbians to marry may also allow us to legitimize "deviant" families, a move that, because it interrogates the traditional, can lead to change. A New York City lesbian couple had two children produced through artificial insemination. In1993 the sperm donor for one child sued to be declared the father and to get visitation rights. Fathers in these cases are not on the birth certificates. In other sperm donor cases, the plaintiffs have succeeded in getting father's rights. Here the judge argued that the suit itself was harming the child and the man's claim was making her anxious, giving her nightmares. The judge said that for this child, "a declaration of paternity would be a statement that her family is other than what she knows it to be and needs it to be." Although ostensibly a victory for children's rights, it was also a victory for lesbians, who had not previously had the "best interests of the child" principle applied to them in the case of a sperm donor. In his opinion, the judge sustained the notion of the two-parent family, saying that the child had a "parental bond to her second mother," as if a third parent or one parent were unnatural. For this judge, the litmus test of family was two parents, not heterosexuality (*New York Times*, 16 April 1993).

Of course, we could argue that a regressive "romance" with children's rights and a co-option of gays into nuclear familiarity are really what is at stake here. Also, legal rights for children are not the answer to difficult social and psychological problems. Nevertheless, in the shift to individual rights such as children's rights and to increasing public surveillance of the private, notions of family become pluralistic. Court decisions have the feel of temporary, negotiated solutions: a boy can divorce his parents, and a child can have as parents two lesbian mothers. Although such solutions are provisional and still underpinned with emotivism, competing discourses can center on a new object in a new field—a child. Traditional biological claims yield to claims of children who, as Emmanuel Levinas argues, command our moral responsibility because our relationship to them is the "first shape" that our moral responsibility for the other takes, and thus they provide a powerful moral imperative (1985: 71).

Anti-Oedipus and Change

As we grudgingly confront pluralism in family organization, revisions of the oedipal foundation myth increase their explanatory power. As the Father fades, other figures, such as the orphan, a person without family, or, less radically, the mother, come forward. In *Anti-Oedipus: Capitalism and Schizophrenia* (1977), Gilles Deleuze and Félix Guattari describe the oedipal system as a fascist construction and challenge its value as truth: does not the oedipal structure "merely express the history of a long mistake . . . ; the strain of an endless repression?" (53). Writing *Anti-Oedipus* in the wake of the French and American student revolts of the 1960s, Deleuze and Guattari assert that the oedipal grip can be loosened only by dissolving the family structure altogether. They oppose the figure of Oedipus not with other variations on the neofamily but with the figures of orphans (no "daddy-mommy-me"), atheists (no metanarratives), and nomads (no home or territory), each of which is free of attachment (53). The book's argument regarding the oedipal configuration is for total revolt. Such revolt, though appealing, requires more than the culture is willing to give. Its present ambivalence is not rejection, and the forseeable future will include the oedipal family. However, this configuration must now accommodate the pluralism of family organization that is due to new reproductive technologies, feminism, children's and gay rights, and increasing court oversight of families. Perhaps the most powerful lesson of *Anti-Oedipus* is an indirect one, of the oedipal myth's cultural strength as well as its vulnerability, and of the necessarily limited reading we can therefore make of it.

Rather than abandon the family altogether, Luce Irigaray, the feminist psychoanalyst, argues for the recovery of the maternal: "We must not once more kill the mother who was sacrificed to the origins of our culture. We must give her new life, new life to that mother, to our mother within us and between us. We must refuse to let her desire be annihilated by the law of the father" (1991: 43). The primary relationship is between mother and infant, and the primary desire is the return to the womb (39–42). The umbilical cord, representing the connection with the mother, rather than the phallus, dominates this revised foundation myth. The mother is "within us and between us," an alternate source for culture and language and a way to give subjectivity to the other. Irigaray's psychology stresses confluence between mother and child, rather than patriarchal domination.[16]

This de-emphasis of paternal hierarchy and attention to mother-child reciprocity is taken up more practically by feminists interested in an "ethics of care." Indeed, a substantial United States literature regarding ethics has arisen around the maternal. Taking ideas from Carol Gilligan (1982) as well as Luce Irigaray, some maternalists propose that a substitution of the mother for the father will move society toward the good. In a more complex articulation, the maternal becomes part of a heterogeneous ethics. Rather than separating state from family morality, such an ethics tempers universalist ideas of justice and individual rights with values of care (Tronto, 1993: 54–55). This ethics of care can move beyond the domestic realm and into the political, with laws written to serve human needs rather than limited to protect abstract justice or individual rights (161–80). Its advocates claim that such an ethics would allow for moral pluralism. Of course, the danger is that it may reinstate a paternalistic mode by providing a broader field with wider powers to caregivers: the person giving care will decide for the one receiving it, as the mother does for the infant (170–71). The moral high ground claimed for all women in these accounts is, of course, dubious. However, the shift away from authority toward care and respect in these accounts provides a perspective beyond oedipalism. As with *Anti-Oedipus,* such a perspective demonstrates the weakness as well as the resilience of oedipalism. To deal with moral uncertainty, we can neither turn to nostalgic paradigms nor shrug the old off entirely.

In the field of the neofamily, we can see that despite this family's recapitulations of old structures and emotions, some elements of *Anti-Oedipus* and the ethics of care are being played out. In 1994, Cindy Meneghin told a *New York Times* reporter, "We are the all-American family. . . . We pay taxes, cut our lawn and go to church." She works as a technical editor at Princeton University while her partner, Maureen Killian, stays home with their children. But this apparent private conservatism is made possible by an economic reconfiguration that allows a woman to earn a family wage. This lesbian couple reported that the university's benefit package was what gave them the means to organize their family traditionally (*New York Times,* 20 August 1994).

Within television and movies, neofamilies' moral transgressiveness may be especially short-lived. Nevertheless, these neofamilies may still deliver moral uneasiness. *Paris Is Burning* provides some good examples of such residual resistance. The "families" in the movie fall within Malinowski's criteria, retaining the distinction between insiders and outsiders, a familial location, a "home," and an emotional connection of dependency and/or love. But beyond this reinscription of nuclear family support in a black gay context—a "just-like-us" parallelism that is ironic, subversive, and pathos-inducing all at once—these vogueing families break with the oedipal stability we expect of families. Although the families are effective, they often change their size, structure, and dynamics. "Gender roles," though they look traditional, are a pastiche within them, having no necessary correlation with familial propriety or emotion. Across these destabilizations, family members do, however, endorse an ethics of care for the other that demands mutual recognition. In the film *My Own Private Idaho* (1991), a "family" comprising a middle-aged gay man, an aged woman retainer, and a group of teenage male hustlers is directly compared to the upper-middle-class family of one of the hustlers—and the former is emotionally richer and more supportive. This care is valorized even though the "father" falls in love with his "sons," a blurring of parent and lover that removes the suburban mask from this gay household. Within the more conventional virtual families of television drama, such as those of *NYPD Blue, Homicide,* and *ER,* "family" survives as it is supposed to, but the transgressions are often extreme. "Daughters" and "sons" are undutiful, "fathers" and "mothers" fail in their duties of nurturing, and "incest" again occurs.

The most dramatic change in television representations of family has been the surge in representations of families that break the Christian Coalition's "Contract with the Family" as well as other common moral assumptions about family. A flood of series show women working outside the home, men caring for children, single-parent families, and reconstituted families involving stepchildren, adopted children, and groups of single parents joining together to live with their children. Even relatively anodyne programs such as *Party of Five, Fresh Prince, The Nanny,* and *Third Rock from the Sun* retain some traces of rebellion when they assert conventional familial emotions and authority while letting audiences explore a riot of deviant structures. In daytime soap operas, plots relentlessly turn on discovering which child is whose and on the choreography of marriage and divorce, but the casts of characters are enormous and endlessly recombine. On *All My Children,* Erica marries again and again as if for the first time—dressed in white, dewy-eyed, murmuring promises of eternal love. Television neofamilies also provide pictures of untraditional gender relations: unemployed men do household chores, and women work outside the home. In this way, working-class women and men get opportunities similar, televisually, to those of more obviously gender-fluid middle-class "new men" and professional women. Women in television virtual families seem, in addition, able to be louder than they are in more conventional television representations. The women in *Roseanne, Grace under Fire, Ellen, Cybill,* and *Murphy Brown* rely on images of female disruption that offer women viewers fantasies of strength to which they do not often have access.[17] Such televisual redistributions of assertiveness and independence to women and nurturing to men may perhaps provoke some shifts in the cultural agenda.

Many television representations of families break with the cultural ideal in other important ways: by not being nice, as in *Married with Children,* which transmits the blue-collar id of the U.S. family; or not being white, as in *The Cosby Show* and *Fresh Prince;* or not being middle-class, as in *Married with Children, Grace under Fire,* and *Roseanne,* or simply by being workplace or leisure-time families, as in *Seinfeld, ER,* and *Brooklyn South,* for example, which set up loci of intense emotional investment against the assumed repository of such investment, the biological family. The title character in the prime-time sitcom *Ellen* is a lesbian who treats her homophobic friends as if they were backward children. Homophobia, here, is a foible of the immature that rarely engenders anything more serious than Ellen's parentlike impatience. For Cybill, in the TV comedy of the same name, her two ex-husbands and two daughters, one from each husband, form an extended family, and she varies in the familial role with which she confronts them. For her ex-husbands she plays breadwinner, mother, or lover—never wife—and to her daughters she appears capriciously as friend or as the "cool" or traditional mother. In return, the other characters, all monitor, with varying degrees of good humor, her adventures in middle-age dating. In a much-discussed IKEA ad, a gay couple's commitment to each other and to buying a table with a leaf may suburbanize them, but it is also an initially startling reconfiguration of shopping for furniture. These flirtations with the dysfunctional, ersatz, or outlaw family are ways of recalling the traditional oedipal constellation. But they are also ways of enjoying and half-normalizing anti-oedipal configurations.

This double effect of both reinscribing and overwriting Oedipus applies particularly to *The Cosby Show*. Although the show used common sitcom devices—clever, biting exchanges between family members, children neglecting household chores, ever-vigilant mothers—to reproduce the all-American family, it persistently challenged stereotypes of the African American family.[18] It overwrote white Oedipus by presenting images of present, caring fathers; responsible, professional mothers; achieving, respectful children who love their family, and a cycle of nurturing rather than deprivation in a black family. It also gave us a young black man who cooks for himself, loves his family, and is intensely engaged with the American literary canon; a black woman, his mother, who can further that engagement; and a nurturing, powerful black father who makes dinner and always gets the last laugh in the scene. In addition, the show made some political gestures, with grandchildren named Winnie and Nelson and African American art on the walls. In one episode (broadcast 17 January 1992), as the family sits around the dinner table, they discuss *Moby-Dick*, a text the son is studying in college. But rather than reading it traditionally, they suggest that the text's depiction of the struggle between good and evil can be read in terms of America's relationship to the other, implicitly the racial other.

A more dramatic deviation from the oedipal model occurs in Geoffrey Biddle's photo of Amy Zapata with her sister Lillian leaning on her in a New York City street (1988). Here, a family already aberrant by virtue of its non-whiteness and its poverty becomes structurally peculiar but emotionally

Figure 11. Amy Zapata (right) *with her sister Lillian. © 1988 by Geoffrey Biddle.*

normalized when a daughter heroically claims the nurturing role that the mother and father do not fulfill. The photo appears in a 1991 *Granta* issue entitled, after a Philip Larkin poem, *The Family: They Fuck You Up* (published later as *The Granta Book of the Family* [1995]). In the accompanying text, the photo's innocent realism is undermined as the daughter constitutes herself as the mother:

> AMY ZAPATA: I'm twenty-three now. Then I was twelve. My mother had money. . . . She used to go to Peru, Spain, and come to New York City with drugs taped to her body. She came home with a lot of hundred-dollar bills. Then after that she started shooting up drugs.
>
> One day, she brought a man to the house. They did whatever. She left him sleeping and stole his wallet. The man could have raped me or my sisters, could've hurt us. That's when I found out my mother didn't really care about us. So that night, I went to this place and worked all night bagging up dope and coke. When I made enough money, I called my aunt in Puerto Rico, got the tickets right in the airport and sent my sisters off.
>
> My mom's in prison. She looks good but she has AIDS. She used to sleep in abandoned buildings. She used to use the vein in her neck. Any vein she could find in her body. (158)

This self-generated female family, sprung from the labor and care of a girl, is reported as an imitation of the real thing, but over that report is positioned the image of the two sisters linked together, smiling, not objects of pity.

Moral Multilingualism

A fluid negotiation between family moralities can be and often is the result of having a number of such paradigms in play at the same time. In *Paris Is Burning*'s families, for instance, the oedipalism of phallic mothers, the anti-oedipalism of competition and flux, and the ethics of care coexist, and each gets a hearing. In Alison Moore's novel *Synonym for Love* (1995), the biological family is surrendered for a series of chosen families, suggesting that family love has numerous synonyms, even if some are more desirable than others. Although some representations of the black family recapitulate—with a difference—the idealized white family, like *Cosby* and *Boyz N the Hood*, other representations de-emphasize nuclearity. For Robeson and Williamson, "community" functions as a family, but unlike Lasch's and the communitarian moral communities, this African American community is child-centered rather than being a neighborhood rewriting of the nuclear family. These models have problems. Most obvious are their romanticism and nostalgia. Visions like that of Robeson and Williamson and that inspired by the Million Man March on Washington, D.C., in 1995 assume a common commitment and a unity that may not exist. Such optimism gets repeated in popular culture, in lyrics by Coolio, for instance, that attempt to produce a new relation to fatherhood even when a father is not living with his children. Addressing his own child in "Smilin'," Coolio sings, "Even though we're not together like we used to be / D-A-D-D-Y you can count on me." He acknowledges that his family is not *Cosby*-perfect: "This ain't the Huxtables and my name ain't Cliff," but then tells how looking into his children's eyes makes him smile. These hopes of values that will be shared between young black men in the city are too high. Even within such a circumscribed community, the pluralism of a modern democratic society breaks up common notions of the good. A member of this community may also be a member of several others that have incongruent goals (Mouffe, 1993: 83). Yet such brave forays into the discourse of family allow various moralities to circulate and, beyond that, allow them to be articulated, albeit locally, across differences. They face the complex problems they can see in family morality and make moves toward an ethical beyond, toward better possibilities for living together.

In contrast to the oedipal and class metanarratives that directed the therapists, social workers, and judges to make decisions in the Baby M case in the name of the "best interests of the child" but actually in the interests of the middle-class biological father and adoptive mother, a more pragmatic, pluralistic, and negotiatory settlement of the case occurred on appeal. Judge

Birger Sween, who reinstated Whitehead's visitation rights in New Jersey Superior Court, explained that

> Melissa is a resilient child who is no less capable than thousands of children of broken marriages who successfully adjust to complex family relationships when their parents remarry. . . . William and Elizabeth Stern must accept and understand that Melissa will develop a different and special relationship with her mother, stepfather, siblings, and extended family, and that these relationships need not diminish their parent-child relationship with Melissa. (qtd. in Whitehead with Schwarz-Noble, 1989: 217–18)

Here is a judgment that appreciates the contemporary moral complications of family. In Judge Sween's view, the best interests of the child do not depend on the traditional bases of biology or class. Neither one parent nor the others, but all three, are factors in the child's life. Here the "interests of the child"—including those of all the parents—are taken into account. Sween's judgment does not reproduce the expediency that led parents to chain Linda Marrero to her bed. Under the "best interests" banner, he acknowledged the difficult moral context of family life as well as affirming the network of relationships around Baby M, a recognition that offers a glimpse of an ethical beyond.

4 | Body

Our bodies are the common denominator.
Gerald Edelman, "The Wordless Metaphor: Visual Art and the Brain"

My hair is . . . a revolution.
RuPaul, "Back to My Roots"

As well as the cooked and the raw, there is also the rotten.
Peter Wollen, *Raiding the Icebox*

Moral Contests

A couple holding hands, heads shaved, made up like dolls, and dressed identically in short pink plastic raincoats and white high heels stroll around New York's Museum of Modern Art (MOMA). They hand out cards announcing themselves as Eva and Adele, artists and hermaphrodites. Fascinated onlookers scrutinize height, shoulder width, and hand size: are they men? women? one of each? (Yes.) Does such a collision of bodies, genders, and Barbie-doll clothing really qualify as art? The possibility that a man might be wearing women's clothes not just in a gallery but perhaps on the street provoked the ethical queasiness that always accompanies the sight of people refusing their biological sex. When cross-dressing is presented as art, does it clarify or confront such unease, or does an aesthetic presentation remove cross-dressing from the realm of morality entirely?

    A 1989 Benetton campaign included the image of two infants, one black, one white, with the white infant's blond hair curling down his neck and the black infant's hair twisted into little horns at either side of his head. In another photograph, two muscular, naked arms, one black and one white, were handcuffed together. A third ad, which U.S. magazines refused to run, showed a black woman breast-feeding a white infant. Black activists opposed the campaign, arguing that the ads' aestheticizing and eroticizing style, together with their references to black convicts and slavery, trivialized slavery, criminalized blacks, and effected a new slavery of black bodies in the white marketplace. The company countered that it was trying to represent an enlightened multiculturalism that showed that "we're all in this together" and that left the past behind (Kanner, 1992: 28). Should we treat bodies as Benetton does, as if they are all the same, regardless of history and cultural differences? Can tolerance come from such amnesia, or only slogans?

Since the 1960s, one million American women have had breast implants, 20 percent for reconstruction after mastectomy, the rest for enlargement. In 1992, an FDA panel recommended restricting silicon breast implants because they leak, and around one in a hundred rupture (*New York Times*, 21 February 1992). From then on, implant surgery would be treated as experimental and would be monitored. Some doctors and many patients defended the procedure, claiming that it helped women feel better about themselves and that no firm scientific evidence existed for the implants' causing connective-tissue disease (Angell, 1996). Defenses of women's right to do what they want with their bodies clashed with the new medical orthodoxy. By emphasizing scientific uncertainty, the controversy questioned medicine's moral regulation of the body. Within feminism, it split those who thought stereotyping was the issue from those concerned first about women's control over their bodies.

The body is integral to discourses of morality. It is the apotheosis of immorality, the place where Western culture seeks and finds unnaturalness, depravity, and chaos. Yet the culture also constitutes the body as the place of life, labor, and pleasure. Across these disordered ethics, the body's materiality—its physical characteristics and our experiences of them—remains. Bodily materiality seems the source of all being and knowledge, and we must always reach some accommodation with it. This necessity propels us into furious and continuous arguments about what a good or a bad body really is, and also leads us to challenge the ethical limits it represents.

Regulating the Body

To deal with the immoral body, we try to regulate it, creating discourses that tell us what good and bad bodies are, and practices to manage them. Today we control the body not only by the old, crude methods of purification, punishment, and confinement, but also by researching and treating the body, trying to improve it, teaching it, and socializing it. "The body" is always many different bodies—a combination of all the bodies that regulatory discourses describe. This clutter of discourses turns the body into a contested and uncertain moral territory. The pregnant body, for instance, is fought over by doctors, medical ethicists, elected officials, religious leaders, the Supreme Court, the pro-choice movement and Operation Rescue, and the woman's parents and the biological father, as well as the woman herself. Bodies such as those that Eva and Adele paraded at MOMA set in motion a rather different combat, that between "body" artists, art critics, the Moral Majority, and institutions such as museums and the National Endowment for the Arts, with feminists and other artists as interested onlookers.

Confusing bodily morality further is the coexistence of regulations dating from different times. Although the doctor, rather than the priest, has become "the moral preceptor of society," science has not entirely supplanted religion (Laqueur, 1990: 213). When Dr. Jack Kevorkian rejects legal challenges to his assistance at suicides, he is reverting to an older law, trying to be priest rather than physician, playing "Dr. God" (*New York Times*, 25 October 1991). When it comes to bodies, our ideas are sometimes a strange mixture of nostalgia for the past and relief at the present. In the Benetton ads, these emotions blur together as the images recall several moments in the ethical history of the United States: slavery, its defeat, and current racial tensions. Similarly, new discourses of the body operate in the present even before they have widespread practical effects, as if in vitro fertilization, surrogacy, artificial wombs, and cloning, for instance, were already majority experiences. More generally, the body's subjection to what Christopher Lasch calls the "scientific habit of mind," a habit that expects knowledge always to progress toward truth, imbues the body with the future (1991: 527, 528).

As with moral discourse generally, the history of the body's regulation is marked by moral breaks. Within institutions such as the prison, the psychiatric clinic, the army, the factory, the school, and the family, knowledge of the body has, since the eighteenth century, been equated with power over it (Foucault, 1977a: 200ff.). In this schema, the body is secular and scientific. Secular social policies focus on monitoring and controlling the body. Science shows us what is empirically available as evidence of the body and displays this evidence as the body's truth.[1] The scientific body has democratic rights, but it is subjected both to the authority of state institutions and to its own self-monitoring.[2] Not everyone is granted citizenship in this body. In the nineteenth century, the new biological science of race constituted an important break in the black body's moral regulation. This racial science legitimized the "ladder of being," the hypothesized biological chain stretching from inanimate matter, through animals governed by their passions, through rational humans, to angels and divinity (see Dennett, 1995: 64; Gilman, 1985: 83). Supported by social Darwinism's interpretations of evolution, biologists associated blackness with leprosy and ranked humans in terms of evolving female pelvis size, with Hottentots at the bottom and Europeans at the top (Gilman, 1985). This bodily hierarchy, in which pathology is revealed through anatomy, justified white ownership of black bodies during slavery and, afterward, these bodies' oppression and segregation. At the same time, the work of writers and artists such as Zola, Poe, Twain, Manet, and Picasso connected the black body to animality, sexuality, madness, and childishness, as well as to "primitive" virtues such as strength, nurturance, and intuition.[3] A reverse occurred in the 1950s, though, when scientists, many of them black, rejected evolutionary theories of race differences and argued that individuals' development was damaged irredeemably by segregation. This scientific shift facilitated social change, particularly school desegregation (Gates, 1993: 251).[4]

Changes in the moral regulation of the female body are sometimes more elusive. The "Queen of Temperance," Frances Willard, wrote a bestseller on women and bicycle riding, in which she declared that activity could "help women to a wider world"; Susan B. Anthony believed bicycles "did more to emancipate women than anything in the world" (qtd. in Willard, 1991). A more obvious change occurred when in the early twentieth century women fought for access to contraception, a precondition for the success of other feminist campaigns for employment rights and sexual freedom (Cott, 1987: 48). With *Roe v. Wade,* women gained a right to regulate their bodies that signaled a more general acceptance of their individual rights. Today, technological developments in medicine that allow the maintenance of life in conditions where previously it would have ceased, are producing new formulations of good medical practice and humane care for those you love. AIDS, too, has wrought specific changes in the policing of first-world bodies. Heterosex without a condom now carries a charge that it never did in the days of *Bob and Carol and Ted and Alice* (1969), when spouse swapping was good clean fun. In a range of contemporary movies, from *Frankie and Johnnie* (1991) to *Hangin' with the Homeboys* (1990), rubbers are casual but essential parts of the action. AIDS has also reactivated movie genres that depend on the exchange of bodily fluids—vampire and epidemic movies (see Ricaputo, 1995; Taubin, 1995).[5] And young men's deaths now raise loaded questions about cause that obituaries must answer, with silence, a specific explanation, or a revealing vagueness about "a long illness" or "lymphoma."

Often, too, it looks as though historical breaks in the body's regulation are being reversed. The body ethics of AIDS resurrects a nostalgia for 1970s sexual permissiveness, pre-1970s intolerance of gay sexuality, and pre-1960s sexual restraint. From the stage, a finalist in the 1995 Miss America pageant called for abstinence. Rodney King's body was a lot like the nineteenth-century body of the beaten, animal black, its degradation seen everywhere, its voice hardly heard (Baker, 1993: 44, 48). Injected and implanted contraceptives, prescribed extensively to poor women of color since the 1980s, make women pay for a moral and political right to control their sexuality with lack of control and medical risk. Since the late 1980s, the nation has again tolerated high rates of urban tuberculosis (Ryan, 1993: 389ff.). However, the changes still leave a mark. AIDS, for instance, is imbued with post-colonial fears of the invading "other"—the Haitian, the African (Patton, 1990; Watney, 1989). Nostalgia for spontaneous, unprotected sex, whether it is acted upon or just talked about, is an AIDS-era emotion, a remembrance, not a return. King's beating ended up legally condemned and forced his voice on the national ear through the sounds of uprising.[6] TB's contemporary inextricability from AIDS fears makes current representations of it much more than a moral retread of the nineteenth century. The tubercular body is no longer associated with a romantic sensibility like that of Keats, or Dickens's Little Nell, who were too good for this world.

Moral discourses of the body are historically inconsistent. If you are religious, bodily goodness is hard to attain or be sure about. Jimmy Carter's confession, "I've committed adultery in my heart many times," spoke for every believer who has tried to silence whispers of adulterous desire (qtd. in Glad, 1980: 383). What science "knows" about the body changes rapidly, making its moral lessons uncertain, too. Doctors often cannot distinguish clearly between different ailments or predict the outcome of a medical procedure, let alone give a biological explanation of mental disorder, explain homosexuality, or tell us where the dividing line falls between "life" and "not-life" for the fetus or the person. Viruses cannot be seen directly and are themselves emblematically unstable, changing their shape and effects. Under the microscope, even the shape of *Ebola*, the deadly hemorrhagic fever virus, "assumed the appearance of a '?'" (Horton, 1995: 24). The prejudices of science also weaken its moral force. In the early days of the AIDS epidemic, doctors looked fruitlessly to stereotypes of promiscuous, "receptive anal," drug-using gay and bisexual men, and Haitians, as incubators of the disease (Treichler, 1989: 46, 49). Current attention to infectious viruses and bacteria seems based less on their biological interest than on their potential impact on "American lives," now that they are all "within a day's flying time of the US" (Preston, 1992: 62). As if in response to this internal turmoil, many scientists question the relevance of their findings about, for instance, the biological basis of homosexuality or of aggression, suggesting that policy issues be decided on nonscientific grounds (Byrne, 1994: 55; *New York Times*, 15 September 1992, 19 February 1995).

Seemingly irreconcilable discourses—Christian and rationalist, scientific and utilitarian—are mixed up in discussions of the body. On radio shows such as Bishop L. E. Willis's *Crusade for Christ*, Jesus walks hand in hand with science across the field of the believer's body. Sick callers tell hospital test results; then they and the bishop pray. Willis implores the Lord to "step into" the body of a woman paralyzed by a stroke "and correct every ailment, every malfunction, every blood vessel" (30 June 1993). Similarly, antiabortionists' concern with the visible combines a religious emphasis on witnessing and "seeing the light" with a scientific interest in visible proof. Activists claim that if there were a "window" on pregnant women's abdomens, as in a child's scientific model of a pregnant woman, there would be no more abortions. In *If I Should Die before I Wake* (1986), parallel accounts of Jerry Falwell's and a young woman's conversions to the pro-life position, Falwell begins like a good empiricist, describing abortion and its risks scientifically. He also claims to be writing a feminist story in support of young mothers. Listening with perfect feminine receptiveness to God and to women, he turns out to be the book's best feminist. Helping women keep their babies, he is helping them fulfill their true selves (see Harding, 1992: 80–85; and Ginsburg, 1992: 71). Pro-lifers may also use a morality of costs and benefits. Some accept federal abortion funding, but only if it is restricted to rape and incest cases, for instance, on the grounds that it is better to save some fetal lives than lose them all. Scientific judgments are also compromised by other moral frames. Doctors and patients choose mastectomy in cases where outcome studies suggest that lumpectomy is just as good, as if sin, not a tumor, must be purged: "I can't tell you how many women I talk to who say, 'I just want to get it out,'" says Nancy Brinker, an advocate for women with breast cancer (qtd. in *New York Times*, 5 May 1993).

When everyday actions are in question, moral authority is even more confused. In 1991, a Seattle woman who was eight months pregnant ordered a raspberry daiquiri at the Red Robin restaurant. Trying to dissuade her, a waiter showed her a warning against pregnant women's drinking that he had torn from a beer bottle, and she did not get her drink. The waiter, along with a coworker involved in the incident, was fired for being disrespectful to a customer. A subsequent statewide campaign asking that restaurants be allowed to refuse alcohol to pregnant women restated science's public moral force. In this case, several moral rules vied for authority: warnings from the Surgeon General and a broader sense of women's responsibility to fetuses versus constitutionally guaranteed freedom of action and giving customers what they want (*New York Times,* 30 March 1991).

The regulatory discourses of the body are also disrupted by the body's involvement with discourses of, for instance, art, family, nation, gender, and race. Through these interactions, the body acts as a powerful metaphor for other moral issues. Benetton's kaleidoscope of bodies ignoring racial boundaries assumes a worldwide consumer "family." Antiabortion and viral narratives share a post-Vietnam sense of the body as a fortress-nation, vulnerable to attack (Ginsburg, 1992: 69; Hoberman, 1995a). Vinnie, the egomaniacal and ineffectual Don Juan in *Hangin' with the Homeboys,* thinks of his nonoxynol-9-lubricated condom as an ultimate deterrent, capable of zapping even herpes. Richard Preston's "Crisis in the Hot Zone" (1992), the first popular account of hemorrhagic fever viruses, gives a step-by-step account of bodily denaturing that echoes 1980s lists of the effects of nuclear weapons. The article even invokes Joseph Conrad, describing an infected area of Zaire as "the silent heart of darkness" (68). Other discussions of infectious diseases construe the United States as under attack from within, by migrated strains of TB rampant in "ethnic minority groups" or by the general "urban Thirdworldization" of U.S. health (Horton, 1995: 26).

The body can also signify an ethics of nation more directly. U.S. media pictured the Dream Team at the 1992 Barcelona Olympics as infinitely more skilled than the other basketball teams and as an emblem of the moral stature of the United States in the post–cold war world. Though the team's modest performance raised the specter of U.S. vulnerability, it did not entirely vitiate the dream. And although the players' overwhelming blackness representing a majority-white, race-divided nation suggested that blacks have to play great basketball to do well in America, that blackness also signified the irrelevance of race in a democracy: they were, after all, successful Americans. More subtly, though, these young black men's national-hero status in basketball and athletics, while seeming to proclaim nation, also erodes it. When young black men appear elsewhere in the popular media, they usually have a geographically and racially specific underclass identity: They are not Americans but "inner-city black youth." Even in music, young black men's greatest contemporary success comes from mythologizing this local identity. Thus, the fast and powerful bodies of young black athletes that stand for an expanded "nation" are bodies that at the same time stand for the disunity of "nation." On a dark city street, Michael Jordan might appear a potential criminal, not a national hero.

The moral regulation of the body is compromised by the very regulatory activities it requires. Regulation demands that we speak and write continually about the bodies we want to prohibit. It therefore reinstates prohibited bodies at the same time that it represses them. The paradox has its own pleasures to counterbalance its logical shortcomings (Foucault, 1977b: 31). We enjoy the prohibitions and talk avidly about the forbidden. Gender transgressions such as those of Eva and Adele, drag queens, transvestites, and transsexuals sustain numerous television talk shows. The sexualization of children's bodies is well publicized in abuse cases or in art such as the photographs of Sally Mann. Religions that conceptualize children as innocents maintain a parallel discourse of childhood corruption and constantly reassess young people's sexual-moral states through the apparatuses of confession, Sunday schools, Bible classes, confirmation classes, public campaigns against "kiddie porn," retreats, and and crusades (see Foucault, 1979: 27–32; Observer [London], 26 June 1994; and Weeks, 1985: 224). Anti-abortion campaigners endorse the visual moral power of what they hate most—the aborted fetus—as they did when, for instance they presented one such body in a salad box to presidential candidate Bill Clinton.

It may be that the transgressive, immoral body has more power than the legitimate, moral body, which comes to exist primarily as the obverse of prohibitions. Foucault noted how the prohibited forms of sexuality are the ones that sustain the immense machinery of bodily regulation (1979: 32–35). We know the "natural" body, perhaps the most generally elevated yet vaguely defined of moral bodies, primarily through the unending parade of the "unnatural" —transsexuals, surrogate mothers, anorexics, bulimics, cosmetic surgery veterans, people in comas—across our television screens and front pages, or under our noses, as when Eva and Adele stroll by. We know drinking and smoking "can damage your health," but images of bodies using these fatal substances cover the public landscape, ten feet tall. Such negative knowledge attenuates the "moral" body even further. What is moral is even less clear than what is not.

Finally, within the category of immoral bodies are some that we cannot know or even really speak about. These are bodies of our imagination, fantasy, and memory. They are irrational, fascinating, and horrible; abject bodies, Julia Kristeva calls them, provoked by their prohibition, lurking slyly on the verge of consciousness (1982: 4, 11). Bodily abjection does not announce itself clearly. Often our more ordered thoughts suppress it, leaving its moral challenge unanswered. For moments of abjection are the limit of the body's moral authority. Examples are the repeated poor-quality, clearly made-up freak images on tabloids' front pages—a child with a dog's head, Newt Gingrich meeting a space alien. These images confront us with the strangeness implanted within our own bodies. Readers may not believe in them, but they buy the papers. Horror films deal even more explicitly with abjection, playing out anxieties about sexual polymorphism, racial difference, childhood, growing up, and the vulnerability of the body surface. In the early-1990s movies and books about infectious diseases, the body's disintegration is a clear lure (Squire, 1998). "Crisis in the Hot Zone" describes *Ebola Zaire*'s effects with what one reviewer termed "unseemly relish" (Horton, 1995: 24): "You are stuffed with clots, and yet you bleed like a hemophiliac who has been in a fistfight . . . A sort of melting occurs, and the corpse's connective tissue, skin, and organs . . . begin to liquefy" (Preston, 1992: 59). Repeated moral panics about homosexuality indicate a similar fascination with the abject. The gay body has won limited social and political acceptance, a precarious place within the moral mainstream.[7] Although the sitcom *Ellen*, with its out and proud lesbian protagonist, may give its advertisers sleepless nights, the Clintons very publicly welcomed the lead actor and her woman partner at the White House. Nevertheless, the gay body's sterile, purely pleasurable sexuality, its intimations of femininity in men, its folk devil status in debates about children's sexuality, and its association through AIDS with death make it still an object of intense, unnameable fears and wishes (Bersani, 1989: 212; Weeks, 1985: 40).

The sexual body ("the sole substance of universal taboos"), the non-white body, the disabled, the old, the ill, and the dying body also function as sites of abjection where the culture faces the limits of bodily knowledge and experience (Foucault, 1977b: 30). It is, in the end, such abject bodies, unproductive, desiring, and uncontrollable, that discourses of the body try to regulate. These bodies cannot be domesticated or silenced, and they put moral systems in perpetual jeopardy.

My Body, My Self, My Ethics

Many moral arguments about the body are deadlocked. The response to the deadlock tends, as with other such stalemates, to be an emotivist appeal to individuals' feelings of right and wrong. Since the nineteenth century, authority over the body has been taken over by the individual, who must translate moral rules into personal conviction. By tethering those feelings loosely to communication, emotivism proposes that they can be expressed and discussed, and so this manages to look like a solution. Following this pattern, moral emotivism about the body screens out the abject, uncommunicable bodies we have discussed, and thus stills argument. Debates are not resolved or even engaged, so much as adjourned. When a woman wonders whether to have an abortion, she may assess the medical evidence, her rights under *Roe v. Wade*, and the costs and benefits of abortion versus pregnancy, childbirth, and parenting. The main question the culture expects her to ask, though, is, "Which course of action will make me feel better?" All those who put out a moral claim on pregnancy, from the Catholic Church to the National Organization for Women volunteers who escort women into abortion clinics, agree that in the end, a woman should do what feels right. The moral authority given to feelings shunts controversy temporarily onto the sidelines, but the old combatants still hover around the issue, ready to fight over the very next woman who finds herself outside a picketed clinic or whose case becomes a matter for public deliberation.

Perhaps the most obvious successes of emotivism occur when it takes over from religion. In the late 1980s and early 1990s panic over the satanic sexual abuse of children, personal experience crowded out religious feelings, and the devil took a backseat to amnesia and repression. A *Primetime Live* episode on the topic began by pointing to the phenomenon's continuity with medieval legends of "devil worship, black masses, sacrifical altars and secret covenants" and to the difference from them: "Today it's not high priests who are called on to explain the evils of the mind—it's professional therapists" (1993: 4). One accused father charged the United States with "going through a love affair with psychotherapy" (1993: 8). What is at stake here is a transformation of sinful and sinned-against bodies into bodies as containers of emotion, traumatized by either parents or professionals and moral by virtue of their experiences.

Popular music makes some dramatic translations of religious ethics into an ethics based solely on a performer's persona. The secularization of the Mary figure, for instance, reaches an emotivist extreme in its appropriation by Madonna to further her own interests in sex and death (Kristeva, 1980: 253). Crucifixes, she points out, "are sexy because there's a naked man on them" (King, 1991: 175). The musician formerly known as Prince similarly makes faith and sex equivalent and personal. On the cover of *Lovesexy* (1988), the singer is naked, reclining among flowers, in a pose that invokes both Manet's *Dejeuner sur l'herbe* and Saint Sebastian.

The body's materiality fosters its association with stable personal identity. This identity renders the emotivist morality of the body especially powerful. For the body is experienced as the most fundamental and intimate aspect of our lives. Even more than our families, it gives us our "selves." The rights and wrongs of the body are a matter not just of how you feel but of who you are. My body is both my self and my ethics. Such identity ethics carries a powerful charge. A woman who has a breast reconstruction because she says the breast is part of who she is has more moral authority than the woman who says it would make life easier for her, or that it would make her feel better, or simply that she wants it. The book that first comprehensively linked women's liberation to their physical identities, *Our Bodies, Ourselves*, first published in 1971 by the Boston Women's Health Book Collective, is still an iconic feminist text, and its title remains morally powerful in feminist rhetoric, as a slogan of the pro-choice campaign, for instance.

Embodied identity is fragile, however, like all our feelings about the body; it is difficult to pin down. A woman may be brought to recognize her womanhood by menstruation, sexuality, pregnancy, or being whistled at in the street, but such on/off recognition does not reliably define her (Riley, 1988: 96, 98). The equation of particular bodily desires or acts with an identity is also questionable. Does one same-sex experience mean you are gay? As Andy Warhol said, following this criterion, it is difficult to find ten straight men (1989: 339). Are you gay through biological fate, a state that exists regardless of what you say and do? Or must you, in order to be gay, come out and say you are? "Lived" identity, the kind that leads you to say, "As a gay man, I feel . . ." or, "As a woman, I know . . . ," can work only as a holding measure, controlling the moral instability of the body, maintaining a precarious equilibrium.

The body can never act as the moral foundation it appears to be. Material attributes of the body that seem essential and that operate as ethical standards—sex and race, for example—turn out to be suppositions maintained with difficulty. We take for granted the importance of the distinction between women and men and our ability to make that distinction. Such certainty turns being a man or being a woman into moral truth. To cross the boundary between the sexes seems an ethical as well as a bodily impossibility. The boundary varies in permeability, however. In some states, a man cannot get a marriage license as a woman if he has had a sex change. In medicine, whether you are a man or a woman depends on many things: chromosomes, hormones, what your genitals look like, whether your parents brought you up as a boy or a girl, whether you live as a man or a woman, and what you feel yourself to be. Surgeons and psychiatrists cannot change your chromosomes, but they can "reassign" your gender. The clothed body, too, confuses the man-woman divide, giving a visible form to cross-gendered identifications and desires. Finally, the emotivist discourse of personal choice turns your sex from a moral imperative into an individual option. If you are a man but feel yourself to be a woman, shouldn't you be able to choose freely to live as a woman or to become a woman surgically? Women who have breast implants are similarly constructing or reconstructing themselves as culturally valued women. Performers such as Eva and Adele disturb the moral status quo by inventing extra choices such as "artist-hermaphrodite," a third sex that is aesthetic rather than biological. All these events that dispute the equation between body and identity call up abjection. For the destabilization of identity is a horrific possibility, a "narcissistic crisis" that forces abjection upon us (Kristeva, 1982: 54, 14).

Faced with such possibilities, it is difficult to maintain even the most apparently secure aspects of the body as our moral ground. The solid, material body that moral argument assumes ends up looking very insubstantial. We are left, then, with a "body" that is necessary to our moral thinking but whose functions and characteristics are multiple and contradictory.

Naturalness

To contain the body's moral confusion, we try to tell clear, persuasive stories about it. In part we succeed, although no stories subdue entirely the complexity of the body's morality. Naturalness and improvement are two narratives of bodily morality. Although they are not the only ones, they are highly indicative of the body's status as both moral authority and moral limit. Each story tries to impose an ethical order, but each is disrupted by the noise of other stories, or by emotivism that silences ethical doubt temporarily but does not resolve it, or by the immoral bodies against which the story defines itself but which it can never entirely exclude.

The story of naturalness, which presents bodies as moral by virtue of their unmodified state, is perhaps the most ubiquitous narrative of the body. It has a powerful place in food, cosmetics, and cigarette advertising; in popular books on diet, exercise, and sex; and in journalistic coverage of fashion and health. When young people balk at using contraception, they say it doesn't feel "natural." When women protest hospital births, they contrast them with "natural" births in a birthing center. This story is effective because it is so compatible with other morality tales. The narrative of a good, "natural" death, for instance, contradicts neither religious accounts of a divinely ordained death nor scientific accounts of a medically appropriate one.

Given that cosmetics are quintessentially artificial, their selling as "natural" provides clues to what the story of the "natural" body entails. A 1993 ad in *People* magazine for Cover Girl foundation and powder, for instance, raises naturalness to an absolute good through repetition. The product is "the most natural kind of beautiful ... so natural it doesn't look like make-up ... the natural choice for beautiful." The ad associates the natural body with a quasi-sacred perfection yet also associates itself with science when it

claims to "match your skin tone, your skin type." It rises above its imprecision through an emphasis on individual choice and self-expression—the
products are "the perfect choice for you"—and, by stressing the good feeling the product gives that justifies the consumer's choice.

The grand narrative of the natural body is underpinned here by an
emotivism that operates, as always, with skidmarks under it. Is feeling good
a complete ethic? What if the good feeling has nothing to do with naturalness; you simply hate your face without makeup and want to conceal it? The
product is after all a *cover:* perhaps its artifice, its "unnaturalness," makes
you feel good. The ad's ambiguous relationship to beauty dramatizes this
doubt. The copy links feeling good and choosing natural-looking products
with beauty ("the most natural kind of beautiful . . . the natural choice for
beautiful"). This link is not quite convincing. Modern concepts of beauty do
not tie beauty firmly or exclusively to naturalness, let alone to rationality,
good feelings, or morality (Cottom, 1991: 137ff.).

The cosmetic story of the "natural" body must now account for some
bodies that were previously excluded from it. In Western popular culture, a
"natural" body has traditionally been youthful, heterosexual, clearly gendered, and white. Responding to new and newly vocal markets, the Cover
Girl ad reaches out to diverse ages and ethnicities. It pictures five female
models: one Asian, one black, and three white, four of whom look under
thirty. The copy describes "147 naturally true shades" and "7 skin-specific
formulas." Naturalness is a code here for "natural" differences, such as being
over thirty and being of color. But "natural" swallows such differences. We
are all special, beautiful individuals, so differences of age and race are not
important. The photograph reinforces this melting-pot assimilationism.
Each model differs from the others by a few minor individualizing marks,
such as a mole, shorter hair, or a different texture of clothing. The marks of
age are also small, outweighed by a uniform Cover Girl identity. All the
women wear revealing white clothes on lithe bodies. Those who smile present the same gleaming slice of teeth. Facial features and hair are more or
less uniform, and skin color varies slightly, tending toward that beigeing of
the white ideal that has become the preferred tactic of a fashion and cosmetics industry faced with a social and economic requirement to represent
and sell to nonwhites (Willis, 1991: 120).

Cover Girl tackles racial difference by trying to assimilate it into white
naturalness. The fashion and cosmetics coverage in *Essence,* a magazine directed at black women, tells another story. The magazine appeals repeatedly
to a "natural" that includes a wide range of hair, lips, legs, and noses, and a
spectrum of black skins. One 1993 swimwear feature showed "three sisters

with bodies that range from lean to full-figured" ("Take a Dip This Summer," 1993: 62). A woman with big legs and round breasts stares into the marine distance, wearing a suit that "celebrates the best parts of you!" (69). "Natural" functions here both as a rejection of artifice and, like the hairstyle called the "natural" in the 1960s, as a critique of white beauty standards and an assertion of Africanness. It replaces assimilationism with Mayor Dinkins's "gorgeous mosaic." But feeling good about your "natural" and socially devalued body will still not give it the ethical purity the culture invests in images of a thin, white, blond woman. And doesn't the black model's stare owe as much to fashion photography's romance with seductive arrogance as to black pride?

Another strategy is to think about differences of gender and race as elements of pure, natural pleasure. In the mid-1980s, Benetton's United Colors campaign pictured smiling young people from different ethnic backgrounds wearing different Benetton clothes. The image was a kind of multiethnic precursor of the sitcom *Friends*. We were asked to look, to enjoy "natural" differences, and to see across them to a "natural," ethical, human commonality: "Color is an international language, a real and positive source of happiness which communicates across frontiers" (Benetton, 1987: 7). The slight differences between the faces and bodies and between the clothes were equally fun to look at. The visual pleasure that made each Benetton product seem as natural and valid as each physiognomy also erased the wider meanings that body differences have and became the ad's loudest ethical statement. Condensed onto a single page, the ad presented Benetton's vision of the world as a market united by the good, natural pleasures of differences in bodies and clothing.

Later Benetton images of black and white children, black and white arms handcuffed together, and a black woman with a white infant worked in the same way. All the meanings these ads supported—world unity, crime, slavery, homoeroticism, aesthetic pleasure—were invested with an equal degree of significance. The Benetton world is postdifference, postbias, and playful: the only differences that remain are between images. Such uncommitted picture making caused widespread consternation among those for whom the body is heavier with meaning. Images, though, never really exist in the free-floating way Benetton suggests. They cannot wrest themselves entirely from the pull of meanings.

The narrative of natural bodies approaches abjection in a way that is distinct from previous religious and scientific attempts. It does not exclude or fight abjection. Instead, it assimilates it, letting abject bodies be seen but casting them as just another variation in the natural order of things, part of an ongoing system-in-flux (Martin, 1994: 72–81). But this assimilation does not stop abjection from threatening to break the narrative apart. Benetton's handcuffs ad hints at an off-limits sexuality that cannot be passed off as simple visual pleasure. The picture of children is shaded with the uneasy eroticism that always accompanies their use for visual enjoyment. The racial differentiation in the superficially nurturant image of black mother and white child points to other horrors, such as slavery and rape (Kristeva, 1992: 13). The attempt of naturalness to familiarize the abject thus leaves a hazardous strangeness outside the narrative.

Improvement

The improvement narrative does not try, like naturalness, to assimilate abjection but instead takes it on, trying to subdue and win it. Unlike naturalness, improvement tries to change the body, edging it nearer and nearer perfection. Like naturalness, though, the improvement narrative manages at times to bind the morality of the body together across contradictions. The improving body-in-process also echoes the continuing flux of the natural body. Unlike colonial accounts of the body as a kind of nation, a fortress to be defended against external dangers, improvement is postcolonial. It sets up the body, inside and out, as a new frontier, always to be fought for, always vulnerable to the enemy within. Over every T cell, every fragile membrane, a battle goes on (Martin, 1994: 34–35, 49–62).

In the 1980s, the healthy body rather than the sexual body became excessively regulated (Coward, 1989: 126). Improvement through food, exercise, medication and surgery, and clothes and cosmetics is increasingly an ethical imperative in the culture. Ultimately the narrative aims for a good death, or even no death at all. Improvement is complicated, though, by the different bodies—poor, black, ill, unfit, ugly—that it must address. This diversity of abjection cannot be solved by a single program, and elements of it perpetually resist being improved away. As a result, uncertainty chokes the narrative, and emotivism again provides a partial resolution. If you feel better about your body, your mind and life should improve too. "I am much happier now," and "I'm finally free to be the teenager that I am," says a teenage actress after breast reduction surgery (Rosen and Sheff-Cahan, 1993: 84, 87). Because an improved body often does not solve a life, though, the narrative remains troubled.

Narratives of improvement describe multiple and specialized body technologies. In popular guides to nutrition, what *kind* of fiber, carbohydrate, or cholesterol people ingest is crucial. Food supplements include not just technologically simple substances, such as cod liver oil and vitamins, but also trace minerals, such as magnesium; substances made within in the human body, such as mRNA; and ancient elixirs, such as evening primrose oil, newly mainstreamed for big and basically healthy markets—in this case, women who have premenstrual discomfort. The health and fashion status of "ethnic" foods from East and Pacific Asia, Mexico, and southern Europe fluctuates rapidly, reducing whole cultures to cholesterol counts. Some new twist is always arising in exercise culture, too: walking is better than running; suppleness is more important than strength or endurance. A long succession of Asian physical disciplines become novel forms of body conditioning. Often these innovations are attached to products: ever more specialized exercise shoes, StairMasters replacing treadmills, Nautilus machines taking over from weights. The logic of the market and the requirement for individual choice are obviously at work here. But these multiplications and specializations are also ways of addressing the social and historical diversity of the body and the recurrence of abjection.

The body that is physically just right and mentally stress-free, permeated with self-esteem and acceptance, will not develop arteriosclerosis, cancer, or immune system disorders; even AIDS becomes, as the title of Elizabeth Kübler-Ross's book has it, "the ultimate challenge" (1988). More mildly, Betty Friedan describes aging as a quest beginning with "denial and fear" and ending in "acceptance, affirmation and celebration" (1993: 637). Improvement must be worked for, but you are also supposed to improve by trusting your feelings: eating, exercising, and thinking how you want. How, then, can you know when your body has worked enough to vanquish terminal illness or age? How, exactly, does it feel? At its ever-receding end, the improvement narrative uncouples itself from utopia. You can never be too hard-bodied, too thin, or too at peace with yourself; you can never entirely beat back abjection.

The narrative of bodily improvement is also confused by its coexistence with other stories. Now, in the New Age, physical improvement does not just make you feel good about yourself but also leads to spiritual growth. Annie Sprinkle, the sex performance artist, describes sex as her "spiritual path"; in such a journey, there is no bad sex, only a "learning process" (1991: 21, 29). Middle-class Americans associate devoutness with bodily comfort: "Honor the temple, for the Lord has housed thy soul within. Buy that temple a foot massage and a Rolex watch," is how one character in the novel *Pigs in Heaven* satirizes it (Kingsolver, 1993: 88). Secularized concepts of salvation are attached to the improvement of socially disenfranchised bodies. In the best-selling twelve-step genre of self-help, an individually-decided-upon spirituality guides recovery from a variety of out-of-control, abject bodies—those that are drunken, drug-abusing, eating-disordered, and sex-addicted. Books by illness survivors, such as Frances Morani Thompson's *Going for the Cure* (1989), give inspirational accounts of redemption by particular regimes of exercise and nutrition, positive thinking, or lifestyle transformation. The state of dying bodies is imaged as transfigured calm. "I'm ready," breathes Andy, dying of AIDS in the film *Philadelphia* (1993). Religious mortification and ecstasy also remain in the improvement narrative. The body that emerges from the Step class or the one-thousand-calorie-a-day diet is both an expression of right living and a lesson in penance and its pleasures: firmly muscled yet exhaustedly sweaty and aching; healthily slim yet euphorically bony and hungry. Similarly, science acts as a justification of moral improvement. Twelve-step narratives give people who gamble or shop beyond their means, or who keep having the same relationship problems, a medical status as addicts that, though contested, allows for remission or "recovery."

Justifications in terms of costs and benefits also bolster the improvement story. Women's bodily improvement is often interpreted as a matter of economic and social advancement: Barbie earns more. Go-go dancers on *Donahue* all concur that women with implants do best: "Large breasts . . . make all the money" (*Donahue*, 1994: 4). Improving one's black body and improving one's life also have a strong historical connection. The use of illegal drugs, both for recreation and to improve performance, by black athletes who occasionally die of them is publicly condemned but also silently condoned (*New York Times*, 1 May 1993). Polls indicate that well over half the public does not think athletes should be disciplined for past drug use (Harris, 1987: 16).[8] The cost-benefit assessment here seems to be, that's the price of getting the black body to succeed. More generally, the moral imperative to improve the nation's health is always costed out. Behind talk of empowerment, choice, freedom, and responsibility in the early 1990s debate on expanding health coverage lay the assumption that all these good things come in proportion to income. As the political economist Uwe Reinhardt says, "A working majority of Congress (and possibly a majority of the American people) views health care as a *private consumption* good that can legitimately be rationed by income level" (1995: 56).

The powerful are not exempted from the improvement narrative. Since Carter, we have pictured a series of jogging presidents broken only by Reagan. Senator Paul Tsongas, a candidate in the 1993 Democratic primaries whose cancer was then in remission, grimly swam laps for the cameras to demonstrate his electability. The less powerful, with their more abject bodies, are even more subject to the improvement ethic. The moral tale of improving the female body is an epic one of controlling its excesses, its folds and cyclic flows, its softness and liquidity, its multiplicity and monumentality. The horror of fat exemplifies this gendered ethics. When Oprah Winfrey lost sixty-seven pounds, she dragged it onstage in bars of lard. Supermarket tabloids picture the obese and the no longer obese, either trim and complacent or comically trailing yards of surplus skin, alongside alleged Martians and the living Elvis. Fat in a society of nutritional plenty does not mean health or security or prosperity, as it did in the nineteenth century, when, as Stuart Ewen says, "jowled men and ample women proudly displayed a plenitude of flesh" (1988: 177). Now fat is the unproductive element of the body, signifying animality, irrationality, and pleasure, and associated with out-of-control women.

The improvement narrative of the female body follows a number of different story lines. The dieter displays fat's absence, the anorectic pathologizes this absence, the waif model aestheticizes it, and the exerciser displaces it with virtuous, rigid muscle.[9] The call to be just yourself hides the confusions. The narrative equates the female body's multiplicity with a range of equally valid and accessible individual choices. Oprah Winfrey, Madonna, and Demi Moore make their bodies fat, thin, fit, muscular, pregnant, feminine, androgynous, youthful, adult. Even Barbie, with her invariant body, energetically varies her hair, her clothes, and her lifestyle, from "Slumber Party Barbie" to "CEO Barbie." In an issue of the monthly magazine Self, a model with her ribs prominent faces a page on which a woman with a similarly bony rib cage illustrates a piece on anorexia. Perhaps anorexia, too, is OK if it makes you feel good. Even the feminist orthodoxy of eating what you want and feeling comfortable with your body is always a story leading, if not to Barbie, to normal weight (Orbach, 1978). It seems the moral female body can be anything you want it to be, as long as it isn't de trop and it feels good.

In the improvement narrative, the abjection of racial otherness is explicit. Advertisements, endorsements, and the retail display of products still make hair straightening and skin lightening acceptable. Although such narratives of improvement are contested by the religious idea of the soul inside the skin, the rightness of the natural body, and the right to self-determination, these ideas are less important than choosing who you want to be. If you can be anyone, this possibility must include hair relaxers and skin bleach. Personal choice, though, is never a fully convincing explanation. Shopping your way out of racial abjection is different from choosing new shoes. The moral imperative that the black body get whiter has a political and historical force that does not apply to whites when they indulge in cosmetic tourism through tanning, lip implants, hair extensions, or dreadlocks.[10]

The abject resists the improvement narrative through that narrative's incoherencies and insufficiencies. Thus, abjection ensures that the last frontier is never really won. Unimprovable "welfare" bodies, lazy and wasteful, haunt the discourse of health care reform. In the improvement narrative of the female body, the horrors of femininity continually return. But the improvement narrative's commitment to turning abjection into a good feeling about yourself and your body means that it ignores these falterings, repressing abjection's potential to disturb.

Disruption, Co-option, and Negotiation

Although narratives of improvement and naturalness offer moments when the abject body gains a marginal place in moral discourse, other narratives treat abjection with more persistence and more seriousness. These narratives are more able to negotiate conflicting moralities. For instance, narratives that take apart the moral certainties of the body, that denaturalize them, demonstrate how these certainties are put together and maintained. The denaturalizing moral effect of drag is that it exposes the constructed nature of femininity and masculinity. The body seems fluid in its gender, provisionally sexed and ethically uncertain (Butler, 1993: 125). In the film *Paris Is Burning* (1991), the men's drag is a way of "talking back" to a culture that pathologizes them. It shifts their abject "feminine" bodies into moral discourse, managing to "confuse and seduce" the audience by giving gender unfamiliar forms (Butler, 1993: 131). The confusion is heightened by the film's focus on traditionally gendered moralities attached to the "wrong" bodies. Men masquerading as women display stereotypically "feminine" virtues and vices, such as nurturance, subservience, vanity, and bitchiness.

Although not everyone participates in drag balls, the high frequency of television talk shows about transvestism and transsexualism suggests that these topics speak to a large audience. Similar effects may result from more everyday affronts to gender. Some representations of women's bodies as extremely or unjustifiably violent also denaturalize femininity. These representations of female violence obey neither conventional nor feminist moralities but reveal the complementary structures of the two. The violent women of *Thelma and Louise* (1991) and *Basic Instinct* (1992) and of vigilante splatter movies such as *I Spit on Your Grave* (1977; see Clover, 1992: 114–20); and well-known real-life defendants, such as Lorena Bobbitt, who cut off her husband's penis, and Aileen Wuornos, the lesbian sex worker who killed tricks along Florida's Highway 75—all display aggression that goes beyond feminist justification and the conventional expectations of balls-breaking women. More self-consciously, lesbian sadomasochism claims to play out power relations in a healing, nonoppressive way (Califia, 1994: 163, 169). Because it presents its perversity as theatrical and consenting, enacted between two individuals with the same gendered power, it upsets mainstream moral judgments. Lesbian S-M is alien to standard notions of lesbians as tragic, mad, "just like us," or harmlessly woman-centered. In lesbian S-M, the morality of gender gets shaken. What kind of "women" are they? Such denaturalizations expose weaknesses in the Law of the Father that governs morality. They negotiate an ethics that says that moral rules cannot be fixed. In lesbian S-M, the Bobbitt case, and the film *Paris Is Burning* femininity refuses to accept castration and masculinity refuses to fear it. The protagonists show where the edge of moral discourse is by balancing on it. [11]

Exchanges between black and white style can also denaturalize moral certainties, this time turning race into a form of moral drag. Particular bodies do not have single or fixed meanings. RuPaul's lyrics to "Back to My Roots" suggest that black hair styles such as weaves and Jheri curls are not emulating whiteness. They have their own cultural and political traditions as well as personal significances. RuPaul alludes to some of them (see also Mercer, 1990: 248):

> Jheri curls . . . style, sophistication
> Afro-puff . . . uh-ooh, uh-ooh
> Hair weave . . . call her Miss Ross
> Braids . . . pride, respect.

In Malcolm X's autobiography (1964), his red conked hair, bright as a beacon, bleached and pressed into straightness, is a sign of his self-hatred and unsophistication but also an object of admiration to friends and an amazement and terror to whites. Similarly, interpretations of Michael Jackson's self-transformations—his narrowed lips and nose and whitened skin—as routes out of blackness may miss the point: Jackson is one of a long line of black entertainers whose extravagant looks are a kind of confrontation, impossible to ignore (see Mercer, 1990: 247; and Willis, 1991: 121).[12] When white youth wear black fashions, they rarely don a politics to match, but for a brief time they make a miscegenating mark on suburban culture. Such moves denaturalize racial categories: how can we be sure who's white, or what black means?

Horror films, too, seem interested in questioning moral rules beyond the Law of the Father. As well as depicting female victims, they give us androgynous female heroes, clever survivors whom Carol Clover calls "final girls," (1992: 35–41), like the female hero in the *Alien* movies (1979, 1986, 1992, 1997). These films shake the moral fixity of embodied, gendered identity. Cindy Sherman's photographs start where such films leave off—for instance, with images of her own body mixed with organic and inorganic refuse, corpselike. Although her dramatic denaturalizations of bodily integrity drive into our field of vision a femininity that is monstrous and deathly, they also show how identities, particularly those of women, are put together from continuing oscillations between abjection and our efforts to manage it. When dealing with the substances and objects in Sherman's photographs, viewers vacillate between the absolute horror of not knowing what they are and the lesser horror of giving them names such as "blood," "shit," or "woman's face."

Such moral denaturalizations are isolated moments, though, not joined together. Are they mere blips in the climate of moral feel-goodism? Do they really help us negotiate moral solutions, even contingent and temporary ones? It is easy to make sense of Eva and Adele's performance at MOMA by seeing it as just "art." In *Paris Is Burning*, the male-to-female transsexuals like Venus Extravaganza, who want to be rich white women, suburban housewives, or supermodels, reinforce the power and inevitability of gender (Butler, 1993: 125). Often, too, the moral questions that drag poses about gender disappear when drag is understood as entertainment or pathos. Substance seems also to evaporate from many representations of violent women, leaving a picture of them as mad, pathetic, or innocent abuse victims (S. Jones, 1991: 13; Youngblood, 1991: 40). And when you leave a horror movie or a gallery showing Cindy Sherman's work, you step back into an ordered world: a door in your mind slams shut on abjection.

The disruption of body morals by abjection is not always assimilated (Wollen, 1987: 29). However much black styles are exploited in the white marketplace, their diversity "challenges us to cherish plurality politically" and prevents us from simplifying moral debates (Mercer, 1990: 263). We can see that an enormous Cindy Sherman untitled photograph of two heads, eyes closed, almost kissing, is of two mannequins (1995). For a moment, however, we almost believe in a denaturalizing passion that goes beyond the moral possibilities for human relationships. These challenges are like the perverse knowledge of fetishists, who say of their strange love objects, "I know, but all the same . . ." (Mulvey, 1991: 146). That contradiction sustains a desire for something different, keeps the ethics of the body from stabilizing, and makes moral negotiation a continuing possibility.

Denaturalization can also, by reconstructing meanings, allow new values to arise (Butler, 1993: 137). The instability of moral borders can engen-

Figure 12. Cindy Sherman, Untitled, *1995. Courtesy of the artist and Metro Pictures.*

der new forms of representation and living. When the poor, black, gay men in *Paris Is Burning* recreate themselves as women, their masquerade negotiates, albeit tentatively, with the abjection of femininity, blackness, and poverty (Butler, 1993: 132). It makes space for new moral possibilities, moralities less determined by these limits.[13] In a more common instance, women who have mastectomies and do not reconstruct their breasts denaturalize the female body by continuing to assert the "breastless" womanhood of their bodies. When they take photos of their scarred bodies, they dramatize this moral expansion and flexibility. As the artist Matuschka says of her self-portraits, "You can't look away any more" (qtd. in Ferraro, 1993: 58). This art has helped negotiate a shift in mainstream notions of what ought to be seen: now that includes the radical mastectomy, tastefully lit and with the head averted, as in the picture of Matuschka that generated more mail than any other *New York Times Magazine* cover.

Among multiple and shifting moral discourses, denaturalizations of the dominant ethics can initiate a reworking of moral meaning that is micropolitical and pragmatic (Deleuze and Guattari, 1981: 65). Locally and temporarily, morality gets reshaped. Representations of AIDS provide good examples. An early activist poster on San Francisco buses showed, in a visual style that recalled Benetton ads, young, happy, brightly dressed, interracial same-sex couples kissing above the slogan, "Kissing doesn't kill." The image was of a liberal morality, opposed to racism and homophobia, individualistic and pleasure-loving. A similar insistence on negotiating the abjection of AIDS into pragmatic moral sense characterized the attempts of ACT UP through the late 1980s to change the AIDS body from victim to warrior (Saalfield and Navarro, 1991: 344). ACT UP members used their bodies to obstruct medical facilities, newspaper offices, TV studios, and Wall Street. They reached out to make loose, temporary alliances between gay men of widely differing politics, lesbians, drug users, and people of color. ACT UP was also fun: "AIDS, we think, is so unglamorous, so unfestive. That's why we are members of ACT UP" (Saalfield and Navarro, 1991: 365). Although ACT UP's tactics were confrontational, its success consisted in occasional compromises that changed the moral status of AIDS bodies from victims and objects to moral, desiring subjects. ACT UP helped HIV-positive people to gain access to drug trials that do not use placebo conditions and that are bigger and broader-based; to get experimental medicines sooner and easier; to be assessed by wider diagnostic criteria; and to have some legal protection and social acceptance.[14]

After AIDS activists ripped off Benetton, Benetton repaid the compliment with an image of a naked male torso with "HIV-positive" stamped on the arm. Because health and beauty were resignified on this body *as* HIV, HIV's abjection was transformed. Although some criticized Benetton for reducing a potentially fatal medical condition to surface decoration, outing HIV so literally on the healthy body had, in the early 1990s, a moral impact. Although it lacks the moral force of sex and race, such a mark is like a tattoo, introducing transience and conditionality into a whole series of moral laws. Tattoos are outside the body but also part of it, "inside" the skin. Tattoos mark you as outside the social order but still disruptively present within it. They are signs of being working-class, low-life, or outcast—a prisoner, a sailor, a Holocaust survivor (Acker, 1988: 140). Though other phenomena have similar effects—the word "thief" spat at the young Genet, visible Kaposi's sarcoma lesions on a person living with AIDS, the blood of the HIV-positive performance artist Ron Athey flowing from the needles he inserts—tattoos are the clearest stigmata (Sartre, 1963: 163). The HIV stamp in the Benetton ad showed how abjection, the beyond of morality, is not inside or outside but is a threshold where the repressed meets the sanctioned, and is thus never fixed but always negotiable.[15]

Other representations have negotiated the body with AIDS into the moral mainstream more subtly. The memorial AIDS Quilt is depressing for

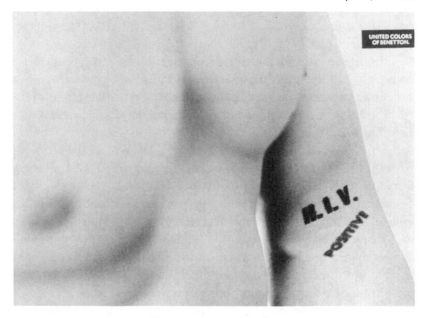

Figure 13. HIV-Positive. *Courtesy United Colors of Benetton.*

many people living with AIDS, and its success could be read as meaning that the only culturally acceptable gay man is a dead one (Nunokawa, 1991: 319). However, the effect of a great expanse of lost lives spread out before the gaze like a graveyard is to turn the morally excommunicated body with AIDS into an object of mourning, both for the bereaved, whose losses previously had no public face, and for those less directly affected.[16] Unique among AIDS representations, the quilt constructs AIDS deaths as a national calamity.

A bridge for the body with AIDS to cross into the moral mainstream is created in recent elegiac AIDS fictions. In the last scene of the film *Longtime Companion* (1990), gay men who died from AIDS are resurrected, sexless and healthy, in a golden haze, on a paradisial pre-HIV Fire Island beach. Although this scene seems in its nostalgia to canonize everyone who has died of AIDS, it can also be understood as the movie's translation of AIDS bodies into a moral discourse held in common by a broad audience (Clum, 1993: 208; Miller, 1993: 300–302). In the newer AIDS movie *Kids* (1995), the strategy, though more confrontational, is equally pragmatic. The narrative's stark posing of a good protagonist, a near-virgin, against a promiscuous, infecting villain seems crude, but it may be what is required to put HIV in the picture for an audience among whom it is often dismissed. At the same time, the film has its own golden moments, its visual hedonism and its excesses of drink, sex, and drugs, with which it keeps the moral ambiguities of abjection in play.

Evangelism is perhaps the tradition least able to recognize the AIDS body. This tradition generally addresses AIDS by loving the sinner while hating and forbidding the sin. Even here, though, a closer integration of the AIDS body into moral communion with the church sometimes seems possible. The Metropolitan Community Church, the biggest gay congregation in the United States, is evangelical. Its minister is Mel White, Falwell's ghostwriter for *If I Should Die before I Wake* and a member of ACT UP, who sets forbidden bodies against texts about Jesus' love: "I find six lines [in the Bible] that can be controversial about gay and lesbian people. But I find a million lines that refer to love and to grace and to forgiveness and to moving together" (*Larry King Live*, 1993: 3). Perhaps only from the inside, with an apocalyptic tone and a commitment to biblical texts, can this negotiation of the profane into the discourse of salvation be achieved.

Evangelists are even more antiabortionist than they are antihomosexual (Stacey and Gerard, 1992: 116). For them, abortion is a kind of crucifixion. Protesters are engaged in a "holy war" that, for some, justifies killing abortionists. Pro-choice arguments seem similarly, though less violently, uncompromising, asserting female rights and fetal nonpersonhood. The antiabortion position, however, is not uniform, unanimous, nor that old. It is also heavily embroiled with other scientific, feminist, and utilitarian positions. Sometimes, too, it invokes the Holocaust or the antiwar movement of the 1960s.[17] Similarly, pro-choice advocates have varied opinions on the beginning of fetal life, federal abortion funding, and welfare restrictions for mothers. Yet it is the confrontational, denaturalizing quality of the positions that allows them to reshape each other's meanings. In the process, they negotiate considerable shifts within each moral discourse and even some points of convergence. "Any person who takes a serious stand on abortion" will have to struggle with some "complex and confounding reality," writes Falwell—and White, who must know a lot about such reality (qtd. in Harding, 1992: 90). Frequently, the pro-life position, describing unwed mothers as victims of unthinking or abusive men, approaches a critique of patriarchy. Women pro-life activists think that other women need support and knowledge to make the right decision. This leniency expresses not just religious paternalism but a quasi-feminist awareness of the difficulties of many women's lives. A similar awareness is apparent in the evangelical emphasis on support for pregnant women and mothers. Falwell's "liberty godparent homes," set up to support pregnant, unmarried women, are concrete examples, as is pro-life refusal to support Republican proposals to deny welfare to pregnant unmarried teenagers.[18]

The pro-life agenda of fetal "rights" often seems to be a cover for asserting the Law of the Father (Tribe, 1990: 234). Nevertheless, it has the effect of subverting individualized women's rights arguments, suggesting the impossibility of a morality in which the fetus does not exist and abortion decisions are strictly private. This subversion of individual "rights" has stimulated pro-choice advocates to adopt a more inclusive ethics, within which female and fetal interests may differ, leading to inevitable but livable conflict.[19] In this ethics, women may be refused abortions if they are not clear about their wishes. "Women would be passive or hostile, or they'd tell us they had to have an abortion so their abusive boyfriend wouldn't leave them," said Charlotte Taft, Dallas abortion clinic founder. "We used to try to be nonjudgmental.... Now we ... work it through" (qtd. in *New York Times*, 10 May 1992). Some abortion activists are also trying to understand the issue more broadly in the context of women's health and are recognizing that many poor women and women of color require support for reproduction, not abortion. Released from the constraints of a zero-sum morality where women's and fetal rights are opposed, both sides begin to sound remarkably alike when they talk about women and children's connectedness and shared lives. Such a resolution in an ethic of "feminine" care is not thoroughgoing, because pro-choice activists are not all committed to the notion of an essentially female ethics, and pro-lifers may step back from ceding decision making to women. Nevertheless, people on both sides are paying respect to principles of moral judgment incompatible with their own, in a way that sometimes produces material changes in discourse and action.

However, such contingent and temporary moral negotiations are not the only means to revalue the moral body. The ideology of the body's privacy makes it easy to ignore such modest moral challenges. Repeated, brash performances of off-limits morality may do more to prevent the assimilation of morally disempowered positions. These performances may involve phenomena that the mainstream culture regards as other, "decorative," "wasteful," "feminine," or "rotten" (Wollen, 1987: 29). Practices associated with homosexuality have been proposed as exemplars. Their effects are disruptive, not redemptive, and their excesses recall to us our presubjective maternal engulfment, passivity, death, and abjection (Bersani, 1989; Edelman, 1991: 14–29). They indicate the limits of morality: "They compel us ... to rethink what we mean and what we expect from communication, and from community" (Bersani, 1994: 18). At such moments, the body of another—her or his carnality and mortality—shows us the ethical necessity, and difficulty, of relationships to others (Lingis, 1995: 177). However, a broader field of events can produce similar effects: the devastating expanse of the AIDS Quilt; the narrative excitement of female violence in movies and press reports; the indrawn breath when a woman aestheticizes her mastectomy scar; the nightmares conjured by a horror movie's slaughterhouse of meanings; the double takes provoked by mixed-race relationships; heads turning, not quite believing, to get a second look at Eva and Adele. When attempts to negotiate bodily morality address such moments rather than trying to forget them, some movement in bodily morality seems possible.

5 | P.C.

The foreigner comes in when the consciousness of my difference arises, and he disappears when we all acknowledge ourselves as foreigners, unamenable to bonds and communities.
Julia Kristeva, *Strangers to Ourselves*

To live in the Borderlands means to
> *put chile in the borscht,*
> *eat whole wheat tortillas,*
> *speak Tex-Mex with a Brooklyn accent;*
> *be stopped by la migra at the border checkpoints . . .*

To survive the Borderlands
> *you must live sin fronteras*
> *be a crossroads.*
Gloria Anzaldúa, "To Live in the Borderlands Means You"

Culture Wars

Oleanna (1992), a play by David Mamet, depicts a war between the sexes on the political correctness battlefield. The two characters, a college student named Carol and her professor, John, face off in his office in each of the play's three acts. The New York opening of the play in fall 1992 found audiences divided on who won and whose side the playwright favored. Even feminists disagreed: Susan Brownmiller, author of *Against Our Will: Men, Women, and Rape* (1975), found the play "exhilarating," while Deborah Tannen, who wrote *You Just Don't Understand: Women and Men in Conversation* (1990), said the play encouraged people to "feel good about a man beating a woman" (*New York Times*, 15 November 1992). In the first act, Carol, who is failing John's course, speaks haltingly and self-deprecatingly as she confesses she doesn't know what he's talking about in class. John, in turn, mouths patronizing assurances with half his attention while the other half is on his tenure battle and purchase of a house.

Mamet structures the dialogue so that the meanings float deliriously. The identities of the two characters metamorphose and worry one another. While Carol appears as self-doubting coed, oppressed woman, and feminist

159

bitch, John appears as condescending patriarch, misogynist brute, and desperate victim. Refusing his argument that grades are unimportant, Carol seems to be speaking of women's dismal history under patriarchy when she says, "I did what you told me. I did, I did everything that, I read your *book*, you told me to buy your book and read it. Everything you *say* I . . . I do" (9). In act 2, they meet at John's request after Carol, on the advice of a "group," has submitted a detailed report to his tenure committee describing John as sexist, racist, and elitist. Particularly damning is her assertion that he offered to allow her to retake the exam if she came "oftener" to his office. The audience heard this offer presented in act 1 as John's ostensibly teacherly, though condescending, effort to help Carol with her studies. In this way, act 2 reinterprets many of John's act 1 words. So, to his incredulity, Carol responds, "If you possess one ounce of that inner honesty you describe in your book, you can look in yourself and see those things that I see" (52). Mamet's dialogue rides such ambiguity to the play's end and thus takes us to an improbable border where sexual harassment meets male bashing.

In act 3, Carol reveals that beyond the damning report, which has endangered John's tenure, she is taking him to court for attempted rape, a charge not warranted by the events on stage. However, after John says, "You vicious little bitch. You think you can come in here with your political correctness and destroy my life? . . . You little *cunt*" (79) and raises a chair against her while she cowers on the floor, his innocence shades into guilt. His act invokes the history of power inequality between men and women, and thus, Carol's charge against him begins to make some historical sense. By shifting the argument onto ideological ground, Mamet keeps the questions in play. Carol has destroyed John's career and jeopardized his family's future, but how else does Carol escape her role as female victim; how else to revise John's alien language; how else to escape his incomprehensible book? Yet does John deserve to be punished for a moral hierarchy he inherited and of which he is not quite conscious? How should moral impasses play out in individual lives? How does one weigh individual injustice against historical injustice; how, indeed, does one separate them?

William Safire traces the origins of political correctness to Mao's "little red book," where one thought is titled "Where Do Correct Ideas Come From?" (1991), but the notion has a longer history in the Communist movement. On the Leninist Left, for instance, it was used approvingly to mean ideas in strict agreement with a certain communist ideology (Berman, 1992: 5). However, since then, debate on the Left has included accusations of rigidity, inflexibility, and overzealous "correctness." According to Safire, the first use of the phrase in the United States was in 1975, when Karen DeCrow, president of the National Organization for Women (NOW), defended NOW's agenda as "politically correct" against attacks by a dissident faction accusing NOW of pandering to the interests of white, middle-class, straight women. DeCrow used the phrase without irony, but it quickly became an ironic commentary from within on the dogmatisms of feminist, Left, and gay politics. In 1993, it was used 4,643 times in periodicals cataloged in the Lexis-Nexis database (Gitlin, 1995: 487). Even conservatives who, for a time, used the term affirmatively did so with a degree of irony. For instance, George F. Will in 1985 described someone as "one of Washington's dozen or so Correct Thinkers" (qtd. in Safire, 1991).[1]

From the early 1990s to the present, P.C. has gathered many moral issues under its capacious umbrella, from the ethics of ethnic slurs to course curricula. A University of Connecticut student, Nina Wu, was disciplined for posting a joke notice of people to be shot on sight on her dorm room door. The people included "preppies," "bimbos," "men without chest hair," and "homos." Wu was evicted from her dormitory and barred from other dormitories and the campus cafeteria. University authorities relented, however, when she launched a federal lawsuit. The strict student code outlawing "personal slurs or epithets based on race, sex, ethnic origin, disability, religion or sexual orientation" was then revised. Ironically, this strict version of the code had been spurred by an incident of severe harassment of Asian American women students who were spat and jeered at as "Oriental faggots" on their way to a dance. The code was formulated to express the university's opposition to all forms of harassment, but the broader community, in this case, judged not only that individual rights took precedence but that the code itself violated the First Amendment (Adler, 1990b: 48). In putting forward the strict code, the university had allied itself with the violated minority, thereby protecting the smaller unit with its larger force, its ability to codify rules. The university offered this newly formulated code as a First Amendment-like protection of freedom, even though it might have violated the letter of the First Amendment.

Grabbing headlines in the spring of 1990 were two City College professors at the City University of New York (CUNY), both accused of racism, both of them claiming their First Amendment rights. Michael Levin, a philosophy professor who espoused the theory that blacks are innately less intelligent than whites, was picketed by students and censured for his opinions by the college faculty senate in 1988, and was removed from his introductory classes midsemester the following year. Later, the City College dean of humanities sent a letter to students informing them of Levin's controversial views on race, gender, and homosexuality and gave them the option of switching to another instructor. A federal court case resulted in which the judge ruled that Levin's civil rights had been violated: The 23 April 1990 issue of CUNY's *Student Advocate* quoted the judge's opinion that Levin's case "raises serious constitutional questions that go to the heart of the current national debate on what has come to be denominated as 'political correctness' in speech and thought on the campuses of the nation's colleges and universities."

Riding on the coattails of this judgment, City College officials stalled in the even more widely publicized case of Leonard Jeffries, chair of the Department of Black Studies. Jeffries created controversy with his argument for the racial superiority of Africans over Europeans (of "sun" people over "ice" people) and with his accusation that a Jewish cabal deliberately excluded and denigrated blacks in Hollywood. In Levin's case the moral conflict between the university community and the Constitution was resolved in federal court, and in the Jeffries affair university officials at first evaded resolution by renewing his contract for chair by just one year rather than the traditional three years.[2] As the *Observer* put it, "When a rightwing Jewish professor won a racism case, a black anti-semite benefitted," but all involved felt they had lost—Jeffries had lost his constitutional right to free speech, and his opponents had lost their right to be protected from hate speech (Tran, 1991). Complicating the free speech issue is the issue of what constitutes evidence in academia. Should professors like Levin and Jeffries be held to a single standard? Given the disagreements in higher education over whether rational argument leads to truth and whether objectivity is even possible, how can such standards be formulated? Critics of Jeffries were accused of Eurocentrism, and Levin's critics, of being unscientific. Institutional indecision regarding proper scholarship becomes embroiled in indecision regarding what constitutes free speech. The moral frames of the university and the Constitution complicate one another.

> When the native hears a speech about Western culture he pulls out his knife—or at least he makes sure it is within reach. The violence with which the supremacy of white values is affirmed and the aggressiveness which has permeated the victory of these values over the ways of life and of thought of the native mean that, in revenge, the native laughs in mockery when Western values are mentioned in front of him. (Fanon, 1968: 43)

These words from Frantz Fanon appear as part of an illustration to a *Newsweek* article on P.C., with a quotation from the Declaration of Independence on the opposing page. The graphic dramatically poses freedom of speech as represented by the Declaration against Fanon's account of anticolonial violence as if Fanon's quote were an endorsement of speech codes and multicultural curricula. In fact, many of the arguments for multiculturalism do involve a Fanonlike critique of the centrality given to Western culture and the violence with which it has been enforced. In this argument, the relationship of oppressed or colonized people to the moral tradition of their oppressors is determined not by the contents of that tradition but by the fact that it belongs to the oppressor. As the oppressors liberate the native, according to Fanon, they "point out to him the specificity and wealth of Western values." When the native hears the phrase "Western values," however, he feels "a sort of stiffening or muscular lockjaw" (qtd. in Adler, 1990b: 48–49).

Multiculturalism, the movement to include a plurality of cultures in textbooks and course curricula, aims to correct the immorality of such cultural hegemony. It was prompted by an egalitarian ethic of direct representation. Mark Twain in *Huckleberry Finn* may speak for white male ambitions to escape restraints on individual freedom, the reasoning goes, but you also need, for instance, Kate Chopin, Richard Wright, Leslie Marmon Silko, and Gloria Naylor in order to include white women, black men, Native Americans, and black women. The most common strategy has been to replace traditional with nontraditional texts. Other strategies are directed more pointedly at renaming and contextualizing the traditional canon. Exemplifying a trend in cultural studies, a panel at the Modern Language Association convention in December 1997 entitled "Whiteness and Heterosexuality" isolated these identity markers in literature, thus making them a bit morally suspect. Another strategy was adopted by a Georgetown University assistant professor of English, Valerie Babb, who offers a course entitled "White Male Writers." This course includes Herman Melville, Nathaniel Hawthorne, James Fenimore Cooper, and Twain on its syllabus. Babb notes that the course presents these writers as "just one small group within a large body of literature. . . . Just as we say native American writers, just as we say black women writers, these are white male writers" (*New York Times,* 4 March 1991). Annette Kolodny suggests that notions of canonicity be dropped altogether and all texts be read in their historical and social contexts (1985: 302–4). For instance, Cooper could be read for the information he provides about nineteenth-century U.S. attitudes toward Native Americans rather than as articulating a universal U.S. narrative, say, about the nation's "manifest destiny" to stretch to the Pacific.[3]

Although across the country "multicultural" courses are part of college general education requirements, the notion of multiculturalism has come under increasing attack from the Center and Left, where these courses originated. Some argue that multiculturalism, despite good intentions, may lead to moral impasse, to another form of ghettoization (Lind, 1995: 3). Or it may "essentialize" cultures, reducing them to a fixed set of qualities that do not accurately reflect their organic, complex, and hybrid nature (Bhabha, 1994: 3).[4]

Underlying these imbroglios are deep ambivalences about personal and national identity that confound moral choice. In the absence of a universal morality, moral decisions depend on at least a momentary agreement about who we are. If we cannot identify the subject position of the person to whom we are speaking or come to an agreement, however transitory, about that position, how can we begin to formulate right action (see Bhabha, 1990: 1–3)? *Oleanna's* John and Carol talk past each other partially because they define one another rigidly as cartoon categories: at first, as underprivileged, underprepared female student versus powerful, omniscient male professor, and later, as man hater versus rapist. Similarly, underlying the debate about the canon are basic disagreements on who we are as a nation and what values we espouse. For some, teaching *Huckleberry Finn,* for instance, means passing on to the next generation moral values, such as radical individualism and freedom, that are consonant with the democratic enterprise. For others, the book documents unreasonable male fear of domesticity and of the women associated with it.

The avalanche of reports documenting clashes over books and appropriate subject matter, such as in the Jeffries case, reveals deep epistemological insecurity—an insecurity that is related to instability in ideas of subjectivity and nationhood. Today, we do not share an understanding of what knowledge is. What does it mean that "Columbus discovered America," in light of the prior presence of Native Americans? What was knowledge is now myth or even prejudice. Moreover, basic democratic vocabulary, such as "equality," is contested. When President Lyndon B. Johnson issued the executive order for affirmative action in 1965, he wrote, "We seek . . . not just equality as a right and a theory but equality as a fact and equality as a result" (qtd. in Lemann, 1995: 41).[5] In a climate of intensified millennial doubt, conservatives and liberals continue to wrestle with the value and meaning of affirmative action. What exactly does equality as a value require? Should we judge job or admissions applications differentially to achieve it? Should affirmative action be based on race and gender, or should it be based on class? If we can't agree on what "equality as a fact and equality as a result" means, how do we move toward it? Once metanarratives are surrendered, moral judgments may issue from specific identity positions, which are themselves fluid and unstable, just as are notions of nationhood. Thus, floating in the

P.C. debates—on sexual harassment, free speech, the literary canon and multiculturalism, and affirmative action—are multiple indeterminacies. The debates raise the question of how we can describe our moral present and plan our moral future, if we cannot agree on what "ours" means.

P.C.-isms

Codes of speech and behavior are pinned to specific identities. Until tested in the courts, the University of Michigan's policy on discrimination by students included "any behavior, verbal or physical, that stigmatizes or victimizes an individual on the basis of race, ethnicity, religion, sex, sexual orientation, creed, national origin, ancestry, age, marital status, handicap or Vietnam-era veteran status."[6] The lengths to which this list goes to name every possible offended category have been exceeded in other efforts to place identity-based curbs on "incorrect" language and behavior. In their heyday, new categories of discrimination included classism, fatism, lookism (the use of a standard for beauty), speciesism (the valuing of humans over other animals), laughism ("inappropriately directed laughter," banned at the University of Connecticut), handism (privileging of the right-handed), scentism (imposing of artificial scents on others), and homeism (oppression of the homeless). In the "correct" vocabulary, the notion of difference replaces that of disability, giving rise to the term "differently abled" to describe the disabled. However, this euphemism does not escape the implication that people with disabilities deviate from the standard or norm. So, too, the words "challenged" and "special" are used as euphemisms for perceived disadvantages, terms that have gained some currency in the popular media, as with the "Special Olympics" for the disabled. Pets' subordinate status is chivalrously corrected with the phrase "animal companion."[7]

Parodies, omnipresent in newspapers, on late-night television, and in popular journals, treat a single personal characteristic as an identity. One journalist wrote that short people should be called the "vertically challenged"; "birthmarkism" was suggested as a suitable designation for the prejudice that Ted Kennedy Jr. spoke of in the *Boston Globe* against people with birthmarks; and the *New Republic* proposed "shavism" to describe negative attitudes toward the hirsute (Leo, 1991). Yet much of what is parodied reappears in serious use: reporting on an antidiscrimination law being considered by the city council of Santa Cruz, California, a reporter interviewed Gloria Nieto, "a 4-feet-11-inch lesbian of Mexican descent" who described herself as "vertically challenged" (*New York Times,* 13 February 1992).

The anxious identity politics that such vocabulary symptomizes occasionally leads to correctives that obscure the ethics they were meant to salve. The Antioch College Sexual Offense Prevention Policy adopted in fall 1993, which became a particular media target, requires verbal consent for every step in a sexual interaction.[8] Although this policy applies equally to men and women, its "correctness" is in its attempt to circumvent identity politics: it aims to separate behavior from culturally constructed roles and to base it on in-progress contractual negotiation. Its strategy is to repress the history and culture of gender and sexual relations, to start over with a new, ahistorical code. But, as psychoanalysts know, the repressed always returns, and intimate relations cannot be micromanaged. P.C. policies based on such amnesia or on the erasure of particular subject positions (man, woman) are always disingenuous, because they were first drawn up in recognition of social and political differentials attached to these positions.

Intuitive Morality

As in other arenas of morality, positions around political correctness are often intuitive. They may feel objective, natural, or universal, but they are not. Pierre Bourdieu's argument regarding art also applies to P.C. morality. Certain espousals feel like truths, like "gifts of nature," but are more like habits or intuitions—related to MacIntyre's idea of emotivist moral decision making (Bourdieu, 1990: 211).[9] In act 3 of *Oleanna*, Carol responds to John's complaint that her accusations are based merely on her personal feelings: "The issue here is not what I 'feel.' It is not my 'feelings,'" she asserts, but "evidence" and "facts" (Mamet, 1992: 63–64). Carol's claims of objectivity and factuality in structuring her moral position are like many such claims: although they feel like truth, they really sit in an individual's guts. Although it is moral emotivism, it is experienced as moral fact.

Feelings are often referenced as grounds for arguments in P.C. discussions. Such references to feelings have a long history, one that strict interpreters of First Amendment rights traditionally argue against. Espousing the traditional pre-P.C. position, Justice Oliver Wendell Holmes wrote that feelings are not part of the free speech calculus: "It's too bad that sensitivity, courtesy, and civility have to take a back seat to free expression, but anything ought to be sayable" (Posner, 1992: 325). But free speech fundamentalism that advocates sacrificing hurt feelings for the greater good of free speech is itself often based on moral intuition, on an intuitive feeling of right. The ex-president of Yale Benno Schmidt asserted that to restrict free speech is to surrender humanity to its anxieties and weaknesses: "It is to elevate our fear and our ignorance over our capacity for a liberated and humane mind" (qtd. in Wortman, 1991: 56). Major terms in Schmidt's argument, such as "our capacity for a liberated and humane mind," are not analyzed but are offered as universal values that everyone understands in the same way.

However, intuitive morality cannot distinguish between free speech and hate speech. What P.C. and multicultural evangelists call hate speech is free speech to others. A waitress, "Barbara," was "highly offended" by a patron's reading *Playboy* at her station in a 1991 incident at Bette's Diner in Berkeley, California. She and her manager approached the patron, a journalist, and demanded he put away the magazine. Mike Hughes, the journalist, retorted that *he* was "highly offended" by the abrogation of his freedom of speech. Spurred on by articles in the *Contra Costa Times*, the *San Francisco Chronicle*, and the *Village Voice*, demonstrators held a *Playboy* read-in at the diner while counterdemonstrators tried to shout them down with accusations of pornography and sexual harassment. Both groups invoked free speech. On one side were those protecting it through the First Amendment; on another side were those categorizing *Playboy* as "hate literature" and the reading of it as a "hate crime"—thus, in their minds, exempt from free speech protection. As one demonstrator's placard demanded, "What about her [Barbara's] free speech?" In reporting on the incident, Nat Hentoff reminded readers of Gloria Steinem's extreme moral judgment of *Playboy*: "A woman reading *Playboy* feels a little like a Jew reading a Nazi manual" (qtd. in Hentoff, 1992). The waitress defended her response in emotional terms: "I was so appalled and shocked. . . . I felt as if I had been struck." Others defended their positions with arguments of "sexual harassment in the workplace" or by saying that the real issue was "power," the "power of white men to impose their standards on anyone, no matter how humiliating" (qtd. in Hentoff, 1992). Thus, the assault on free speech was measured by colliding intuitions, colliding feelings of truth, that made the issue undecidable.

President George Bush's positions regarding the First Amendment were notoriously intuitive, an exemplar of confused, emotional moral judgments in the P.C. wars. Take his vacillations in 1991: in his infamous May 4 University of Michigan commencement address, he slammed P.C. "political extremists" for "abusing the privilege of free speech" but at the same time accused them of denying it, of declaring certain topics "off-limits, certain expressions off-limits" (qtd. in Cockburn, 1991: 1). This inconsistency could be counted on to appear in Bush's other stands on free speech issues despite his many assertions of the importance of free speech. That summer, the Supreme Court upheld his administration's gag order on medical staff counseling patients about abortion in federally funded family planning clinics, even when a woman's health was endangered by pregnancy. In January, his military commanders barred the media from access to the Persian Gulf War front.

The first congressional siege on the National Endowment for the Arts (NEA) in 1989 also demonstrated how easily intuitive morality takes over P.C. issues. Performance artist Karen Finley, who was denied funding by the NEA, points out that by the standards that Senators Alphonse D'Amato and Jesse Helms used, there would be numerous "empty frames" of confiscated art: Jasper Johns for desecrating the flag; Mary Cassatt for painting nude children; and Pablo Picasso, along with his children, for urinating on his sculptures to achieve a certain patina (Finley, 1992: 282).[10] Traditional art, after all, makes quite liberal use of female nudes, and rape and dismemberment are familiar themes. As D'Amato tore up a likeness of Andres Serrano's *Piss Christ* and attacked the NEA on 18 May 1989 during a Senate session, he was banking on unanalyzed intuitive moral judgments about the unacceptable conjunction of body fluids and a sacred subject. The fact that the art of Serrano could easily pass the Miller obscenity standard—the current legal standard—did not lessen the expression of moral outrage that ensued (Vance, 1992: 221).

One lesson of this emotivism, this intuitive morality, is that the speech you most value is your own. It often represents a subject position you identify with. The Guerrilla Girls poster of 1989 that cautions "RELAX SENATOR HELMS, THE ART WORLD *IS* YOUR KIND OF PLACE!" reminds us that art is owned and negotiated mainly by white, heterosexual males. The number of homoerotic representations of the penis, such as in Robert Mapplethorpe's photographs, are very few: "The majority of exposed penises in major museums belong to the Baby Jesus" (Guerrilla Girls, qtd. in Bolton, 1992: 313). Jesse Helms is explicit about what subject positions he excludes. In a 1991 letter to Jerry Falwell soliciting his participation in a campaign to regulate more severely the National Endowment for the Arts, he itemizes them: "the homosexual 'community,' the feminists, the civil libertarians, the pro-abortionists, the flag burners . . ." (qtd. in Bolton, 1992: 306).

Political opportunism counts on mass emotivist morality. Senator Bob Dole's attack on Time Warner gangsta rap labels, which referred to incendiary lyrics from various tracks, is a case in point (*New York Times*, 8 June 1995). Although Dole did not publicly repeat them, popular magazines such as the *New Yorker* were happy to print lyrics such as those by the alternative white band Nine Inch Nails that, in equating a penis with a gun, threaten, "Got me a big old dick and . . . / I'll make you suck it" (qtd. in Gates, 1995: 35). Such lyrics galvanize the intuitive, emotivist moral response of many *New Yorker* readers even if the article palliates the lyrics as an anti-

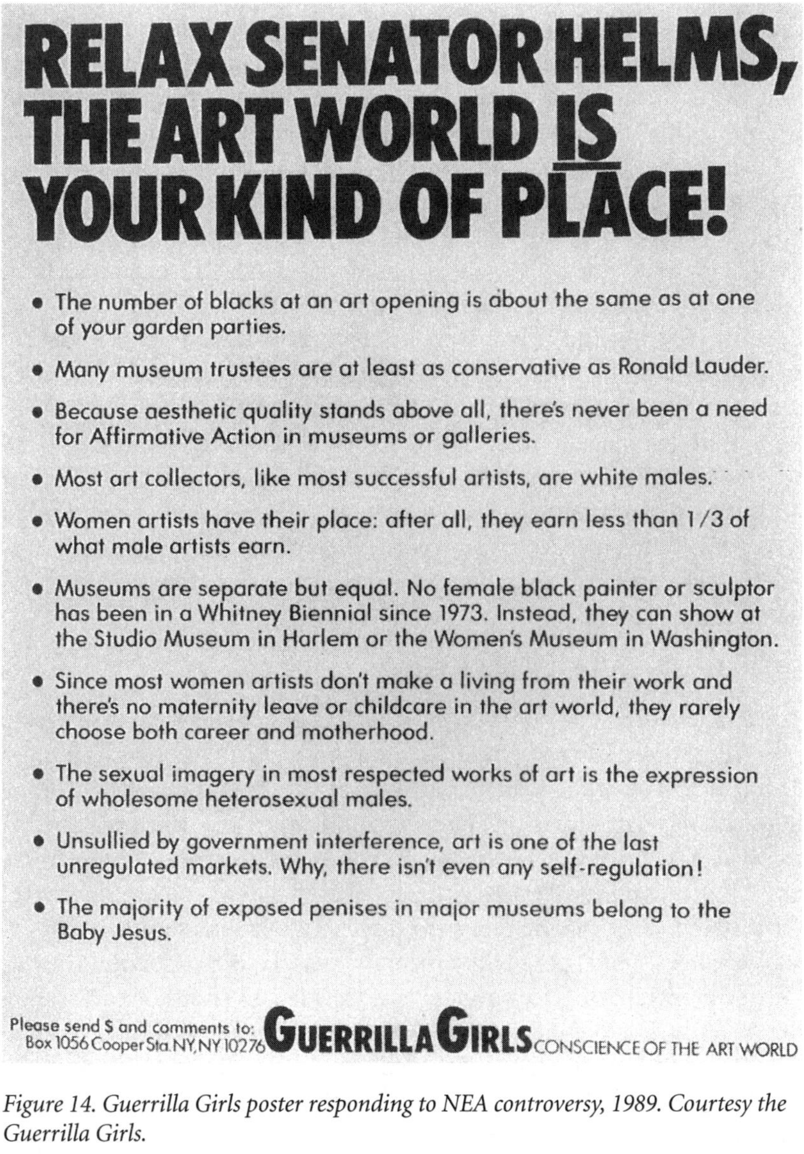

RELAX SENATOR HELMS, THE ART WORLD IS YOUR KIND OF PLACE!

- The number of blacks at an art opening is about the same as at one of your garden parties.

- Many museum trustees are at least as conservative as Ronald Lauder.

- Because aesthetic quality stands above all, there's never been a need for Affirmative Action in museums or galleries.

- Most art collectors, like most successful artists, are white males.

- Women artists have their place: after all, they earn less than 1/3 of what male artists earn.

- Museums are separate but equal. No female black painter or sculptor has been in a Whitney Biennial since 1973. Instead, they can show at the Studio Museum in Harlem or the Women's Museum in Washington.

- Since most women artists don't make a living from their work and there's no maternity leave or childcare in the art world, they rarely choose both career and motherhood.

- The sexual imagery in most respected works of art is the expression of wholesome heterosexual males.

- Unsullied by government interference, art is one of the last unregulated markets. Why, there isn't even any self-regulation!

- The majority of exposed penises in major museums belong to the Baby Jesus.

Please send $ and comments to: **GUERRILLA GIRLS** CONSCIENCE OF THE ART WORLD
Box 1056 Cooper Sta. NY, NY 10276

Figure 14. Guerrilla Girls poster responding to NEA controversy, 1989. Courtesy the Guerrilla Girls.

bourgeois assault or as an attempt to "out" racist stereotypes. Shortly after Dole's campaign, Time Warner began negotiations to sell its gangsta rap interests (*New York Times*, 10 August 1995). However, as Dole must have known, nothing much is accomplished when Time Warner ditches its controversial labels. Bill Adler, president of NuYo Records, which specializes in rap, points out, "Of course, the reality is that you haven't changed what's in the record bins one iota. . . . Imagine if a modern-day temperance society decided to target Seagram, and got it to sell off its liquor divisions. It might be a way for them to flex muscles, but you know it's not going to stop a soul from drinking" (qtd. in Gates, 1995: 36).

Although Dole attacked rap, a few years earlier he had contradictorily campaigned against the Children's Television Act, which would curb violence in children's programming and advertising (*New York Times*, 4 June 1995). Similarly, Senator D'Amato's crusade against the NEA may have been engineered to deflect attention from accusations that he misused Department of Housing and Urban Development (HUD) low-income housing money in his hometown (Vance, 1992b: 113). By presenting *Piss Christ* as sensationally sacreligious, he took center stage as national moral guardian, a position that made him less vulnerable to allegations concerning HUD. How could HUD compete with *Piss Christ* in the media, which themselves are skilled at playing public emotivist morality? Here morality is entangled with the intuitive, media hype, and political expediency, as well as with varying subject positions and public convictions about what makes an ethical nation.

Restless Signifiers and the First Amendment

The implications of the First Amendment are always under discussion. The meanings attached to its signifiers shift continually. Among the most adamant of constitutional defenders of free speech, Thomas Jefferson interpreted the First Amendment as prohibiting only "previous restraint" on free speech—that is, no laws could be made to prohibit speech before it was made. Yet even Oliver Wendell Holmes believed that not only false but also "true statements could be punished" under certain circumstances, for instance, when "speech posed a 'clear and present danger' to society" (qtd. in Dworkin, 1992: 55). Free speech has a long legal history of constraints placed on it, despite fundamentalist rhetoric. Among the exceptions to the First Amendment, the most well known is the "fighting words" ruling of the Supreme Court in 1942, which amends free speech in the case of speech that directly causes violence. Such exceptions themselves are objects of wide interpretation. Although strict interpretations limit the "fighting words" exception to speech that incites immediate violence, Yale law professor Ruth Wedgwood argues that the history of victimization must be considered in determining what speech constitutes "fighting words": "Whether any groups need protection against racial speech may in part be a function of history. In the United States we have the obligation to ask whether our own moral history has any bearing on treatment of racial speech." To bolster her stand, she points to Germany's ban on anti-Semitic speech. She reasons that "Where nothing is unspeakable, nothing is undoable" (qtd. in Wortman, 1991: 62). This interpretation may extend fighting words to include what we know as "hate speech"—even, as in the case of Bette's Diner, to include *Playboy.*

If free speech is, then, a movable moral feast, is it determined, as First Amendment advocate Schmidt fears, by the "politics of the moment," or simply by who yells the loudest (Wortman, 1991: 59)? For Owen Fiss, professor of public law at Yale, the First Amendment protects not the individual right to speak but, rather, "public discourse." According to Fiss, the purpose of the First Amendment is to "enable collectivities to make up their minds in public debate. It is not 'freedom *to speak*' but 'freedom *of speech.*'" Public debate, rather than individual license to say anything, is the guarantee made by the First Amendment. However, argues Fiss, the control of public speech is now in the hands of those who control the means of communication. Thus, speech is vulnerable to the market, to those with the "wealth and the advertising budget." An example of a misinterpretation of First Amendment rights in favor of the powerful, writes Fiss, can be found in the Federal Communication Commission's (FCC) revocation of the Fairness Doctrine. In this doctrine, "equal time" for viewpoints dissenting from those aired by radio and TV stations was required. In rescinding equal time, the FCC argued that it was protecting the First Amendment rights of radio and TV owners. Such reinterpretations of individual rights offer those rights to the privileged. Under such a rule, only the rich and powerful have access to public discourse. Fiss endorses the view that, in order to be in harmony with the spirit of the First Amendment, laws governing speech should be designed to provide dissenters with access to the means of communication, thus guaranteeing free public discourse (1996: 63).

The swamps, snarls, elisions, muddles, competing claims, intuitions, and emotivism around P.C. issues exhibit the moral uncertainties that discourses need to retain. In the interstices of these disagreements, there is room for both Nine Inch Nails and Senator Helms—for all those who speak and capture our attention, which does not include everyone but does include many. Having thrived since the early days of the Republic, contests between First Amendment theories, for this reason alone, are productive. So, too, are contradictions, for instance, between an analysis of oppressive representations of women in advertising and the pleasure that those ads provide. Camille Paglia, media-wise gadfly of academic feminism, multiculturalism, and postmodernism, often tells the story of her challenging an "Ivy-league" feminist lecturer on sexual oppression in fashion photography. Where this lecturer saw "decapitation" and "strangulation" in Revlon and other ads, Paglia saw the birth of Venus and evocations of King Tut. Paglia celebrates fashion photography as "great art" and criticizes the "feminist inability to deal with beauty and pleasure" (1991: 33).

Such contests within feminism have dislodged the moral complacency of the subject position that early second-wave feminists assumed. Paglia was one of the minor blips in feminism. The nature of the challenges to feminism has varied. While the first challenges came from those not included in the white, middle-class feminist agenda of the 1970s, later challenges had less to do with inclusiveness than with the entire notion of gender. A series of antifeminist feminists attacked previous premises. Katie Roiphe targeted the "women-as-victims" discourse, especially regarding rape (1993: 51–84), and Christina Hoff Sommers saw the feminist idea of an all-encompassing "patriarchy" as simply paranoia (1994: 230). So too, woman, the very category of feminist analysis, became elusive. In view of sex-change operations, transvestism, and other biological and cultural variables, where is the precise border between masculine and feminine, anyway (Garber, 1989: 371–75)? Moreover, one is not perpetually identified only as a woman. As Denise Riley writes, it is "not possible to live twenty-four hours a day soaked in the immediate awareness of one's sex" (1988: 96). At any rate, writes Judith Butler, all gender is drag, related to imitation or performance (1991: 21). Such disagreements are more than academic. They complicate our ideas of gender, the political agendas undertaken on its behalf, and the morality attached to it. They may, via Roiphe, decrease the measures taken against rape at a college campus or fuel, via Sommers, an administrator's inclination to cut women's studies, but on the whole, feminist discourse expands, and more positions, all of which have ethical implications, are at least heard.

Like "woman," the word "nigger" also has a multivalence that keeps in view the moral ambivalence of First Amendment arguments. It varies its meanings not just among whites but also among African Americans. It can be used descriptively, to mean dark-skinned and African-looking, or affectionately, in camaraderie. It can be used politically, as Ice-T does in "Straight Up Nigga" (1991), to remind African Americans of their subordinate status in the United States: "BLACK PEOPLE MIGHT GET MAD, / CAUSE THEY DON'T SEE, / THAT THEY'RE LOOKED UPON, / AS A NIGGA JUST LIKE ME." Sometimes "nigga" works as an invocation of powers, including powers that white society finds dangerous: "I'M A . . . GRINDIN GROOVIN FLY-GIRL-GRABBIN HORNY GUN-SHOOTIN LONGHAIRED HAVIN NIGGA." "Nigga" can also be used more directly to evoke the fantasy of an urban black threat to comfortable white and black suburbia. Ice Cube's "Nigga Ya Love to Hate" (1990) says, "Your mother warned you about me," and "It's time / to take a trip to the suburbs," while voices interject, "Yo, you ain't doin nothing positive for the brothers—what you got to say for yourself?" and "I would *love* to shoot you nigger." The word "nigger" also foregrounds the differentials in power between middle-class and inner-city African Americans, but more often than not, as Ice-T recognizes, the word "nigger" is simply rejected by black people of all classes.

P.C. discourse centering on the use of language, of particular vocabulary, assumes that language has power, that, for instance, allowing people to name themselves helps ensure social equality. The assumption is that speaking can change the world, that using "humanity" rather than "mankind" or using "s/he," "him or her," or even "herm" can alter our sense that the masculine is the norm. These language changes seem to stimulate and emblematize social shifts. Many writers, though, contest their real effects. Barbara Ehrenreich points out their economic impotence: "It's silly to mistake verbal purification for genuine social reform. Even after all women are 'Ms.' and all people are 'he or she,' women will still only earn 65¢ for every dollar earned by men" (1991b). Although they will not end racism or sexism, the various values of "nigger" and "woman" enrich the discourse around race and gender. They help to both formulate and demonstrate a multitude of ethical positions on identities.

In addition, this complexity in subject positions opens up opportunities for moral alliances with other subject positions at different locations and moments. Such crossover in subject positions may be partially why *Newsweek* chose the Nina Wu story, in which an undergraduate with an Asian name challenged a policy initially formulated because of an incident of hate speech against Asian American women. Her public declaration against "bimbos" and "homos" allied her morally with a subject position that may well have included Asians on its list of pariahs. Nevertheless, such instabilities, the oscillation between reading Wu as minority (Asian American) and majority (heterosexual), prod not only some thinking about the First Amendment on campuses but also received ideas about identities. The morality of free speech depends on who is speaking. The fluctuations in that identity make moral prescription impossible.

Identity, Moral Evasion, and Pragmatism

Solutions to the moral problems of P.C. are often carved with a crude, utilitarian hand. But decisions made on the basis of calculating the costs and the benefits do not always address the underlying issues. They can come off as moral evasion. The overt purpose of the Antioch College dating policy is to stop acquaintance and date rape, but no one can hope to achieve this goal by writing an unenforceable policy. Rather, the policy's benefit is to convey a sense of largesse and fairness in regard to identity politics, a benefit that not everyone agrees outweighs its cost. This equivocal "at least we're doing *something*" posture avoids the difficulties of truly addressing gender inequality. Ad hoc utilitarian decisions can also cover over prejudice—as, for instance, when a Texas Panhandle State District judge, upon the complaint of a divorced father, ruled in 1995 that his ex-wife, who spoke only Spanish to her five-year-old, was "abusing that child" and would be responsible for eventually "relegating her to the position of housemaid." Although he could have reasoned that the child would benefit culturally and economically from bilingualism, the judge accepted the father's more mainstream cost-benefit reasoning and ordered the mother to speak only English to the child (*New York Times*, 30 August 1995).

Moral evasion was also evident in the moves by City College against Leonard Jeffries. First, the college established an independent African American research institute, headed by Edmund W. Gordon, who took over Jeffries' chair when he was removed, thus circumventing Jeffries (*New York Times*, 13 February 1994). Two years later, citing financial exigencies, it downgraded the Department of Black Studies to a program, a move that many, including Herman Badillo, former city councilman, saw as an effort to "finesse the Jeffries problem" (*New York Times*, 19 March 1996). In 1997, the college moved Jeffries to the political science department, an action that Jeffries attempted to block (*New York Times*, 17 June 1997). These moves, made in the name of scholarship and finances, sidestepped the crucial issues concerning the First Amendment and what constitutes scholarship within the academy.

Of greater consequence is the 1995 Supreme Court ruling on affirmative action that also sidestepped the moral issues involved. The 5–4 decision ruled that federal programs classifying people by race can survive only if they are "narrowly tailored" to forward a "compelling governmental interest," including racial discrimination. The decision overturned Supreme Court decisions of 1990 and 1980 that validated affirmative action set-aside programs (*New York Times*, 13 June 1995). Following the 1995 decision, numerous set-aside programs were revised or rescinded.

Any decision that addresses affirmative action, however limited and unreflective, recalls the original morality that instituted it, a morality that drew a certain portrait of the country. The Court's move against affirmative action seems to avoid the complicated moral issues of subjectivity, equality, and nationhood that affirmative action evokes. Its language tries to contain the issue within the limited, practical sphere of "compelling governmental interest." The Court took a stand against "racial discrimination" but treated the phrase as if it were free of history, sloughing off its accumulated meanings in the United States. "Racial discrimination" is treated in this decision as if it applied equally to white men. This implication picks up on a certain paranoid strain among many whites in the United States who believe it is they who are the new victims of prejudice. On a Los Angeles talk show about the O. J. Simpson verdict, for instance, a caller who identified himself as white said, "It doesn't work for white people anymore. . . . There's a new type of prejudice going on against white people that needs to be talked about" (qtd. in *New York Times,* 5 October 1995). The affirmative action decision, especially in its management of the term "racial discrimination," thus interpreted the Constitution as if its meanings were fixed and ahistorical, without origin or context. It pretended that Supreme Court decisions on affirmative action had limited national moral resonance, and it rigidified subject positions around race.

Because they often lack a moral frame beyond costs and benefits, utilitarian responses seem opportunistic. The coming millennium, for instance, will offer many chances to apply utilitarian logic to affirmative action, but such an application will not engage with the longer-lasting, underlying moral conflicts around the issue. In a society that is divided, especially on the West Coast, between an overclass of Anglos and a large underclass of Hispanics, it makes economic and political sense to encourage Hispanics to go to college and stay until they finish (Fields, 1987: A1). The statistic that the population of women and minorities in the workplace will grow to 85% by the year 2000 has also prompted companies to embark on policies and workshops "valuing diversity" to prepare for changes in their workforce. Describing this phenomenon, Kathy Seal, in a business article published in the *American Way,* summed up the cost-and-benefit logic: "It's a case of demography forging a coincidence between morality and good business" (1991: 15). Similarly, the teaser of a *Chronicle of Higher Education* article cautions, "Affirmative action seen no longer as only a moral responsibility, but as a 'matter of national survival'"—not moral responsibility alone but also a profession's requirements make action advisable. Without women entering science and engineering, the article reported, there would be an insufficient professional pool to meet future demands (McMillen, 1987: 9).

Although such positions answer immediate or impending needs, they fail to engage with moral arguments, so that the positions and the decisions they inspire are simply expedient. Moreover, the determination of costs and benefits is always situated. What is valuable from one point of view may be worth nothing from another. What plaintiffs in an affirmative action suit deem a compelling interest for them and for society generally may not meet the court's criteria for "compelling governmental interest"; it depends on the powerful to sanction action rather than on ideas of right or wrong.

Classic pragmatist positions, which hold a vision of the common good, do not successfully negotiate this issue of competing frames of reference. William James, for instance, held that whether a thing was good or bad could be determined subjectively, by an individual's judgment of its effect. This belief depended on the assumption that there was general agreement on what constituted a satisfying effect, on what was a "good" result (Russell, 1945: 824). Such an assumption is also implicit in the influential definition of truth by C. S. Peirce, a precursor of James, as the "opinion which is fated to be ultimately agreed to by all who investigate" (qtd. in Russell, 1945: 824). James's and Peirce's pragmatism succeeds only if morality can be arbitrated by an oligarchy of the like-minded. But because of the assumption of a shared frame of reference, including a shared ethics, this version of pragmatist morality is not particularly useful when there are competing ethics, competing frames of reference. In the post-1960s United States, such an oligarchical morality translates not just into Rortyesque conversation but also into Newt Gingrich's Contract with America, which fails again to recognize different definitions of moral nationhood and different ethical investments in America. In southern California at the end of the twentieth century, for instance, the common good is hard to agree upon across the disparate histories, ethnicities, and economic positions that fracture citizen identities. The kind of pragmatism that supports moral negotiation understands these differences and speculates about commonality across them rather than imposing commonality on them.

How Many Identities Are Enough?

Operating out of a fixed idea of one's or another's subject position can lead to moral impasse, as it does in *Oleanna*. When Eden Jacobowitz called some noisy black University of Pennsylvania sorority pledges "water buffaloes" in 1993, he and they became locked in a contest of white against black and black against Jew, when the pledges interpreted the phrase as a racial slur (*Trenton [N.J.] Times,* 14 May 1993).[11] Later, the pledges withdrew their charges. Of course, the ambiguity and comedy of a slur such as "water buffaloes" makes it easy in this case to back away from rigid racial subject positions into the position that "we are all students" or "we are all human." In other conflagrations in black and white, as with the beating of Rodney King by the L.A. police, such morally evasive maneuvers do not work, and we are left with severely delineated racial identities.

Sometimes such racial confrontations seem local and transient and therefore manageable, but this was not the case with the O. J. Simpson verdicts, especially the first one, which was registered largely along racial lines on college campuses and in bars and offices all over the United States. Much more than the first Rodney King verdict, which exonerated the police who beat him—the dubiousness of which was not universalized but local, attached only to "Los Angeles"—the first Simpson trial was taken as a general demonstration of the contradictory moral evaluations produced by identity politics. The verdict certified to whites that black justice was being done. For many blacks who listened to reports by the white media about "jury nullification"—juries who ignore evidence—it confirmed that whites regarded the predominantly black jury as too biased to make judgments based on evidence and law (*New York Times,* 5 October 1995).

The trend to define oneself as morally allied with a particular race, gender, ethnic group, or sexual preference is being challenged by a competing trend to define oneself as occupying multiple subject positions. Such multiplicity means you must negotiate the moralities these positions require. One consequence may be that your identity is so fragmented that you are left, if not in pieces, in a state of radical individuality, unclear how to proceed or where you belong. Elaine Chang explores this condition in an essay typical of the new personal-narrative writing about identities: "As a Korean Canadian, middle-class, educated, feminist literary critic Anglophone straight woman, I equivocate between my privileges and my oppressions to the extent that I have sometimes wondered if they could . . . nullify one another." In a pun that reveals the complicated morality of such a position, she describes herself as "equi-vocal," balancing and sidestepping various identities at the same time (1994: 263).

Such fragmentation also affects groups: Jee Yeun Lee writes about a 1993 retreat of the Asian Pacifica Lesbian Network, where just such shredding led to smaller and smaller identity groups:

> East Asians, South Asians, Southeast Asians and Pacific Islanders; women of mixed race and heritage; women who identified as lesbians and those who identified as bisexuals; women who were immigrants, refugees, illegal aliens or second generation or more; older women, physically challenged women, women adopted by white families, women from the Midwest. (1995: 210)

One feminist, surveying a similar dilemma, quipped, "from mass movements to support groups to self-help" (Kaye/Kantrowitz, 1996). However, despite the fragmentation, such a condition may encourage reaching out to others whom you recognize as different from yourself. At the end of the lesbian network retreat, the organization decided that it was a coalition of different subject positions (Lee, 1995: 210).

Just as they bring difference into focus, subject positions asserted with definitive borders may lead to the fetishizing of difference and the exclusion of everyone else's subjectivity. Yet experiencing multiple subject positions or accepting membership in a coalition may make you feel moral responsibility more sharply for identities you do not currently occupy, or flow over with sympathy toward those identities you have never occupied (Levinas, 1985: 95, 99).[12] It means moving toward the the consciousness of *la mestiza*, a consciousness of "the borderlands," where one resides in the ambivalence of a number of identities, estranged yet not estranged from them, knowing them all at least partially, and embracing pluralism (Anzaldúa, 1987: 77).[13] What would hate speech be in such a borderland, where subject positions are so intermingled and hybrid that isolating them is superfluous or irrelevant? Sometimes subject positions get taken over, as happened when the white rap group 3rd Base attacked black rapper MC Hammer for being too melodic, that is, not black enough (Baker, 1991: 203). "Black" is separated from skin color and associated with desirable musical qualities that some white musicians may have more of than some black musicians. Such moves, of course, may be the other face of the cultural imperialism Fanon describes, or they may make a bland stew of cultural traditions. But they also may make difference seem not so foreign and therefore not wrong or immoral. An awareness of your own borderland identity and of fluidity in subject positions may foster a moral sense of "we-ness," not in the sense of unified community but in the sense of moral responsibility to the other. It may encourage a move toward a sense of equivalence that does not erase difference among or fluidity between the subject positions people occupy in a pluralistic democracy (Mouffe, 1992: 32).[14]

Nation

The already complicated morality of personal identities is further complicated by the enveloping context of nation, where these complexities are played out. The dramas of identity are limited, enabled, and qualified by this context. Leonard Jeffries' extreme rhetoric of "sun" and "ice" people and Michael Levin's hierarchies of race are produced in the United States and indigenous to it. For instance, Jeffries and Levin took for granted their First Amendment right to speak no matter how outrageous audiences found their words. Nina Wu's joke notice about "bimbos" and "homos," *Oleanna's* conflicts, and courses such as "White Male Writers" are all animated by the moral assumptions of life within the United States. Inflecting these assumptions is a certain body of law and ideals, a national history, and particular notions of what is due you—however conflicted and shifting—that shape, limit, and contain them. The sexual harassment issues in *Oleanna* derive much of their moral resonance from being post–Anita Hill, coming after the case that, through television, put the legacy of the U.S. women's movement in our living rooms.[15] The Clarence Thomas hearings were themselves tied to the longer history of race and gender relations in the United States. The Antioch College sexual behavior policy, in contrast, strains the legacy of Anita Hill by trying to codify private behavior between men and women and by pretending that men and women are equally in danger in an encounter between them. Yet both *Oleanna* and Antioch are tied to Anita Hill, and they are uniquely U.S. moral events. Even hybrid identities are attached to certain national borders and framed by them. The identity of *la mestiza*, for instance, accrues meaning from a particular border, a specific nation and citizenship. Impossible in some nations—Germany and Japan, for instance, where citizenship is largely reserved for the relatively ethnically pure—it is more characteristic of others, such as the United States, in which a large part of the population or their ancestors come from someplace else.

The ethics of nationality is tied to a long history and found quintessential expression in a lecture delivered by Ernest Renan in 1882, who asserted that nation is more a moral than a geographic entity: "Man is a slave neither of his race nor his language, nor of his religion, nor of the course of rivers nor of the direction taken by mountain chains. A large aggregate of men, healthy in mind and warm of heart, creates the kind of moral conscience which we call a nation" (qtd. in Bhabha, 1990: 11). In this view, then, the ethical nation is a mass agreement on national history, the values that that history implies, and the actions necessary to insure that those values are carried into the future (Renan, cited in Bhabha, 1990: 19). Such reasoning is used by conservatives when they argue that subject positions, such as "woman," "African American," "Latino," and "homosexual," on behalf of which separate moral claims are made, subvert the national ethical quest for equality.

Currently, the most developed one-nation arguments come out of the war over academic curricula. The dumbing of America, its moral disintegration, the danger that, should current trends continue, "being itself" may "vanish" beyond the "dissolving horizon"—one or another version of

Armageddon is risked, it is said, when an affirmative action policy is applied to the choice of texts. The extravagant "dissolving horizon" metaphor is from Allan Bloom's *The Closing of the American Mind* (1987: 63). Bloom and others share the notion that a collective memory, contained in a repository of sacred texts, sustains national cohesion. Their anxiety is that, should collective memory fade, the nation will fall into moral anarchy and, according to Bloom, face extinction (39). In the same year as *The Closing of the American Mind* appeared, E. D. Hirsch published *Cultural Literacy: What Every American Needs to Know*, self-described as a set of "quick pragmatic fixes." It was endorsed by William Bennett, President Reagan's secretary of education, whose own more ideologically prescriptive *Book of Virtues: A Treasury of Great Moral Stories* (1993), as well as a sequel and a children's book, has appeared on the best-seller list. In the widely discussed appendix to his book, Hirsch offers a national vocabulary that, if mastered by the U.S. citizenry, would provide a common body of knowledge that Hirsch sees as the path to a shared national ethics.

The nostalgic, one-nation portrait appears even among traditional liberals such as Arthur Schlesinger Jr. Dissenting from the New York Board of Regents' decision to make the curriculum more diverse, Schlesinger argued that what holds U.S. democracy together is its "common ideals, common political institutions, common language, common culture, common fate" (1991: 138). Conservative columnist George F. Will echoes these thoughts in a *Newsweek* article when he defends the academy against what he calls Marxist academics: "The real Constitution, which truly constitutes America, is the national mind as shaped by the intellectual legacy that gave rise to the Constitution and all the habits, mores, customs and ideas that sustain it." For Will, all that is sacred in U.S. culture is threatened by P.C. courses in which Shakespeare's *Tempest* is described as reflecting the "imperialist rape of the Third World" and "Emily Dickinson's poetic references to peas and flower buds are encoded messages of feminist rage, exulting clitoral masturbation to protest the prison of patriarchal sex roles." Such courses, complains Will, cause "collective amnesia and deculturation" (1992; see also Delbanco, 1997: 208).

Yet one-nation, one-culture advocates do not always agree on the moral legacy they wish to preserve. Camille Paglia, in the preface to *Sexual Personae* (1990), writes: "*Sexual Personae* seeks to demonstrate the unity and continuity of western culture.... The book accepts the canonical western tradition and rejects the modernist idea that culture has collapsed into meaningless fragments" (xiii). However, Paglia's sense of Western culture is hardly consistent with that of Will and Schlesinger. In her view, the domi-

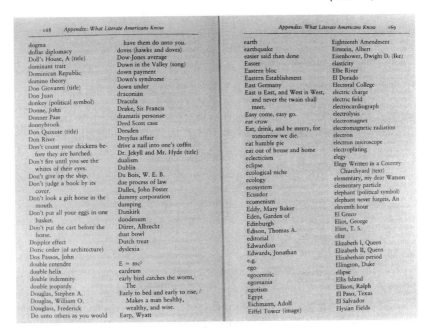

Figure 15. Excerpted from the appendix of Cultural Literacy, by E. D. Hirsch. Copyright 1987 by Houghton Mifflin Company. Reprinted by permission of Houghton Mifflin Company. All rights reserved.

nant threads of Western culture are decadence and paganism, which she celebrates.

The set of "great words" advocated by Hirsch and Bloom is culled from a tradition that less and less expresses the present moment in the United States, when one out of every three schoolchildren is not white (see U.S. Department of Education, 1994: 60).[16] In addition, Arnold Rampersad traces a "continuum" of attacks on U.S. culture by antiestablishment writers—William James, Gertrude Stein, Wallace Stevens, Robert Frost—the very ones that Schlesinger and Will may have in mind. Rampersad quotes Ralph Waldo Emerson: "We have listened too long to the courtly muses of Europe" (1991: 14). Emerson, like the curricular multiculturalists, objected to a universal required reading list. He wrote, "The only objection to *Hamlet* is that it exists" (1976: 485). Rather than conveying a unified culture, argues Rampersad, U.S. literature is distinguished by antiestablishment, antihierarchical positions (1991: 14). Of course, one-nation advocates might argue that such dissent is a result of an ethics of freedom and individualism—important pieces of U.S. moral ideology—not of the anarchic ethics of multiculturalism. Yet if one concedes that the relationship between the national literature and the sense of nationhood cannot be separated, perhaps this relationship is complicated beyond easy distinction and exceeds calculation. As Michael Berubé writes,

> You can't imagine an American literature that isn't grounded in *some* US narrative of self-definition, whether you rely on stories about "self-reliance" or on the multicultural "salad bowl" into which more and more foreign ingredients get tossed. And yet I wonder. Perhaps an American literature that *exceeds* the boundaries of the American nation-state, temporally and conceptually, can be thought—and brought into the classroom. (1994: 220)

Whatever the view is on one-nation, one-culture ideology, everyone agrees that multiculturalism is a legacy of the political movements of the 1960s and 1970s, times obsessively revisited by Hollywood. In advising the editors of a U.S. literary history, Annette Kolodny warns that they must keep faith with certain explosive historical moments, such as the 1963 March on Washington, where Martin Luther King Jr. delivered his "I have a dream" speech; the Berkeley free speech movement; the antiwar protests; the formation of the National Organization for Women in 1966; the assassinations of Jack and Robert Kennedy and Martin Luther King Jr.; the first Gay Pride march in New York City in 1970; and the showdown by Native Americans at Wounded Knee in 1973. To Kolodny, a consciousness of these moments leads to a reinterpretation of "American" literature. No longer can this literature imply a "harmonious commonality"; rather, it implies "diversity, division, and discord" in a "vocabulary of plurality" (1985: 307). Unlike Kolodny, who lists each disruptive historical moment to chart the route to the current multiculturalism, James W. Tuttleton, a conservative literary critic, lumps these moments together as the "dissensus of the Sixties and Seventies," which ruined a generation of graduates, the very graduates who are now attempting multicultural U.S. literary histories (1986: 8). Kolodny and Tuttleton, however, both trace a moral break in U.S. intellectual life to the social fissures in the 1960s and 1970s.

Like other breaks in the moral continuum, contemporary ambivalence toward the metanarrative of nation has been traced to World War II. Julia Kristeva writes that the nineteenth-century ideals of nation collapsed in the horrors of National Socialism: "It could be demonstrated that World War II, though fought in the name of national values . . . , brought an end to the nation as a reality: It was turned into a mere illusion which . . . would be preserved only for ideological or strictly political purposes, its social and philosophical coherence having collapsed" (1986: 188). The nightmare of German nationalism, the postwar redrawing of national borders that in some cases embraced a mixture of hostile ethnic groups, the precarious nation-lessness of the remaining Jews, and the profound internal divisions between collaborators and resistance fighters made nation more morally suspect than it had been before. Even from the singular vantage point of the United States, thinking it had won an ethical victory in the war, the moral meta-narrative that cast "America" as the land of freedom and fairness for the huddled masses was eroded by the legacy of Hiroshima, concentration camps for Japanese Americans, and U.S. rejection of Jewish refugee children.

The nostalgia of those who cling to an Edenic, unified notion of America, already served up to a wildly receptive public as satire in the Stephen Sondheim lyrics of "America" ("Everything free in America, / For a small fee in America") in the 1950s musical West Side Story (1957), can be maintained only with vigilance. Despite this difficulty, "America" is an ever seductive morality, partially because its status is endangered and nothing appears on the horizon to replace it. Newt Gingrich can offer a Contract with America implicating every American citizen. Corporations can also assert "America" effectively. Lee Iacocca urged U.S. consumers to "buy American" despite the fact that many Chrysler Corporation products had a Japanese design and were made of Japanese parts. When a single corporate enterprise requires multinational participation, the question what consti-tutes an "American" product becomes more and more difficult to answer. In fact, the Japanese workers at the Mitsubishi plant in Nagoya, Japan, ex-pressed confusion at Iacocca's "buy American" campaign, since they were producing the Dodge Stealth on their own assembly line (New York Times, 27 February 1992).

At the same time that moral expectations of nation are idealized, then, nation is an undependable narrative, a moral tale that is repeatedly shored up but that defies these efforts. The historical breaks that have contributed to the erosion of nationalism have also fed the postmodern sensibility that sees all monolithic structures, including nation, as constructions. As Benedict Anderson sees it, the nation is only an imagined entity, a mythical community where most people are strangers (1984: 15). If it is not reliable, it is also, in some manifestations, not desirable—especially in the double wake of Nazi and Serbian ideas of "ethnic cleansing," in which national identity is tied to slaughter (Bhabha 1994: 5).

Identities and Nationality

Thus, the story of "nation" is ideologically ambivalent and, some believe, historically transient (Tom Nairn, cited in Bhabha, 1990: 2; Bhabha, 1990: 1, 4). Its moral legitimations, besides having deteriorated, are complicated by the competing allegiances required of fractured or fluctuating identities. The rift between individual identity and nation is no longer accounted for by the classic distinction between "community" and "society," between systems that emphasize integrated values and tradition and systems that emphasize differentiated values (Lipset, 1990: 75). This rift was early identified as a problem in democracy that had to be resolved. For Federalist John Quincy Adams a stable nation was essential to guaranteeing individual rights into the future.[17] But for Thomas Paine, the cost of such stability was inflexibility and an arrogant authority that wished to rule "beyond the grave."[18] Now, however, this rift, the unresolved relationship between individual rights and the shape of the moment and nation, may be a starting point for moral negotiation.

The borders within which we play out our identities are partially a result of our negotiation with the past. Yet each time we imagine it, we reinvent that past as well as its moral traditions. Indeed, Will's "national mind" and Gingrich's "America" may not originate in identical moral traditions as they suppose. Even in calling on the same history, they inevitably re-create it differently. For Will, the Constitution evokes a unified national morality derived from European intellectual traditions, but for Gingrich, it offers an individually focused morality, emphasizing both accepting responsibility and seizing opportunity. However, constructions of tradition and nationality do get repeated, despite inexactness in these repetitions. Individuals continually engage with these constructions to arbitrate their own identity and their relation to the state.[19] Such engagement was a theme in the 1993 Whitney Museum of American Art biennial exhibition, which was widely criticized for its blatant political correctness. *What You Lookn At?* a 96-by-192-dot screen mural by Pat Ward Williams, dominated the Madison Avenue museum window as passersby looked in from the outside (Sussman, 1993: 248–49). It pictures five young men of color sitting in front of a brick wall. Their faces register defiance, anger, and coolness, emotional qualities reiterated in the spray-painted legend "WHAT YOU LOOKN AT," scrawled across the mural. The mostly white, middle-class Madison Avenue pedestrians outside the museum were faced with a ghetto scene inside a mainstream institution, the Whitney. In so positioning the mural, the exhibit curator bolstered Williams's ironic play with race relations in the United States—who is outside and who is inside being looked at with desire. In its moral challenge, the mural marks a sly negotiation between identities of color and U.S. culture, the artist of color and the mostly white art establishment.

A similar, though more historically freighted, negotiation appears in

Figure 16. Pat Ward Williams, What You Lookn At?, *1993. Courtesy of the artist and PPOW, New York.*

the work of Chinese American artist Hung Liu. *Trademarks* is a lithograph based on an old photograph of Chinese child prostitutes offered to Americans and other foreigners during the Boxer Rebellion at the turn of the century. Such photographs, in which Chinese prostitutes were pictured in European settings and in some cases wore European clothes, were fairly common. In *Trademarks,* the row motif of girls seated on a bench is repeated in a row of mah-jongg pieces placed beneath them, from the Chinese board game also popular in white middle-class American homes. Glued on each mah-jongg piece is an identical photograph of an attractive Chinese woman in native dress. A complaint about the bitter and trivial moral legacies ("trademarks") of encounters between her native and adopted culture, this lithograph, in terms somewhat similar to *What You Lookn At?* negotiates between Hung Liu's subject position and her status as a naturalized U.S. citizen. Both of these artworks expose different, often conflicting moral claims on the individual artist. These claims result in what Homi Bhabha calls cultural hybridity, a condition in which one is poised at several borders of identity and nation at the same time (1994: 2).[20]

As Williams and Hung Liu variously demonstrate, sometimes you bristle at border conflicts, and sometimes you wonder what you owe at each border or how each border is endangered by the others, but at other times, as in Williams's work, you revel in the possibilities such choices and mix-

Figure 17. © *Hung Liu,* Trademarks, *1992. Photo lithography on paper with photography on woodblocks, edition of 16. 24¼ x 33⅝ x 1 inches. Courtesy Steinbaum Krauss Gallery, New York City. From the collection of Ellen and Max Friedman.*

tures afford. Hybridity is thus an alternative to multiculturalism as a way of honoring diversity. It is a less limiting way to view individual identity within the context of nation. It avoids the danger in multiculturalism of essentializing an identity category, that is, identifying all individuals within a group as having a fixed set of qualities, a process that may lead to balkanization, as *Oleanna* and the cases of Nina Wu, Jeffries, and Levin demonstrate (Bhabha, 1994: 3). Yet in the shift from the multicultural to the hybrid, something may be lost: the keen awareness of power differences that allegiance to a group can provide, an awareness that stimulates political action. By representing extreme subject positions, Carol and John in *Oleanna,* as well as Jeffries and Levin and even the Antioch College dating policy, mark borders from which, once defined, it is then possible to rebound into more reasonable ethical terrain. Even the Nina Wu story demonstrates the arbitrariness of allegiances and implacable positions on identity.

Both identity and nation oscillate between instability and stability, and they are interactive (Kristeva, 1995). The interactive, interdependent nature of identity and nation is evident in Serrano's 1990 exhibition *Nomads,* Cibachrome portraits of homeless people and Klansmen, juxtaposed. A Latino and a successful artist, Serrano self-consciously chose these subjects because, he says, of "being who I am racially and culturally" (qtd. in Fusco, 1995: 84). The portraits reflect and define his subject position within the United States. As a Latino, he is in a sense "homeless" in the United States, the object of KKK scorn. But by making the homeless and Klansmen objects of his art, he puts both of them in his power. With these photographs Serrano both surrenders to and exploits his position as successful Latino artist. At the same time that he demonstrates his and others' strangeness in the nation, their status as foreigners, as different, he also uses this strangeness, this abjection, to make himself and others a little less abject, negotiating away some of this strangeness through public art.

Negotiations between identities and nation can lead to a serendipitous truce between two enemies that find themselves strangers in the United States, uniting against the "bad influence of American culture." A *New York Times* article, "Jews and Muslims Share a Piece of Brooklyn" (Kennedy, 1995) reports on the relatively happy coexistence of Muslims and Orthodox Jews in Borough Park, Brooklyn. They patronize one another's businesses and professionals and, apart from certain topics—"We don't talk about religion, we don't talk about news"—they have similar dietery laws and similar restrictions on behavior: "You don't see the legs of the women or the chest here," says Abdul Majeed Tabusan. "This is a place where children learn the right things: no kissing in the streets, no drugs or alcohol, everybody well behaved" (qtd. in Kennedy, 1995: B3). Although they have formed an alliance of sorts against the "bad influences" of pluralistic U.S. culture, their effort nevertheless demonstrates the oscillating effects of the interactions between identity and nation. A hybrid identity also requires such negotiation. Its opposition to the one-nation, one-identity, melting-pot ideal gives it power. The hybrid is always several and never coalesces, and each part makes bargains not only with the others but also with the culture in which it lives.

In John Sayles's 1996 film *Lone Star*, it is toward this sense of hybridity that the moral narrative moves. Set in Frontera, Texas, a border town, this film juxtaposes several stories, each revolving around identity. A black owner of the only bar in Darktown, who operates just this side of the law, must confront the son whom he abandoned, now returned as an army colonel. A Mexican American woman, who owns a restaurant, ideologically renews her U.S. citizenship each time she yells at her help to "speak English" and each time she calls the border patrol to report the "wetbacks" sneaking through her yard having just survived crossing the Rio Grande. But when a young, pregnant woman emerges from the river and appears at her house, she is forced to recall her own illegal entry into the United States. Even the film's humor is about how mutable the values attached to identity are. When a character is told that the family of his male friend's black fiancée will be so relieved that she is not a lesbian that they won't care that his friend is white,

Figure 18. Lone Star. Left, *Private Johnson and* right, *Colonel Payne.*

he says, "It's always heartwarming to see one prejudice supplanted by a deeper prejudice." None of these identities—white, black, Native American, Mexican, Mexican American—is stable, even within an identity group. When Colonel Payne, the barkeeper's son, asks Private Johnson, a black woman, what she's doing in the army, he expects to hear about patriotism, but he is made to rethink his status as a black man in a white institution when she says, "It's their country. It's the best deal they offer. . . . They got people to fight—Arabs, yellow people. Why not use us?" These stories about identity also detail conflicts between fathers and sons, here a trope for the conflict between history and the present. The film's protagonist, Sheriff Deeds, wants to prove that his dead father, revered in Frontera, was evil, but instead he discovers that he was complicated: his father separated him from his high school sweetheart not because she was Mexican but because she was his half-sister. Kristeva says that to achieve "heterogeneity is to disidentify our identities."[21] Almost every major character in the movie disidentifies in this way in order to live in this borderland, this Frontera. The film's last words are "Forget the Alamo." Thus, the final disidentification in the film is with a history that in this southern border town is powerfully associated with racism. Of course, such disidentifications are never complete, but they do invite hybridity and heterogeneity.

So, too, within the borders of the United States, Borough Park Muslims and Jews find it preferable to "disidentify," at least to some extent, the

I'm Eladio Cruz.
Welcome to Texas.

Figure 19. Lone Star. *Mexican woman greeted by a Texan upon illegally crossing the border into Texas.*

identities they brought with them from the Middle East in order to salvage their religious moral values. They bargain with their identity for a minimal heterogeneity, a small but significant move to accommodate life in the United States. Some degree of such disidentification is inevitable even if you propose, as Jeffries does, to speak universally for your identity group. Speaking as a universal subject, for all black men, gives Jeffries cultural authority, but his speech also transpires within the parameters of a universalism, a universalism of nation that is neither neutral nor fixed but that mediates his speech just as it mediates the neighborhood ethics in Borough Park and the ethics of identity in Serrano's *Nomads,* Hung Liu's *Trademarks,* and Sayles's *Lone Star* (see Schor, 1995: 32–33). The significance of this ethics of identification and disidentification is a gift of postmodernist tolerance of ambiguity. One does not have to side ethically with either Paine or Adams, community or society, the group or the individual, tradition or the present, responsibility or freedom. One can say, with Jacques Derrida, that "the *same duty* dictates respecting differences, idioms, minorities, singularities, but also the universality of formal law, the desire for translation, agreement and univocity, the law of the majority, opposition to racism, nationalism and xenophobia" (1992: 78).

6 | Lite

Reality used to be a friend of mine.
P. M. Dawn, *Of the Heart, of the Soul, and of the Cross: The Utopian Experience*

It's hard for me to get excited about the prospect of new and better modes of fake experience....
I don't want better fake; I want better real.
Candi Strecker, *Sidney Suppey's Quarterly and Confused Pet Monthly*

Is Lite a (New) Wave or a (BAD) Particle?

In Red Bank, New Jersey, in 1992, local people told a New Age store owner she was selling evil (*New York Times,* New Jersey Weekly, 5 January 1992). The owner, Mrs. Midose, said, "It's a place where people come to find hope, to give life meaning, to give them the tools to enhance the quality of their lives." Opponents found an old rule, passed before the borough started dating its ordinances, prohibiting the practice of "physiognomy, palmistry, phrenology and crafty sciences." Some claimed the store would bring the neighborhood down. Mrs. Midose countered with the First Amendment. To those who said incense was used to disguise the smell of marijuana, she replied that incense is a staple of Catholicism; thus she claimed a parallel moral legitimacy for New Ageism.

Pretending to be Sidney Poitier's son got David Hampton, a young black man from Buffalo, into clubs and the homes of well-off Manhattanites. While he was sitting at their table, he *was* Poitier's son. Hampton was given a twenty-month sentence for fraudulent deception. The moral angst about the case as it was expressed in a hit play by John Guare, *Six Degrees of Separation* (1992), a movie of the same name, and talk show interviews with

Hampton went deep. According to Phil Donahue, "These wealthy people, insulated and probably feeling guilty about their own separation, more than six degrees, from the real New York City, get to be sort of very progressively integrated when you arrive" (*Donahue*, 1991: 7). The play suggested that the duped bourgeoisie genuinely loved Hampton, who—briefly—meant more to them than their own children. Then he broke their trust. Hampton sued Guare for $60 million, claiming that his lifestyle was a performance over which he owned the rights. The court decided that the play was art but his life was not (*Guardian*, Weekend Section, 8–9 February 1992; *New York Times*, 7 May 1991 and 19 July 1993) .

Mrs. Midose's retailing of spirituality and David Hampton's fabrication of identity spark concern about when and whether spirituality and identity are real. Such phenomena, whose reality is a cause for moral panic, we shall call "lite." The word started as a description of low-calorie products and cheerful pop radio stations. Its irreverence about conventional spelling signaled a liberation from heavy food and serious music. This liberating aspect of lite is also important in the moral domain, where such phenomena seem newly creative and democratic. Conventional wisdom, though, says that only in a morally "unreal" society could foodless food and trivial music receive a name that connotes progress and modernity. What people condemn about lite is its abdication of reality. Television, which provides people with most of their information, is often seen as the main culprit. The medium's cultivation of a short attention span and its emphasis on the visual are condemned as making for less real communication than speech or print. "Reality" programming—crime reenactments and docudramas—and "advertorials," which mix fiction with fact are accused of blurring dangerously the boundaries of "real" knowledge. Comics, read seriously by many young adults, are dismissed by a previous generation, who cannot see them as "real" literature. New Ageism like that on sale in Red Bank is denounced for simulating enlightenment and transcendence: "The American conviction that actuality imposes cruel, and really unfair limits upon desire leads naturally to the ambition to TRAVEL OUT OF YOUR BODY," says Paul Fussell, quoting an ad in *Fate* magazine (1991: 46). The representation of history in Hollywood movies such as *JFK* (1991), Wild West theme parks, and restorations such as colonial Williamsburg are decried as fake (Horvath and Bin, 1991: 108). The porn-free, retroneon reconstruction of Times Square in New York is "a denial of everything that's not squeaky clean and brightly colored," a "Candyland" (qtd. in Schoofs, 1995: 16). The transformation of the retail sector by malls, catalogs, and television and computer shopping channels is condemned for abandoning "real" community.

For lite haters, "private," domestic life is real. Life lived in the public gaze by celebrities, or through open-access Internet communication, is not. E-mail is divorced from the richness of nonverbal cues in interpersonal speech. Other forms of lite language are thought similarly to eviscerate representational power because, the argument goes, they have had reality refined out of them. Nothing is "really" being said, for instance, in knee-jerk politically correct coinages or on talk shows. People who are not "real" professionals but have some professional skills also cause moral suspicion; the span ranges here from computer hackers, through self-help devotees, to writers whose amateur magazines, " 'zines," circumvent established distribution systems. When the law is televised, it is widely said to pass from reality to fiction, with sound bites drowning out due process and the audience conducting a parallel lite justice.[1] After the not guilty verdict in the first, criminal trial, O. J. Simpson pulled out of a planned interview with *Dateline NBC*. He claimed that the presenters, Katie Couric and Tom Brokaw, whom he renamed Katie Clark and Tom Darden, after the prosecution lawyers, aimed to "retry" him (*New York Times,* 12 October 1995).

Politics, too, is more and more lambasted for its media-fostered unreality. This critique gained strength in the 1980s with Ronald Reagan and culminated in denunciations of the Persian Gulf video war. It takes in Bill Clinton's saxophone playing on *The Arsenio Hall Show,* the cross-media blitz of Republican '96 candidates, and the metamorphosis of presenters into policy makers—Diane Sawyer becoming an expert on welfare mothers, for instance (Cockburn and Silverstein, 1996: 2). When entertainers appropriate political authority, a similar moral unease arises, as with rappers acting as social analysts and activist movie actors and musicians. The Creative Coalition, whose members include Ron Silver, Susan Sarandon, and Christopher Reeve, focuses on abortion rights, the environment, the homeless, and the National Endowment for the Arts. Of it, Richard Bernstein asks, "Should stars set the agenda? . . . Does their presence make a media circus out of what should be sober reflection on complicated problems?" (*New York Times,* 10 March 1991). Individuals who live out made-up identities are also suspect. That includes Hampton but also more long-lived media figures, such as Madonna and Clinton, whose "real" achievements are suspected of being smaller than their celebrity.

Cultural critics who describe something as "lite" are being ironic, indicting it as a cultural descent from a nostalgically imagined, unspecified past. The loss has a number of characteristics. First, lite phenomena are faulted for deserting complexity—for "overstatement and simpleminded literalism" (Fussell, 1991: 75). The medium of television, even when it aspires to quality, is said to provide emotional gratification quickly, without the concentration "real" art demands. New Ageism provides quick and easy salvation for which established religions make you work hard. As in Red Bank, it is one-stop shopping rather than regular and long-term commitment to a community of faith. Lite's crude organization is also castigated, accused of making it a playground for special interests. Critics lambaste the undifferentiated mix of information, entertainment, and advertisement on the television news, accusing it of abdicating journalistic objectivity and authority and of reducing politics to popularity ratings and self-interest. The columnist Barbara Ehrenreich, for example, suggests that our concept of essential American interests now includes "oil in the Gulf, those lovely coral earrings in Grenada," and baseballs from Haiti (1994).

The second charge is that the ease and theatricality of lite phenomena seduce people away from the real world, blurring the boundaries between real and unreal, even replacing reality. The result is a reduced potential for action. Bill McKibben, in an article titled "TV or Not TV," worries that "TV is becoming more real than life" (*New York Times,* 27 May 1992). He cites the political debates on Murphy Brown's single motherhood, the Discovery Channel's encouragement to "get this close to the thrill of real life," and the transformation of the Gulf War into a miniseries. In McKibben's view, morality is fading into a spectacle we passively absorb, rather than intervene in or participate in ourselves. This change, he says, makes it "hard to summon lasting outrage, lasting determination to go do something that might help." At the same time, the lite realm can give you the illusion of complete control. In this imaginary present, as in the nostalgically imagined "real" past, moral choices are comfortingly cut-and-dried. In cyberspace you can have virtual sex, be a virtual neurosurgeon, or regulate a virtual ecology. In the self-help movement, where morality rests primarily in your responsibility toward yourself, the larger structures of problems recede in the doable day-to-day program of self-actualization. When you reduce political success, as both Clinton and Newt Gingrich apparently do, to the "seven habits of highly effective people" described in the book of that name (Covey, 1989), achieving that success seems misleadingly possible. When you visit Disneyland, its China and Polynesia exhibits offer attainable substitutes for world travel while assuring your safety and fixing the parameters of your pleasure.[2] When you are impersonating Sidney Poitier's son, the world is a friendly place and you are a nice person—but for how long?

In these moral critiques, lite betrays authenticity. For although lite is too simple, it is at the same time too artificial—too cooked as well as too raw. Mass media generate misleading forms of communication and community. Television personal ads, for example, offering safety and "the privacy of print along with the immediate impact of TV," are soulless, evading the realities of intimate relationships (*New York Times*, 25 August 1991). Often such accounts suggest that the more technical the medium, the further from the raw materials of production, the more alienating it is. Susan Willis finds a saving grace in the commodification of blackness only when it preserves something of the "black vernacular." Michael Jackson's video for "Speed Demon" qualifies, because it invokes Brer Rabbit; his "Smooth Criminal" video, trading in cyborg images, does not (1991: 126–29). Such critics believe that power now accrues not to substantive figures but to media-generated shadows. Oprah becomes our TV Eleanor Roosevelt, speaking out against social inequities. Politicians themselves are no longer convincing in their authority. Reagan for all his media savvy, still looked like a ham actor, and George Bush was pictured as an empty space in the *Doonesbury* cartoons. Clinton seemed as flimsy as a cardboard cutout, folding on gays in the military and gay marriages, and blowing with the prevailing electoral winds on welfare policy.

The pretense of lite events is often judged as more unethical than their content. Beyond the race issue, Hampton's willful deceptiveness rankled; he didn't have to play Poitier Jr., and he didn't really gain anything. "I'll tell you my real crime," he said, "that a young black man made a fool" out of upper East Siders (qtd. in Haselden, 1992: 11). Fear of being tricked also seems to underlie Internet panic, which derives not only from sexuality but also from the Internet's uncertainties, from the chance that when you exchange fantasies with someone who calls himself or herself a woman, that person may be a man; from the dangers and possibilities of gender play when you are "just" talking (Turkle, 1996: 210–32).[3] Movies directed by Quentin Tarantino, such as *Reservoir Dogs* (1991) and *Pulp Fiction* (1994), attract the same kind of unease. They seem so in love with movies that they can only play at being movies themselves. Tarantino himself says, "Violence is one of the looks of a movie" (qtd. in Brooks, 1994: 14). Authenticity anxiety also appears in lite critics' tendency to reserve their strongest moral indictments for phenomena that lay claims to being high, "authentic" culture—"educational" television, such as *Sesame Street* (Postman, 1985: 146–48), or Hollywoodized films of literary classics, such as *The Scarlet Letter* (1995). At such points, the critique often descends into curmudgeonly elitism. Perched on Olympian cultural heights, Paul Fussell assumes that the masses cannot see through the pretensions of what he calls "BAD culture." Sometimes his disdain descends into clear snobbery, as when he regrets the postwar "proletarianization" of air travel, before which it "used to be almost elegant, or at least pleasant" (1991: 23).

However, others advocate lite. They see it not as escapism but as liberation from the tyranny of the real. At Disney World, for instance, the actors inside character heads are not allowed to take them off in public, despite their weight and stuffiness, but they themselves also seem committed to this rule, dedicated to maintaining the Disney "magic" (Klugman et al., 1995).[4] Sometimes this commitment focuses on representation itself. At Sesame Place, you can take part in a videotaped enactment of "Elmo and Zoe's Adventure" and then see yourself on-screen. As the teenage hosts confide to a largely preschool audience, being on TV is what every child wants, an absolute goal and good. Lite representations may even be interpreted as redemptive, as in Ron Rosenbaum's rendering of Elvis worship as national self-cure: "finding a way to love . . . the heartbroken, pain- and pill-filled impersonator of greatness, may be our way of finding, in our *own* decline, some forgiveness, some humor, even some healing" (1995: 64). What is considered authentic and real may create undemocratic limitations that lite can subvert. The paranormal, attacked as a betrayal of rationality, is defended as a full look at reality in opposition to the narrowness of science. For his supporters, David Hampton's case raises a similar point: your "lite" is my reality, a reality you don't know. If you have never met a middle-class young black man, the first one who comes to your door can easily persuade you that he is Poitier's son.

At its most extreme, this argument suggests that each individual has an important, authentic voice of his or her own. If you listen well, you can hear what is going unrepresented in the culture. In this account, personal experience is not lite knowledge—anecdote masquerading as truth—or an emotivist reduction of ethics to feelings, but real scholarship, extending the range of what is known. Patricia Williams, a black legal theorist, describes how law journals refuse autobiographical writing, thus shutting out as "lite" large swathes of relevant material, such as women's and blacks' experiences of discrimination (1991: 47). Those who value cultural democracy often see lite's rawness as a moral corrective to overrefined civilization. Commentators repeatedly remark on how "real" Oprah Winfrey is, for instance, seeing in her an emotionality so rich that it can break through television's traditional artificiality (Zoglin, 1986).

Lite may also extend reality through the expanded access and audiences of media such as public access TV, the Internet, shareware and freeware, desktop publishing, faxes, and individually produced magazines, or 'zines. Because these media do not depend on authenticity and are multiple in their meanings, no one can monopolize them. In them, the nonelite acquire new possibilities for making and interpreting art and knowledge.[5] Inspirational and self-help books, for example, are available across all social groups and promise equal ethical authority to everyone who uses them. Lite is cheap, too: Hampton's "lite" life as Poitier's son was his only entrée to moneyed white people. Graffiti, an art form with unusually accessible materials and forums, is able to claim public space for those who cannot own it. Anyone with an America Online subscription can have a home page on the Net. Alvin and Heidi Toffler, Third Wave pundits, brush aside the barriers to technological access that lack of expertise and money pose. They think the new communications technologies signify a general possibility of empowerment: "An educated citizenry can for the first time in history begin making many of its own political decisions" (1994: 98).

Access can, some argue, generate new communities that have moral functions in themselves. Talk radio, defined in the 1988 film of the same name as "the last community in America," is, says talk host Gary Byrd, who broadcasts from the Apollo Theater for the black-owned New York station WLIB, "the one medium left where people can interact with each other with a sense of immediacy. . . . In the black community radio is a tribal drum" (New York Times, 7 June 1992). Sites on the Net allow young gays and lesbians to discuss their sexuality and feel accepted. Access to others like yourself generates "a sense of true community, of belonging," and cyberspace seems safer and more confidential than interpersonal space (New York Times, 2 July 1995; Walker, 1995).

With access come possibilities of empowerment and accountability. Lite media are often decentralized and communicate directly with their audiences, and those audiences can themselves become producers, as with Star Trek fans who move from watching TV to making videos, from reading to writing fan literature and publishing stories, or with repeat callers on the Rush Limbaugh Show—Eli from Westchester, John from Staten Island—who become minor celebrities (New York Times, 7 June 1992; Penley, 1991: 139–40). If television in the Simpson courtroom encouraged playing through the cameras to the nation rather than only to judge and jury, black viewers could see for themselves that nothing was hidden, and in this way maintained their belief in the justice system as an expression of ethics (Graham, 1995).

Against the puritanism of the anti-lite argument, proponents of the lite realm argue for its pleasures, a part of "reality" the mainstream ignores.

If there is banality in lite's pleasures, there is also a powerful transgressive and creative force that puts together historically or socially divided elements of the culture, as with the post-Christmas festival Kwanza, which draws on African harvest and New Year rituals to affirm an African American heritage. At the Disney Institute, which proposes vacation as creation, the "more than 80 offerings" of activities may be carefully scripted and limited, but a vast menu of options is nonetheless available "to make a music video, go rock climbing, craft a storybook, dabble in architecture, [or] enhance a golf swing," and guests may indeed put options together inventively (Walt Disney World, 1995: 1). Even the authors of a highly critical study of Disney World, *Inside the Mouse*, which explains away the enjoyment people get from the park by referring it to childhood, economic oppression, or exhaustion, allow that the "big heads" of the parading character figures have a strong carnivalesque allure (cited in Klugman et al., 1995: 5).

Banality may simply be the perception of those not attuned to these new media and new realities or not literate in these media. Shopping looks trivial within a traditional political analysis, but consumerism is for many their only arena for effective social action: buying a black Barbie can be a moral act. Even if the impact of such acts is limited, the acts may still be worthwhile: so what if Shani, Aisha, and Nichelle, proud African American dolls, all have long, "combable" hair? Disney, a relatively gay-friendly employer, stages an annual Gay Day in the Magic Kingdom. Although it is merely tolerant of its gay "family" of workers, that tolerance means a lot in an enterprise centered on heterosexual family (Klugman et al., 1995: 155). And despite the un-ironic stance of those who attend Gay Day and who "but for sodomy . . . *are* the middle class," the high-camp inclusiveness of the event, meshing seamlessly with the Magic Kingdom's regular activities, is a kind of victory (Hannaham, 1995: 36).

As such examples suggest, pro- and anti-lite moral arguments are not always firmly divided. People contradict themselves, approving or disapproving of different lite phenomena depending on their personal or social interests. Lite-busters almost inevitably enjoy aspects of the culture they despise, praising their First Amendment openness or morally redeeming vigor. The cultural critic Neil Postman calls television "theater for the masses" and acknowledges its emotional power (1985: 28–29). Even Paul Fussell accepts that television is good at reporting events and selling things (1991: 185–87). Lite advocates, like their opponents, are preoccupied with possibilities of misuse: the Net's commercialization, the manipulation of minors through it, its degeneration into trivia and inaction (Godwin, 1995). Howard Rheingold, though strongly optimistic about cyberspace's potential for "stronger, more humane" communities, still thinks the issue of who will control it must be addressed (1993: 300). Even lite moguls declare their concern about lite's intensification of isolation: Disney CEO Michael Eisner suggested that the company's planned Times Square redevelopment, including a Disney superstore, would deliver people from their electronic "cocoon" back into public space (qtd. in Hrabi, 1995: 173).

Despite pro-lite arguments' focus on the future, nostalgia haunts them, as it does critics of lite, most notably in a Habermasian longing for civilization and community (Postman, 1985: 8). Literacy in the new media is said to resurrect the Renaissance ideal of a common citizenship, broadened to include all who produce and consume information (Lanham, 1995: 200). In much "cyberpunk" writing, complex moral problems get solved by a reincarnation of preindustrial community. In William Gibson's *Virtual Light* (1993), for instance, a romantic, anarchic group of the homeless and dispossessed of all races, nations, and ages toughs it out in a postearthquake, postplague San Francisco, camped high up on the walkways and towers of the Golden Gate Bridge. Lite's futurism works sometimes as visionary plan, sometimes as bitter moral commentary on the existing state of affairs: *Virtual Light's* dystopian future, for instance, is a rigidly stratified society where rich and poor meet only for crime, sex, or drugs (Gibson, 1993: 123). Those on both sides of the lite issue also draw on past images of nation, such as Disneyland's benevolent postwar, "small world" colonialism. Moreover, lite nostalgia recapitulates the 1950s and 1960s romance with technology. One Web site was set up in 1995 as a virtual World's Fair (Van Tassel, 1995: 44).

Moral panic about lite is complicated by its interconnections with other moral debates. Because lite is new and nontraditional, we often define it morally through a safely established discourse: that of the law. Courts have to adjudicate David Hampton's claim that his life story should not be used without permission by comparing life stories with images and with books, both of which already have legal status as property. Fears about lite also converge with fears about the body, especially regarding HIV. In the paranoia about computer viruses, sharing software, like sharing body fluids, seems to be dangerous to the individual and the national "body," and recommendations for safe Net conduct recall AIDS risk reduction guidelines.[6] Anti-lite arguments often have familial underpinnings. In undermining traditional cultural forms, these new forms of technology seem to be challenging the traditional domestic realm. If children can escape into unmonitored chat rooms, how can family authority be maintained? If people of any age can enter these Net spaces, how can young people be protected and concepts of "childhood" preserved? The pro-lite side also uses family to promote its views. One cable TV service offers itself as the uniter of generations split by different interests; the last scene in its ad shows father and son side by side on a sofa, watching together. And the Disney experience is recounted by visitors as an occasion when for once the family is united.

All in the Past?

Moral debates about lite phenomena are not new; all are extensions of previous moral concerns with reality. Yet they also break with those concerns. Virtual reality, for instance, replays a long history of fears about the mechanization, and then the computerization, of work and play. On the one hand, contemporary virtual reality panic is exacerbated by a sense that the nation is growing apart. As melting-pot unity yields to salad-bowl separateness, so communal participation yields to individual isolation within the virtual world. On the other hand, cyberpioneers, despite their cynicism, hark back to the social change movements of the 1960s, awaiting the "dawn of a new humanism" (qtd. in Sobchak, 1994: 14–15). Moral panics over self-help panaceas and New Ageism have continuities with previous concerns about the self-absorption of the 1970s "me generation" and the "culture of narcissism" (Lasch, 1979). The furor over tabloid press and television fictionalization of the news replays 1950s moral panic over sleazy tabloids and scurrilous scandal magazines such as *Confidential, On the Q.T.,* and *Cheesecake,* featuring stories such as "I Was a Japanese Love Dope Slave," "Bad Girls USA," and "The Belly Dancer Who Stole an Atom Bomb" (Strausbaugh, 1991: 10). Now, though, it seems to many that such jumbled-up media forms have taken over the legitimate press.

The identification of lite with an expanding democracy also goes way back. Victorian intellectuals derided popular religious writing for a "feminine" sentimentalism that ignored real history and politics, yet they recognized that this writing gave new power to women (Douglas, 1977: 328). A similar dichotomy exists today in our awareness of New Ageism as mushy, "feminine" thinking that nonetheless touches many who are unaffected by other intellectual and spiritual traditions. Marianne Williamson, a guru of New Ageism, connects herself with the female spiritualism founded in the nineteenth century and bases her *A Return to Love* (1991) on the spiritualist Helen Cohen Schucman's *A Course in Miracles* (1975). Today, however, New Ageism's lite spirituality is associated less closely with gender marginality, and its audience is far larger than was the class-restricted readership of Victorian ladies' improvement stories. Thus, lite's morality of democratization has a new, broader form.

Radio was thought to hold the promise of cultural universality at the beginning of the century, much as cyberspace is seen today. In the 1970s, CB radio seemed to many to offer fabulous possibilities for community building and empowerment. Although different media appear to have this potential at different times, the particular features of the media are significant. The national communities of radio and television, for instance, are in sharp contrast to on-line communities, which are less easily defined, local as well as international, and divorced from physical reality. Debates over Internet regulation thus extend issues of democracy and privacy to a newly "unreal" forum.

Finally, the nostalgia that is common to all moral discourse about lite phenomena has a very mixed set of historical reference points. Defenses of hacking evoke 1960s politics and the 1950s angst of the "rebel with a modem," as well as frontier Westerns and science fiction (Ross, 1991: 116). New Ageism looks back to the 1960s but also to the romantic preindustrial state of nature. Fantasizing about diverse pasts is probably inevitable. What is new is the extent to which these fantasies question the reality of the present and speculate about future realities.

Lite Theology

As in other moral debates, many irreconcilable explanations of morality coexist. Questions about the adequacy of scientific truth, for instance, animate many arguments about the paranormal. Often, lite morality is a utilitarian cost-benefit calculation. New Age rhetoric, despite its emphasis on an incalculable good, associates that good with personal and social gain, suggesting that spiritual progress leads to "efficiency" (Peck, 1993: 171–72). Religion, however, is a dominant subtext in lite, as if, in a climate of millennial anxiety, lite is a less dogmatic substitute for more conventional beliefs, as were the utopian movements of the nineteenth century. However, lite spirituality continually undermines itself by an imprecision that makes it seem trivial and, in comparison to worked-out theological systems, inconsistent. Williamson's work, based in Christianity, nevertheless concocts a nondenominational spiritual stew, with the usual exotic Eastern ingredients, that ignores important conceptual differences between religions. God, she says, is merely a metaphor for the love inside each person (1992: 13). M. Scott Peck, the author of two best-selling meditations on right living, *The Road Less Travelled* (1985) and *Further along the Road Less Travelled* (1993), declares that this spiritual route need not go through the organized church (1993: 153) and provides no firm means of distinguishing spiritual from personal improvement. Feminist New Ageism, focusing on the Goddess, raises the dilemma of whether feminist politics is compatible with a divine femininity. Virtual reality discourse sets up a basic dichotomy between good and evil, but it too displays a theologically unnerving flexibility. It lets programmers and corporate whizzes alike be heroes, and likes nothing better than when, as with Bill Gates, the two seem to coincide.

Much of the lite critique looks religious in its denunciations of pleasure and ease, though it articulates a puritan edict against consuming time and resources rather than against offending God. The theological focus on lite as evil also comes into direct conflict with the rationalist critique of lite's unreality. If lite is unreal, where can its evil effects come from? Can virtual sex be at the same time a substitute for sex that diverts us from the real thing and a dangerous influence on sexual behavior? Critiques of talk television call attention to the theatrical unreality of the representations. The same mother-daughter pair appeared on several shows in the mid-1990s, for instance, alleging the daughter was jealous of her sexy mom and graphically demonstrating this conflict for the cameras. Later they admitted they got on well and just liked being on the shows (*New York Times*, 11 June 1995). Media interest in such manipulations is high, but this interest accords poorly with the parallel concern about talk shows' malignant, powerful reality—about, for instance, the 1995 *Jenny Jones* guest who, shortly after the show, murdered the man who had revealed he had a "secret crush" on him (Benson, 1995b; Dempsey, 1995). It becomes unclear whether the critics think talk shows are evil because they are misleading, because they dissemble, or a bit of both.

Whose Reality?

Empowerment is a major moral claim of the pro-lite argument, and elitism a major failing on the anti-lite side. But whose reality is at stake in the lite realm and how much empowerment lite can achieve are complicated issues that cut across pro- and anti-lite positions. The equation of lite with a new democracy, for instance, is highly questionable. Hampton is an emblematic figure, admitting of the casually powerful social stratum his masquerade infiltrated, "I love it and I despise it" (*Donahue*, 1991: 11). Often lite seems to make a new set of interests powerful. Rush Limbaugh says his audience and those of other right-wing shows are disenchanted with mainstream media and are "cutting into [opinion leaders'] influence" (*New York Times*, 30 April 1995). But this radio community is a monarchy, not a republic. It is not the listeners but Limbaugh who is the new influencemonger, the gatekeeper of public response. Moreover, the shows' absolutism does not reflect a great unheard-from middle America, for the majority of Americans, as we have

seen, express moral ambiguity. Radio talk shows' totalitarianism is more attributable to the medium itself, which is verbal, suited to clear, conservative
sound bites, not liberal waffle (Hoberman, 1995b). The new masters of the
computer universe also turn out to be less revolutionaries than establishment figures in the making. Demographically similar to CEOs, only younger,
they turn cyberspace into a geek heaven crammed with white-bread, unironic pop-cultural enthusiasms and "flaming"—argument by bombast and
insult that provides a safe form of masculine, if not male, confrontation
(Dery, 1994: 6). Spin-off products such as *Wired,* a print magazine about
cyberspace, maintain this macho tone. In the August 1995 issue, on the letters page, itself called "Rants and Raves," a reader praises a combative article and pleads, "Let's have more food fights" (Lemon, 1995). Where the
cyberspace market diversifies, it often appeals to another conventional audience, professional thirtysomethings with young children, as in the print
magazine *Virtual City,* which, in its fall 1995 issue, tells about sites that give
investment advice and health information, and lets the reader preview
"software sandboxes for kids."

Perhaps, then, the effects of lite media forms are predominantly traditional. Black talk radio, for instance, forms a community, but it is no more
able than established black institutions to bring about social improvement.
As Gary Byrd, the talk show host, says, "There's a tremendous amount of
frustration people feel—not just black people—about not being able to affect change." Yet for some listeners, Limbaugh's or Byrd's shows realign the
real, producing moral gains that are not calculable in conventional terms.
Byrd says, "In a certain way, [the show is] better than a vote" (*New York
Times,* 7 June 1992). Talk radio is cheap and profitable, but it can also have
widespread political effects, such as mobilizing people for demonstrations
or consumer boycotts.

Although lite advocates stress the democratic possibilities of new
media such as computing, this conclusion seems naive. Maybe it is just that
such media, being less regulated, intensify the argument for individual
rights that in a democracy is always in conflict with the need for collective
responsibility. As Clifford Stoll points out, journalism is legally accountable,
whereas electronic bulletin boards are not. Here, "people get away with
things . . . that they'd never be able to pull off on the street," and they need
this freedom if the medium is to continue (1995: 217). The question, then,
is whether a lite, virtual morality is really a threat to the social fabric. Many
pro- and anti-lite arguments take on this concern. They discuss the dangerously unfettered nature of computer communication, for example, and
whether and how to encrypt on-line communications to preserve privacy.

The *degree* of liteness is also at issue. For some, Macintosh-type operating systems are disempowering, because they do not give access to the machines' processes. Others think the Mac aesthetic is creative, encouraging them to "dance" and "dream" as they work (Turkle, 1996: 36–43). It may be that questions about access and control will go away as computer media age. When corporations get a firm grip on the Internet, or when particular users—the Limbaugh Right or computer nerds—become dominant, perhaps even its present hints of democratization will disappear. In such confused moral circumstances, many commentators are unsure whether computers will lead to "Athens without slaves" or "slaves without Athens" (Ross, 1991: 125).

The moral debate about television talk shows also has to do with democracy. The perception of their moral degeneracy emerges from concern about their expressions of social and sexual marginality. Many guests—poor blacks, white racists, families with tales of incest and abuse—would not otherwise be on television except as statistics. The shows are also woman-dominated, fronted by women and watched largely by women. Blacks and other people of color often host daytime shows, but they don't in prime time (*New York Times*, 21 May 1995). Black issues, from hair care through interracial relationships to racism in education, and women's issues, such as sexual harassment and abortion, appear much more frequently on daytime talk shows than in primetime. However, it could be argued that the shows act simply as cautionary tales for middle-class whites, setting up black people as caricatures—loud, aggressive women and shifty, no-good men (hooks, 1995). [7] White trash with nothing to lose act out family horrors that those in more economically and culturally privileged milieus can afford to keep private. On one episode of *The Bertice Berry Show* (1994), for instance, a white, seventeen-year-old high school dropout, Joy, was revealed to have a one-year-old black daughter from a previous relationship and a twenty-year-old boyfriend, Billy, whom her mother and stepmother hated, who had not finished high school, had a dead-end job, and was alleged to be wanted by the sheriff, to have seen another woman, to call Joy "bitch," and to shove her around. Even when the shows take up important feminist issues such as male violence, it often seems like the prurient replay of a stale reality, not the forging of a new one. As a result of these divided and uncertain allegiances, talk shows' moral messages multiply and seem contradictory. [8]

Additionally, the debate about lite and democracy is about cultural conservatism. Critics of lite phenomena pit it against print, arguing that only the latter requires the interpretation of complex symbol systems (Postman, 1985: 25). Lite media do not have to be understood on this level—you can watch a horror movie, for instance, without being aware of the genre conventions it is obeying or flouting. Moreover, just as printed texts may be simple or difficult, visual media, such as film and comics, have the same variety. Lite thus transgresses a cultural elitism of considerable intellectual and moral power.

Feeling Lite

Those who see moral potential in lite and those who see moral collapse in it usually accept the idea that lite is finally as real as you feel it to be. Emotivism allows all the moral perspectives on lite to remain in play, without needing to address their differences. Lite advocates see New Ageism, television, the personal growth movement, shopping, and virtual reality as setting up a moral agent, the self, in the domains of, respectively, religion, entertainment, politics, economics, and everyday life. When everything around you is uncertain, the self is the only sure object of belief and hope. By taking the self as moral standard, lite disclaims moral comparisons with other modalities—of New Ageism with religion, for instance—and thus disarms criticism of its hokeyness. Marianne Williamson declares the limitless, practically divine power of the individual to conquer hate, falsity, and self-pity: "In every heart, there is the power to do it" (1992: 254). Similarly, the lite 1990s feminism of self-improvement grounds itself in how you feel. Gloria Steinem declares that social justice comes before self-esteem—yet writes a whole book about the impact of the latter, ending with the advice, "There is always one true inner voice. Trust it" (1992: 22, 323). Even a company with the concrete aim of helping women develop their own businesses starts from low self-esteem. "There's a lot of pain there," its creator says (*Philadelphia Inquirer*, 23 February 1992). *Essence* magazine tries to construct a black feminism that pulls together activism and spirituality. Again, an emotivist self-affirmation dominates. Trying to build this black feminism, Susan Taylor, the editor, writes that at a difficult time "I . . . slowed my breath, closed my eyes and asked my inner wisdom" (1995). Despite their very different aims and methods, electronic media also assume a shared emotional truth as their moral justification. Speaking of the televised spectacle of the Gulf War, producer Michael Mitchell said, "All over the planet at the same time, people will see and hear and feel the same set of emotions" (*New York Times*, 19 December 1991). Virtual reality games such as *SimCity* let you construct a city to stroll through, untrammelled and safe. Here urban exploration, a pervasive trope for modernity's pursuit of reality, is reclaimed, safely out of social context, for the individual imagination.

Lite's "I feel it's good because it feels good" solipsism is easy to parody. However, its emotivism clouds its moral claims. First, this emotivism simplifies issues by its focus on the individual. In novels about virtual reality, such as *Virtual Light* (Gibson, 1993), as in conventional thrillers and Westerns, it is the bravery of exceptional people that solves moral difficulties. In this book, our heroes, a virtual cowgirl–bike messenger and a millennially disillusioned ex-cop, win the day in a shopping mall shootout. Even in more nuts-and-bolts writing about the future, such as that on nanotechnology—engineering at the level of atoms and molecules—which starts from scientifically accepted reality, the potential moral consequences of a technology that could end work, disease, ageing, and pollution has to vie with the simpler picture of frontier mavericks campaigning against the conformity and shortsightedness of existing science (Regis, 1995: 216).

Lite emotivism leaves us with no moral options other than ourselves, no course of moral action other than feeling. You have a moral right to the reality of your choice. "Finally!" the "out of your body" ad promises, "You can learn to safely and easily leave your physical body—at will—to travel to distant lands, visit family, meet absent lovers, even communicate with spirit beings" (qtd. in Fussell, 1991: 46). Lite's emotivism even absolves it of effectiveness: lite needs merely to make you *feel* that it has effects. Thus, controversial television talk shows can justify themselves merely by getting participants to say they feel better afterward. During *The Bertice Berry Show,* Billy, Joy's boyfriend, read a conciliatory statement, and her stepmother said she was ready to compromise, statements Berry hailed as the first step toward a solution, "working towards things" (1994: 29).

In the lite realm, emotivism leads to a careless treatment of rationalist distinctions that is more obvious and less acceptable than in other areas of moral debate. Lite's emotivism leaves no way to adjudicate between feelings or to negotiate between one moral decision and another. On television talk shows, all opinions, from those of murderers to those of pack rats, become morally equal—a disturbing consequence for many. Anyway, how much do we really hold in common emotionally? Important social differences in the morality of the real get flattened by lite's emotivism. On the same day that *The Bertice Berry Show* raked through Joy's and Billy's lives, *The Oprah Winfrey Show* considered "moral dilemmas." Winfrey wondered whether you should tell someone if a length of toilet paper is protruding from his or her pants. She asked whether toilet paper wasn't "the common bond in the human experience. . . . There isn't a person on the planet who doesn't use it" (1994: 6). The mild insensitivity to difference in this universalist empathy—"United States" would do just as well as "planet"—

illustrates the drive in lite phenomena to emotional unity. On *Sally Jesse Raphael,* racial specificity disappeared in a similar universalism about "relationships." Gwendolyn Goldsby Grant, *Essence's* advice columnist, expounded the usual line about finding yourself first: "Selfishness is a courageous stand. . . . You need to take care of yourself so when the ship sinks, you can help others, too." A black guest agreed that in problematic relationships, "you seem to be incorporated . . . and you can't find where you are." When a lesbian in the audience endorsed the same perspective, the remedy was the same, only more so: "I'm a lesbian. . . . I knew I would have to work that much harder [on my relationship]. . . . we are both selfish. . . . We had to come in whole" (*Sally Jesse Raphael,* 1994: 5). Such homogenization around the category of the self can swamp the varieties of reality fighting to get a hearing on talk shows.

Anti-lite arguments are emotivist as well. The person who asserts that computer models of mind cannot capture mind's essence believes that important aspects of subjectivity cannot be modeled but only felt (Wright, 1995: 16). Yet lite's opponents often find traces in lite of this morality of feeling that they praise. Guare's play *Six Degrees of Separation* treats David Hampton's theatrical life as an allegory for lost feeling, lost reality. The longings of the impostor become a measure of our own anomie, of the bond we do not have with our children or the world. "This paltry thing, our life—he wanted it," says the duped woman to her husband. "He did more for us in a few hours than our children ever did. . . . Don't let that go" (1992: 116–17). An impostor incapable of moral thought has, nonetheless, powerful yearnings that can indicate to us our ethical failings.

It seems more egalitarian to ground differences in opinion about lite in the realm of emotion—some people like lite, some people don't—than in the realm of intellect. But because lite phenomena are so derided, anti-lite pundits *can* say, undemocratically, that some people think better than others. Grassroots art, for example, has as strong a claim as do the products of art school artists to emotional authenticity. Yet it is acceptable to exclude grassroots art from the category of "real" art, because its interiority is not clearly accompanied by complex intellectual deliberation (cited in Metz, 1989: 5). Emotivism is thus inadequate to moral distinctions in the domain of lite.

Lite Excess

Whether we think lite is real or not, moral or not, we reach that understanding through its representations. If, for instance, we disapprove of television for deserting reality, we are denouncing television as bad representa-

tion. Such disapproval is really nostalgia for an imaginary perfect fit between representation and reality. If, however, we approve of cyberspace for
extending our reality, we are upholding cyberspace as a good representation
of reality, one that takes account of phenomena that, though often dismissed
as trivial or marginal, are important. If, finally, we praise the unreality of
horror movies, comics, or romance novels, we are, again, endorsing the
moral value of specific forms of representation, in this case melodramatic
and excessive forms. In this section, we shall argue that when we understand
the moral debates about lite in this way, as debates about what is good and
bad representation and what representation's relationship to reality should
be, the possibility grows of negotiating, beyond emotivist placation, toward
contingent moral solutions.

Television talk shows provide good examples of moral negotiation.
With their cast of people on the edge of rationality and their ethical incoherence, the shows are often denounced as sensational. But their emotional
excesses, pointing beyond easily available meanings, hint at subjective, irrational horrors that usually lie outside representation.[9] The *Geraldo*
episode airing against *Sally Jesse Raphael*'s "relationships" show was characterized, its host said, by "the most hatred I have ever seen expressed between a mother and a daughter." Disjointedly, the show uncovered a history
of physical and sexual abuse. One young woman said her stepfather "beat
me one time so bad he broke a belt on me and put me in a bathtub that had
salt in it. And he turned up *Charlie's Angels* so that no one would hear me
scream." "I did beat her," responded the man. "The main reason was ciga-
rettes and lying" (*Geraldo*, 1994: 2–3). Then daughter and mother started
fighting and said they hated each other. "I no longer have a daughter," said
the mother. "You are dead in my book," replied the daughter (13, 15). The
mother made incomprehensible, threatening comments: "What about Big
E, Angie? What about Big E?" (5). The host's mediating revulsion—the event
"is very embarrassing and very painful to me. . . . I feel almost sick to my
stomach" (13)— did not mitigate the sense of something half-unveiled and
inexplicable, escaping representation. On the contrary, Geraldo's overblown
disgust served as a mark of the event's ethical challenge. By suggesting that
some things cannot be represented, such talk show rhetoric diverts us toward an ambivalence that can move us beyond familiar ethics. Such lite excess demands that we negotiate it into our own moral frames, changing it,
and the frames, in the process.

At its simplest, lite excess appears as a strategic amorality, an insistence on a morality of the surface. David Hampton's life as an impostor
worked as such a representational resistance to conventional reality, assert-

ing a morality of masquerade that had nothing to do with who you "really" are. So do the virtual "worlds" created on the Internet, where you take on a persona constructed solely for cyberspace. The creators of such "game realities" defend the rules of the game as the only applicable ethical standards (Dibbell, 1994: 251). A similar fictional morality is developed by those who participate in the Net's academic discussions, discussions that run parallel to real life or the "RL" academic world but are dissociated from it. These discussions, even if they have their own hierarchies, allow new patterns of debate, new communities, where graduate students may drown out professors and no one can judge you by your color or gender.

Lite is a highly empirical realm, generating information and experiences beyond counting or comprehension. This excess transcends the boundaries of what can be represented, sometimes moving moral debate toward new, nonlite realms. Talk shows' insoluble narratives of sexual abuse and battering suggest an explanatory frame beyond the one we see and hear. The demographics of these shows, in which children and women repeatedly report the abuse of men, turn moral consideration away from the truth, falsity, or sensationalism of what is being said, and toward the social, gendered structuring of these wrongs. Similarly, the ignoring of racial difference in the shows, for instance, in parent-child reunion episodes that feature children who look black and mothers who look white, or in episodes on education and poverty, points away from the emotivist morality the shows articulate, toward the racial structure of social realities, perhaps more effectively than do self-conscious "race" shows.

Talk shows also put forward innumerable sagas of white-trash abjection—violence; failed relationships; multiple, variously cared-for children—in which white failure is coded as miscegenation, a stain or soiling. When Joy appeared on *Bertice Berry*, her stepmother said she was called white trash because she had a black baby (1994: 14). In many episodes, too, guests play out stereotypes of passive white and aggressive black femininity and powerful white and impotent black masculinity, through cross-raced figures of "whitened" black princesses or "blackened" white trash like Joy. This repetitive tonal uncertainty about who is black, who is white, and who is right points to the racial structuring of established morality.

Cultural Mixing

Negotiating toward moral solutions in the realm of lite is often a matter of recognizing and promoting a kind of hybridity. Lite's inclusiveness and mixed-media nature produce a horror among its moral opponents that looks a lot like "guess who's coming to dinner" panic. It is by acknowledging rather than downplaying the moral challenge of lite's tainted realities and confused genres, of lite as "the invisible spy in perfect disguise that slipped past the barricades in an unguarded moment," that some accounting and understanding of its effects becomes possible (Piper, 1991: 26; Bhabha, 1994).

In the lite realm, the mixing of forms conventionally considered unmixable is a sign of ethical challenge or change. Often, the miscegenation is fairly literal. For instance, African American women's articulation on talk shows and in magazines of an emotivism drawn largely from white New Age writers and pop psychologists sometimes becomes a briefly effective moral coalition that also calls on the work of Maya Angelou, Gloria Naylor, Toni Morrison, and Alice Walker, and on the black church. The mixture is irreconcilable but amiable and productive; it manages to be more, ethically, than the sum of its parts. *Essence,* for instance, makes self-esteem, long part of white self-help discourse, central to black self-affirmation as well. In a feature on "the winner within," motivational rhetoric is combined not just with "goddess-wisdom" but also with the "Creator." However, the article speaks to its black readership by presenting a more woman-friendly and ecumenical view of the black church and by emphasizing help from "older, wiser" people, being a good daughter, and contributing to the "community" (Corbett, 1995: 66). The magazine modestly suggests that "a cheerful smile" is sometimes the only positive work contribution you can make, and advises you not to take a job "just for the money" (70). *Essence* mixes white New Ageism and self-help with black referents—a woman-empowered church, the history of black women's achievements against the odds—to promote self-advancement for black women. By such miscegenations, bringing unrelated domains together, lite breaks the grip on individualist emotivism, undoes polarities of good and bad representation, of high and low culture, and suggests new moral possibilities for living—particularly for living within a racially divided culture.

The ethical effect of such hybridity is perhaps most explicit when cultural forms are deliberately mixed. White music that acknowledges its black history, as some white soul does, or black music that uses white-identified forms, as black rock music does, is a kind of play that is serious in its morality of cross-race affirmation. Ice-T, for instance, says of "Cop Killer," the banned song by his rock group Body Count, that it "injected black rage into white kids" (1994: 170). Rap draws as heavily on white horror movies, superhero comics, white rock, and mainstream TV as it does on the history of black cultural production. It threatens the dominant moral order, not just with explicit sexuality, misogyny, and gangsta anger but also with a hybrid creativity, a constant refashioning of diverse materials.[10] "Our way of thinkin' ain't industrialized," says RZA of the Wu-Tang Clan, a long-established rapper collective (Malone, 1995: 74). *Enter the Wu-Tang,* a hard-core album recorded by the Wu-Tang Clan in 1995, is peppered with drive-bys, grim beats, and ferocious rhymes: it sounds like a war. But it is a rap war, a war between rhymes and sounds. The Glocks and Lexuses repeatedly invoked are comic-book images; the rhymes outdo the most self-consciously gory movies in their gleeful plays with dismemberment—"We're more deadly than the stroke of an ax, choppin' through your back, ffsshhh" ("Bring Da Ruckus," 1995). The music pays respect to 1970s soul and funk, with a mellow, reflective piano tinkling through many of the tracks and references to sentimental 1970s icons such as the television show *Fame* and the song "Chim Chim Cheree." The whole is presented as a reincarnation of the ancient Asian monk-warrior power of the Wu-Tang sword, a secret physical and mental discipline portrayed in kung fu movies. The work thus follows a strong tradition in postwar black American music of piecing together imaginatively reconstructed history and future fantasy. Such mixing ignores respected boundaries that have become ethical distinctions between types of music and speech—black and white, serious and lite—contesting them with more fluid and fantastic ethics—of Buddhism and Afrocentrism, rhyme and rhythm-mixing.

Rap's miscegenation also affects producers, who include white rappers such as 3rd Bass, and audiences. Although it is a significant part of the economic and moral order of black consumerism, rap also has an audience about 50 percent white. In an important, though limited, way, rap can make whites "black" (Wood, 1991: 11). This means that rap's effect as a moral negotiator is not only to represent ignored realities but also to use representation itself to reformulate "race," though not to deny it. Radically different forms of rap, such as P.M. Dawn's New Ageism, operate with a similar ethical tension between reality and a mixed-up, consciously utopian possibility: "I can understand realistic ways / But I invent the next phase of forever / I, like you, freewrite the next page" ("Sometimes I Miss You So Much," *Jesus Wept,* 1995).

Can lite radio, which is much less self-conscious about its combinations and innovations but whose very name conjures the moral ambivalences of this chapter, supply similar moral possibilities? Lite stations play not the seamless music made under the Muzak trademark—music that never had a history—nor popular versions of classical music, but tunes from the last twenty-five years, well-known songs that act as markers of the culture's history but that the stations divorce from that history. After a string of songs, titles and singers are announced, but dates are never mentioned. Songs are linked not by chronology but by mood, a scheduling that preserves them from social and historical specificity. Every ten minutes or so, listeners hear a song they sort-of like: that is lite radio's emotivist glue. The music is mixed in its genres and racial identifications, and never insistent in either. One typical Friday, for instance, WLTW, New York's lite FM station, preceded the 8:30 A.M. news with four lovelorn, medium-tempo songs dating from three decades, sung by women and men of varying ethnicities. Although it ignores historical and cultural distinctions, the medium is also a democratization, treating everyone alike, a good strategy for the economically and racially integrated workplace. Leading into the news, WLTW's disc jockey followed Jennifer Warnes's song "Right Time of the Night" with a reminder to the disparate audience that it was the "right time of the week" for them all. But the station still has to bridge different lifestyles and the different genders associated with them: later the DJ reassured those working at home that the station was "there for" them too.

The ads bracketing the news ran the class and gender gamut, from cars and gasoline through *Good Housekeeping* magazine. Chevrolet's "heartbeat of America" spot and *Good Housekeeping*'s promise of definitive "American baking" recipes appealed to a nationally unified market. Nutri-System, said, like the station, to make you feel better, was a sponsor. The news itself covered all social bases, including items on a Brooklyn cop, a Hispanic arsonist, a bid-rigging trial, a New Delhi plane crash, a Paul Simon concert, and New York sports teams. Around this date, television ads for WLTW showed a middle-aged white man and a younger Latina, positioned at his side like a secretary, agreeing that the station helped them both get through the day. Setting itself up as music for citizens to live by, lite radio holds out a modest moral possibility of keeping the social fabric together. If an executive and his secretary can both listen to the same stream of sound and find value in it, perhaps they can reach a similar, though equally limited, consensus at work and even find some common ground outside the workplace.

"The Art of the Weak"

If you were trying to build citizenship through popular culture, lite radio might not be a vital part of the program. Nevertheless, in the contemporary workplace it often seems to function not just as background entertainment or as a denial of difference, but as a way of negotiating commonality. Rap may be merely a soundtrack to many listeners, but to others it is a "voice of the ghetto" to fear or to learn from, or a way to get yourself and others out of the ghetto, or a genre whose stylistic openness and dynamism confer moral possibility (RZA, cited in Malone, 1995: 75). It may be that television talk shows' endless repetitions of moral dilemmas and glib pop-psychological solutions are all that many viewers get from them. But viewers seem to like the shows' competing moral frequencies, a white noise that is never entirely reduced to an individual's moral feelings. The shows offer these competing moralities not just as entertainment, but as ways to understand the world, to bridge the gap between ourselves and ethical otherness without forgetting it. As a mother says, dismissively yet tolerantly, in a short story about her lesbian daughter coming out to her, "You don't have to tell me. . . . It's on all the shows. Donahue. Oprah" (Anshaw, 1995: 315; see also Squire, 1994). The effects of such minor tactics of resistance, which Michel de Certeau calls "the art of the weak" (1980: 37–38), are subtle, convoluted, often short-term, and easy to lose sight of. Moreover, an audience's own circumstances limit the interpretations it can make of lite cultural forms. Nevertheless, lite culture sometimes manages to introduce the other into the moral mainstream.[11]

How does lite support these moral possibilities? The fact that lite media are poorly regarded seems to help, by allowing heterogeneity. Compared to prime-time television, for instance, there is little commitment to regulating talk shows. Events such as the *Jenny Jones*-associated murder produce outbursts of concern from policy and program makers about the shows' reality-fantasy mix, but these concerns fade, as if the genre and the people watching are too unimportant to think about for very long. Lite seems innocuous enough both to allow sensational topics and to limit their effects. Yet its mutable sensationalism enables these effects. When lite exhausts one topic, it can junk it, an appropriate fluidity for changing moral circumstances. Barbie religion is not forever: even Billy Name, who had a collection of 16,000 dolls and organized Barbie fashion shows, tired of Barbie and fantasized another doll, "Mdvani, a trendy *Parisienne* with lesbian and multiracial friends" (White and Sorin, 1994: 44).

Moreover, consumers are also producers of lite.[12] Lite media have proliferated enough to allow everyone to produce something—a clip for *America's Funniest Home Videos,* a home page on the Net, a self-help group. But these productions themselves depend on lite consumption. Making videos for television requires you to know about the home video conventions—pratfalls, good lighting, but clumsy camera movement—that work in that medium. When you set up a home page, you must be familiar both with the genre and with cyberspace's structuring through metaphors of place—the domesticated space of "chat rooms," "moos," and "playrooms," the sense people get that virtual reality approximates a neighborhood, city, or world.

For your support group to work, you need to understand the importance of expressing how you feel, "growing," and twelve-step principles such as "Let go and let god," and "One day at a time."

In a postindustrial economy, where power relations are unstable and it is hard to know what "real" productive work is, consumption itself can be seen as a form of production, producing a new kind of surplus value, an excess of meaning that challenges existing moralities and provides a kind of everyday resistance (Certeau, 1980: xvii, 95). Think about walking through a city. Let's assume that you are doing that lite thing, shopping. You may be using this word in the new, nonbuying, "lite" sense, to mean window-shopping. You are consuming by moving and looking. If you were in New York in the 1990s, you might take a stroll around the "new" Times Square. This promenade allows many possible interpretations of its ethics. You might understand it as a celebration of a kitsch aesthetic, a happy unreality; or as participation in a safe, inclusive urban pleasure, a "micropolis," a new reality we all can share in, where even the homeless are being given gainful employment by the local retailers. Alternatively, you might see your walk as a kind of collusion in the usurpation of the real by real estate, as entertainment conglomerates, Gaps, and cappuccino bars swallow up pieces of the cityscape and the homeless are swept out of sight.[13] But as you walk, lite pulls itself apart before your eyes, offers up new possibilities of moral drift to your pacing feet. You have to take in not one but several contending Times Squares, each with its own economic, representational, and moral orders. Coffee bars, symbols of confidence, as were fast-food chains before them, have replaced the porn shops, now reduced to nostalgic local color on the periphery of the district but still viable. The Gap turns out to be on a stately corner of Forty-second Street and Broadway, and discount tourist stores surround the Disney and Virgin emporiums. In the square, a steel-drummer plays Bach to lines waiting to see a revived musical. Times Square's redevelopment is itself stylistically and ethically diverse. The Virgin Mega-store aims to become a place of pilgrimage: "If music is your religion, we are building your shrine," said its billboards during construction. Not far away, like a displaced conscience, the news runs by on an LED display, momentarily refocusing the attention of walkers. To the north, the unsubtle aesthetic of the Radisson Renaissance Hotel, glittering black slabs atop the promise of crude cheer in its basement Medieval Tavern, competes with the upmarket investment display of the Morgan Stanley building, contoured cream stone and reflecting steel displaying times from around the world—Johannesburg, London, Los Angeles. However much you enjoy variety, there will be something on this route through conflicting orders of urban moral-

Figure 20. E Walk®, the entertainment/retail/hotel complex being developed on Forty-second Street in New York, creates a new multimedia icon for Times Square. Photograph copyright Tishman Realty & Construction.

ity that you disapprove of, dislike, or feel uneasy about. Contrarily, however much you morally resist Times Square, old or new, there will be something here that speaks to you. As you walk, you hold the moral traditions together in uneasy coexistence. You have to tolerate its ambivalence or get out.

During the reconstruction on the street now called "new Forty-second," artist Jenny Holzer made the ambiguity more explicit. In black letters like those that make up the titles on low-rent movie theaters, Holzer's aphorisms adorned glitzy but fading theaters such as the Pandora and the Selwyn. Approaching World AIDS Day, they talked of death—"The driver palms his cigarette, opens the hearse door," "All farewells should be sudden"— while adjoining signs declared that Times Square and Forty-second Street welcomed Julie Andrews in *Victor/Victoria*.

Prosaically and modestly, passersby did this kind of moral negotiation for themselves. As part of its renovation, the Victory, a not-for-profit theater for young people, acquired a rococo entrance, salvaged from an earlier Forty-second Street. People walking by saw a solid sweep of steps, with old-fashioned, ornate light clusters, standing dignified below brand-new signs in primary colors loudly announcing the theater. They laughed at this happy cohabitation of incongruity. Evoking a generous old municipal building, the steps symbolized the area's proclaimed new safety and friendliness and held a promise for the still-dilapidated street. The laughter of the pedestrians, many of whom worked or lived, as well as shopped, nearby, was hopeful, though also cynical. This laughter, like their walk, negotiated the liteness of Times Square, taking from its patchwork of realities some possibilities for new moral conditions, though no guarantee.

The political is no longer a singular or easily identifiable space (Laclau and Mouffe, 1985: 159ff.). Consumption itself—who consumes what, and how—is not just a successor to or replacement for production. It is a complicated political phenomenon that needs understanding in its own terms. Moral possibilities can sometimes get identified and developed, not just presented, through lite media. At the least, such possibilities change the cultural agenda, suggesting other, nonemotivist ways of negotiating moral conflicts about lite. A purely pragmatic approach to morality, to what works, can lead us to ignore what might be possible, and what is impossible but still important; lite provides a window on this ethical indeterminacy.

Conclusion

In democratic politics, all destinations are temporary.
Michael Walzer, *Spheres of Justice*

Mass Morality

As the twenty-first century approaches and moral uncertainty intensifies, resistance to this uncertainty seems to be represented by hundreds of thousands of people rallying around programs of moral renewal. Of particular interest to us are the Million Man March of black men on 16 October 1995 and the Promise Keepers rallies all over the country, which have drawn more than 2.5 million mainly white men in Christian solidarity since 1995, and in September 1997 drew more than 500,000 men to a single rally in Washington, D.C. The media's recitations of participant numbers at these events came off as arguments for the success of moral absolutism. Hundreds of thousands strong make a compelling declaration. The spectacle the camera offered as it nervously hunted for an edge to the densely packed crowd or zoomed in on those with arms entwined or in postures of atonement and resolve stirred public feelings of empathy and fear. While one viewer saw the "American values" of "taking control of your community and destiny" in the Million Man March, another felt it spelled "separatism, racism, and hypocrisy" (*USA Today,* 17 October 1996).[1] Nevertheless, the image of a huge community of the moment delivers to all those who see it a message of

Figure 21. Million Man March. © 1995 Harlee Little.

unity, even unanimity. Although such gatherings may have been stimulated by the uncertain prospects of the approaching new century and millennium, they have a tradition. At the turn of the twentieth century, Billy Sunday, an evangelist of the "muscular Christianity" movement, preached that "real men" give themselves to Jesus, a sentiment echoed on the T-shirts sold at Promise Keepers rallies (*New York Times,* 6 August 1995). In the United States, while white men's movements may historically rise with fin de siècle moral ambiguity, black men's movements are additionally driven by un-certainties that are attached to being black in America. The rhetoric of Marcus Garvey, head of the United Negro Improvement Association of the 1920s, concerning black manhood and white oppression is echoed in the rhetoric of Louis Farrakhan, the main mover of the Million Man March (Wilentz, 1995: 16-18).

At such evangelical gatherings, organizers ask those who are there to commit themselves to a program of moral rejuvenation and certainty. A se-ries of pledges extracted from the crowd was the centerpiece of Farrakhan's speech during the Million Man March rally, beginning with, "I pledge that from this day forward I will strive to love my brother as I love myself. I, from this day forward, will strive to improve myself spiritually, morally, mentally, socially, politically, and economically for the benefit of myself, my family and my people."[2] In the same spirit, the Promise Keepers have formalized the commitments they require their followers to make in seven specific promises having to do with "obedience to God's Word," "building strong marriages," "practicing . . . purity," and "reaching beyond any racial and de-nominational barriers to demonstrate the power of biblical unity." The pledges associated with the Million Man March and the Promise Keepers seem part of a current trend to counter moral ambiguity with promises,

THE SEVEN PROMISES OF A PROMISE KEEPER

1. A Promise Keeper is committed to honoring Jesus Christ through worship, prayer and obedience to God's Word in the power of the Holy Spirit.
2. A Promise Keeper is committed to pursuing vital relationships with a few other men, understanding that he needs brothers to help him keep his promises.
3. A Promise Keeper is committed to practicing spiritual, moral, ethical, and sexual purity.
4. A Promise Keeper is committed to building strong marriages and families through love, protection and biblical values.
5. A Promise Keeper is committed to supporting the mission of his church by honoring and praying for his pastor, and by actively giving his time and resources.
6. A Promise Keeper is committed to reaching beyond any racial and denominational barriers to demonstrate the power of biblical unity.
7. A Promise Keeper is committed to influencing his world, being obedient to the Great Commandment (see Mark 12:30-31) and the Great Commission (see Matthew 28:19-20).

Figure 22. Promise Keepers pledges from the Web (October 1997, at http://www.tdksoft.com/pk/7proms.html).

vows to specific principles of action and thought that will hold this ambiguity at bay. This trend includes the Republicans' Contract with America and Clinton's "New Covenant," the response to the Contract with America announced in his 1995 State of the Union address. Rather than using the Republicans' legalistic designation, Clinton chose a religious name for his plan, trumping the Republicans with a name that evokes more ethical certainty. The intent to counter moral doubt marks much of the address itself: "Our New Covenant is a new set of understandings for . . . how we can repair the damaged bonds in our society and come together behind our common purpose" (*New York Times,* 25 January 1995). But attempts to convert the promises of politicians into laws and the pledges made at mass rallies into actions are altered, moderated, or rescinded when they enter the complicated congressional structures and the ambivalent social contexts where such attempts must be played out.

By limiting participants to men only, both the Million Man March and the Promise Keepers rallies suggest that moral certainty has a gender. Against the charges of sexism, each constructed its own justification: at the Million Man March, the benign intention of this discrimination was expressed over and over. For Farrakhan, it was a day of "atonement," an opportunity for black men to apologize to black women and to voice their intention of relieving them of the burdens they have carried (*New York Times,* 8 October 1995). For Marcia Gillespie, editor of *Ms.* magazine, these movements tell men, "We've been bad masters. Let's now become better masters" (qtd. in Goodman, 1995). At the Promise Keepers official Web site in 1997, the question "Why for men only?" was answered with the rationale that the "specific calling to minister to men has helped to fill a void in Christian resources." The void is a reference to the fact that although Christian clergy are predominantly male, female parishioners outnumber male (*New York Times*, 6 August 1995).[3] Thus, imply the Promise Keepers organizers, the emphasis on men is to establish a balance that will favor moral certainty. The familiar subtext in these cases is that women in control means weakened or even dissipated morality; it requires men to guarantee moral stability and growth. Although eschewing evangelism's methods, David Blankenhorn, a leading communitarian, offers a secular version of these ideas. In his book *Fatherless America: Confronting Our Most Urgent Social Problems* (1995), he both describes men as rescuers of moral certainty and asks them to take a pledge to accomplish this rescue. He directs American men to pledge fealty to fatherhood and marriage, because he attributes immorality to the loss of such fealty: "If we encourage men to pursue a manhood that is untempered by norms of responsible fatherhood, the primary results will be more violence" (225). Although the emphasis on men has a rationale specific to each movement, it is also connected to a general tendency we have remarked on before. It expresses a nostalgic wish to reaffirm male power eroded by feminism, to restore the patriarchal family, and to re-oedipalize society—a nostalgia that, although it implicitly recognizes moral uncertainty, also evades it.

There is no guarantee that the hundreds of thousands participating in the Million Man March and the Promise Keepers rallies will remember their vows. Participants are likely to return to communities momentarily impressed but untransformed and still locked in an ethically uncertain America. Moreover, the pledges and promises, if acted upon, translate into a large variety of programs and practices that may be only vaguely related to their source. Seven months after the Million Man March, the Black Ministers Council of New Jersey sponsored a "follow-up" rally in Trenton for "men, women and children," thus changing the original exclusive appeal to black men; the call to rescue black masculinity is converted to the much more familiar appeal of the black church for community solidarity and action (*Trenton [N.J.] Times*, 7 May 1996). A year later, Farrakhan himself organized an anniversary rally to which he invited women and Hispanic and Native American speakers, thus, like the Trenton church, edging the ideology of the march closer to familiar terrain (*New York Times*, 17 October 1996). And two years later, in October 1997, the oppressed returned again several hundred thousand strong when black women staged their own Million Woman March in Philadelphia, which refocused attention on health care, education, and jobs (*New York Times*, 26 October 1997). In similar moves, local chapters of Promise Keepers posted letters and editorials from followers on the

World Wide Web that violated some of the tenets of the national organization. Despite a national masculinist rhetoric that nevertheless disavows a misogynist agenda, letters circulated on the home pages of local Promise Keeper chapters went beyond the canonical Pauline hierarchy of God, man, and woman. One letter writer, complaining of the leniency toward women in official Promise Keepers rhetoric, implored men, "I'm not suggesting that you ask for your role back. I'm urging you to take it back.... There can be no compromise here." Individual emotivist moral judgments qualify or even displace Promise Keepers' communal ethics. Once the rallies end, each Promise Keeper can interpret, amend, or forget his pledges. Additionally, the extrachurch nature of the Promise Keepers works against the solidarity upon which the message of moral certainty depends. As participants go back to their own churches, which they are supposed to do as Promise Keepers, they are enveloped in the local parish and the particular denomination—each with its own demands (Spalding, 1996: 260). They also return to their variously organized families and diverse communities, as well as to morally contentious and unstable workplaces, schools, and associations. Having tasted short-lived communal certainty, they return necessarily to the moral ambiguities of citizenship, of everyday life.

Pragmatic Indecision

In contrast to these uneasy public attempts at moral rejuvenation are demonstrations of adapting to moral uncertainty. These demonstrations often have a utilitarian cost-benefit shape, especially in the hands of politicians. They are meant to settle the issue, but since some uncertainty remains, they are never quite convincing. Such excursions into moral ambivalence are particularly vexed around the issue of abortion. During the 1992 presidential campaign, the media treated a candidate's stand on abortion as a litmus test of voter acceptability, though it was unclear whether a particular stand on abortion would, in the end, decide many votes. Grilled on *Meet the Press* and by various news anchors, the presidential and vice presidential candidates shifted positions or slipped from one to another. Both Clinton and Gore moved toward a stronger pro-choice position than they had held before the campaign. Bush shuffled between a firm advocacy of a constitutional amendment to protect the "unborn" to a promise, should the occasion arise, to stand by his granddaughter no matter what her decision regarding an abortion might be (Toner, 1992). As the 1996 presidential campaign heated up, this moral ambivalence in the Republican camp was foregrounded and institutionalized. In an attempt to seem inclusive, the Republican National Committee appointed temporary cochairs of the

Republican National Convention, each representing an opposing position on abortion: Governor Christine Todd Whitman of New Jersey for choice and Governor George W. Bush of Texas against choice (*Trenton [N.J.] Times*, 1 May 1996). With one position negating the other, Dole officially proclaimed his acceptance of abortion's moral undecidability. This inconclusiveness spilled over into the convention itself. The Republican platform included an antiabortion plank, but Governors Pete Wilson and George Pataki rejected the plan, and others, including Dole, pretended it did not exist. Moral undecidability toward abortion also was the message Dole delivered in choosing a young mother, Representative Susan Molinari, to give a keynote speech. Although her pro-choice stand was well known and was often repeated by TV anchors, she did not mention it. Rather, her speech was marked by many references to her new baby girl, upon whom the cameras lingered during the speech, bottle-feeding in the arms of her appropriately family-minded father, though this division of labor also signaled untraditional family roles.

Dissenting Supreme Court justices in April 1996 saw a similar logic at work in the decision not to hear South Dakota's challenge to a U.S. Court of Appeals ruling. This ruling struck down South Dakota's 1993 parental notice law that required teenagers who wanted an abortion to notify a parent forty-eight hours before the procedure was to take place. The court of appeals declared the law unconstitutional because the best interests of *some* of the teenagers would not be served if their parents were involved in the abortion decision. The decision not to hear the South Dakota appeal struck Justices Scalia, Rehnquist, and Thomas as a "stealthful" "ad hoc nullification machine" regarding state abortion laws. By refusing to hear such an appeal, according to the minority opinion, the Supreme Court was surreptitiously condoning the negation of state restrictions on abortion (*New York Times*, 30 April 1996). Although both the majority and minority justifications turned on constitutionality, the decision mirrored the general moral ambiguity regarding abortion. Mainstream politicians and the courts, who are supposed to speak for all of us, seem increasingly reluctant to resolve the issue when the status quo is complicated and contested.

Even though undecidability regarding it persists, abortion, of course, remains legal. However, as the South Dakota case suggests, *Roe v. Wade* is vulnerable to state and federal laws restricting access, whether it be state bills requiring parental notification or federal bills outlawing forms of late-term abortion.[4] Yet these restrictions are themselves subject to legal appeals and Supreme Court review. This situation means that, rather than a thumbs-up or thumbs-down issue, abortion has, for the moment, become a matter of myriad piecemeal negotiations, often with pragmatic results such as the court of appeals ruling in the South Dakota case, that the best interests of all teenage girls seeking an abortion are not served by requiring parental consent. Like the ruling in the Baby M case, this decision is an example of pragmatic moral negotiation in the legal sphere, recognizing complicated contemporary familial relationships. Honoring parental prerogative, the court majority implied, may not yield the most moral result. Not all parents make decisions based on the best interests of their teenage daughter. Some may sacrifice her well-being to religious beliefs she may not share. In other cases the parent in authority may be abusive, irresponsible, or spiteful. Therefore, legal solutions cannot be based on the assumption of a moral family. Although the larger issue of abortion remains morally ambivalent, isolated aspects of it are open to pragmatic solutions.[5] Moral undecidability does not always prompt such a pragmatic outcome, but one of the purposes of this book is to demonstrate the opportunities such undecidability can provide for negotiating contentious moral issues.

Uncertainty Principles

The 1996 Democratic National Convention opened with a performance of Jonathan Larson's song "Seasons of Love," from the Broadway musical *Rent* (1996), based on *La Bohème* and set, as one of its lyrics declares, at the end of the millennium. Isolated from the context of the script, the song delivers expected Broadway musical optimism: "Measure, measure your life in love." But this mid-1990s *Bohème* about artists, writers, and composers in poverty is shadowed not by tuberculosis but by a fatal disease that sunshine, good nutrition, and antibiotics cannot touch. Many of *Rent*'s East Village characters, which include a Latino drag queen, a white ex-junkie, a black lesbian lawyer, a performance artist, a Latina prostitute, and a homeless man, are dying of AIDS in illegal lofts in the East Village. They create songs, film, and performance art while bonding over AZT cocktails. In its context, the gospel-like "Seasons of Love" is a kind of dirge, despite its celebration of love. It begins by counting the minutes in a year—"Five hundred twenty-five thousand six hundred minutes"—poignantly suitable in a play that dwells on the uncertainty of a life that may not extend beyond your twenties. The Democratic Party hoped to buy an image of happy diversity with *Rent*'s rainbow cast and the seemingly upbeat lyrics of "Seasons of Love," but it could not shake loose from the play's disquieting context. It seems that Broadway plays can no longer be depended upon to deliver an uncomplicated and definite morality. Unlike *Bohème*, in which death seems clearly linked to a socially remediable poverty, AIDS gives *Rent* a more muddled morality in which blame cannot be fixed. It wraps the play in an impenetrable uncertainty that means to express the times and that invades even meticulously bland media events, such as political conventions.

Our understanding of the world in this century has been mediated by moral uncertainty. It is an insistent, though largely unacknowledged, understanding that we resist but that keeps resurfacing. In this book, we have pointed to a series of historical events such as the Holocaust, Vietnam, the assassinations of Martin Luther King Jr. and John F. Kennedy, and Watergate that in their repeated representations reiterate and strengthen the doubt attached to universal ideas of good and evil. It is largely an ethic of feeling that tentatively cobbles together the fragments from secular and religious received ideas, professionalism, and cost-benefit analyses out of which everyone, from evangelists to atheists, makes moral judgments that consequently have an emphemeral and unstable life.

Morality is not an isolated uncertainty. Uncertainties invade the categories we rely on to know our world and have a role in shaping the rhetoric of the Million Man March and the Promise Keepers, as well as David Blankenhorn's Communitarians. Uncertainty has also become more strongly attached to realms we rely on to be dependable, such as biology, medicine, and technology, making it difficult to believe that gaps in knowledge are temporary and correctable by science. The vocabulary of probability, relativity, the uncertainty principle, black holes, and chaos filters out from contemporary physics and unsettles popular notions of a stable and knowable world, of physical reality itself. Like many physicists, David Lindley in *Where Does the Weirdness Go? Why Quantum Mechanics Is Strange, but Not as Strange as You Think* (1996) has opted to look at this indeterminacy with a utilitarian eye: "In quantum mechanics nature is, at the most fundamental level, genuinely unknowable, but despite that, the world at large, the world of which quantum mechanics is the foundation, can be known and understood" (226).[6] "Science still works," despite quantum mechanics (223). But for many, such cost-benefit logic is an inadequate counter to a sense of fundamental unpredictability, which informs their sense of the world at large.

Basic questions shadow other categories of knowledge, such as, What is history, literature, identity, nation, justice, family? What determines gender? What is my body? Whether these questions get sophisticated analyses in the academy or are simplified in political discourses and on talk TV, they are left unsettled when we act. Also, the connections between moral certainty and sexism, racism, homophobia, and totalitarianism have made such certainty less and less acceptable. Moral uncertainty is, then, the condition of life in the United States. Because the immediate future does not seem to include a transformation that would stem moral uncertainty, what we can do is face up to this condition. We can explore its possibilities in ways that are more conscious and deliberate, less accidental, than those in many of the instances we have presented.

The Uses of Uncertainty

From the sea captain who abandoned his ship before his passengers did— the story with which we began this volume—to the lite phenomena in the last chapter, the resulting shocks to moral certainty and the welling up of moral anxiety and doubt also move us from old assumptions. Although such shocks give rise to a feeling of strangeness about other people and the conditions in which we live, they may also nudge us into recognizing a companion strangeness in ourselves. Such a recognition characterizes the responses of movie critics who regarded *River's Edge* (1987) as an event that precipitously made them reevaluate their culture (Rosenbaum, 1987: 80). Such strangeness can be productive. It may give us the distance from the familiar required to make overtures to the unfamiliar, to moral uncertainty. Ariel Dorfman's *Death and the Maiden* (1992a) provides an extreme instance of one type of overture, in this case made to torturers and murderers. Although painful and morally complicated, such overtures seem required for peace and democracy to have a chance in countries such as Chile and South Africa. Such explorations of the unfamiliar, though, are not only mandated by political circumstances. Much more often, they are commanded by local and personal conditions—a son with AIDS or a daughter who wants her mother to carry her child. These situations may pull you out of the quotidian and put you into an alien moral zone where you must negotiate moral decisions with few precedents, the results of which may not be measurable against traditional or consensus standards of right and wrong.

In this uncertain moral zone, contradictions and complications proliferate. At the same time that the Tawana Brawley case gave permission to distrust blacks and women again, on another level it also complicated categorical moral assumptions made on the basis of race and gender. Although Brawley may not have told the truth about being raped and sodomized, Al Sharpton worked the racism in the culture as surely as Susan Smith did when she accused a black man of murdering her two sons. Even if Brawley was not the victim of a brutal hate crime, her case raised public understanding of racism's power to victimize. Yet her story also refocused the public gaze on the particular details of a case and made generalizing from one case to another more difficult and more suspect. As the case developed, lessons about the unpredictable and multifarious relationships between race, gender, family, law enforcement, opportunism, and the white establishment spilled out. In the ensuing ambivalence, "Tawana Brawley" ceased to evoke received ideas about race and gender and became about paying attention to the complex factors involved. Here, the moral strangeness and unfamiliarity that sloughed off comfortable assumptions may have yielded a heightened sensitivity to the multiple ethical views one can hold about a case and to a greater attentiveness to its particularity—a yield that is transferable to other situations of moral ambiguity.

Even discourses in complete disarray, in which moral uncertainties can only expand, offer instructive encounters with the ethically unfamiliar. Despite the legal definition spelled out in a 1973 Supreme Court case, the meaning of obscenity became a topic of public controversy in debates on congressional censorship of the National Endowment for the Arts in 1989 (Vance, 1992: 221).[7] Deciding on the definition of obscenity is no small matter, because "obscenity" marks moral borders for speech and action. Attempts at definition demonstrated, first, emotivism's power to pulverize such issues and, second, the law's inability to resolve uncertainty, particularly in a pluralistic democracy. Conservative positions varied: Patrick Buchanan saw S-M as evidence of an "explosion of anti-American, anti-Christian, and nihilist 'art'"; William F. Buckley reiterated the right of art galleries to "continue to express . . . childish fascination for blackmass profanity or kinky sex," but wanted to protect a "taxpaying Christian heterosexual from finding he is engaged in subsidizing blasphemous acts of homoeroticism"; and Hilton Kramer vaguely called for "public standards of decency." President Bush was characteristically telegraphic: "Barbara and I are bothered about the raunchy stuff . . . urine . . . fist up rectum." Beat writer William Burroughs dismissed the issue as a matter of "semantics": after all, he said, we exalt as great art Greek vases showing sadomasochistic scenes and naked boys and girls chasing each other. Novelist David Leavitt took this argument to an anarchic conclusion: "I don't think anything is obscene," he declared. The artist John Baldessari adopted a purely personal emotional standard, calling the obscene what "offends me," while another artist, Benny Andrews, called porn "whatever is in a person's mind." Privatism also led to some logically questionable distinctions. Liberal congressman Barney Frank, offended by Andres Serrano's urine but not Robert Mapplethorpe's leather masks and black penises, asserted matter-of-factly that "religion is sacred, but sexuality is not."[8]

The volume of this moral cacophony, and the uncertainty it exposed, guaranteed that these opinions were circulated and opportunities for an exchange of meanings were created. The art in question was widely described, reproduced, and viewed. As the record crowds at Cincinnati's Contemporary Art Center exhibit of Robert Mapplethorpe's *The Perfect Moment* demonstrated and as TV interviews confirmed, people who would not ordinarily come out for such art did (Brookman and Singer, 1992: 353). The photographs' unfamiliarity and abjectness were now crowded into many people's familiar world. If it did not modify that world, it did make such art less foreign. Where it found resonance with exiled regions of the self, it may have affected the border one drew around morality.

Confrontational engagements over obscenity led to a 1989 congressional amendment introduced by Jesse Helms. This amendment barred the NEA from supporting "obscene" art that involved sadomasochism, homoeroticism, child sex (or any sex), and the denigration of particular religious beliefs. After it was contested by art advocates, the amendment was declawed so that it matched the provisions of the existing obscenity standard of 1973 (Brookman and Singer, 1992: 347). But in the rhetorical battle that preceded this negotiated moral truce, the application of First Amendment rights was scrutinized, the line between art and pornography inspected and variously reinvented, and the place of art in culture and its relationship to action seriously reviewed. Both parties claimed moral victory: the art community because it had not lost anything, and the Helms contingent because an amendment had passed (Vance, 1992: 220). The value of this result, however, is not the stalemate itself and not even the rethinking of received ideas it stimulated.[9] The point is that many people were forced to grapple with a moral vocabulary that they had not imagined existed but that now was becoming part of their own.[10]

Faced with an unfamiliar moral lexicon, you may begin to acquire that lexicon and perhaps move toward moral negotiation. For instance, the men of color in *Paris Is Burning* (1991) use a language of family that takes in both an ethics of care and one of competition. Thus, this language opens up the possibility of divisions of interest in family traditionally conceptualized as a unity. Because socially marked aspects of the body have overtones of deviance and wrongness, the strangeness attached to a black Santa Claus provoked the *New York Daily News* headline "St. Ethnic" (17 December 1991). Although the headline conveyed the uneasiness of such an image, it also delivered a sense of the moral correctness of equal-opportunity Saint Nicks. An "ethnic" Santa may be a visual oddity, but he is on the front page of a daily tabloid. Framed half as freak and half as news item, he is here to stay. As a secularized, unifying cultural icon, he is invested with explicit commonality, and through his emblematic though superficial difference, he is, the paper suggests, black like "you," and white like "me"—a

Figure 23. In a show for New York City officials and the press, Mayor Rudolph W. Giuliani, right, cross-dressed and performed with Julie Andrews, the star of the cross-dressing musical Victor/Victoria. *Photography by Joe DeMaria. Courtesy of NYT Permissions.*

Santa for all of us. More publicly unnerving than the ethnic Santa, New York City's Mayor Rudolph Giuliani, dressed as Marilyn Monroe, in a blond wig and high heels, left the audience at a charity dinner open-mouthed as he sang "Happy Birthday, Mr. President." Despite the just-in-fun context, this gesture was calculated to convey the mayor's acceptance of New York City's extravagant diversity of lifestyles, a diversity that could be safely, if warily, embraced in a Hilton Hotel gala dominated by Republicans (*New York Times*, 3 March 1997).

New-style advertising for disability charities shows the disabled body unflinchingly, exhibiting its abnormality, long associated with evil, but also establishing it as a presence usually ignored in representations of the body and, through this presence, endorsing the contemporary disability politics, which affirms an identity rooted in physical difference. Associating their party with such a politics, the Democrats brought two speakers in wheelchairs to address their 1996 national convention: James Brady, President Reagan's press secretary, wounded during an attempt on Reagan's life; and Christopher Reeve, Superman of the movies, paralyzed in a horse-riding accident. Brady, in a gesture evoking evangelical healing, said, "I'm cured by the Democratic Party," and arose from his wheelchair and walked to the podium. When Christopher Reeve spoke, the podium was slowly lowered to reveal his immobile body in a high-tech wheelchair. Unlike St. Ethnic, whose blackness was normalized by the icon he represented, Reeve had another sort of normalizing vehicle: access to top-of-the-line medical care and technology. Speaking with obvious difficulty and with the help of a breathing device, he associated his disabled body with his Superman movie role. By quipping about Clinton's campaign train, "I think I can beat it. I'll even give you a head start," he translated his disability into a new claim for Superman status and the public eye. He spoke about FDR, implying a similarity. But the appearance suggested he was better than Roosevelt, who was rarely shown in his wheelchair, and better than the celluloid Superman, whose strength is derived from another planet. Reeve sat deliberately, defiantly exposed, stiff, barely able to puff out his words, disabled but still heroic, still humble and morally superior to the citizens of Metropolis, Superman's city. Indeed, for politicians, the disabled seem to represent the "difference" of choice, easier than blacks or gays to defend against discrimination. In response to a question about gay and lesbian discrimination at the second presidential debate in 1996, Bob Dole, who was severely injured during World War II and lost the use of his right arm, said, "I'm against discrimination. We suffered discrimination in the disability community. I'm one myself" (American Broadcasting Corporation, 16 October 1996).

Definitions of homosexuality also became morally complex and uncertainties spilled out after "outing," the campaign to reveal the sexuality of closeted public figures who either denied their homosexuality or campaigned against it. Part of the opposition to outing focused on its equation of gay identity with particular acts of the body. What homosexuality means is uncertain (Butler, 1991: 15).[11] Does it reduce to one act? many acts? Do you have to acknowledge you are a homosexual to be one? Can you, conversely, call yourself gay if you have not had gay sex? Can you, like Brett Anderson of the British rock group Suede, call yourself "a bisexual man who has never had a homosexual experience" (*New York Times*, 17 May 1992)?[12]

Some critics, using a cost-benefit calculus, suggested that outing should concentrate on people who make a difference on policy. Who cares what an actor, whose views on homosexual marriage have minimal political clout, does in bed? Outers were also challenged: Where did they get the right to speak for all lesbians and gay men, and what would they do if they got a person's sexuality wrong? Is a reluctant homosexual, dragged out of the closet, really a valuable role model—really "gay" or "lesbian" at all? The shattering of a totalized homosexuality produces not only disconcerting ambiguities but also a more flexible moral lexicon. People on different sides can find themselves saying similar things. A common understanding of "individuality" and "diversity," for instance, may have facilitated "don't ask, don't tell" privatism about homosexuality in the military. These shared terms committed people on both sides of the issue to a consideration of social variability. For them all, sexuality implied a certain freedom within the "personal" realm.

In the Baby M case, the Babel of class, gender, biological, legal, and psychological vocabularies heard through a series of court appeals was finally resolved in an ethical multilingualism that comprehended that one did not have to choose between kinds of parents—biological, surrogate, or adoptive—that a democratic society embracing diverse familial organizations had room for one more variation. The conclusion of the Baby M case, which legitimized all the parents, was the result of a long and complicated process. It entailed negotiation between moral positions and demonstrated that moral multilingualism, despite the disorderly process of translating across ethical vocabularies, is more compatible with the ambiguities in our world than is any of the single ethical vocabularies applied to the case.

Moral negotiation is often not deliberate but an accidental result of a process in which elements of the opposition are imported. The stalemates over abortion legislation are symptomatic of the cross-fertilization of positions on the right and the left of this issue that have allowed in the opposition's thinking and vocabulary. The process of listening to and answering the opposition's case has left few political or religious stands on abortion uncontaminated by the other's vocabulary, despite the very real differences between them. Pro-choice advocates may agree with pro-lifers who believe that life begins at conception, and may even endorse some of the opposition's thinking on restricting federal funding for abortion. Some in each camp base their arguments in a feminine ethics of care. Although the emphasis in defining the care ethic may differ, their differences occasionally seem subdued by a mutual concern with the welfare of women and children. We are suggesting increasing the consciousness of overlap in the negotiation of moral issues. Perhaps there can be no agreement across discourses of pro-choice and pro-life on abortion itself, but it may be possible to find some common ground on issues of prenatal care, child support, and day care facilities. Here an "ethics of care" can support a pragmatic moral commonality between citizens. Respect for principles of moral judgment that are strange to us can thus help us shape local accords and actions that most people involved agree are moral.

Commonality among seemingly distinct moral vocabularies is not always a sign that an exchange, much less a negotiation, of meanings has taken place. Sometimes the convergence conceals widely different meanings held together by shared assumptions about morality. Noting commonality where it does not seem to belong may produce another kind of estranging awareness, instructive but not necessarily leading to moral negotiation or agreement. For many, the Million Man March declared a new black male solidarity that engaged optimistically with ethical possibility, with the ethical beyond. Its spiritual antecedent seemed to be Martin Luther King Jr.'s civil rights March on Washington. But Patricia J. Williams recasts the Million Man March. Its rhetoric, she argues, is situated somewhere between the Promise Keepers and the Contract with America. The ideologies of these three resemble one another in their ethnic slurs, misogyny, and homophobia. In her view, Farrakhan's and Pat Buchanan's programs of moral purity and patriarchy are not dissimilar. Also, Farrakhan's theme of atonement for the past sins of black men repeats the stereotype of criminality and deviance attached to them and may do the Right's bidding in having black men concentrate on their guilt rather than on positive programs (1995). Although you may not completely buy Williams's association of the Million Man March with the radical Right, you may attach some moral significance to the confluence of these vocabularies. If your rhetoric coincides with that of your would-be oppressors, it does not necessarily mean, as with the pro-choice and pro-life confrontations, that an incipient sense of common citizenship has developed. It could mean that your rhetoric is simply oppressive in the same way as theirs is.

"The Multitude of Dreams Is Irreducible"

In a democracy, an ethics compatible with moral uncertainty and strangeness requires a new understanding of citizenship, an understanding that lets us make moral agreements across differences. As we have said, this citizenship is not the same as "community." Communitarianism calls on individuals to act in accordance with an agreed-upon common good. In this framework, not only individual rights but also the many and conflicting positions an individual subject may hold in the social world are subordinated to a notion of the "citizen."[13] This citizen is likely to be white, male, and Christian, and to define the common good within that particular "universality."

Even when the common good is defined permissively, communitarianism cannot fully accommodate ethical pluralism. The Free City of Christiania, an experimental Danish alternative community located in Copenhagen, which dates from 1971, was constituted to protect radical individuality and is widely thought to make few sacrifices to notions of citizenship. A self-selected community of a little more than one thousand people, it practices governance by consensus. However, because it is a small, protected enclave within a nation, it can throw out people not in tune with what it sees as the common good—as it did, for instance, in the late 1970s when it threw out not only heroin dealers but also addicts who refused treatment. Asterix, a resident since 1971, confesses: "We are very, very conservative really. It's very ironic" (qtd. in Bellos, 1996: 2). Christiania's existence is thus dependent upon a relatively homogeneous population of the morally like-minded, despite its ideology of nonconformity. Described as a "social dustbin" by its own people, the citizens of Christiania may be different from the citizens in the rest of Denmark; they may be viewed by other Danes as assaulting law and order; a third of their population may receive public assistance; and they may attract Copenhagen's runaways, mentally ill, and other refugees from the middle class; but they nevertheless have a clear sense of who is allowed in and who has to stay out (3). A *Guardian* reporter describes Christiania as exerting "more control than any other local council in the Western world—they must 'approve' who lives there, they work out who can do what to their homes" (2). A pluralist democracy does not have such options. Indeed, in Danish democracy, pluralism is what makes room for Christiania (Kinzer, 1996). A society espousing communitarianism, no matter of what stripe, has committed itself to homogeneity. It has not acknowledged, as is necessary in a democracy, that the "multitude of dreams is irreducible" (Mouffe, 1992c: 5).

Given this multitude, given the turn to emotivist ethical judgment and the uncertainties such judgment engenders, and given the general moral uncertainty and the multiple contesting forces of a democracy, we need a radical concept of citizenship. But the citizenship we have in mind is only one of the ways in which we are bound to others. It does not jeopardize other identities a person may have, nor does it reconcile them. This citizenship does not compromise other ties we may have, but it does allow us to mediate between them and to negotiate moral judgments that take them into account.[14] Because such negotiations usually involve a process over time, they do not often make the news, which is more attentive to single, dramatic events. In popular representations, citizen morality is more often heroic than mediated, dependent on a character taking personal risks in a well-defined, single moral act rather than negotiating a path through a contested field. Matty Grover, the adolescent orphan-photographer of *Synonym for Love* (Moore, 1995), for instance, becomes a citizen-hero when she sends a photograph of a "black man with a white man's dog tearing at his arm (111)," documenting a racial incident in her small Virginia town, to the *Washington Post*. This act costs her her job and her already fragile standing in the white community. Similarly, the Nazi Oskar Schindler, who saved

Jews from death camps, becomes the focus of a powerful 1990s Holocaust representation in *Schindler's List* (1993).

Even acts that look like moral mediation are wrapped in heroism in the movies, where it is easier to be an exemplary citizen than it is in the world. To unite factions of the black community against the destruction of low-income housing, Wynn, the black councilman in *City of Hope* (1991), must mediate a variety of his associations: the conservative council he serves on, a corrupt white city government, a prejudiced police hierarchy, black militants from the Nation of Islam, and a more moderate black constituency. He must also convince a white professor to drop assault charges against a black boy who attempts to escape these charges by accusing the professor of making a homosexual overture to him. A Hollywoodized Reverend Al Sharpton, Wynn, with conventional hair and white speech inflections, is only celluloid: he has a clear moral victory. When the professor drops the charge, the black community unites behind Wynn. What's more, the kid apologizes to the professor. Sharpton's actions with Tawana Brawley, on the other hand, led to muddier moral effects. Meditating on the distance between Wynn and Sharpton, we see the kind of complexities that are usually left out of fictional representations, where they would sidetrack or derail the plot or artistic necessity, but that must be negotiated in the world.

In the real world, the repressed can be counted on to return again and again, complicating our sense of moral citizenship and signaling repeated reinterpretations, rendering the meanings of events open and revisable. The people involved in front-page news reappear, perhaps on back pages and sometimes with minor players taking center stage, cuing an ethical reevaluation of their situation. For instance, Steven A. Pagones, a former assistant district attorney, did not want Tawana Brawley's charge that he raped her to stand unanswered by him when his three daughters became old enough to find out about it. Although he was cleared of all charges, vindication for him as a father meant winning his suit against Brawley's advisers, Al Sharpton, Alton Maddox, and C. Vernon Mason (*New York Times*, 24 October 1997). But his lawsuit further complicates an already morally contentious case, hooking onto it new issues, such as that of moral fatherhood and, more generally, the moral beyond of law cases, making the case and its relation to justice and citizenship ever more undecidable.

Real-world stories have long, though perhaps intermittent, life spans; they do not end with the waning of media attention. They resurface, having changed their course, and as a result, their meanings must be renegotiated. On what moral scale do we now weigh Hedda Nussbaum, the abject mother, who returned to the news as an Avon lady in 1997, ten years after her daughter Lisa died, bent on suing Joel Steinberg for physical and psychological abuse (Russo, 1997)? If she wins the suit, does that make her less responsible for Lisa's death? Would it be a victory on behalf of all abused women? In view of her horrific past, her use of normal legal channels seems to introduce abjection into the structures of citizenship.

Real-world verdicts, unlike most verdicts in novels and films, can be contradictory. How do we distribute citizenly moral responsibility when the high-profile accused are found both innocent and guilty and when both verdicts stand at the same time? Lemrick Nelson, a black man, was acquitted in 1992 on murder charges in the death of Yankel Rosenbaum, a Hasidic Jew, during racial violence in Crown Heights, Brooklyn, in 1991. In 1997, Nelson was found guilty, in federal court, of violating Rosenbaum's civil rights by stabbing him at least twice (New York Times, 11 February 1997). So, too, O. J. Simpson, acquitted of the murder of his wife in criminal court, was convicted for the same crime in civil court.

This real-world complexity makes for a messier, more contested citizenship in which moral agreements across differences are prone to be vexed, transitory, and small, but in which they do occur. The incident reported by an African American gang member about the L.A. riots exemplifies such agreement. Here gang members gave up to the police the Mexican American youth from outside the neighborhood who burned down a popular, Asian-American-owned neighborhood grocery store. This one citizenly act does not presage repetition, but it does provide a model of what can be practiced across differences as citizenship. Small instances of citizen morality are, of course, common, some even inspired by legislation. A California crime bill called the Street Terrorism Enforcement and Prevention Act (California Penal Code, 186.22) inspired cooperation in Redondo Beach. Police and neighborhood residents got a restraining order against gang members in Perry Park, making the park safe for local children to play in.[15] Elected officials can also facilitate agreement across differences. In 1995, when Hispanic small grocery store owners in East Harlem united against a mainly black development consortium backing a 53,000-square-foot Pathmark supermarket in their neighborhood that they feared would put them out of business, Mayor Rudolph Giuliani forged an agreement that allowed the project to go ahead. In a move to make cheaper groceries available in the neighborhood, the mayor kept a 49 percent share in the enterprise for the city, a share that he planned to turn over to a Hispanic East Harlem group, thus attempting to counteract the negative effect of the new Pathmark on the local Hispanic community (New York Times, 3 August 1995).

However, economic plans such as Giuliani's can be undermined or found unsound, just as Perry Park can become a hostile place for children again while community, press, and mayoral attention turns elsewhere. But this possibility does not lessen the moral authority of the citizenship that was practiced. As Michael Walzer argues, "In democratic politics, all destinations are temporary" (1983: 310). Fluidity and pluralism in U.S. democracy resist moral permanence and absolutism. Sometimes such transience means that good moral solutions erode, but it also means that what is no longer a good decision may be qualified or rescinded. The moral debates between citizens can always be reopened, and the formerly persuaded may entertain new doubts.[16] This citizenship may be regarded as a new kind of universalism, a universalism that does not lay claim to neutrality as the old one did. It is a universalism that is contingent and mediating and responds to changing historical contexts as well as to personal and community contexts (Schor, 1995: 32–33). It also makes claims for the stranger.

Such citizenship proposes a "complex equality," what we have been calling equivalence, a notion that embraces difference (Walzer, 1983: 308). In contrast, traditional political theory takes citizenship to mean excluding the foreign or alien and largely limiting it to the native-born members of a nation focused on secure borders (Jones, 1994: 263).[17] The radical citizenship we have been describing, however, makes use of moral ambiguities, tries to find common ground with the stranger and the foreign, accepts citzens' hybrid, mestiza state, and does not recoil from, but negotiates, the borderlands.[18] Such citizenship can be unconscious, as exemplified in some lite phenomena that dwells in the hybrid, in multiple moral allegiances briefly held together. The talk show or the popular magazine feature offers daily, temporary moral coalitions of, say, New Ageism, psychology, medicine, and utilitarian calculations of costs and benefits: a *Psychology Today* article, for instance, entitled "Kicking the Habit: It's No Longer All-or-Nothing," tells you to use a combination of "holistic" medical techniques to stem drug and alcohol addiction—including massage, hatha yoga, good nutrition, acupuncture, hypnosis, counseling, and family and community support—depending on what works for you (Veronsky, 1996). Although such a melange may seem incongruous, incompatible, and emotivist, it sometimes manages a specific moral uncertainty pragmatically, with an attitude of respect to difference and without recourse to absolutism. Addiction, in the article, is both a disease and a personal problem, something not far beyond normal personality variance, so that the addict's position as alien is reduced. The article thus makes a citizenly overture to extend democracy without reducing addiction to a mere personal quirk.

Sometimes opportunities for citizenship are simply made more likely by circumstances. The identical towers of Lefrak City, a cluster of twenty eighteen-story apartment buildings on forty-two acres in Queens, New York, hold a vastly diverse population. More than half are foreign-born, and more than 3,000 of its 60,430 residents documented by the 1990 U.S. Bureau of the Census speak languages other than the nineteen different languages spoken by ten or more people there—languages as various as Tagalog and South Slavic.[19] At John Bawne High School, which Lefrak students attend, one-third of the students attend English-as-a-second-language classes. Sufficient numbers of students are qualified and interested to warrant the high school's offering bilingual programs in Mandarin and Spanish. In 1996, fifty-five seniors out of six hundred graduating took reading and writing proficiency exams in languages other than English, such as Urdu, Farsi, Hindi, and Haitian Creole. In such an environment, practicing a citizenship of equivalence seems the pragmatic way to coexist. The vice principal, in fact, said that there is such diversity in the school that no single group dominates. Even among the large Spanish-speaking population, there is little solidarity between people coming from many different countries. In Lefrak City, the Muslim African and Jewish central Asian immigrant groups have separate places of worship, but they traverse the same public spaces and have similar moral investments in getting ahead in the United States, in fostering a safe community, and in educating their children. Eighty-five percent of the John Bawne graduating class goes to college.[20] Aside from undependable neighborliness, formal programs and events call for equivalence between the diverse groups: their children meet not only in the public schools but also on Lefrak's soccer field and basketball and tennis courts, as well as in after-school programs, and senior citizens may choose to socialize in the vegetable garden or at the occasional community barbecue (Onishi, 1996: B1). It may be that tolerance is the price residents pay for peace, but it may also be that sharing the status of foreigners makes an ethic of equivalence more likely. Of course, moral agreements about education and safety are apt to be less contentious than, say, interracial marriage. But, as in the United States generally, in Lefrak City, a domain of in-your-face difference, the extension of citizenly equivalence may be the best way to imagine an ethical beyond, of continuous negotiation of morally ambiguous terrain.

Notes

Introduction

1. Although ethics in the Aristotelian sense of an abstract good often obtrudes on our project, we are not trying to oppose a compromised morality and an ideal ethics. In popular representations, the distinction gets blurred. Representations of morality can themselves assume the force of ethical truth.

2. However, participants in the march were predominantly middle-class and in their thirties and forties, and almost all (95 percent) were not associated with the Nation of Islam.

3. In the United States, the contradictions are exacerbated by a powerful religious tradition, now expressed in a need for secular grand narratives; and in a forceful individualism, developed largely to contain religious absolutism.

4. People live "accepting usually unquestioningly the assumption of the dominant . . . forms of public life, but drawing in different areas of their lives upon a variety of tradition-generated resources of thought and action, transmitted from a variety of familial, religious, educational and other social and cultural sources" (MacIntyre, 1989: 397).

5. Despite evangelism's high profile and political clout and the fact that nine out of ten people claim belief in God, religion seems morally unpersuasive, and extreme beliefs suspect. "We have lost this common [biblical] language," Ralph Reed,

now the former executive director of the Christian Coalition, claims (*Wall Street Journal,* 16 March 1993).

6. Much U.S. moral philosophy simply equates emotivism with rationality. John Rawls justifies our concept of justice by "its congruence with our deeper understanding of ourselves and our aspirations and our realization that . . . it is the most reasonable doctrine for us" (1972: 519).

7. As Hirst points out, "We are not helped greatly by being told . . . that our ways of doing things are historically limited and not inevitable. True, but we . . . are not living in a perpetual sociology seminar" (1990: 18).

8. If MacIntyre seems at such moments to echo Habermas or Rorty, he draws more attention to the limitations in such communications and understandings. Unlike Habermas, he places little emphasis on the intrinsic rationality of the individual; unlike Rorty, he is pessimistic about consensus. Nevertheless, in concrete situations incommensurability between traditions is not, MacIntyre says, a serious problem.

9. Drucilla Cornell, though, suggests that communities can occupy a borderline position, recognizing both identity and difference, acknowledging "the sameness that marks each one of us as an individual and thus . . . both different and the same" (1992: 60).

10. As Chantal Mouffe says of such arguments, "There cannot be an absolute separation between validity and power" (1993: 38).

11. Such arguments receive a sophisticated articulation in Lacan's work on ethics (1995), where desire, rather than what we have termed pleasure, is at stake.

12. Such a pragmatism translates the past into a present frame of understanding and achieves its "conditional resolution" through a vision of the future (Cornell, 1993: 29). "The only controllable conduct is Future conduct," says Charles Sanders Peirce (qtd. in Cornell, 1993: 29).

1. Strangers to Ourselves: Movies, Books, Art

1. In *Strangers to Ourselves,* Julia Kristeva writes, "The foreigner comes in when the consciousness of my difference arises, and he disappears when we all acknowledge ourselves as foreigners, unnameable to bonds and communities" (1991: 1). Although her subject is not morality as such, in writing of the stranger or the other within us, her notions have powerful implications for moral discourse.

2. Mann suggests not only physical abuse but also child pornography, in the photo of her older daughter at five (*Jessie at 5, 1987*), half-nude and wearing lipstick, gaudy costume jewelry, and a provocative look.

3. In analyzing two "nostalgia" films, Frederic Jameson makes the following observation, which can be more widely applied: "These two films can be read as dual symptoms: they show a collective unconscious in the process of trying to identify its own present at the same time that they illuminate the failure of this attempt, which seems to reduce itself to the recombination of various stereotypes of the past" (1991: 296).

4. For instance, Marlin Fitzwater, White House spokesperson, said, "We believe that many of the root problems that have resulted in inner city difficulties were started in the 1960s and 1970s and that they have failed" (*New York Times*, 5 May 1992).

5. The two significant deaths in the movie are of a black friend in Vietnam who gives Gump the idea of owning a shrimp boat, with which he later succeeds, and Jenny, a hippie whom Gump marries and who bears him a child. Blacks and hippies, although they may be useful in evoking the 1960s, are disposable in this film.

6. This quotation is from the program distributed at the play's performance in February 1996 at the MCC Theater in New York City.

7. The units of the Sonderkommando were nevertheless short-lived, because they were periodically killed and replaced.

8. E. L. Doctorow's book *Billy Bathgate* (1989, later turned into a popular film), about the gangster Dutch Schultz, and the film *Bugsy* (1992), which celebrates the mafioso Bugsy Siegel as a dreamer responsible for the glamour and success of Las Vegas, both portray the mobster's life as offering opportunities for creativity and self-expression unavailable in the bourgeois straight life. They are squarely in the U.S. tradition of constructing the mobster as a romantic antiestablishment figure, someone freed from suffocating institutional forces.

9. Alasdair MacIntyre argues that emotivism is accompanied by attempts to maintain the objectivity and impersonality of moral judgments. That is, although the judgments are personal, they are offered as impersonal and universal (1984: 19).

10. Pete Dexter's novel *The Paperboy* (1995) reverses this liberal humanist take on moral privatization. Here, a reporter successfully campaigns to free a convicted murderer, whom he believes is innocent but who turns out to be outrageously guilty.

11. *Kids* was coupled with *River's Edge* in reviews. A *New York Times* article was accompanied by a graphic that categorized "bad kids" films from 1955 to *Kids* according to their crimes, drugs, parents, and motivations (Pareles, 1995: 23).

12. Casper's joke name, referring to a cartoon ghost, takes on new meaning after he exposes himself to HIV.

13. Other such flirtations with the taboo include many of Kathy Acker's books, especially *Empire of the Senseless* (see Friedman, 1989). Also see Dennis Cooper's *Try* (1994).

14. Tammy Bruce, heading the Los Angeles chapter of NOW, organized a boycott of Random House books to protest the publication of *American Psycho* (see Kennedy, 1991: 427). For objections based on the novel's violence against women, see Barbara Grizzuti Harrison's comments in *Mademoiselle* (1991). See also Norman Mailer's account of *American Psycho's* "new" immorality (1991).

15. The students' behavior inspired visits from Spielberg and Governor Pete Wilson to their high school. California, as well as New Jersey, offered free viewings of the film to students (*New York Times*, 13 April 1994).

16. This point is elaborated at the end of chapter 2 in regard to justice. See also Young (1986: 20).

2. Justice Post-Tawana

1. E. R. Shipp, the only African American journalist at the *New York Times* who was involved with the entire case, summarized this confusion when she said on *Donahue*, "A black person lied, but I don't want white people out there to feel so smugly, because white people have lied in the same manner for many, many years, and many blacks have been punished for that" (*Donahue*, 1990: 19).

2. The case also spawned a tell-all book, *Lethal Lolita* (Eftimiades, 1992), episodes of *Hard Copy* and *A Current Affair*, and a TV miniseries running, uniquely, across all three networks.

3. Another example comes from the Lincoln Center Theaters. In 1931, black intellectuals complained that *Mule Bone*, Langston Hughes and Zora Neale Hurston's play, exposed the embarrassing vernacular of southern blacks to the hostile gaze of whites. When the play was revived in 1988, Gregory Mosher, the theaters' artistic director, asked the audience what its merits were for the "post Tawana Brawley decade" (*New York Times*, 10 February 1991).

4. Carol Gilligan's thesis that women have a different moral voice, concerned more with responsibility and caring than is men's rights-and-duties voice (1982: 164–65), addresses this omission but leaves open the question whether the difference between the voices is essential or contingent, and whether race and class make significant differences in either.

5. Endorsing these alternative temporal perspectives, 41 percent of whites said that evidence other than the video might change their view; only 8 percent of blacks agreed (*New York Times*, 11 May 1992). Many commentators have remarked on the varying narrative times of justice in this case; see Gooding-Williams (1993).

6. The jogger was, Joan Didion says, "a sacrificial player in the sentimental narrative that is New York public life" (1992: 255).

7. Lesbians and gay men, whose culturally defining sexual orientation is also viewed as a private matter, experience similar limitations of justice. At Jeffrey Dahmer's 1991 trial in Milwaukee, it was alleged that even when one of Dahmer's victims ran into the street begging for help, he was treated by police as a consensual participant in a predictably baroque and emphatically private homosexual dispute, and was returned to Dahmer.

8. Black commentators compared this demonization with the canonization of the white Central Park jogger (*Donahue*, 1990).

9. Notoriously, the defense supported one aspect of this strategy, picturing Tyson as wildly libidinous but just rational enough to listen if a woman said "no." However, it tried to keep Washington "black," describing her as instinctually sexual, a "lascivious, hot-blooded, willing young thing who could not wait to screw the savage" (Morgan, 1992: 39).

10. If the Simpson case at first had the potential to call on this regular-guy ideology using Simpson's peculiar crossover appeal as a nonblack black man, the media and trial arguments about race quickly restored his blackness. Hence, many white

men assessing the case became linked ideologically to critiques of domestic violence that they might in other circumstances have opposed.

11. Also implicated were the prosecution's lack of preparedness and the judge's decision that statements about previous alleged attacks by Smith were inadmissible (Booth, 1991; Taylor, 1992: 37–38).

12. The same argument is made by those who believe in Simpson's guilt yet support his acquittal on the grounds of police ineptitude. In this case, though, the question of how much the justice system messed up causes much wider dissensus.

13. Even this complexity takes no account of the fact that only 51 percent of those arrested during the riot were Latino, and only 36 percent were African American (Gaiter, 1994).

3. Family

1. The former question, posed in a large-type headline, was prompted by a fifty-nine-year-old British woman who gave birth to twins after receiving fertility treatment (*Toronto Globe and Mail,* 28 December 1994). See also Linda Wolfe's op-ed piece "And Baby Makes Three, Even if You're Gray" (1994).

2. The two Baby M judgments discussed in this chapter were decided in the Superior Court of New Jersey, Bergen County, 31 March 1987, by Judge Sorkow (525 A. 2d, 1128) and the Supreme Court of New Jersey, 3 February 1988, by Judge Wilentz (537 A. 2d, 1227). See Roberts (1993).

3. *Father of the Bride Part II,* about simultaneous mother and daughter pregnancies, depicts Steve Martin attempting to deal with his simultaneous fatherhood- and grandfatherhood-to-be. The movie hit cineplexes in the 1995 Christmas season.

4. This episode is probably a fictionalization of a real case, in which the "brain-dead" Marie Odette Henderson's fetus was brought to term. See Hartouni (1991).

5. A second case replicates some of the complexities in this one: In 1993, Kimberly Mays, a fourteen-year-old Florida girl, went to court to sever all ties with her biological parents. She had been given to the wrong parents at birth, a mistake discovered ten years later by her biological parents, who then sued for custody. The court gave them visitation rights, which Mays successfully thwarted in court. But every case has its own twists. In 1994, as a result of what her lawyer described as typical adolescent problems, Mays moved in with her biological parents (*New York Times,* 23 August 1993 and 10 March 1994). The point is that the child chose her parents—twice.

6. In New Jersey at the time, no laws regulated surrogacy, although prostitution, a more public commerce, was illegal. Katha Pollitt wrote, "It seems that a woman can rent her womb in the state of New Jersey, although not her vagina, and get a check upon turning the product over to its father" (1987: 681).

7. No matter how the statistics are described, the unreality of this pattern emerges. A 1996 Census Bureau study found, for instance, that only 25.5 percent of households comprised married couples with children in 1995 (Kilborn, 1996).

8. Coco Fusco points out that "'nontraditional' extended and otherwise re-

invented families are a historical constant in Latin American societies," particularly among the poor. Her point is that the *Paris Is Burning* voguers are not subverting the traditional model, which is white, but in some respects continuing another tradition (1995: 73–74).

9. Feminist economists see this thinking reiterated in contemporary economic theory. Gary A. Becker, Nobel laureate in economics, describes the head of the household as naturally altruistic in making economic decisions in his family's best interests, in his book *A Treatise on the Family* (1981). A man is assumed to be acting for the good of all, a moral force for family and thus for civilization. In rejecting the assumptions behind such theories, Smiley's novel documents contemporary forces challenging nostalgic ideas of family as moral center. See Coughlin (1993).

10. Brownmiller published a novel, *Waverly Place* (1989b), based on the case.

11. The opening sentences in an Associated Press account of another arrest of a parent photographer read, "Professional art photographers like Sally Mann have made international reputations for their sensitive portraits of their children, sometimes nude. But Toni Marie Angeli is no Sally Mann. She's just a student in a beginning photography course." Police were called by the manager of the Boston photo lab where Angeli developed portraits of her four-year-old son. In one he is urinating, and in another his penis is erect (*Trenton [N.J.] Times*, 5 January 1996).

12. Concerning abjection, Kristeva writes, "We may call it a border; abjection is above all ambiguity" (1982: 9).

13. The *New York Times Book Review* for 9 January 1994, an article by Richard W. Schweder, "What Do Men Want? A Reading List for the Male Identity Crisis," with titles including *In a Time of Fallen Heroes: The Re-creation of Masculinity, The End of Manhood: A Book for Men of Conscience, Boys Will Be Men: Masculinity in Troubled Times, Not Guilty: The Case in Defense of Men*, and *Why Men Hate Women*.

14. The Sunday after *Junior* was released, an article titled "How to Get a Man Pregnant" appeared in the *New York Times Magazine* (Teresi, 1994), an account of attempts to get experiments for male pregnancy going.

15. According to Donzelot, "Neither destroyed nor piously preserved, the family is an agency whose incongruity with respect to social requirements can be reduced, or made functional, through the establishment of a procedure that brings about a 'floating' of social norms and family values" (1979: 8). Donzelot rejects the Marxist view of family as "an apparatus indispensable to the bourgeois order. This is owing to its function as an anchorage point for private property and its function of reproduction of the ruling ideology, for which purpose alone its authority is recognized and mandated" (xx).

16. Here, the father becomes the despised, because he is responsible for cutting the link with the mother "in order to take over the creative power of all worlds, especially the female world" (Irigaray, 1991: 42). Jessica Benjamin writes, "The father's ascendancy in the Oedipus complex spells the denial of the mother's subjectivity, and thus the breakdown of mutual recognition. At the heart of psychoanalytic theory lies an unacknowledged paradox: the creation of difference *distorts*, rather than

fosters, the recognition of the other. Difference turns out to be governed by the code of domination" (1988: 135).

17. Danae Clark points out that in *Cagney and Lacey,* "women (i.e., Chris and Mary Beth) assume the voice(s) of judgment [rather than men] concerning female sexuality while attempting to resolve the trouble that patriarchal structures create for women" (1990: 124). Moreover, as Clark intimates, the two women form a "virtual" family to compensate for the "broken, perverted, peripheral family relations" outside their relationship (125).

18. Of such attempts Paul Gilroy argues that "the family is not just the site of cultural reproduction; it is also identified as the mechanism for reproducing the cultural dysfunction that disables the race as a whole. And since the race is nothing more than an accumulation of families, the crisis of black masculinity can be fixed. It is to be repaired by instituting appropriate forms of masculinity and male authority, intervening in the family to rebuild the race" (1992: 312).

4. Body

1. In science, the body provides a "vision of our place in nature" (Edelman, 1995: 47). See Frank Ryan (1993: 12) on the first showing of the tubercle bacillus. Also see Alexandra Juhasz (1993: 152) on the visualization of AIDS knowledge in TV representations.

2. Nikolas Rose provides an exposition of this phenomenon (1985: 36–37, 146–75).

3. Sander Gilman describes the development of a science and culture of racism (1985: 83, 101–7).

4. Jeannette Murphy, Mary John, and Hedy Brown, though, question the significance of the social scientists' intervention (1984: 49).

5. Ellis Hanson (1991: 325) argues that the vampire myth has a particular structural resonance not just with homosexuality, as is often argued, but also with the deathly homosexuality of AIDS.

6. Houston A. Baker Jr. suggests that the most insistent voice of this resistance was rap (1993: 43, 48).

7. Before AIDS, homophobia seemed to be waning in the United States (Altman, 1982, 1987). AIDS reduced such acceptance. Gay-bashing, political resistance to lesbian and gay marriage and parenting, and opposed military and general fundamentalist opprobrium are continual reminders of the gay body's inadmissibility.

8. Cocaine use to enhance performance rather than for fun is estimated to be practiced by 40–50% of baseball players, 40–75% of NBA players, and around 50% of NFL players (Harris, 1987: 9–11). Blacks are disproportionately represented among athletes in these sports: they comprise 74% of pro basketball players, 55% of those in pro football, and around 20% of those in major-league baseball (Harris, 1987: 53). This drug use therefore implicates them.

9. As Stuart Ewen says, the masculine physique "has been the tablet on which modern conditions of work, and of work discipline, have been inscribed" (1988:

188). Muscle once signified economic hardship. Now, though, for men and women, it carries work's moral valence without its social stigma. It means you work hard and are therefore moral, but it does not bear the stigma of working-class economic hardship.

10. See Morrison (1992: 44–59) on similar processes within U.S. literature.

11. Judith Butler suggests that in *Paris Is Burning,* the laws of class and especially race are as significant as the law of the father in constituting subjects (1993: 130). However, Catherine Millot, writing of transsexuality, argues that it "is a response to the dream of forcing back and even abolishing the frontiers of the *real"* (1990: 15)—a response, that is, arising from the denial of sexual difference, whatever the other forms it takes. We would argue that whatever their psychic status, confrontations with and explorations of abjection around class and race, like those in the film, are significant for moral discourse.

12. However, the dichotomy that Susan Willis sees between culture and the commodity (1991: 129–30) makes her very ambivalent about the possibilities offered by such image making. See also bell hooks (1992b: 27).

13. Butler asserts this reconfiguration only of the voguers' mutated families; see chapter 3. Like Butler, though, we are assuming that getting one's image and voice on-screen leaves a residue beyond the director's control: these are not media entirely determined by single authors (1993: 137; see also hooks, 1992a: 155–56, and Phelan, 1993: 93–94). However, an important group of critics has argued that Butler, forgetting that a film is very largely determined by those who make it, in this case by a white woman, neglects race issues (hooks, 1992a: 149-53; Fusco, 1995: 71–74; Phelan, 1993: 104).

14. However, ACT UP has been said by some to have been compromised by victim talk or militaristic language in its efforts to get results (Marshall, 1991: 88, 95–96; Sherry, 1993: 49).

15. A similar but less accessible example of such negotiatory images is the artist Diamanda Galás's tattoo, "We are all HIV positive," on the fingers of her left hand; she says everyone ought to get it (1991: 18; *New York Times,* 4 July 1993).

16. It is, though, both inadvisable to substitute politics for grief completely (Marshall, 1991: 96) and impossible to drive out the image of the tragic homosexual, though it may be challenged, as Jeff Nunokawa suggests (1991: 320–21). The quilt is not one of his examples of how to sustain these ambiguities, but it seems a good one to us.

17. Examples of these connotations appear in Jerry Fallwell (1986: 143) and Faye Ginsburg (1992: 68–69).

18. Ginsburg (1992) provides a thorough account of the contradictory opinions of one group of pro-life women, while Harding (1992) usefully dissects Falwell's own ambivalent relationship with feminism.

19. A number of writers have both noted and tried to encourage this move. Roger Rosenblatt usefully explores the ambivalence about abortion and advocates "learning to live with uncommon ground" (1992: 31) but suggests that we simply

divorce personal from political morality around this issue and thinks that a consensus could arise on ways to reduce abortion, such as support for the family and children, privacy, and better contraception. Ronald Dworkin (1993) emphasizes the "sacred" basis of the consensus on life's importance. Laurence Tribe points out that "there is a profound difference between recognizing that persuasion in a dialogue of mutual respect is all we have and suggesting that there are no moral truths" (1990: 241). See also George McKenna (1995).

5. P.C.

1. For additional sources on the history of the term "political correctness," see Ruth Perry (1992) and Deborah Cameron (1994).

2. The Jeffries case has been through several court decisions. For instance, on 5 April 1995, the *New York Times* reported that a panel of the U.S. Court of Appeals for the Second Circuit Court of Manhattan reversed its 1994 decision and ruled that City College acted within its rights in removing Jeffries as chair of the Department of Black Studies for making incendiary remarks about Jews. See subsequent discussion later in this chapter.

3. In 1994, Harold Bloom published *The Western Canon: The Books and School of the Ages* as a defense against the "school of resentment—feminists, Marxists, and others." His list includes twenty-six authors who are "the best" and three thousand other works that merit attention. *Time* magazine trumpeted his book with the headline "Hurray for Dead White Males" (Gray, 1994).

4. Yet another objection is given by Robert J. C. Young: "The need for organic metaphors of identity or society implies a counter-sense of fragmentation and dispersion" (1995: 4).

5. This order was targeted to blacks, not women, who would wait a few years until they were included.

6. According to Mary Louise Antieau, assistant to the vice president of student affairs, this policy, adopted in April 1989, was overturned in September of the same year in the U.S. District Court. The University of Massachusetts at Amherst imposed a new code toward the end of 1995. Targeted speech includes "epithets, slurs and negative stereotyping" based on "race, color, national or ethnic origin, gender, sexual orientation, age, religion, marital status, veteran status or disability." To this list, the graduate student union added "citizenship, culture, H.I.V. status, language, parental status, political affiliation or belief and pregnancy status" (Lewis, 1995).

7. Our list is derived from Henry Beard and Christopher Cerf (1992) and *Harper's* (1991), which got its glossary of politically incorrect terms from a handout for students at Smith College. The 27 May 1991 cover of *Maclean's* magazine pictures two white students in graduation caps with gags over their mouths and the caption "The Silencers: 'Politically Correct' Crusaders Are Stifling Expression and Behavior."

8. Revised in 1996, but not substantially changed, the relevant stipulation reads: "Obtaining consent is an ongoing process in any sexual interaction. Verbal

consent should be obtained with each new level of physical and/or sexual behavior in any given interaction, regardless of who initiates it. Asking 'Do you want to have sex with me?' is not enough. The request for consent must be specific to each act" (from a copy of the policy graciously provided by Karen Kovach, director of Public Relations and Publications at Antioch College).

9. Bourdieu writes, "The danger of academism is obviously inherent in any rationalized teaching which tends to mint, within one doctrinal body, precepts, prescriptions, and formulae, explicitly described and taught, . . . which a traditional education imparts in the form of a *habitus*, directly apprehended *uno intuito*, as a global style not susceptible to analytical breakdown" (1990: 208).

10. Finley's list is much longer. See Richard Bolton (1992: 282–84).

11. The incident came on the heels of public debate about whether a follower of Louis Farrakhan spouting anti-Semitic rhetoric should be allowed to speak on campus. The case made it into Richard Bernstein's *Dictatorship of Virtue* (1994), a compilation of egregious prosecutions of P.C. cases.

12. Emmanuel Levinas writes of moral responsibility, "I understand responsibility as responsibility for the Other, thus as responsibility for what is not my deed, or for what does not even matter to me; or which precisely does matter to me, is met by me as face" (1985: 95).

13. We use *mestiza* in the sense that Gloria Anzaldúa gives: *la mestiza* is an "Aztec word meaning torn between two ways, . . . a product of the transfer of the cultural and spiritual values of one group to another" (1987: 78).

14. At such borders, as in literal border towns in the United States, different identities meet, working and living together. It is important, though, not to romanticize such border identities. One side of the border is usually more powerful than the other, and this imbalance is well recognized. In U.S. border towns such as Columbus, New Mexico, for instance, the economic and educational traffic is one-way: Mexicans provide labor, send dollars home, and obtain, on sufferance, a highly valued education for their children (*McNeil-Lehrer Newshour,* 19 June 1991). See also T. Coraghessan Boyle's *The Tortilla Curtain* (1995), which dramatizes this inequality in a novel about the encounter between migrant Mexican workers and the Anglo middle class in L.A.

15. The *New York Times* made this link explicit: "A year after the Clarence Thomas–Anita Hill hearings, charges of sexual harassment lead to battle in 'Oleanna'" ("He Said . . . She Said," 1992).

16. In 1954, when the Supreme Court desegregated schools in the *Brown v. Board of Education* decision, one out of every ten schoolchildren was not white. See U.S. Department of Commerce (1975: 371).

17. Here is a sample of Adams on this topic: "If, therefore, a majority . . . are bound by no law human or divine, and have no other rule but their sovereign will and pleasure to direct them, what possible security can any citizen of the nation have for the protection of his unalienable rights[?] The principles of liberty must be the sport of an arbitrary power, and the hideous form of despotism must lay aside

the diadem and the sceptre only to assume the party-colored garments of democracy" (qtd. in Parrington, 1927: 331–32).

18. In *Rights of Man*, Paine wrote: "Every age and generation must be free to act for itself *in all cases* as the ages and generations which preceded it. The vanity and presumption of governing beyond the grave is the most ridiculous and insolent of all tyrannies. . . . Every generation is, and must be, competent to all the purposes which its occasions require. It is the living, and not the dead, that are to be accommodated" (qtd. in Parrington, 1927: 341).

19. As Bhabha succinctly writes, "Restaging the past . . . introduces other, incommensurable cultural temporalities into the invention of tradition. This process estranges any immediate access to an originary identity or a 'received' tradition. The borderline engagements of cultural difference may as often be consensual as conflictual; they may confound our definitions of tradition and modernity, realign the customary boundaries between the private and the public, high and low; and challenge normative expectations of development and progress" (1994: 2).

20. See Coco Fusco's "Bilingualism, Biculturalism, and Borders" (in 1995) for an account of the Border Art Workshop/Taller de Arte Fronterizo (BAW/TAF), an art collective devoted to "deconstruct[ing] the mythology of the border" through a process of "inter-, trans-, and multiculturalization" (147–49). Guillermo Gómez-Peña speaks of the "tricontextuality" of border art, which includes Mexican, Chicano, and Anglo contexts (qtd. in Fusco, 1995: 151).

21. For Kristeva, the relation between identity and nation can be either benign or malignant. The heterogeneity that comes from weaker allegiances to our identities, therefore, is not necessarily good or bad (1995).

6. Lite

1. In shifts that indicated the entertainment function of the O. J. Simpson case, the large evening audiences at the first trial's end were poached from dramas such as *Murder One* (*New York Times*, Arts and Leisure, 28 September 1995). Similarly, afternoon audiences for the trial came largely from older talk show viewers (Benson, 1995a: 156).

2. Edward Ball (1991) and Karen Klugman et al. (1995: 78) provide indictments of this vicarious and themed tourism.

3. Mark Slouka provides negative examples of gender impersonation in his comprehensive attack on cyberlife (1995). See also Julian Dibbell's account of a notorious "virtual rape" (1994).

4. Thus they seem to be pursuing, as an ethics, the order of representation that Jean Baudrillard identifies at Disneyland. Disneyland, Baudrillard says, has no relation to reality. Instead, it masks and mitigates the loss of the real world: Disneyland's imaginariness persuades us to believe in the reality of Los Angeles (1989b: 172).

5. Walter Benjamin (1970: 236) makes this argument. Much later, John Fiske (1989: 159ff.) develops it within the contemporary context of expanding access to some forms of cultural production.

6. Andrew Ross has explored these parallels in viral panic (1991: 112).

7. In many ways, race is written out of talk shows; they are a white genre within which black spectatorship must always be problematic, never straightforwardly empowering (Gaines, 1988).

8. See Sylvia Livingstone and Peter Lunt's discussion of the playing out of expression and control in talk shows (1993:175ff.).

9. Although this superreal, existing beyond representation, has some similarities with what Jacques Lacan theorized as the Real (see 1977: 95), we are using the term in a much more limited and culturally situated way.

10. Such creativity has little regard for "the ethics and outputs of wage labor" (Baker, 1991: 203). Rap's disruption is, like jazz, a kind of poetic break in a homogeneous culture (Baker, 1991; Bernard, 1991; Poulson-Bryant, 1991).

11. Since the 1980s, a series of analyses by cultural theorists has pointed to actual and potential subversive uses for, among other things, romantic fiction (Radway, 1984) and television soaps (Ang, 1985).

12. This indistinctness was commented on by Walter Benjamin: "detachment of the reproduced object from the domain of tradition" allows access to and production by everyone; "There is hardly a gainfully employed European who could not, in principle, find an opportunity to publish somewhere or other comments on his work, grievances, documentary reports, or that sort of thing" (1970: 231–34).

13. In this progression, Los Angeles's Citywalk, a Disney-fied version of the city itself, is an intermediate step. The new Times Square seems, indeed, like New York's own version of Citywalk.

Conclusion

1. Newt Gingrich did not shy away from the contradiction of empathy and fear when he said that the Million Man March, unlike Martin Luther King's 1963 March on Washington, "will polarize and drive us apart," but he hoped the march would inspire "reassertion of values" (USA Today, 17 October 1996).

2. In 1997, this pledge could be found at any Million Man March Web site, such as http://www.acsu.buffalo.edu/~sww/mmmloc.html.

3. Under the general Promise Keepers category, in 1997 at the official Web site (www.promisekeepers.org) could be found a subcategory entitled "The Feminization of the Church," urging men to counter the church's domination by women.

4. A battle regarding late-term abortions took place between the president and Congress in 1996, with Congress moving on banning "intact dilation and evacuation" abortions and the president threatening to veto if exceptions were not made for cases in which the life or health of a woman was at risk. Clinton vetoed the bill Congress passed (New York Times, 28 February 1996).

5. A group called Common Ground Network for Life and Choice has arisen around this very posture and held its first national conference at the University of Wisconsin in June 1996 (New York Times, 3 June 1996).

6. The debate between physicists and intellectuals who use ideas gleaned from

physics to substantiate their attack on certainty and objectivity was brought to a head by the physicist Alan Sokal, who fooled the editors of *Social Text* by publishing a joke article parodying such attacks (1996). Once the hoax was revealed, a print war between these two factions ensued. See Stanley Fish (1996), Bruce Robbins and Andrew Ross (1996), and Steven Weinberg (1996).

7. In the Miller standard established in 1973 in *Miller v. California,* a Supreme Court case, a work of art must meet all three of the following criteria: (1) "The average person, applying contemporary community standards, would find that the work, taken as a whole, appeals to prurient interest. . . . (2) the work depicts or describes, in a patently offensive way, sexual conduct specified by statute, and (3) the work, taken as a whole, lacks serious literary, artistic, political, or scientific value" (qtd. in Vance, 1992: 221).

8. These opinion snippets are drawn from Richard Bolton (1992), where the warring rhetoric about NEA funding is gathered.

9. Many in the art world analyzed the total effect of this fracas as negative: the head of the NEA at that time, John Frohnmayer, put the amendment in NEA contracts, where it became known as the "loyalty oath," and denied grants to performance artists whose work supporters of Helms had singled out as obscene (Vance, 1992: 225).

10. Pertinent here is Julia Kristeva's idea that a sense of "we-ness," of overcoming separation and strangeness, always begins with separation and strangeness (1991: 82).

11. See Stuart Michaels et al., *The Social Organization of Sexuality* (1994), which gives an account of the complexities of identifying homosexuals.

12. A University of Chicago study of 3,432 Americans aged eighteen to fifty-nine concluded that "there is no agreement whether homosexuality is a matter of self-identification, behavior, desire or a combination of these" (*New York Times,* 18 October 1994).

13. See Chantal Mouffe's discussion on "civic republicanism" in "Democratic Citizenship and the Political Community" (1992b: 226–28).

14. Mouffe, paraphrasing Michael Walzer's "The Civil Society Argument," writes of Walzer's notion of " 'critical associationalism' in which citizenship, while being only one among our several commitments . . . enables us to mediate among the others and act across them" (1992c: 6).

15. Information is based on a telephone conversation on 10 October 1996 with Marion Lagatree in the Redondo Beach city prosecutor's office, who reported that residents and police had cooperated to make this park safe for children.

16. As Walzer writes, in a pluralistic democracy, "no citizen can ever claim to have persuaded his fellows once and for all" (1983: 310).

17. Citizenship is an idea undergoing interrogation among political theorists. It is our intent not to enter this debate but, rather, to limit our discussion to the ethical implications of a certain notion of radical citizenship, which we have been developing throughout this book. Examples of such interrogation may be found in, for

instance, Walzer (1983), Mouffe (1992c), Young (1990), Kathleen Jones (1994), and Mary Dietz (1987).

18. Kathleen Jones writes: "As an alternative to the exclusionary model of citizenship, I propose a model of the synthetic or 'naturalized' citizen, ironically named the *mestiza*- or *mulatto*-, or even the *cyborg*-citizen" (1994: 263).

19. These statistics were obtained in October 1997 from the Web site http://www.queens.lib.ny.us/branches/branches/lK37/demograp.html, which provides demographic statistics for Lefrak City.

20. Conversation with Glenn Nadelbach, vice principal of John Bawne High School, on 8 November 1996.

Works Cited

Absolute Power. 1996. Produced by Clint Eastwood and Karen Spiegel. Directed by Clint Eastwood. Castle Rock Entertainment.

Acker, Kathy. 1988. *Empire of the Senseless.* New York: Grove.

———. 1993. *My Mother: Demonology.* New York: Pantheon.

Adler, Jerry. 1990a. "The Killing of a Gory Novel." *Newsweek,* 26 November, 85.

———. 1990b. "Taking Offense." *Newsweek,* 24 December, 48–54.

Adorno, Theodor. 1973. *Negative Dialectics.* Translated by E. B. Ashton. New York: Seabury.

Alexander, Paul. 1995. "The War on Time Warner." *George,* October–November, 160–65, 258–60.

Alien. 1979. Produced by Gordon Carroll, David Giler, and Walter Hill. Directed by Ridley Scott. Twentieth-Century Fox/Brandywine.

Aliens. 1986. Produced by Gale Anne Hurd. Directed by James Cameron. Twentieth-Century Fox/Brandywine.

251

Alien 3. 1992. Produced by Gordon Carroll, David Giler, and Walter Hill. Directed by David Fincher. Twentieth-Century Fox/Brandywine.

Alien 4: Resurrection. 1997. Produced by Gordon Carroll, Bill Badolato, Walter Hill, and David Giler. Directed by Jean-Pierre Jeunet. Twentieth-Century Fox.

Allison, Dorothy. 1992. *Bastard out of Carolina*. New York: Dutton.

Altman, Dennis. 1982. *The Homosexualization of America, the Americanization of Homosexuality*. New York: St. Martin's.

———. 1987. *AIDS in the Mind of America*. New York: Doubleday.

American Historical Review. (1992). April, 487–511. Articles by Marcus Raskin, Robert A. Rosenstone, and Michael Rogin on Oliver Stone's *JFK*.

Anderson, Benedict. 1984. *Imagined Communities: Reflections on the Origins and Spread of Nationalism*. London: Verso.

Ang, Ien. 1985. *Watching* Dallas: *Soap Opera and the Melodramatic Imagination*. London: Methuen.

Angell, Marcia. 1996. *Science on Trial: The Clash of Medical Evidence and Law in the Breast Implant Case*. New York: Norton.

Anshaw, Carol. 1995. "Old Souls." In *Tasting Life Twice*, edited by Ellen J. Levy. New York: Avon.

Anzaldúa, Gloria. 1987. *Borderlands: The New Mestiza = La Frontera*. San Francisco: Aunt Lute.

Atwood, Margaret. 1986. *The Handmaid's Tale*. Boston: Houghton Mifflin.

Baker, Houston A., Jr. 1991. "Hybridity, the Rap Race, and Pedagogy for the 1990s. In *Technoculture*, edited by Constance Penley and Andrew Ross. Minneapolis: University of Minnesota Press.

———. 1993. "Scene . . . Not Heard." In *Reading Rodney King / Reading Urban Uprising*, edited by Robert Gooding-Williams. New York: Routledge.

Ball, Edward. 1991. "Theme Player." *Village Voice*, 6 August, 81.

Barton Fink. 1991. Produced by Ethan Cohen. Directed by Joel Coen. Twentieth-Century Fox/Circle.

Basic Instinct. 1992. Produced by Alan Marshall. Directed by Paul Verhoeven. Carolco/Tri-Star.

Baudrillard, Jean. 1989a. *America*. New York: Routledge, Chapman & Hall.

———. 1989b. *Simulations*. New York: Semiotext(e).

Bauman, Zygmunt. 1995. *Life in Fragments*. Oxford: Blackwell.

Beard, Henry, and Christopher Cerf. 1992. *The Official Politically Correct Dictionary and Handbook*. New York: Random House.

Beauvoir, Simone de. 1968. *Force of Circumstance*. Harmondsworth, England: Penguin.

Becker, Gary A. 1981. *A Treatise on the Family*. Boston: Harvard University Press.

Bellah, Robert N., Richard Madsen, William M. Sullivan, Ann Swidler, and Steven M. Tipton. 1985. *Habits of the Heart: Individualism and Commitment in American Life*. New York: Harper & Row.

Bellos, Alex. 1996. "Whatever Happens to Hippies When They Grow Old?" *Guardian*, 25 September, 1–3.

Benetton. 1987. *Benetton Color Style File*. London: Octopus.

Benjamin, Jessica. 1988. *The Bonds of Love: Psychoanalysis, Feminism, and the Problem of Domination*. New York: Pantheon.

Benjamin, Walter. 1970. *Illuminations*. London: Cape.

Bennett, William J., ed. 1993. *The Book of Virtues: A Treasury of Great Moral Tales*. New York: Simon & Schuster.

Benson, Jim. 1995a. "Syndie Slide Hits Oprah, Phil, Hard." *Variety*, 29 May–4 June, 25, 156.

———. 1995b. "Talkshows Rate Murder Case an Ethical Dilemma." *Variety*, 20 March, 6, 23, 61.

Berman, Paul, ed. 1992. *Debating P.C.: The Controversy over Political Correctness on College Campuses*. New York: Dell.

Bernard, James. 1991. "It's a Jazz Thing." *Village Voice*, 22 February: 69.

Bernstein, Richard. 1994. *Dictatorship of Virtue: Multiculturalism and the Battle for America's Future*. New York: Knopf.

Bersani, Leo. 1989. "Is the Rectum a Grave?" In *AIDS: Cultural Analysis/Cultural Activism*, edited by Douglas Crimp. Cambridge: MIT Press.

———. 1994. "The Gay Outlaw." *Differences: A Journal of Feminist Cultural Studies*, summer–fall, 5–19.

The Bertice Berry Show. 1994. "My Daughter's Sleeping with a Jerk." 14 July. Livingston, N.J.: Burrells Information Service.

Berubé, Michael. 1994. *Public Access: Literary Theory and American Cultural Politics*. London: Verso.

Bhabha, Homi, ed. 1990. *Nation and Narration.* New York: Routledge.

———. 1992. "A Good Judge of Character: Men, Metaphors, and the Common Culture." In *Race-ing Justice, En-gendering Power,* edited by Toni Morrison. New York: Pantheon.

———. 1994. *The Location of Culture.* New York: Routledge.

Blankenhorn, David. 1995. *Fatherless America: Confronting Our Most Urgent Social Problems.* New York: Basic Books.

Bloom. Allan. 1987. *The Closing of the American Mind.* New York: Simon & Schuster.

Bloom, Harold. 1990. *The American Religion.* New York: Simon & Schuster.

———. 1994. *The Western Canon: The Books and School of the Ages.* New York: Harcourt Brace.

Bly, Robert. 1990. *Iron John: A Book about Men.* New York: Addison-Wesley.

Bob and Carol and Ted and Alice. 1969. Produced by Larry Tucker. Directed by Paul Mazursky. Columbia/Frankovich.

Bolton, Richard, ed. 1992. *Culture Wars: Documents from the Recent Controversies in the Arts.* New York: New Press.

Booth, Kathy. 1991. "The Case That Was Not Heard." *Time,* 23 December, 38.

Boston Women's Health Book Collective. 1971. *Our Bodies Ourselves.* New York: Simon & Schuster.

Bourdieu, Pierre. 1990. "Outline of a Theory of Art Perception." In *Culture and Society: Contemporary Debates,* edited by Jeffrey Alexander and Steven Seidman. New York: Cambridge University Press.

Boyle, T. Coraghessan. 1995. *The Tortilla Curtain.* New York: Viking.

Boyz N the Hood. 1991. Produced by Steve Nocolaides. Directed by John Singleton. Columbia/Tri-Star.

Bradshaw, John. 1987. *Bradshaw on The Family: A Revolutionary Way of Self-Discovery.* Deerfield Beach, Fla.: Health Communications.

Brookman, Philip, and Debra Singer. 1992. "Chronology." In *Culture Wars: Documents from the Recent Controversies in the Arts,* edited by Richard Bolton. New York: New Press.

Brooks, Richard. 1994. "A Hard-Hitting Sense of Humour at Work." *Observer* (London), 29 May, Review section, 14–15.

Brownmiller, Susan. 1975. *Against Our Will: Men, Women, and Rape.* New York: Simon & Schuster.

———. 1989a. "Hedda Nussbaum, Hardly a Heroine . . ." *New York Times,* 2 February, A25.

———. 1989b. *Waverly Place.* New York: Grove.

Broyles, William, Jr. 1992. "Letter from L.A." *Esquire,* July, 37–38.

Bugsy. 1991. Produced by Mark Johnson, Barry Levinson, and Warren Beatty. Directed by Barry Levinson. Columbia/Tri-Star.

Butch Cassidy and the Sundance Kid. 1969. Produced by John Foreman. Directed by George Roy Hill. Twentieth-Century Fox/Campanile.

Butler, Judith. 1991. "Imitation and Gender Insubordination." In *Inside Out: Lesbian Theories, Gay Theories,* edited by Diana Fuss. New York: Routledge.

———. 1993. *Bodies That Matter.* New York: Routledge.

Byrne, William. 1994. "The Biological Evidence Challenged." *Scientific American* 270, no. 5: 50–55.

Califia, Pat. 1994. *Public Sex.* Pittsburgh: Cleis.

Camelot. 1967. Produced by Jack L. Warner. Directed by Joshua Logan. Warner/ Seven Arts.

Cameron, Deborah. 1994. "Words, Words, Words: The Power of Language." In *The War of the Words: The Political Correctness Debate,* edited by Sarah Danant. London: Virago.

Carson, Kit. 1986. "Texas Chainsaw Massacre." *Film Comment* 22 (July–August): 9–12.

Cary, Lorene. 1991. *Black Ice.* New York: Knopf.

Castine, Jacqueline. 1989. *Recovery from Rescuing.* Pompano Beach, Fla.: Health Communications.

Certeau, Michel de. 1980. *The Practice of Everyday Life.* Berkeley: University of California Press.

Chang, Elaine K. 1994. "A Not-So-New Spelling of My Name: Notes toward (and against) a Politics of Equivocation." In *Displacements: Cultural Identities in Question,* edited by Angelika Bammer. Bloomington: Indiana University Press.

Cisneros, Sandra. 1991. *The House on Mango Street.* New York: Random House.

City of Hope. 1991. Produced by Dan Bishop. Directed by John Sayles. Columbia.

Clark, Danae. 1990. "Cagney and Lacey: Feminist Strategies of Detection." In

Television and Women's Culture: The Politics of the Popular, edited by Mary Ellen Brown. London: Sage.

Clockers. 1995. Produced by Martin Scorsese, Spike Lee, and Jon Kilik. Directed by Spike Lee. Universal/Forty Acres and a Mule Filmworks.

Clover, Carol. 1992. *Men, Women, and Chainsaws: Gender in the Modern Horror Film.* London: BFI Publications.

Clum, John. 1993. "'And I Once Had It All': AIDS Narratives and Memories of an American Dream." In *Writing AIDS,* edited by Timothy F. Murphy and Suzanne Poirier. New York: Columbia University Press.

Cockburn, Alexander. 1991. "Bush and P.C.—A Conspiracy So Immense . . ." *Nation,* 27 May, 1, 690–91, 704.

Cockburn, Alexander, and Ron Silverstein. 1996. "What the Papers Don't Say." *Observer* (London), 26 May, Review section, 1–2.

Collier, James. 1991. *The Rise of Selfishness in America.* New York: Oxford University Press.

Collier, Jane, Michelle Z. Rosaldo, and Sylvia Yanagisako. 1992. "Is There a Family?" In *Rethinking the Family: Some Feminist Questions,* edited by Barrie Thorne. Boston: Northeastern University Press.

Contact. 1997. Produced by Robert Zemeckis and Steve Starkey. Directed by Robert Zemeckis. Warner Bros.

Coontz, Stephanie. 1992. *The Way We Never Were: American Families and the Nostalgia Trap.* New York: Basic Books.

Cooper, Dennis. 1994. *Try.* New York: Grove.

Corbett, Corynne. 1995. "The Winner Within: A Hands-on Guide to Healthy Self-Esteem." *Essence,* June, 65–70.

Corliss, Richard. 1991. "Vidiocy." *Film Comment* 27: 53–56.

Cornell, Drucilla. 1992. *The Philosophy of the Limit.* New York: Routledge.

———. 1993. *Transformations.* New York: Routledge.

Cott, Nancy. 1987. *The Grounding of Modern Feminism.* New Haven: Yale University Press.

Cottom, Daniel. 1991. *Abyss of Reason.* New York: Oxford University Press.

Coughlin, Ellen K. 1993. "Feminist Economists vs. 'Economic Man': Questioning a Field's Bedrock Concepts." *Chronicle of Higher Education,* 30 June, A8–A9.

Covey, Stephen. 1989. *The Seven Habits of Highly Effective People.* New York: Simon & Schuster.

Coward, Rosalind. 1989. *The Whole Truth.* London: Faber & Faber.

Crawford, Christina. 1978. *Mommie Dearest.* New York: Morrow.

Crimes and Misdemeanors. 1989. Produced by Robert Greenhut. Directed by Woody Allen. Rollins/Joffe.

Daughters of the Dust. 1991. Produced and Directed by Julie Dash. Geechee Girls/ American Playhouse.

Dead Man Walking. 1995. Produced by Jon Kilik, Tim Robbins, and Rudd Simmons. Directed by Tim Robbins. Gramercy.

Death Wish. 1974. Produced by Hal Landers, Bobby Roberts, and Michael Winner. Directed by Michael Winner. Paramount.

Death Wish 5. 1994. Produced by Damien Lee. Directed by Allan A. Goldstein. Vidmark.

Defending Your Life. 1991. Produced by Michael Grillo. Directed by Albert Brooks. Warner Bros.

Delbanco, Andrew. 1995. *The Death of Satan.* New York: Farrar, Straus & Giroux.

———. 1997. *Required Reading: Why Our American Classics Matter Now.* New York: Farrar, Straus & Giroux.

Deleuze, Gilles. 1979. Foreword to *The Policing of Families,* by Jacques Donzelot. Translated by Robert Hurley. New York: Pantheon.

Deleuze, Gilles, and Félix Guattari. 1977. *Anti-Oedipus: Capitalism and Schizophrenia.* Translated by Robert Hurley, Mark Seem, and Helen R. Lane. New York: Viking.

———. 1981. "Rhizome." *Ideology and Consciousness* 8: 49–72.

DeLillo, Don. 1985. *White Noise.* New York: Viking.

———. 1988. *Libra.* New York: Dutton.

DeMott, Benjamin. 1990. *The Imperial Middle.* New York: Morrow.

Dempsey, J. 1995. "Jenny's Incident Raises Specter of Control." *Variety,* 13 March, 9, 36.

Denby, David. 1987. Review of *River's Edge* (Hemdale movie). *New York Magazine,* 18 May, 90–93.

Dennett, Daniel. 1995. *Darwin's Dangerous Idea.* New York: Simon & Schuster.

Derrida, Jacques. 1992. *The Other Heading: Reflections on Today's Europe*. Bloomington: Indiana University Press.

Dery, Mark. 1994. "Flame Wars." In *Flame Wars: The Discourse of Cyberculture*, edited by Mark Dery. Durham, N.C.: Duke University Press.

Dexter, Pete. 1988. *Paris Trout*. New York: Random House.

———. 1995. *The Paperboy*. New York: Random House.

Dibbell, Julian. 1994. "A Rape in Cyberspace; or, How an Evil Clown, a Haitian Trickster Spirit, Two Wizards, and a Cast of Dozens Turned a Database into a Society." In *Flame Wars: The Discourse of Cyberculture*, edited by Mark Dery. Durham, N.C.: Duke University Press.

Didion, Joan. 1992. *After Henry*. New York: Simon & Schuster.

Dieckmann, Katherine. 1987. "The Way We Weren't: Adultery in '50s Films: Exploring the Great Unknown." *Village Voice*, 16 December, 92.

Dietz, Mary G. 1987. "Context Is All: Feminism and Theories of Citizenship." *Daedelus*, fall: 1–23.

The Doctor. 1991. Produced by Laura Ziskin. Directed by Randa Haines. Touchstone.

Doctorow, E. L. 1989. *Billy Bathgate*. New York: Random House.

Donahue. 1988. Transcript no. 061588. Cincinnati: Syndication Services.

———. 1990. "What Really Happened to Tawana Brawley?" 4 September. Transcript no. 3026. New York: Journal Graphics.

———. 1991. "Deceivers, Imposters, and Impersonators." 5 April. Transcript no. 3178. New York: Journal Graphics.

____. 1994. "True Confessions of a Go-Go Dancer." 18 July. Transcript no. 4035. Denver: Journal Graphics.

Donzelot, Jacques. 1979. *The Policing of Families*. Translated by Robert Hurley. New York: Pantheon.

Dorfman, Ariel. 1992a. *Death and the Maiden*. New York: Viking.

———. 1992b. Letter to the editor. *New York Times*, 24 May.

Do the Right Thing. 1989. Produced and directed by Spike Lee. Forty Acres and a Mule Filmworks.

Douglas, Ann. 1977. *The Feminization of American Culture*. New York: Knopf.

Driving Miss Daisy. 1989. Produced by Richard D. Zanuck. Directed by Bruce Beresford. Zanuck/Warner.

Dworkin, Ronald. 1992. "The Coming Battles over Free Speech." *New York Review of Books*, 11 June, 55–64.

———. 1993. "Life Is Sacred. That's the Easy Part." *New York Times Magazine*, May 16, 36, 60.

East of Eden. 1955. Produced and directed by Elia Kazan. Warner.

Edelman, Lee. 1991. "Seeing Things: Representation, the Scene of Surveillance, and the Spectacle of Gay Male Sex." In *Inside/Out*, edited by Diana Fuss. London: Routledge.

Edwards, Audrey. 1988. "The Rape of Tawana Brawley." *Essence*, November, 79–80, 136.

Eftimiades, Maria. 1992. *Lethal Lolita*. New York: St. Martin's.

Ehrenreich, Barbara. 1990. *The Worst Years of Our Lives: Irreverent Notes from a Decade of Greed*. New York: Harper.

———.1991a. "Beating Parents at Their Own Game." *Guardian*, 16 October.

———. 1991b. "Teach Diversity with a Smile." *Time*, 8 April, 84.

———. 1994. "Another Dread Mission Creep." *Guardian*, 1 October, 26.

Ehrenreich, Nancy. 1989. "Wombs for Hire." *Tikkun* 6: 71–74.

Ellis, Bret Easton. 1990. "The Twentysomethings: Adrift in a Pop Landscape." *New York Times*, 2 December, Arts and Leisure Section, 1, 37.

———. 1991. *American Psycho*. New York: Vintage.

Emerson, Ralph Waldo. 1976. *The Journals and Miscellaneous Notebooks of Ralph Waldo Emerson*. Edited by William H. Gilman. Vol. 12. Cambridge: Harvard University Press, Belknap.

Escape from New York. 1981. Produced by Larry France and Debra Hill. Directed by John Carpenter. Avco Embassy.

Ewen, Stuart. 1988. *All Consuming Images*. New York: Basic Books.

Falwell, Jerry. 1986. *If I Should Die before I Wake*. Nashville: Nelson.

Fanon, Frantz. 1968. *The Wretched of the Earth*. New York: Grove.

Father of the Bride Part II. 1995. Produced by Linda DeScenna. Directed by Charles Shyer. Touchstone.

Ferguson, Andrew. 1998. "It's the Sex, Stupid." *Time*, 2 February, 47.

Ferraro, Susan. 1993. "The Anguished Politics of Breast Cancer." *New York Times Magazine*, 15 August, 24–27, 58–62.

Fields, Cheryl M. 1987. "Closing the Education Gap for Hispanics: State Aims to Forestall a Divided Society." *Chronicle of Higher Education,* 16 September, A1, A36–A38.

Finley, Karen. 1992. "It's Only Art." In *Culture Wars: Documents from the Recent Controversies in the Arts,* edited by Richard Bolton (New York: New Press). First published in *Village Voice Literary Supplement,* October 1990.

Fish, Stanley. 1990. *Doing What Comes Naturally.* Durham, N.C.: Duke University Press.

———. 1996. "Professor Sokal's Bad Joke." *New York Times,* 21 May, 23.

Fiske, John. 1989. *Understanding Popular Culture.* London: Routledge.

Fiss, Owen M. 1996. *The Irony of Free Speech.* Cambridge: Harvard University Press.

Fleming, Anne Taylor. 1987. "Our Fascination with Baby M." *New York Times Magazine,* 9 March, 32–36+.

Forrest Gump. 1994. Produced by Rick Carter. Directed by Robert Zemeckis. Paramount.

Foucault, Michel. 1977a. *Discipline and Punish.* Translated by Alan Sheridan. London: Allen Lane.

———. 1977b. *Language, Countermemory, Practice.* Translated by Donald F. Bouchard and Sherry Simon. Ithaca, N.Y.: Cornell University Press.

———. 1979. *History of Sexuality.* Vol. 1. Translated by Robert Hurley. London: Allen Lane.

Frankie and Johnny. 1991. Produced and directed by Garry Marshall. Paramount.

Friedan, Betty. 1993. *The Fountain of Age.* New York: Simon & Schuster.

———. 1998. "Dear Bill and Hillary." *Guardian,* 29 January, 5.

Friedman, Ellen G. 1989. " 'Now Eat Your Mind': An Introduction to the Works of Kathy Acker." *Review of Contemporary Fiction* (fall): 37–49.

———. 1993. "Where Are the Missing Contents? (Post)Modernism, Gender, and the Canon." *PMLA,* March, 240–52.

Fukuyama, Francis. 1992. *The End of History and the Last Man.* New York: Free Press.

Fusco, Coco. 1995. *English Is Broken Here: Notes on Cultural Fusions in the Americas.* New York: New Press.

Fussell, Paul. 1991. *BAD; or, the Dumbing of America.* New York: Simon & Schuster.

Gaines, Jane. 1988. "White Privilege and Looking Relations: Race and Gender in Feminist Theory." *Screen* 29: 12–27.

Gaiter, Leonie. 1994. "Revolt of the Black Bourgeoisie." *Guardian,* 30 June, 26.

Galás, Diamanda. 1991. "Diamanda Galás." In *Angry Women,* edited by Andrea Juno and V. Vale. San Francisco: Re/Search Publications.

Galassi, Peter. 1991. *Pleasures and Terrors of Domestic Comfort.* New York: Museum of Modern Art.

Garber, Marjorie. 1989. "Spare Parts: The Surgical Construction of Gender." *Differences: A Journal of Feminist Cultural Studies* 1, no. 3: 366–94.

Gates, Henry Louis, Jr. 1993. "Two Nations . . . Both Black." In *Reading Rodney King / Reading Urban Uprising,* edited by Robert Gooding-Williams. New York: Routledge.

———. 1995. "Sudden Def." *New Yorker,* 19 June, 34–42.

Geraldo. 1994. "I Have a Terrible Secret: Women Confront Their Past." 18 July. Livingston, N.J.: Burrells Information Service.

Gibbs, Nancy. 1993. "Bringing Up Father." *Time,* 28 June, 52–61.

Gibson, William. 1993. *Virtual Light.* New York: Bantam.

Giddings, Paula. 1992. "The Last Taboo." In *Race-ing Justice, En-gendering Power,* edited by Toni Morrison. New York: Pantheon.

Gilligan, Carol. 1982. *In a Different Voice.* Cambridge: Harvard University Press.

Gilman, Sander. 1985. *Difference and Pathology.* Ithaca, N.Y.: Cornell University Press.

Gilroy, Paul. 1992. "It's a Family Affair." In *Black Popular Culture,* edited by Gina Dent. Seattle: Bay Press.

Ginsburg, Faye. 1992. "The Word-Made Flesh: The Disembodiment of Gender in the Abortion Debate." In *Uncertain Terms: Negotiating Gender in American Culture,* edited by Faye Ginsburg and Anna Lowenhaupt Tsing. Boston: Beacon.

Gitlin, Todd. 1995. "The Demonization of Political Correctness." *Dissent* (fall): 486–97.

Glad, Betty. 1980. *In Search of the Great White House.* New York: Norton.

The Godfather. 1972. Produced by Albert S. Ruddy. Directed by Francis Ford Coppola. Paramount.

The Godfather, Part II. 1974. Produced and directed by Francis Ford Coppola. Paramount.

The Godfather, Part III. 1990. Produced and directed by Francis Ford Coppola. Zoetrope/Paramount.

Godwin, Mike. 1995. "Net Backlash = Fear of Freedom." *Wired*, August, 70.

Goldberg, Jeffrey. 1995. "Marion Barry Confronts a Hostile Takeover." *New York Times Magazine*, 19 October, 38–45, 54–58, 76.

Gooding-Williams, Robert, ed. 1993. *Reading Rodney King / Reading Urban Uprising*. New York: Routledge.

Goodman, Ellen. 1995. "Two Men's Movements Expressing a Single Desire." *New York Newsday*, 24 October, A36.

Graham, Fred. 1995. "The Ground Glass of Reality." *New York Times*, 5 July, 21.

The Granta Book of the Family. 1995. New York: Granta Books.

Gray, Paul. 1994. "Hurray for Dead White Males." *Time*, 14 October, 62–63.

The Grifters. 1991. Produced by Martin Scorsese, Robert Harris, James Painten, and Peggy Rajski. Directed by Stephen Frears. Cineplex Odeon.

Groner, Jonathan. 1991. *Hilary's Trial: The Elizabeth Morgan Case*. New York: Simon & Schuster.

Guare, John. 1992. *Six Degrees of Separation*. London: Methuen.

Habermas, Jürgen. 1990. "Ethics, Politics, and History." In *Universalism vs. Communitarianism: Contemporary Debates in Ethics*, edited by David Rasmussen. Cambridge: MIT Press.

Hampshire, Stuart. 1983. *Morality and Conflict*. Oxford: Blackwell.

Hampton, Howard. 1994. "American Maniacs." *Film Comment*, 16 December, 2–4.

Hangin' with the Homeboys. 1991. Produced by Richard Brick. Directed by Joseph B. Vasquez. New Line.

Hannaham, James. 1995. "Deep Disney: Gay Day in the Magic Kingdom." *Village Voice*, 27 June, 34–36.

Hanson, Ellis. 1991. "The Undead." In *Inside/Out*, edited by Diana Fuss. New York: Routledge.

Harding, Susan. 1992. "If I Should Die before I Wake: Jerry Falwell's Pro-life Gospel." In *Uncertain Terms: Negotiating Gender in American Culture*, edited by Faye Ginsburg and Anna Lowenhaupt Tsing. Boston: Beacon.

Harris, Jonathan. 1987. *Drugged Athletes: The Crisis in American Sports*. New York: Four Winds/Macmillan.

Harrison, Barbara Grizzuti. 1991. "*American Psycho*: Bestseller from Hell." *Mademoiselle*, May, 148, 150.

Harrison, Michelle. 1987. "Social Construction of Mary Beth Whitehead." *Gender and Society*, 1 September, 300–316.

Hartouni, Valerie. 1991. "Containing Women: Reproductive Discourse in the 1980s." In *Technoculture*, edited by Constance Penley and Andrew Ross. Minneapolis: University of Minnesota Press.

Haselden, Rupert. 1992. "Whose Life Is It Anyway?" *Guardian*, 8–9 February, Weekend Section, 10–11.

Hebdige, Dick. 1987. "The Impossible Object: Towards a Sociology of the Sublime." *New Formations* 1: 47–76.

Hemingway, Ernest. 1926. *The Sun Also Rises*. New York: Scribner.

Hentoff, Nat. 1992. "What Really Happened at Bette's Ocean View Diner?" *Village Voice*, 7 January, 24.

Herron, Carolivia. 1991. *Thereafter Johnnie*. New York: Random House.

"He Said . . . She Said . . . Who Did What?" 1992. *New York Times*, 15 November, Arts and Leisure section, 6.

Himmelfarb, Gertrude. 1994. *On Looking into the Abyss: Untimely Thoughts on Culture and Society*. New York: Knopf.

———. 1995. *The De-moralisation of Society*. London: IEA Health and Welfare Unit.

Hirsch, E. D. 1987. *Cultural Literacy: What Every American Needs to Know*. Boston: Houghton Mifflin.

Hirst, Paul. 1990. *Representative Democracy and Its Limits*. New York: Oxford University Press.

Hoberman, J. 1995a. "Life's Fitful Fever." *Village Voice*, 21 March, 47.

———. 1995b. "Rush to Stern." *Artforum*, April, 34.

Hoffer, Richard. 1997. "Feeding Frenzy." *Sports Illustrated*, 7 July, 32–38.

Home Alone. 1990. Produced by John Hughes. Directed by Chris Columbus. Twentieth-Century Fox.

hooks, bell. 1992a. *Black Looks: Race and Representation*. Boston: South End.

———. 1992b. "My 'Style' Ain't No Fashion." *Z Magazine*, May–June, 27–30.

———. 1995. Women's History Month address, 1 March 1995, at the College of New Jersey, Ewing, New Jersey.

Horton, Ralph. 1995. "Infection: The Global Threat." *New York Review of Books*, 6 April, 24–27.

Horvath, August, and Bin, Lin. 1991. "From Reality to Hyper-reality: Simulation and Images at Greenfield Village." *Communication Research* 18, no. 1: 103–14.

House Party 3. 1994. Produced by Carl Craig. Directed by Eric Meza. New Line.

Hrabi, Dale. 1995. "Will the 'New' Times Square Be New Enough?" *Wired*, August, 128–33, 172–73.

Hughes, Langston, and Zora Neale Hurston. 1991. *Mule Bone: A Comedy of Negro Life*. 1931. Reprint, New York: HarperPerennial.

Hughes, Robert. 1992. "Art, Morals, and Politics." *New York Review of Books*, 23 April, 21–27.

Ice-T. 1994. *The Ice Opinion*. New York: St. Martin's.

Independence Day. 1996. Produced by Dean Devlin. Directed by Roland Emmerich. Twentieth-Century Fox.

"In the Name of the Family." 1996. *Economist*, 29 June–5 July, 23–24.

Irigaray, Luce. 1991. "The Bodily Encounter with the Mother." In *The Irigaray Reader*, edited by Margaret Whitford. Cambridge, Mass.: Blackwell.

I Spit on Your Grave (aka *Day of the Woman*). 1978. Produced by Meir Zarchi and Joseph Zbeda. Directed by Meir Zarchi. Jerry Gross Organization.

Jacobus, Mary. 1990. "In Parenthesis: Immaculate Conceptions and Feminine Desire." In *Body Politics: Women and the Discourses of Science*, edited by Mary Jacobus, Evelyn Fox Keller, and Sally Shuttleworth. New York: Routledge.

Jameson, Frederic. 1991. *Postmodernism; or, The Cultural Logic of Late Capitalism*. Durham, N.C.: Duke University Press.

Janowitz, Tama. 1986. *Slaves of New York*. New York: Simon & Schuster.

Jencks, Charles. 1992. "Leap-Frogging the Cultural Pyramid." *Guardian*, 16 January, Review Section, 25.

JFK. 1991. Produced by A. Kittman Ho and Oliver Stone. Directed by Oliver Stone. Warner Bros.

Johnson, Diane. 1992. "Something for the Boys." *New York Review of Books*, 16 January, 13–17.

Johnson, Joyce. 1990. *What Lisa Knew: The Truths and Lies of the Steinberg Case*. New York: Putnam.

Johnston, Jill. 1992. "Men and Their Myths." Review of *Women Respond to the Men's Movement*, edited by Kay Leigh Hagan. *Women's Review of Books*, October, 8–9.

Jones, Kathleen B. 1994. "Identity, Action, and Locale: Thinking about Citizenship, Civic Action, and Feminism." *Social Politics* (fall): 256–70.

Jones, Lisa. 1991. "A Doll Is Born." *Village Voice*, 26 March.

Jones, Sonny. 1991. "*Thelma and Louise:* Reality Meets Movie Myth." *Women and Guns*, no. 1: 12–16.

Juhasz, Alexandra. 1993. "Knowing AIDS through the Televised Science Documentary." In *Women and AIDS*, edited by Corinne Squire. London: Sage.

Juice. 1992. Produced by David Heyman, Neal H. Moritz, and Peter Frankfurt. Directed by Ernest R. Dickerson. Paramount.

Jungle Fever. 1991. Produced and directed by Spike Lee. Universal/Forty Acres and a Mule Filmworks.

Junior. 1994. Produced and directed by Ivan Reitman. Universal.

Kanner, Bernice. 1992. "Shock Value." *New York*, 24 August, 26–28.

Kantrowitz, Barbara. 1988. "A Tale of Abuse." *Newsweek*, 12 December, 56–59.

Kaplan, E. Ann. 1992. *Motherhood and Representation.* New York: Routledge.

Kaye, Elizabeth. 1982. "Growing up Stoned." *California* 7: 80.

Kaye/Kantrowitz, Melanie. 1996. "Sexualities." Talk delivered at National Women's Studies Association Conference, 16 June, at Saratoga Springs, New York.

Kennedy, Pagan. 1991. "Generation Gaffe." *Nation*, 1 April: 426–28.

Kennedy, Randy. 1995. "Jews and Muslims Share a Piece of Brooklyn." *New York Times*, 17 August, A1, B3.

Kids. 1995. Produced by Cary Woods. Directed by Larry Clark. Excalibur Films.

Kilborn, Peter T. 1996. "Shifts in Families Reach a Plateau, Study Says." *New York Times*, 27 November, A18.

Kincaid, Jamaica. 1991. *Lucy.* New York: Dutton.

King, Norman. 1991. *Madonna: The Book.* New York: Morrow.

Kingsolver, Barbara. 1993. *Pigs in Heaven.* New York: HarperCollins.

Kinzer, Stephen. 1996. "Copenhagen Journal." *New York Times*, 16 May, A4.

Klugman, Karen, Jane Kuenz, Sheldon Waldrup, and Susan Willis. 1995. *Inside the Mouse: The Project on Disney.* Durham, N.C.: Duke University Press.

Kolata, Gina. 1997a. "Childbirth at 63 Says What about Life?" *New York Times*, 27 April.

———. 1997b. "Scientists Face New Ethical Quandaries in Baby-Making." *New York Times,* 19 August, C1, C8.

Kolodny, Annette. 1985. "The Integrity of Memory: Creating a New Literary History of the United States." *American Literature* 57 (May): 291–307.

Kristeva, Julia. 1980. *Desire in Language.* Oxford: Oxford University Press.

———. 1982. *Powers of Horror: An Essay on Abjection.* Translated by Leon S. Roudiez. New York: Columbia University Press.

———. 1986. *The Kristeva Reader.* Edited by Toril Moi. New York: Columbia University Press.

———. 1991. *Strangers to Ourselves.* Translated by Leon S. Roudiez. New York: Columbia University Press.

———. 1995. "Proust: Issues of Identity." Gauss Lectures, 10–12 October, Princeton University, Princeton, N.J.

Kübler-Ross, Elizabeth. 1988. *AIDS: The Ultimate Challenge.* New York: Macmillan.

Kunen, James. S. 1988. "Trials of Tawana." *People,* 4 July, 62.

Lacan, Jacques. 1977. *The Four Fundamental Concepts of Psychoanalysis.* London: Hogarth.

———. 1995. *The Ethics of Psychoanalysis.* London: Routledge.

Lacayo, Richard. 1987a. "In the Best Interests of the Child." *Time,* 13 April, 71.

———. 1987b. "Whose Child Is This?" *Time,* 19 January, 56–58.

Laclau, Ernesto, and Chantal Mouffe. 1985. *Hegemony and Socialist Strategy.* London: Verso.

Lanham, Richard. 1995. "Digital Literacy." *Scientific American,* September, 198–200.

Laqueur, Thomas. 1990. *Making Sex: Body and Gender from the Greeks to Freud.* Cambridge: Harvard University Press.

Larry King Live. 1993. August 13. Transcript no. 892. Denver: Journal Graphics.

Lasch, Christopher. 1979. *The Culture of Narcissism.* New York: Norton.

———. 1991. *The True and Only Heaven.* New York: Norton.

The Last of the Mohicans. 1992. Produced by Michael Mann and Hunt Lowry. Directed by Michael Mann. Warner Bros.

Laumann, Edward O., et al. 1994. *The Social Organization of Sexuality.* Chicago: University of Chicago Press.

Lawson, Mark. 1991. "Driving Men Wild." *Independent Magazine,* 31 August.

A League of Their Own. 1992. Directed by Penny Marshall. Columbia.

Leavitt, David. 1989. *Equal Affections.* New York: Weidenfeld & Nicolson.

Lee, Jee Yeun. 1995. "Beyond Bean Counting." In *Listen Up: Voices from the Next Feminist Generation,* edited by Barbara Findlen. Seattle: Seal.

Lemann, Nicholas. 1995. "Taking Affirmative Action Apart." *New York Times Magazine,* 11 June, 36–44+.

Lemon, Clifton. 1995. "Intellectual Food Fight." *Wired,* August, 24.

Leo, John. 1991. "The Political Taboos of the '90s." *U.S. News and World Report,* 4 March, 21.

Levinas, Emmanuel. 1985. *Ethics and Infinity: Conversations with Philippe Nemo.* Translated by Richard A. Cohen. Pittsburgh: Duquesne University Press.

Levy, John, and Ruth Munroe. 1964. *The Happy Family.* New York: Knopf.

Lewis, Anthony. 1995. "Living in a Cocoon." *New York Times,* 27 November, A15.

Lind, Michael. 1995. *The Next American Nation: The New Nationalism and the Fourth American Revolution.* New York: Free Press.

Lindley, David. 1996. *Where Does the Weirdness Go? Why Quantum Mechanics Is Strange, but Not as Strange as You Think.* New York: Basic Books.

Lingis, Alphonso. 1995. *The Community of Those Who Have Nothing in Common.* Bloomington: Indiana University Press.

Lipset, Seymour Martin. 1990. "Values and Democracy." In *Culture and Society: Contemporary Debates,* edited by Jeffrey C. Alexander and Steven Seidman. New York: Cambridge University Press.

Little Caesar. 1931. Directed by Mervyn LeRoy. Warner.

Livingstone, Sylvia, and Peter Lunt. 1993. *Talk on Television.* London: Routledge.

Lone Star. 1996. Produced by R. Paul Miller and Maggie Renzi. Directed by John Sayles. Castle Rock Entertainment.

Longtime Companion. 1990. Produced by Stan Wlodkowski. Directed by Norman Rene. American Playhouse.

Lost in America. 1985. Produced by Marty Katz. Directed by Albert Brooks. Geffen.

Lyotard, Jean-François. 1986. "Defining the Postmodern, Etc." Translated by Geoff Bennington and edited by Lisa Appignanesi. In *Postmodernism,* ICA Documents 4–5. London: Institute of Contemporary Arts.

———. 1989. *The Lyotard Reader*. Edited by Andrew Benjamin. Cambridge: Blackwell.

———. 1993. *Moralités Postmodernes*. Paris: Galilee.

MacIntyre, Alasdair. 1984. *After Virtue: A Study in Moral Theory*. 2d ed. Notre Dame, Ind.: University of Notre Dame Press.

———. 1989. *Whose Justice? Which Rationality?* Notre Dame, Ind.: University of Notre Dame Press.

———. 1991. *Three Rival Versions of Moral Enquiry*. Notre Dame, Ind.: University of Notre Dame Press.

MacKinnon, Catharine. 1989. *Toward a Feminist Theory of the State*. Cambridge: Harvard University Press.

Mailer, Norman. 1965. *An American Dream*. New York: Dial.

———. 1991. "Children of the Pied Piper." *Vanity Fair*, March, 154–59, 220–21.

Malcolm X, with Alex Haley. 1964. *The Autobiography of Malcolm X*. New York: Ballantine.

Malinowski, Bronislaw. 1913. *The Family among the Australian Aborigines*. London: University of London Press.

Malone, Bonz. 1995. "Offa Space Nine." *Vibe*, June–July, 71–75.

Mamet, David. 1992. *Oleanna*. New York: Random House.

Mann, Sally. 1992. *Immediate Family*. New York: Aperture.

Marshall, Stuart. 1991. "The Contemporary Political Use of Gay History: The Third Reich." In *How Do I Look? Queer Film and Video*, edited by Bad Object Choices. Seattle: Bay Press.

Martin, Emily. 1994. *Flexible Bodies*. Boston: Beacon.

McCauley, Stephen. 1987. *The Object of My Affection*. New York: Simon & Schuster.

McFadden, Robert, Ralph Blumenthal, M. A. Farber, E. R. Shipp, Charles Strum, and Craig Wolff. 1990. *Outrage*. New York: Bantam.

McInerney, Jay. 1984. *Bright Lights, Big City*. New York: Random House.

———. 1996. *The Last of the Savages*. New York: Knopf.

McKenna, George. 1995. "On Abortion: A Lincolnian Position." *Atlantic Monthly*, September, 51–68.

McMillen, Liz. 1987. "Step up Recruitment of Women into Science or Risk U.S. Competitive Edge in Field, Colleges Are Warned." *Chronicle of Higher Education*, 12 August, 9, 12.

Menace II Society. 1993. Produced by Darin Scott. Directed by Allen Hughes and Albert Hughes. New Line.

Men in Black. 1997. Produced by Walter F. Parkes and Laura MacDonald. Directed by Barry Sonnenfeld. Columbia.

Mercer, Kobena. 1990. "Black Hair/style Politics." In *Out There,* edited by Russell Ferguson, Martha Gever, Trinh Minh-ha, and Cornel West. Cambridge: MIT Press.

Merck, Mandy. 1990. "A Case of AIDS." In *Ecstatic Antibodies: Resisting the AIDS Mythology,* edited by Tessa Boffin and Sunil Gupta. London: Rivers Oram.

Metz, Holly. 1989. *Two Arks, a Palace, Some Robots, and Mr. Freedom's Fabulous Fifty Acres.* Newark, N.J.: City without Walls Gallery.

Michaels, Walter Benn. 1996. "'You Who Never Was There': Slavery and the New Historicism, Deconstruction and the Holocaust." *Narrative,* January, 1–16.

Miller, James. 1993. "Dante on Fire Island: Reinventing Heaven in the AIDS Elegy." In *Writing AIDS,* edited by Timothy F. Murphy and Suzanne Poirier. New York: Columbia University Press.

Miller, Mark Crispin. 1988. *Boxed In.* Evanston, Ill.: Northwestern University Press.

Millot, Catherine. 1990. *Horsexe.* New York: Autonomedia.

Minson, Jeffrey. 1985. *Genealogies of Morals: Nietzsche, Foucault, Donzelot, and the Eccentricity of Ethics.* New York: St. Martin's.

Monroe, Sylvester. 1996. "Race Man." *Emerge,* January, 31–36.

Moore, Alison. 1995. *Synonym for Love.* San Francisco: Mercury.

Morgan, Joan. 1992. "A Black Woman's Guide to the Tyson Trial: Rape, Racial Tension, and the Will of Desiree Washington." *Village Voice,* March 3, 37–40.

Morrison, Toni. 1987. *Beloved.* New York: New American Library.

———. 1992. *Playing in the Dark: Whiteness and the Literary Imagination.* Cambridge: Harvard University Press.

Mouffe, Chantal. 1992a. "Citizenship and Political Identity." *October* 61 (summer): 28–32.

———. 1992b. "Democratic Citizenship and the Political Community." In *Dimensions of Radical Democracy: Pluralism, Citizenship, Community,* edited by Chantal Mouffe. London: Verso.

———, ed. 1992c. *Dimensions of Radical Democracy.* London: Verso.

———. 1993. *The Return of the Political.* London: Verso.

Mr. and Mrs. Smith. 1941. Directed by Alfred Hitchcock. RKO.

Mulvey, Laura. 1991. "A Phantasmagoria of the Female Body: The Work of Cindy Sherman." *New Left Review* 188: 136–50.

Munk, Erica. 1988. "The Trials of Hedda: Is It Worse to be a Bad Mother than a Bad Father?" *Village Voice,* 20 December, 12+.

———. 1989. "Short Eyes: The Joel Steinberg We Never Saw." *Village Voice,* 21 February, 16+.

Murphy, Jeannette, Mary John, and Hedy Brown. 1984. *Dialogues and Debates in Social Psychology.* London: Erlbaum.

My Own Private Idaho. 1991. Produced by Laurie Parker. Directed by Gus Van Sant. Fine Line.

Nash, J. Madeleine. 1991. "All in the Family." *Time,* 19 August, 58.

Natural Born Killers. 1994. Produced by Jame Hamsher, Don Murphy, and Clayton Townsend. Directed by Oliver Stone. Universal.

Naylor, Gloria. 1989. *Mama Day.* New York: Vintage.

Nelson, Tim Blake. 1996. *The Grey Zone.* Typescript.

New Jack City. 1991. Produced by Doug McHenry and George Jackson. Directed by Mario Van Peebles. Warner Bros.

Nietzsche, Friedrich. 1973. *Beyond Good and Evil.* Translated by R. J. Hollingdale. 1886. Reprint, New York: Viking Penguin.

———. 1989. *On the Genealogy of Morals.* Translated by Walter Kaufmann and R. J. Hollingdale. New York: Vintage.

Nixon. 1995. Produced by Clayton Townsend, Oliver Stone, and Andrew Vajna. Directed by Oliver Stone. Hollywood Pictures.

Nunokawa, Jeff. 1991. "'All the Sad Young Men': AIDS and the Work of Mourning." In *Inside/Out,* edited by Diana Fuss. New York: Routledge.

Oates, Joyce Carol. 1980. *Bellefleur.* New York: Dutton.

———. 1996. *We Were the Mulvaneys.* New York: Dutton.

Okin, Susan Moller. 1989. *Justice, Gender, and the Family.* New York: Basic Books.

Onishi, Norimitsu. 1996. "Stabilizing Lefrak City." *New York Times,* 6 June, B1, B4.

The Oprah Winfrey Show. 1994. "What Would You Do?" 18 July. Livingston, N.J.: Burrells Information Service.

Orbach, Susie. 1978. *Fat Is a Feminist Issue.* New York: Paddington.

Paglia, Camille. 1990. *Sexual Personae: Art and Decadence from Nefertiti to Emily Dickinson.* New Haven: Yale University Press.

———. 1991. "Ninnies, Pedants, Tyrants, and Other Academics." *New York Times Book Review,* 5 May, 1, 29, 33.

Pareles, Jon. 1995. "They're Rebels without a Cause, and Couldn't Care Less." *New York Times,* 16 July, sec. 2, pp. 1, 23.

Paris Is Burning. 1991. Produced and directed by Jennie Livingston. Twentieth-Century Fox.

Parrington, Vernon L. 1927. *Main Currents in American Thought: The Colonial Mind, 1620–1800.* New York: Harcourt.

Patterson, James, and Peter Kim. 1991. *The Day America Told the Truth.* New York: Dutton.

Patton, Cindy. 1990. *Inventing AIDS.* New York: Routledge.

Peck, M. Scott. 1985. *The Road Less Travelled.* New York: Simon & Schuster.

———. 1993. *Further along the Road Less Travelled.* New York: Simon & Schuster.

Penley, Constance. 1991. "Brownian Motion: Women, Tactics, and Technology." In *Technoculture,* edited by Constance Penley and Andrew Ross. Minneapolis: University of Minnesota Press.

Perry, Ruth. 1992. "A Short History of the Term Political Correctness." In *Beyond PC: Toward a Politics of Understanding,* edited by Patricia Aufderheide. St. Paul: Graywolf.

Phelan, Peggy. 1993. *Unmarked: The Politics of Performance.* New York: Routledge.

Philadelphia. 1993. Produced by Edward Saxon and Jonathan Demme. Directed by Jonathan Demme. Tri-Star.

Piper, Adrian. 1991. "Flying." In *you/know.* Birmingham, England, and Manchester, England: Icon Gallery and Corner House Gallery.

The Player. 1992. Produced by David Brown, Michael Tolkin, and Nick Wechsler. Directed by Robert Altman. Fine Line.

Plummer, William. 1991. "A Mother's Priceless Gift." *People,* 26 August, 40–41.

Pollitt, Katha. 1987. "The Strange Case of Baby M." *Nation,* 23 May, 681–82.

Pope, Kenneth S., and Valerie A. Vetter. 1992. "Ethical Dilemmas Encountered by Members of the APA." *American Psychologist,* March, 402–3.

Posner, Richard A., ed. 1992. *The Essential Holmes.* Chicago: University of Chicago Press.

Postman, Neil. 1985. *Amusing Ourselves to Death*. New York: Viking.

Poulson-Bryant, Scott. 1991. "Tales of the Banjy." *Village Voice*, 2 April, 41–42.

Preston, Richard. 1992. "Crisis in the Hot Zone." *New Yorker*, 26 October, 58–81.

Primary Colors, 1996. New York: Random House.

Primetime Live. 1993. "Devilish Deeds." 7 January. Transcript no. 279. Denver: Journal Graphics.

Pulp Fiction. 1994. Produced by Laurence Bender. Directed by Quentin Tarantino. Miramax.

Quindlen, Anna. 1993. "Let's Anita Hill This." *New York Times*, 28 February, 15.

Radway, Janice. 1984. *Reading the Romance*. Chapel Hill: University of North Carolina Press.

Rampersad, Arnold. 1991. "Values Old and New." *Profession '91* (Modern Language Association): 10–14.

Rawls, John. 1972. *A Theory of Justice*. Oxford: Clarendon.

Regarding Henry. 1991. Produced by Scott Rudivard and Mike Nichols. Directed by Mike Nichols. Paramount.

Regis, Ed. 1995. *Nanotechnology*. Boston: Little, Brown.

Reinhardt, Uwe. 1995. "Post-mortem on Health Care." *Princeton Alumni Weekly*, 22 February, 55–56.

Renan, Ernest. 1990. "What Is a Nation?" Translated by Martin Thom. In *Nation and Narration*, edited by Homi Bhabha. New York: Routledge.

Rent. 1996. Written by Jonathan Larson. Produced by Jeffrey Seller, Kevin McCollum, Allan S. Gordon, and the New York Theatre Workshop. Directed by Michael Grief.

Reservoir Dogs. 1991. Produced by Lawrence Bender. Directed by Quentin Tarantino. Miramax.

Rheingold, Howard. 1993. *The Virtual Community*. London: Secker & Warburg.

Ricaputo, Maria. 1995. "Creeping Back into Vogue." *New York Times*, 13 August, 1, 20.

Riley, Denise. 1988. *Am I That Name? Feminism and the Category of "Women" in History*. Minneapolis: University of Minnesota Press.

Riley, Glenda. 1991. *Divorce: An American Tradition*. New York: Oxford University Press.

River's Edge. 1986. Produced by Sarah Pillsbury and Midge Sanford. Directed by Tim Hunter. Hemdale.

Robbins, Bruce, and Andrew Ross. 1996. "Mystery Science Theater." *Lingua Franca,* July–August, 54–57.

Roberts, Melinda A. 1993. "Good Intentions and a Great Divide: Having Babies by Intending Them." *Law and Philosophy* 12: 287–317.

Robeson, Paul, Jr., and Mel Williamson. 1989. "Accountability and Higher Morality." *Amsterdam (N.Y.) News,* 6 June, 15.

Roger and Me. 1989. Produced and directed by Michael Moore. Dog Eat Dog.

Roiphe, Katie. 1993. *The Morning After: Sex, Fear, and Feminism on Campus.* New York: Little, Brown.

Rorty, Richard. 1990. *Objectivity, Relativism, and Truth.* Vol. 1 of *Philosophical Papers.* Cambridge: Cambridge University Press.

Rose, Nikolas. 1985. *The Psychological Complex.* London: Routledge & Kegan Paul.

Rosen, Marjorie, and, Vicki Sheff-Cahan. 1993. "Now I Can Be Free." *People,* 26 April, 82–87.

Rosenbaum, Ron. 1987. Review of *River's Edge* (Hemdale movie). *Mademoiselle,* August, 80+.

———. 1995. "Among the Believers." *New York Times Magazine,* 24 September, 50–57, 62–64.

Rosenblatt, Roger. 1992. *Life Itself.* New York: Random House.

Ross, Andrew. 1991. "Hacking Away at the Counterculture." In *Technoculture,* edited by Constance Penley and Andrew Ross. Minneapolis: University of Minnesota Press.

———. 1992. "The Private Parts of Justice." In *Race-ing Justice, En-gendering Power,* edited by Toni Morrison. New York: Pantheon.

Rousset, David. 1946. *L'univers concentrationnaire.* Paris: Editions du Pavois.

Rubinstein, Carin. (1994). "New Advice on How to Raise Little Boys to be Good Men." *New York Times,* 11 August, C4.

Russell, Bertrand. 1945. *A History of Western Philosophy.* New York: Simon & Schuster.

Russo, Francine. 1997. "The Faces of Hedda Nussbaum." *New York Times Magazine,* 30 March, 26–28.

Ryan, Frank. 1993. *The Forgotten Plague.* Boston: Little, Brown.

Saalfield, Catherine, and Ray Navarro. 1991. "Shocking Pink Praxis: Race and Gender on the ACT UP Frontlines." In *Inside/Out,* edited by Diana Fuss. New York: Routledge.

Safire, William. 1991. "Linguistically Correct." *New York Times Magazine,* 5 May, 18.

Sally Jesse Raphael. 1994. "I'm Sorry I Did It." 18 July. Transcript no. 1529. Denver: Journal Graphics.

Sartre, Jean-Paul. 1947. *No Exit* and *The Flies.* New York: Knopf.

———. 1963. *Saint Genet.* New York: Braziller.

The Scarlet Letter. 1995. Produced by Roland Joffé and Andrew Vajna. Directed by Roland Joffé. Tri-Star.

Schindler's List. 1993. Produced by Steven Spielberg, Gerald R. Molen, and Branko Lustig. Directed by Steven Spielberg. Universal.

Schlesinger, Arthur M., Jr. 1991. *The Disuniting of America.* Knoxville, Tenn.: Whittle Direct.

Schoemperlen, Diane. 1996. *In the Language of Love: A Novel in One Hundred Chapters.* New York: Viking.

Schoofs, Mark. 1995. "Beat It." *Village Voice,* 27 June, 14, 16.

Schor, Naomi. 1995. "French Feminism Is a Universalism." *Differences: A Journal of Feminist Cultural Studies* 7 (spring): 15–47.

Schucman, Helen Cohen. 1975. *A Course in Miracles.* Mill Valley, Calif.: Foundation for Inner Peace.

Seal, Kathy. 1991. "Know Thy Neighbor." *American Way,* 15 August, 15–16.

Sennett, Richard. 1992. *The Conscience of the Eye.* New York: Norton.

Shapiro, Marilyn. 1991. *Our Town,* 12 May, 9.

Shaughnessy, Mary. 1987. "All for Love of a Baby." *People,* 23 March, 50–52.

Sherry, M. 1993. "The Language of War in AIDS Discourse." In *Writing AIDS: Gay Literature, Language, and Analysis,* edited by Timothy F. Murphy and Suzanne Poirier. New York: Columbia University Press.

Shklovsky, Victor. 1989. "Art as Technique." Translated by Lee T. Lemon and Marion Reis. In *The Critical Tradition: Classic Texts and Contemporary Trends,* edited by David H. Richter. New York: St. Martin's.

Showalter, Elaine. 1991. *Sexual Anarchy.* New York: Viking Penguin.

Shweder, Richard W. 1994. "What Do Men Want? A Reading List for the Male Identity Crisis." *New York Times Book Review,* 9 January, 3, 24.

Silence of the Lambs. 1991. Produced by Edward Saxon, Kenneth Utt, and Ron Bozman. Directed by Jonathan Demme. Orion/Strong Heart.

Silko, Leslie Marmon. 1977. *Ceremony.* New York: Viking.

————. 1991. *Almanac of the Dead.* New York: Simon & Schuster.

Slouka, Mark. 1995. *War of the Worlds.* London: Abacus.

Smiley, Jane. 1991. *A Thousand Acres.* New York: Knopf.

Smith, Nick. 1992. "The Spirit of Modernity and Its Fate: Jürgen Habermas." *Radical Philosophy* 60 (spring): 23–29.

Sobchak, Vivien. 1994. "Reading *Mondo 2000.*" In *Flame Wars: The Discourse of Cyberculture,* edited by Mark Dery. Durham, N.C.: Duke University Press.

Sokal, Alan D. 1996. "Transgressing the Boundaries—Toward a Transformative Hermeneutics of Quantum Gravity." *Social Text* (spring–summer): 217–52.

Sommers, Christina Hoff. 1994. *Who Stole Feminism? How Women Have Betrayed Women.* New York: Simon & Schuster.

Spalding, John D. 1996. "Bonding in the Bleachers: A Visit to the Promise Keepers." *Christian Century,* 6 March, 260–65.

Sprinkle, Annie. 1991. "Annie Sprinkle." In *Angry Women,* edited by Andrea Juno and V. Vale. San Francisco: Re/Search Publications.

Squire, Corinne. 1994. "Is the *Oprah Winfrey Show* Feminist Television?" *Feminism and Psychology* 4, no. 1: 63–79.

————. 1998. "AIDS Panic." In *Body Talk,* edited by Jane Ussher. London: Routledge.

Stacey, Judith, and Susan Elizabeth Gerard. 1992. "'We Are Not Doormats': The Influence of Feminism on Contemporary Evangelicals in the United States." In *Uncertain Terms: Negotiating Gender in American Culture,* edited by Faye Ginsburg and Anna Lowenhaupt Tsing. Boston: Beacon.

Stan, Adele M. 1995. *Debating Sexual Correctness: Pornography, Sexual Harassment, Date Rape, and the Politics of Sexuality Equality.* New York: Delta.

Staples, Brent. 1994. *Parallel Time: Growing Up in Black and White.* New York: Pantheon.

Steinem, Gloria. 1992. *Revolution from Within.* New York: Little, Brown.

Steiner, George. 1976. *Language and Silence: Essays on Language, Literature, and the Inhuman.* New York: Atheneum.

Stephen, Andrew. 1991. "Wild Night at Kennedy Beach." *Observer Magazine* (London), 19 May, 16–25.

Stoll, Clifford. 1995. *Silicon Snake Oil.* New York: Macmillan.

Straight out of Brooklyn. 1991. Produced and directed by Matty Rich. American Playhouse/Goldwyn.

Strausbaugh, John. 1991. "Sleazy Does It." *New York Press,* 20 February, 1, 10, 12.

Sussman, Elisabeth, Thelma Golden, John G. Hanhardt, and Lisa Phillips, eds. 1993. *Nineteen Ninety-three Biennial Exhibition Catalogue.* New York: Whitney Museum of American Art.

Swerdlow, Amy, Renate Bridenthal, Joan Kelly, and Phyllis Vine. 1989. *Families in Flux.* Westbury, N.Y.: The Feminist Press.

Taibbi, Mike, and Anna Sims-Phillips. 1989. *Unholy Alliances.* New York: Harcourt Brace Jovanovich.

"Take a Dip This Summer in Suits You Can Actually Swim In." 1993. *Essence,* May, 62–69.

Talk Radio. 1988. Produced by Edward R. Pressman and A. Kitman Ho. Directed by Oliver Stone. Cineplex Odeon/Ten Four Productions.

Tannen, Deborah. 1990. *You Just Don't Understand: Women and Men in Conversation.* New York: Morrow.

Taubin, Amy. 1995. "Bloody Tales." *Sight and Sound* 5, no. 1: 8–11.

Taylor, John. 1992. "A Theory of the Case." *New York,* 6 January, 34–38.

Taylor, Susan. 1995. "Practicing the Principle." *Essence,* June, 57.

Teresi, Dick. 1994. "How to Get a Man Pregnant: My (True) Adventures on the Frontiers of Science." *New York Times Magazine,* 27 November, 54–55.

The Texas Chainsaw Massacre. 1974. Produced and directed by Tobe Hooper. Vortex/Henkel/Hooper.

Thelma and Louise. 1991. Produced by Ridley Scott and Mimi Polk. Directed by Ridley Scott. Pathé/Main.

Thompson, Frances Morani. 1989. *Going for the Cure.* New York: St. Martin's.

Thorne, Barrie. 1992. "Feminism and the Family: Two Decades of Thought." In *Rethinking the Family: Some Feminist Questions,* edited by Barrie Thorne. Boston: Northeastern University Press.

Toffler, Alvin, and Heidi Toffler. 1994. *Creating a New Civilization*. Atlanta: Turner.

Toner, Robin. 1992. "Drawing a Line in the Shifting Politics of Abortion." *New York Times*, 8 September, 16.

To Sleep with Anger. 1990. Produced by Caldecott Chubb, Thomas S. Byrnes, and Darin Scott. Directed by Charles Burnett. Sony.

Tran, Mark. 1991. "US College Breeds Uneasy Bedfellows." *Observer* (London), 8 September.

Treichler, Paula. 1989. "An Epidemic of Signification." In *AIDS: Cultural Analysis/ Cultural Activism*, edited by Douglas Crimp. Cambridge: MIT Press.

Tribe, Laurence. 1990. *Abortion: The Clash of Absolutes*. New York: Norton.

Tronto, Joan C. 1993. *Moral Boundaries: A Political Argument for an Ethic of Care*. New York: Routledge.

True Colors. 1991. Produced by Herbert Ross and Laurence Mark. Directed by Herbert Ross. Paramount.

Turkle, Sherry. 1996. *Life on the Screen*. London: Weidenfeld & Nicolson.

Turow, Scott. 1987. *Presumed Innocent*. New York: Warner Bros.

Tuttleton, James W. 1986. "Rewriting the History of American Literature." *New Criterion*, November, 1–12.

Udovitch, Mim. 1995. "Sister Act." *George*, October–November, 156–58, 256–58.

Unforgiven. 1992. Produced and directed by Clint Eastwood. Warner Bros.

Updike, John. 1990. *Rabbit at Rest*. New York: Knopf.

U.S. Department of Commerce. 1975. *Historical Statistics of the United States: Colonial Times to 1970*. Bicentennial Ed. Pt. 1. Washington, D.C.: U.S. Department of Commerce.

U.S. Department of Education. 1994. *Digest of Educational Statistics*. Lanham, Md.: Department of Education.

Vance, Carole S. 1992a. "Misunderstanding Obscenity." In *Culture Wars: Documents from the Recent Controversies in the Arts*, edited by Richard Bolton. New York: New Press.

———. 1992b. "The War on Culture." In *Culture Wars: Documents from the Recent Controversies in the Arts*, edited by Richard Bolton (New York: New Press). First published in *Art in America*, September 1989.

Van Tassel, Joan. 1995. "The WWWorld's Fair." *Wired*, August, 43–44.

Veronsky, Frank. 1996. "Kicking the Habit: It's No Longer All-or-Nothing." *Psychology Today,* September–October, 33–43.

Volunteers. 1985. Produced by Richard Shepherd and Walter F. Parks. Directed by Nicholas Meyer. EMI/HBO/Tri-Star.

Vorenberg, Elizabeth. (1993). Letter to the editor. *New York Times.* 28 June, A16.

W., Kathleen. 1988. *Healing a Broken Heart: Twelve Steps of Recovery for Adult Children.* Pompano Beach, Fla.: Health Communications.

Waiting to Exhale. 1995. Produced by Ezra Swerdlow and Deborah Schindler. Directed by Forest Whitaker. Twentieth-Century Fox.

Walker, Eric. 1995. "We're Here, We're Queer, and Now We've Got Virtual Support." *Wired,* August, 68.

Wall Street. 1987. Produced by Edward R. Pressman. Directed by Oliver Stone. Edward R. Pressman/American Entertainment/Twentieth-Century Fox.

Walt Disney World. 1995. "The Disney Institute, a New Disney Discovery Resort." *New York Times,* Winter Travel Guide, 1 October, 1–6.

Walzer, Michael. 1983. *Spheres of Justice: A Defense of Pluralism and Equality.* New York: Basic Books.

Warhol, Andy. 1989. *Diaries.* Edited by Pat Hackett. New York: Warner.

Watney, Simon. 1989. "Missionary Positions: AIDS, 'Africa,' and Race." *Critical Quarterly* 31 (autumn): 45–62.

Weeks, Jeffrey. 1985. *Sexuality and Its Discontents.* London: Routledge & Kegan Paul.

———. 1989. "AIDS, Altruism, and the New Right." In *Taking Liberties,* edited by Erica Carter and Simon Watney. London: Serpent's Tale.

Weiley, Susan. 1988. "Prince of Darkness, Angel of Light." *Art News,* December, 108–11.

Weinberg, Steven. 1996. "Sokal's Hoax." *New York Review of Books,* 8 August, 11–15.

Weiss, Naomi. 1989. "A Love Betrayed, a Brief Life Lost." *People,* 13 February, 82–84+.

West, Cornel. 1986. "Ethics and Action in Fredric Jameson's Marxism Hermeneutics." In *Postmodernism and Politics,* edited by Jonathan Arac. Minneapolis: University of Minnesota Press.

———. 1989. *The American Evasion of Philosophy.* Madison: University of Wisconsin Press.

———. 1992. "Black Leadership and the Pitfalls of Racial Reasoning." In *Race-ing Justice, En-gendering Power*, edited by Toni Morrison. New York: Pantheon.

———. 1993. "The Traps of Tribalism." *Emerge* 4, no. 5: 42–44.

West Side Story. 1957. Book by Arthur Laurents. Lyrics by Stephen Sondheim. Music by Leonard Bernstein. Produced by Robert E. Griffiths and Harold S. Prince. Directed by Jerome Robbins.

Whitaker, Charles. 1992. "The Browning of White America." *Ebony*, August, 25–26.

White, Edmund, and Hubert Sorin. 1994. *Sketches from Memory*. London: Chatto & Windus and Picador.

Whitehead, Mary Beth. 1986. "A Surrogate Mother Describes Her Change of Heart—and Her Fight to Keep the Baby Two Families Love." *People*, 26 October, 46–52.

Whitehead, Mary Beth, with Loretta Schwarz-Noble. 1989. *A Mother's Story*. New York: St. Martin's.

Wideman, John Edgar. 1990. *Philadelphia Fire*. New York: Holt.

Wiesel, Elie. 1982. *One Generation After*. Translated by Lily Edelman and Elie Wiesel. New York: Schocken.

Wilentz, Sean. 1995. "Backward March." *New Republic*, 6 November, 16–18.

Will, George F. 1991. "Getting a Handle on Behavioral Poverty." *Trenton (N.J.) Times*, 26 September.

———. 1992. "Literary Politics." *Newsweek*, 22 April, 72.

Willard, Frances. 1991. *How I Learned to Ride the Bicycle*. 1895. Reprint, Sunnyvale, Calif.: Fair Oaks.

Williams, Patricia J. 1991. *The Alchemy of Race and Rights*. Cambridge: Harvard University Press.

———. 1995. "Different Drummer Please, Marchers!" *Nation*, 30 October, 493–94.

Williamson, Marianne. 1992. *A Return to Love*. New York: HarperCollins.

Willis, Susan. 1991. *A Primer for Everyday Life*. New York: Routledge.

Wolfe, Linda. 1994. "And Baby Makes Three, Even if You're Gray." *New York Times*, 4 January, A15.

Wolfe, Tom. 1987. *The Bonfire of the Vanities*. New York: Farrar, Straus & Giroux.

Wollen, Peter. 1987. "Fashion/orientalism/the body." *New Formations* 1: 5–34.

Wood, Joe. 1991. "Who Says a White Band Can't Play Rap?" *Village Voice*, March, Rock and Roll Supplement, 10–11.

Wortman, Marc. 1991. "Fighting Words." *Yale*, October, 56–63.

Wright, Robert. 1995. "It's All in Our Heads." *New York Times Book Review*, 9 July, 1, 16.

Young, Iris Marion. 1986. "The Ideal of Community and the Politics of Difference." *Social Theory and Practice* 12 (spring): 1–25.

———. 1990. *Justice and the Politics of Difference*. Princeton, N.J.: Princeton University Press.

Young, Robert J. C. 1995. *Colonial Desire: Hybridity in Theory, Culture, and Race*. New York: Routledge.

Youngblood, Linda. 1991. "After the Fact." *Women and Guns* 1: 38–40.

Zentropa. 1992. Directed by Lars von Trier. Miramax.

Zoglin, Richard. 1986. "People Sense the Realness: Look Out, Phil Donahue, Here Comes Oprah Winfrey." *Time*, 15 September, 99.

Index

Numbers in italics refer to the pages where figures appear.